Michigan
Folklife
Reader

T.M.

Michigan Folklife Reader

Editors:
C. Kurt Dewhurst
and
Yvonne R. Lockwood

Michigan State University Press
1987

Design and Production: Julie L. Loehr
Line Art and Calligraphy: Kathryn Darnell
Typography: the Copyfitters, Ltd., Lansing, MI

Michigan State University Press
East Lansing, Michigan 48823–5202

Library of Congress Cataloging-in-Publication Data

Michigan folklife reader / edited by C. Kurt Dewhurst and Yvonne R. Lockwood.

Bibliography

ISBN 0-87013-259-8   Cloth   ISBN 87013-266-0   Paper

1. Folklore–Michigan. 2. Michigan–Social life and customs.
I. Dewhurst, C. Kurt. II. Lockwood, Yvonne R.

GR110.M6M53 1988   88-42622
398.2'09774–dc 19   CIP

Contents

Acknowledgments

Special thanks are extended to our contributors who painstakingly prepared essays that help us all to understand better not only folklife in Michigan but also the nature of that folklife. Their dedication to the discipline of folklore and respect for the cultures of their informants make us proud to have them as colleagues. In addition, a number of archives, museums, and publications graciously complied with our requests for photographs, information, and rights for reprinting articles in this collection for which we wish to express our appreciation. We also want to recognize the generous financial support of the Michigan Department of Commerce YES 150 Grant Program which provided partial financial support for this publication.

Most important to the making of this publication, however, are those individuals who have shared information about their cultures and traditions. They have patiently taught us to view their cultural expressions as they themselves do, and we in turn have attempted to pass on our understanding to our readers. We sincerely hope that this collection of essays will enrich your lives as it has ours.

Finally, we want to thank the following individuals who assisted in the preparation of this volume: Dick Morscheck, Russ McKee, and Norris McDowell who encouraged us to pursue this collection of essays; Marsha MacDowell for her input at the initial stages and advice throughout; Kathleen McKevitt, who provided early editorial advice; Francie Freese, who typed the manuscript; our colleagues in the MSU Museum Folk Arts Division for their support and encouragement; Kate Darnell for her fine illustrations and design work; and Dick Chapin, Julie Loehr, and Jo Grandstaff from the MSU Press for their careful attention to all phases of the production of this book and commitment to the success of this project.

Michigan Folklife Reader

The history of folklore collecting &

study in Michigan begins in the nineteenth century with the first Agent of Indian Affairs for the federal government, Henry Rowe Schoolcraft, who documented Ojibwa culture and narratives. Based in part on Schoolcraft's collection in *Algic Researches* (1839) and influenced by New York Iroquois elements and the *Kalevala*, the national epic of Finland, Henry Wadsworth Longfellow published his *Song of Hiawatha* (Boston, 1855). Longfellow's work caused great controversy and spawned many articles and books about his use and misuse of Schoolcraft's work and the *Kalevala*. A former Michigan governor, Chase Osborn, along with his daughter Stellanova, became involved in the discussion, publishing *Schoolcraft-Longfellow-Hiawatha* (Lancaster, Pennsylvania, 1942), which contributed to folklore scholarship by actually bringing the traditional myths of the Ojibway alongside those of Hiawatha. The work of Chief Andrew J. Blackbird is an important contribution to Michigan Native American history, as well as to folklore. His 1887 publication, *History of Ottawa and Chippewa Indians of Michigan* (Ypsilanti), is a history and study of language which utilizes traditional narratives.

In 1923 Emelyn Gardner from the faculty at Wayne State University (then Wayne College of Detroit), was collecting the traditions of rural children. She encouraged Thelma James who was then a student, to study with Archer Taylor, the renowned scholar of the folktale, at the University of Chicago—advice Ms. James followed. During the summers of 1927–1929, Gardner and James taught courses at Wayne College on the epic, the ballad, and mythology. James joined the faculty, retiring in 1968. In the late 1930s they created the folklore archives at the college, today known as the Wayne State University Folklore Archives, which has become a major repository of urban folklore. In 1939 Gardner, with Geraldine Chickering, published *Ballads and Songs of Southern Michigan*.

During this same period, Ivan Walton, a faculty member of the English Department in the College of Engineering at The University of Michigan, began actively to pursue his long-time interest in Great Lakes folklore, especially concerning the lives and work of sailors between 1860–1918. From 1932 to 1960, Ivan Walton conducted fieldwork among sailors and their families along the Great Lakes and on Beaver Island. In 1940, he founded the Michigan Folklore Society, which was the outgrowth of a folklore group he started in 1938. During this time he also initiated the first folklore course at the University of Michigan (which is still on the books, but is not taught regularly).

Ivan Walton's entire collection of professional documents (field notes, field recordings of songs, reprinted articles, lecture notes, manuscripts, as well as miscellaneous papers, correspondence and minutes of the Michigan Folklore Society dating from 1938–1962) is now at the Bentley Library (The University of Michigan) and the Wayne State University Folklore Archive, with partial copies at the Archive of Folklife at the Library of Congress.

The 1930s witnessed much folklore activity in Michigan. For example, Alan Lomax made a survey of Michigan folksongs for the Library of Congress and with the help of E. C. Beck, who had done research on lumberjack culture, discovered that lumberjack songs and traditions still existed around Mt. Pleasant, Newberry, and Munising.

In 1938 Lomax recorded lumber songs in these areas, some of which are available on the album "Songs of Michigan Lumberjacks" (see bibliography). The complete field collection is at the Archive of Folklife at the Library of Congress.

Some of the first collecting of Michigan lumberjack songs was done by Franz Rickabey; although most of his documentation was done in Wisconsin and Michigan, his publication "Ballads and Songs of the Shanty-boy" (Harvard, 1926) contains some Michigan songs. The research of E. C. Beck, Professor at Central Michigan Teachers College, on the folklore of Michigan lumberjacks is a valuable cultural legacy about an occupational group that no longer exists and of which there are few, if any, survivors. His publications based on his research are classics (see bibliography).

Our knowledge about Michigan folklife has been greatly enriched by the pioneering research of Richard M. Dorson. While on the faculty of Michigan State University from 1944 to 1957, Dorson compiled a corpus of Michigan folklore which included campus culture. This entire collection of Michigan folklore is now at the Indiana University Folklore Archive and the Wayne State University Folklore Archive. More significant is his fieldwork in the rural black population of southwest Michigan and in the multi-ethnic Upper Peninsula which resulted in two classic books and numerous articles. Dorson wrote, "The folklorist belongs in the field as much as in the library."[1] He described his first fieldwork foray into Michigan this way:

> When I left Harvard in 1944 for a teaching post at Michigan State College, as it was then called, my initiation into the mysteries of folklore had aroused my desire to taste the field, and the Upper Peninsula of Michigan seemed to be made to order. Here a variety of ethnic and occupational groups co-existed under the same regional roof, and my purpose was to penetrate equally these separate traditions, rather than to identify with one alone, as collectors may want to do. For five months I traveled around the friendly towns of the Peninsula talking to lumberjacks, copper and iron miners, Great Lakes sailors, Finnish farmers, cousin Jacks, French Canadians, and Ojibwa Indians. The Peninsula offered very much of an oral, even a garrulous culture; this was a folk and open society, still close to its frontier spirit, devoid of bookstores but abounding in taverns. Now the great advantage of the folklore method for establishing personal relations became at once apparent, for with no previous contacts or acquaintances, I was able to make conversation with hundreds of strangers and to enter quickly into their minds and memories.[2]

What resulted from that fieldwork was *Bloodstoppers and Bearwalkers*, a folklore classic in the field of American, as well as Michigan, traditional culture. The skills, methods, and perspectives that folklorists bring to their fieldwork yield a deeper understanding of everyday aesthetics of communal groups or experiences. It is hoped that these selections will enable the reader to "enter quickly into the minds and memories" of Michigan's greatest resources—its people.

---

1. Richard M. Dorson, *American Folklore and the Historian* (Chicago: University of Chicago, 1971), 85.
2. Ibid.

Introduction
to the Reader

This volume is an introduction to the wealth of folklore and folklife in Michigan. The essays offer a glimpse into the folklore of the past, and more importantly, the living folk traditions that thrive in Michigan today. Included are articles by pioneering Michigan folklorists Ivan Walton and Richard M. Dorson, whose collecting and active scholarly careers are recognized nationally. The balance of the articles are drawn from recent studies by folklorists working on Michigan traditions today.

In a volume entitled *Indiana Folklore: A Reader*, Linda Degh offers a powerful description of the value of a collection of articles on a state's folklore:

> Viewing folklore as the most natural, unselfconscious, and sensitive expression of the human mind, we must decode its symbolic language and learn how people feel and what they confess about themselves, their lives, their work, their hopes, and their fears. [1]

Such an undertaking requires not only documenting folklore, but also providing the reader with a sense of the context in which the folklore was collected. The articles chosen for this volume were selected to introduce the general reader, high school or college student to the nature of Michigan folklife. Though far from comprehensive, this collection illustrates a variety of approaches and folklore genres. Most important, it enables the reader to come to know how Michiganders "feel and what they communicate about themselves" through their folk traditions.

The volume has been organized in six sections. The first five chapters are devoted to: (1) Folk Art and Architecture; (2) Storytelling and Meaning; (3) Folk Music and Song; (4) Occupational Folklore and Play; and (5) Symbols and Identity. The final chapter is a brief guide to Michigan folklife resources, including archives, museums, and a selected bibliography for those educators and students interested in reading more about the folklore and folklife of Michigan. For each of the first five sections the editors have selected some previously published articles and added some new contributions. Each section has a brief introduction to help set these articles in the broader perspective being examined. Clearly, three or four articles could never truly represent the genre; however, it is hoped that these selections will stimulate a richer understanding of Michigan folklife and encourage other scholars to turn their attention to the Michigan experience in the years ahead.

What the reader may take away from these collected essays regarding folklife in Michigan may be hard to predict. It is hoped though that certain stereotypes may be set to rest.

The volume demonstrates that folklife is not just rural, it is urban and even suburban; that folk artists and tradition bearers are of all ages, and they are like you and me; that folk music, art, architecture, legends and tales are not crude or primitive but are in fact sophisticated in form and meaning, and that folklife is not old or pre-industrial, but rather it is with us today and new forms emerge even in industrial contexts. And finally, the reader should see that the supposed anonymity of folk traditions and those who practice them is a function of who is doing the looking. Folk traditions are cultural specific and we each create meaning in our lives by including these practices of our family, ethnic, regional or occupational distinctive folk traditions. We are all tradition bearers.

---

1. Linda Degh, Ed., *Indiana Folklore: A Reader* (Bloomington: Indiana University Press) 1980, vi.

Folk Art and Architecture

Vernacular
Architecture

Cedar Fan Carving

Michigan Hmong
Textiles

Museums for the
People

rt and architecture found in

Michigan provide the material evidence of the way in which people have interacted with the land and each other. When associated with traditional behaviors or customs, these man-made (or sometimes man and machine-made) objects are referred to as folk, or traditional, arts. They involve skills learned by observing and imitating a traditional creative act or through oral transmission. Though many revivalists are engaged in so-called folk art production and some forms of traditional arts have been widely commercialized and popularized, most traditional material culture forms are closely tied to a small group experience. This association usually relates directly to an occupation, a religion, an ethnic affiliation, a region, a family, or a community.

With the variety of occupational, cultural, and geographic regions in Michigan, it follows that a wide variety of folk arts also exist in this state. For instance, one can find folk art connected to such occupations as lumbering (carvings) and ice-fishing (spear and lure making); to such ethnic groups as Hmong (embroidered and appliqued textiles) or Afro-Americans (strip quilts); to such religious groups as Mennonites (fundraising quilts) or Shakers (spirit drawings); and to such regions as the Upper Peninsula (pasties) and mid-Michigan (round roofed barns). Some forms of folk art such as rag carpets are made for more lasting purposes; others such as snowmen or carved jack-o-lanterns serve more temporary functions. Not only is the existence and prevalence in Michigan of certain folk art forms influenced by its function within a group, it is also contingent on the larger economic, social, and cultural factors that are at work.

The articles selected provide but a glimpse into this variety of folk art expression. Marshall McLennan's article, "Common House Types in Southern Michigan," traces the settlement of southern Michigan by examining the house types found in this area. By focusing on the interaction of regional and national influences on rural Greek Revival houses, McLennan demonstrates that regional cultural traditions reinterpret national architectural styles.

The tradition of cedar fan carving in Michigan is examined in the next article by C. Kurt Dewhurst and Marsha MacDowell. This type of fan carving has its origins in Scandinavia and was brought to Michigan lumber camp settings by Scandinavian immigrants. No longer exclusively practiced by Scandinavians, Michigan lumbermen learned a fan carving tradition that continues today, even after the decline of lumbering in Michigan. The article illustrates how the material cultural tradition of one nation can assume new meaning through an association with an occupation and emerge also as an occupational tradition.

"Michigan Hmong Textiles," by C. Kurt Dewhurst, Yvonne Lockwood, and Marsha MacDowell, documents the substantial changes that a material culture tradition undergoes when it is subjected to cultural disruption and transplantation. In this case, Hmong refugees who have resettled in Michigan have utilized their traditional needlework skills to produce textiles in America which reflect drastic alterations in their original and traditional function, appearance, and technique. Such alterations provide material evidence of the changes traditional arts undergo when a group is adapting and acculturating to a new environment.

Because of the long history of settlement by such a wide variety of ethnic groups, the range of folk art adaptations found in this state is great. MacDowell and Dewhurst's article on Michigan's museum bars widens the perspective on what constitutes art and art collections. Examined here is a series of eating or drinking establishments which operate as collection centers for material culture related to a local community. Participants in the development of these "living museums" make significant statements about what is culturally important in a community. Not only is the museum building itself an artifact to be studied, but the collection of objects within can clearly shed light on community values and history.

Studying how and why folk art and architecture in Michigan is produced will help bridge our understanding of how other forms of art and architecture are learned, created, and used. Without becoming aware of and understanding the history and strength of the traditional artistic life of Michiganders, it is impossible to fully understand the history of art in general in this state.

Vernacular Architecture: Common House Types in Southern Michigan

Marshall McLennan

majority of the settlers who took up land and pioneered farms in southern Michigan during the thirty-seven years preceding the Civil War came from upstate New York and from New England. The New Yorkers themselves were separated from their New England roots by no more than a generation and sometimes less. In clearing the land, building homes and farm structures, erecting grist- and sawmills, and laying out townsites and road systems, the settlers brought into being a cultural landscape in Michigan combining visual elements of their New England regional background with emerging national landscape characteristics.[1] One element of the cultural landscape which exemplifies this synthesis of New England and national influences in Michigan is the Greek Revival farmhouse.[2]

The Settlementscape in Southern Michigan

To better understand the context of this interaction on the dwelling, it is useful to first examine the interplay of regional and national influences on the larger settlement landscape within which the houses were immersed. The strong sense of community characteristic of New England social organization continued to be formulated in Michigan not only by means of congregational association

A shorter version of this paper, "The Cultural Landscape in Southern Michigan: The Interaction of Regional and Natural Influences as Exemplified by Rural Greek Revival Houses," was presented at the annual meeting of the Pioneer America Society, Galena, Illinois, November 1987.

but also by the traditional New England township form of political and spatial organization. While townships varied in size and shape in colonial New England, experience eventually led to a general consensus that 36 square miles was the ideal township size—any larger and it became difficult for outlying farm families to effectively participate in the activities of the township center. Congress drew upon the New England experience in 1785 when it passed legislation creating the 36-square-mile township and range system for the survey and alienation of the public domain.[3] Use of the township and range system in Michigan nevertheless created a landscape of property, field, and road boundaries very different from that of New England because the system consisted of a hierarchy of grids. While the size of the Michigan township has New England ancestry, the square form of the township, together with its one mile square sectional subdivisions, must be associated with the emergent nineteenth-century national landscape. Modification of the New England township first occurred in upstate New York, and the model was carried to southern Michigan by immigrants from that region.

The cultural landscape of the Michigan township, except for its checkerboard spatial organization, is, nevertheless, only modestly modified from that of its colonial period New England progenitor. The New England township was conceptually neither urban nor rural, but rather was intended to be a cohesive social entity.[4] In most instances, colonial period New England townships were entirely rural, and contrary to the myth of the nucleated colonial New England agricultural village, the farm population was dispersed throughout the township.[5] The population periodically congregated at the "town(ship) center" for community meetings, religious services, and the like. Landscape elements that characterized the "center" included a meetinghouse, eventually a separate church and perhaps a schoolhouse, a green used for various "common" purposes, a graveyard, the clergyman's residence, and occasionally, from the eighteenth century onward, a smithery or tavern.[6] Although the township center provided limited services for the farm population, to a time-traveler from the twentieth century, the average center would have appeared completely rural in aspect. The only colonial period nucleated New England agricultural villages, in the real sense of the word, were the linear broadstreet settlements of the Connecticut River Valley. While a few townships developed port or market-town functions and enjoyed a more urbanized, populated, and nucleated center during the colonial period, the stereotypical

16

nucleated New England village characterized by a group of amply proportioned residences grouped in association with church, meetinghouse, and commons emerged only in the 1790s and the first decades of the nineteenth century. These residences were the homes of merchants and artisans, not farmers. Population growth and productivity gains in New England agriculture after the Revolutionary War stimulated the growth of market towns which focalized at the preexisting township centers, or more frequently, as a "main street" oriented along one of the approaches to the center.[7]

The New England township was undergoing its metamorphosis during the decades in which upstate New York was being settled. In New York urban settlements were incorporated entities distinct and separate from the townships, which again became essentially rural in character. Settlement organization in Michigan followed the model formulated in upstate New York. Washtenaw County serves as a case in point. Ypsilanti and Ann Arbor became incorporated villages independent of their townships in 1832 and 1833, respectively. Other incorporations followed, although frequently not before the settlement had functioned as a commercial and service center for several townships for two or three decades. Saline and Manchester are two such examples, offering church, post office, mercantile, banking, medical, milling, and artisan services by 1837, but not incorporating until shortly before the Civil War. Dixboro, first settled in 1824, remains a part of Superior Township even today, and with its church facing a common, it is the epitomy (except in the size of its residential area) of an 1800 New England township center. More commonly, however, the practice has been the legal separation of urban nucleations from their mother townships.

Turning to the Michigan townships, we find that, separated from urban settlements, they took form along lines similar to those of the pre-urban agricultural townships of colonial New England. A dispersed rural population took root throughout the individual townships. Sectional crossroads became the most popular location for erecting a town hall (successor to the meetinghouse), country church, or a schoolhouse. Even today, such examples of these buildings as the Webster United Church of Christ and the Dexter and Superior townships halls are found standing in isolation at rural intersections or along country roads. Because of the diversity of denominations in Michigan, usually more than one church was erected in a township. Sometimes two or more of these community-serving buildings were clustered together. If these clusters were located on a stage road or route of extra-local travel, other proto-urban establishments such as a tavern, general store, smithery, or wagon manufactory might materialize and a crossroad hamlet come into being.[8] Lima and Sylvan Centers, and the much smaller and ephemeral Carpenter Corners, are examples of this settlement type in Washtenaw County. Cherry Hill is a surviving example in Wayne County. In other instances, such as Hudson Mills, Mooreville, Foster City, Lowell, Delhi, and Scio, nucleated hamlets developed around water-powered mills. It was not uncommon for two hamlets to take form within a township.

Larger settlements in Michigan deviated more from their equivalents in New England than did the rural farmsteads, centers, and hamlets. In New England nucleated urban settlements remained part of the body politic of the township. The Michigan State Legislature followed the national trend in providing for the separate incorporations of cities and villages.[9] Urban settlements constituted separate political entities. Although Michigan was settled by Yankees, they came as individuals and families, not as congregational groups. Town sites were laid out by speculators in real estate. While most nucleated settlements in New England were characterized by informal, irregularly laid out street patterns, the growing acceptance of Renaissance-inspired town planning concepts conspired with the formal geometry and utilitarian logic of the sectional survey system to influence most Michigan speculators to lay out their town sites in street grids. In the Western Reserve of Ohio, settlers from Connecticut, despite the utilization of a formal geometric spatial organization, fashioned their town centers to serve administrative and religious needs in a manner consistent with their regional landscape traditions. In Michigan, where the heyday of town-founding lagged a decade or two behind Ohio, the town center more typically was dominated by commercial land uses. Town plats in Michigan frequently included a park-like square in the tradition of the common, but either commercial enterprises dominated the space fronting the common, or commercial development along one of the streets leading from the square led to the emergence of a linear main street which became the real center of the town.

A hierarchical integration of county and township political entities gave rise in Michigan to a type of urban center completely foreign to traditional New England—the county seat. As a settlement type, the county seat associated with a courthouse square complex appears to have originated at Lancaster, Pennsylvania. The courthouse square complex comprises a centrally located courthouse in a square surrounded by the town's main commercial enterprises. A pioneering study of the courthouse square phenomenon by Edward Price suggests that New England settlers in the Great Lakes states accepted this feature of the national landscape only half-heartedly.[10] While Ann Arbor possessed a centrally located courthouse square until the 1950s, most Michigan county seats appear to have shunted the courthouse square off to the periphery of the downtown area. A detailed study of town planning practices in Michigan county seats is needed, but preliminary observations indicate that a compromise between regional landscape traditions and national practice occurred in Michigan.

Urban settlements, because of their commercial and intellectual connectivity with the outside world, are centers of change. They are more innovative and receptive to new ideas and fashions than rural areas. Consequently, it is not surprising that Michigan's cultural affinity with New England remains more apparent in the countryside than in the towns.

Approaches to the Study of Buildings

Of all the elements of the cultural landscape, the rural dwelling is the most basic, and, with the exception of road and property lines, the most resistant to change. In the academic world two approaches, each with its own objectives and value biases, have developed for the study of buildings. One has been called the "culturogeographic" approach.[11] Primarily involving cultural geographers and folklife scholars, this school of thought looks upon traditional buildings as expressions of vernacular culture. The other approach, that of the architectural historian, has focused on architecture as an expression of innovative high style design influenced by fashionable intellectual currents.

The culturogeographic view has been interested in folk structures and common houses, using house form, massing, floor plan, number of bays, facade orientation, and sometimes other morphological elements to identify "house types."[12] The cultural geographer identifies and analyses house types as an element of the cultural landscape of regions, an element that contributes to the regional sense of place, and in fact, functions as "spoor" that gives evidence of the existence and spatial distribution of culture regions.[13] The

19

folklorist regards the same building more as an artifact of material culture from which evidence can be derived about the workings and evolution of folk culture.[14] Nevertheless, both groups are linked by a common concern with and appreciation for the importance of the vernacular built environment. On the other hand, until very recently academic architectural history has emphasized the aesthetics of architectural style and its changes through time.[15] Analysis is directed to buildings that are monumental, conceptually sophisticated, unique, progressive, pivotal, evolutionary, or client-oriented. To a great extent these are buildings produced by wealth and power and are reflective of the literate segment of society's highest ideals, aspirations, and abilities.[16]

An approach that integrates the two perspectives is necessary for a full understanding of Greek Revival architecture in rural southern Michigan because the period during which these structures were built bridged the transition from tradition-based regional folk construction to fashion-oriented national construction. Most of Michigan's Greek Revival structures can be divided into "types" because they adhere to massing and floor plan traditions that can be traced to New England folk antecedents.

The "Great Tradition" and the "Little Tradition"

In a sense, the field of architectural history has emphasized architecture as art—as a beacon of society's "Great Tradition"—while the culturogeographic approach is concerned with the "little tradition." Anthropologist Robert Redfield formulated the "Great Tradition-little tradition" dichotomy to argue that illiterate folk or peasant societies are, in reality, part societies existing in a dependent relationship with an educated urbanized national elite.[17] The rural inhabitants of colonial New England and nineteenth-century southeastern Michigan were not peasants. In fact, until eighteenth-century mercantile commerce fostered the rise of wealthy merchant families, colonial New England was a literate but essentially middle-class society. Yet there are some useful insights that can be drawn from Redfield's analysis of social structure in traditional societies to help us to understand the architectural vocabulary of Greek Revival buildings in rural southern Michigan.

The little tradition expresses vernacular culture. In peasant societies vernacular culture is oriented to local tradition; it is conservative and unreflective. The way something is done, such as building a house, is based on what has always been done in the past. Conversely, the Great Tradition is worldly, self-conscious, and reflective. It is influenced by the fashionable, forever seeking higher truths. Despite the contrasts, the two traditions are interdependent, two expressions of the same culture. Folktales are filtered and reformulated as epics by the Great Tradition, while moral lessons from the sacred scriptures of the Great Tradition are explained to and passed on among the peasantry as parables.

The idea of a two-class social hierarchy is, of course, too simple to apply to New England or to the Stewart England from which the New England Puritans emigrated. By the end of the medieval period a middle class of country gentlemen, yeoman farmers, and artisan-merchant buyers had inserted itself between the Great Tradition of the nobility and the little tradition of the peasantry. In rural areas this middle class was to a fair degree literate and cognizant of, though not intimate with, the Great Tradition, but with roots immersed in the little tradition. The cultural hearth from which the Puritan New Englanders came was East Anglia—"a rural society comprised of country squires, prosperous yeomen, and small crofters."[18] The house types that emigrants from the eastern counties brought to New England reflected this mix of middle and little traditions. The early Puritans introduced dwellings ranging in size from single room cots to multistory manor houses, but as time went on a few standard types emerged to comprise the New England house type tradition. Whether yeoman farmhouse or simple cottage, these New England house types were all derived from a provincial East Anglian medieval folk tradition.[19] Over the course of two hundred years East Anglian house types were remolded into distinctly New England types.

Greek Mania

Surviving rural houses built in Michigan prior to the Civil War clearly reveal their New England folk ancestry, but many of the houses also incorporate national design elements associated with the popularity of Greek Revival architectural motifs during the first half of the nineteenth century. During Greece's war of independence from the Turks, America's perception of Greece as the cradle of its own democratic institutions was fanned into a national enthusiasm for adopting other elements of ancient Greek culture as well. In the South, where social stratification closely coincided with the Great

Tradition-little tradition dichotomy, the architectural impact of this cultural fashion was largely limited to the gentry, and the Greek Revival style became the hallmark of patrician endeavor. It was in New England and upstate New York that "Greek mania" became manifest throughout all elements of society. A romanticized "new Greece" sprang up in the Yankee landscape, particularly on the upstate New York frontier. Greek-temple churches and dwellings populated brand new settlements named after places of classical antiquity.[20] Many of these classical names reappeared in Michigan as New York Yankees migrated westward.

Outside the towns, in New York and Michigan, literate yeoman farmers also embraced the Greek fashion with enthusiasm. They clothed their traditional New England folkhouses with Greek Revival ornamentation. Sometimes they even reorganized the spatial arrangement of their houses to better accommodate the style. In so doing, the early nineteenth-century settlers of Michigan combined fashion and tradition. This architectural synthesis, drawing from a regional heritage while at the same time partaking of a national cultural enthusiasm, contributed to the fashioning of a new regional landscape in the eastern Great Lakes region. Considerable experimentation took place during the 1810s and 1820s in upstate New York in the achievement of this synthesis. Greek Revival structures were built by Michigan pioneers primarily between the 1830s and the 1860s, and the similarities between houses of the same folk type reveal that by the time the New Yorkers began to settle in Michigan a general consensus had been achieved regarding the integration of classical architectural vocabulary with restructured vernacular forms and plans. It is now time to examine specific Greek Revival house types characteristic of rural southern Michigan and attempt to identify their respective Great Tradition-little tradition elements.

New England One-and-a-Half Cottage

The New England one-and-a-half cottage is the simplest farmhouse type built in the Greek Revival mode in southern Michigan between 1830 and 1865.[21] It was also built in towns wherever lot frontages were wide enough to accommodate it. The type takes its name from its most fundamental distinguishing characteristic, its one and a half story height. It has a gable roof with the eave oriented so as to parallel the street or road (fig. 1).

Robin Haynes

Figure 1. New England one-and-a-half cottage.

Above the ground floor, the loft area is raised sufficiently to function as living space for the occupants. Because the floor of the loft is lower than the height of the eave, one-and-a-half cottages frequently feature a row of small, horizontally oriented knee windows (usually with three lights) under the eave of the facade. In cottages adhering carefully to high style principles, these windows are located in a frieze, but in most Michigan examples they are placed below or partly protruding into any frieze board that may be present. Double sash windows located in the gable end of the loft generally break the plane of the eave line. The typical Michigan one-and-a-half cottage is two rooms wide with the entry placed centrally in the eave side of the dwelling and opening into a central hallway, but the floor plan varies because this house type is descended from two distinct, though related, colonial New England prototypes—the two room hall-and-parlor dwelling and the two room wide, one-and-a-half room deep Cape Cod cottage, which possesses the "New England floor plan."[22]

One of the distinguishing features of the New England folk-housing tradition is the central placement of the chimney. Both

23

colonial ancestral prototypes of the one-and-a-half cottage share this characteristic. As classical architectural influences penetrated New England in the second half of the eighteenth century and introduced the conceptual ideal of symmetry in which rooms were arranged in a mirror image of each other on each side of a central hallway, the older tradition of a centrally placed chimney gradually gave way. A single central chimney was replaced, in new constructions, by chimneys located at the gable ends of the house. This change took effect more slowly in rural and small town housing than in the cities. Central chimneys remained common in turn of the century one-and-a-half cottages in upstate New York, but they are only infrequently seen in Michigan versions of this house type. Displacement of fireplaces and chimneys by stoves and flues occurred concurrently with the building of many one-and-a-half cottages in Michigan, thereby further dissipating chimney location traditions. Consequently, the Michigan version of the one-and-a-half cottage varies from a narrow, one room deep structure patterned after the hall-and-parlor house to a one-and-a-half room deep Cape Cod plans, both modified by alternative chimney and flue placements and the inclusion of a central hallway (fig. 2).

In colonial New England the hall-and-parlor house and the Cape Cod cottage are recognized as distinct folk types. The floor plan of the Cape Cod cottage, however, suggests that it originated as an expansion of the hall-and-parlor plan by the addition of a half depth rank of rooms behind the hall and parlor. The steep pitch of the gable roof—a medieval trait—of the hall-and-parlor house gave way in the Cape Cod cottage to a somewhat shallower pitch, and the horizontality of the structure was further accentuated by a lowering of the eave to rest just above the top of the ground floor windows.

In the second and third decades of the nineteenth century, however, the distinction between the two types was blurred by subordinating the exterior appearance of new cottages to the dictates of national fashion, and the New England one-and-a-half cottage materialized as a new type. In New England and upstate New York many of the one-and-a-halfs retained their traditional central chimney floor plans, but the exteriors were exuberantly reformulated in the architectural idiom of the Greek Revival style. Door surrounds made use of entablatures, pediments, pilasters, and, if the house had a central passage, entry sidelights. Most fundamentally, the angle of the roof pitch was lowered to conform with the characteristic roof slope of a Greek temple. The profile of the temple-like roof was

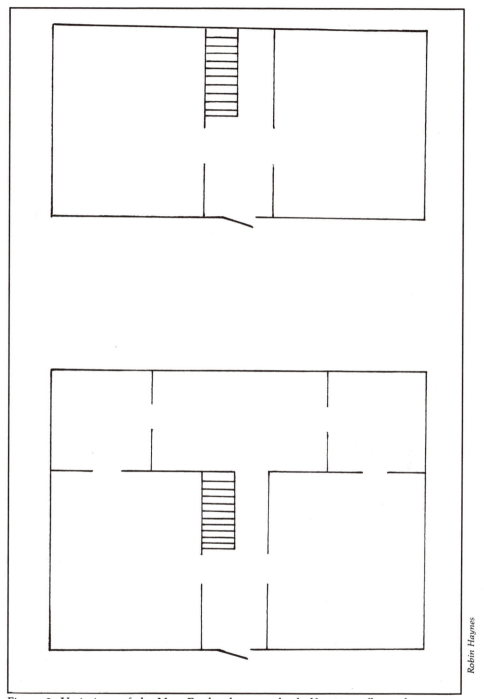

Figure 2. Variations of the New England one-and-a-half cottage floor plan.

Robin Haynes

further emphasized by the use of classical cornice moldings or a box cornice along the eaves and across the gable to form gable-end pediments. Alternatively, and more commonly, the pediments were merely suggested by employing abbreviated cornice returns. Sometimes the facade cornice was visually, though not structurally, supported by pilasters which replaced end boards.

Some of Michigan's one-and-a-half cottages adhered to the one-and-a-half room depth of the traditional New England floor plan, not by encompassing the two ranks of rooms under a single gable roof like the Cape Cod cottage, but rather by employing a separate leanto roof over the one story, half-depth rooms in the rear. Undoubtedly this arrangement resulted when the occupants decided to expand a one-and-a-half cottage with a hall-and-parlor plan. One alternative was a new roof, but that was expensive. In colonial New England the less expensive solution was a saltbox roof. However, in pre-Civil War Michigan a saltbox roof could not be conjoined with the existing classical gabled roof without doing injustice to the symmetry of the gable-end pediments. The separate leanto roof was made compatible with the classicism of the rest of the cottage by utilizing a shallow pitch emphasized by a single boxed raking cornice, raking board, and cornice return. Most Michigan one-and-a-half cottages employing elements of the Greek Revival style were constructed between 1835 and 1860. Three variations have been identified: the hall-and-parlor, the hall-and-parlor with classical leanto, and a Cape Cod plan type, in all of which the central chimney usually had been replaced by a central hallway. Lateral dropwings and rear outshoots added living space and individuality to the three basic variations but they did not modify the conceptual essence of the core block of the subtypes. While the leanto of the one subtype may be structurally exterior to the core block, it is conceptually an integrated part of the New England floor plan and visually integral as well because of the classical cornice trim. A few dwellings are in reality two stories high in terms of scale and could be designated as I-houses except that the second story windows are placed so high as to necessitate their abbreviation, thereby maintaining the visual integrity of the one-and-a-half cottage's facade.

Whatever the variation, these are second generation one-and-a-halfs. By the time they were being built in Michigan, the first flush of Yankee enthusiasm for the Greek Revival style had somewhat abated. Consequently, the use of classical motifs was generally more restrained than with the first generation cottages built in New

England, New York, and the Western Reserve of Ohio. This restraint, characterized by more modest door surrounds, simple wooden pedimented lintels over windows instead of molded pediments or entablatures, and less frequent use of corner pilasters, reflects the age old process of absorption, simplification, and reinterpretation of Great Tradition motifs by little tradition practitioners. Some Michigan one-and-a-halfs are so vernacular as to show their allegiance to Greek Revival fashion only by the shallow pitch of the roof, extension of the roof a few inches beyond the vertical plane of the exterior walls, and by the use of wide frieze and raking boards. Conversely, the reorganization of interior space and chimney or flue placement testifies to a breaking down of traditional regional folk habits and to the appearance of a greater degree of individual innovation.

In 1860 the Greek Revival one-and-a-half cottage may have been the most common farmhouse type in southern Michigan. Because it is a small house, there has been a tendency over the years to add wings, absorb the original structure within a larger structure, subordinate the original cottage as the wing of a larger unit, or to build a new house and either tear the cottage down or use it as an outbuilding. In observing upright-and-wing houses in southern Michigan, it is apparent that in many instances the wing was originally a one-and-a-half cottage predating the larger upright block. Nevertheless, a rural survey of some 4,000 buildings in rural Washtenaw County in 1981–1982 revealed the one-and-a-half New England cottage to still be the second most common nineteenth-century Greek Revival farmhouse type.[23]

The I-House

The I-house is more commonly associated, in the minds of house type scholars, with regional traditions other than New England. This is largely due to Fred Kniffin, the father of American house type studies, who was the first to identify and define the I-house in the literature. He defined the I-house as a structure that was two or more rooms wide, one room deep, two stories high, with end chimneys. It is the last diagnostic element that poses problems in associating the I-house with the New England building tradition. The meaning of "I-house" has been evolving, however, in recent scholarly literature. Some scholars now refer to "central-chimney I-houses," as well as "I-cottages," thereby taking liberties with chimney placement and the number of stories. The "garrison house" is a well-known seventeenth-century New England house type, which can be considered a central-chimney I-house. The garrison house, however, is uniquely characterized by its second story jetty or overhang.

After the turn of the eighteenth century few garrison houses were constructed, but this is merely to say that the practice of constructing a jetty ceased; the first half of the eighteenth century saw the building of many central-chimney I-houses in New England. A possible alternative name for this regionally specific New England house type, which has been completely ignored in the literature, is the "postgarrison house."

From the mid-eighteenth century onward, the New England tradition of the central chimney began to decline because of the growing influence of the Georgian style, which called for a central hallway. Georgian period I-houses with end chimneys began to appear in New England, which were virtually identical in morphology to those in the Middle Atlantic and Tidewater colonies. At the same time, however, the I-house, whether with central or end chimney placement, began to decline in popularity as another house type with the preferred New England floor plan gained favor. This was the New England Large. The I-house was part of the repertoire of house types brought to Michigan by upstate New York and New England immigrants, but it was not a preferred type. For instance, among the 506 Greek Revival dwellings currently surviving in rural Washtenaw County, only 9 are I-houses.

Observed from the front, a five bay I-house looks exactly like a New England Large, but it differs in that it is only one room deep.[24] Three bay I-houses have more modest proportions, but otherwise are similar in appearance to five bay examples. I-houses with irregular fenestration patterns were built in Michigan in the second half of the nineteenth century and are more numerous than the earlier Greek Revival ones. Most surviving rural examples of the later nineteenth-century type I-house lack ornamentive association with any style and appear to represent lower middle-income housing.

With both the one-and-a-half cottage and the I-house, it is the long dimension of the dwelling that presents its facade to the public, consequently, use of Greek Revival decorative elements is similar in both types except that the two-story I-house has no need for frieze windows (fig. 3). Interior spatial arrangements of the Michigan Greek Revival I-house reflect the influence of both New England folk building tradition and Georgian classicism. In southern

Robin Haynes

Figure 3. Three Bay Greek Revival I-house.

Michigan an occasional I-house can be found which retains the central chimney, but the central-passage I-house is more common. The one room depth of the dwelling, whatever the chimney and hallway arrangement, has roots that can be traced back through New England to English folk practice.

The New England Large

The New England Large is a traditional house type of eighteenth-century New England, a two-story rectangle with the long side of the structure, commonly of five bays, facing the front. The interior spatial arrangement is the traditional New England plan. This type represents the pre-Greek Revival end point in the evolutionary sequence of New England folkhousing which began with the traditional English hall-and-parlor house. The typical initial expansion was the addition of a two-room, second story (garrison and postgarrison I-houses), then with the addition of a narrow rank of rooms to the rear on the ground floor, the house evolved into a saltbox type. With the expansion of the second story to the rear over the leanto rooms on the ground floor, the evolutionary sequence had arrived at the New England Large. Further expansion generally was in the form of a variety of rear ells which were external to the core block of the dwelling. The New England Large is regionally distinct as a folkhouse type from the Pennsylvania four-over-four type because of its centrally placed chimney and by the fact that the rear rooms are of a shallow depth because of their leanto conceptual origins. Some structures became a New England Large by means of expansion; others were built as such, but the proportions of the rear rooms in comparison to the front rooms remained much the same. The full-scale Georgian manses with central hallways, which were built primarily in the port cities and towns in New England late in the eighteenth century, represented a shift in Great Tradition architectural values and are not to be confused with New England Large houses even though the latter often utilized Georgian decorative mannerisms.

At the end of the eighteenth century the New England Large dominated the "large farmhouse" end of the spectrum. However, because of "Greek mania" the upright-and-wing house emerged as a new and increasingly popular alternative to the New England Large as a large scale dwelling early in the nineteenth century. Among the New England Large dwellings which continued to be built in Michigan, the effect of the downward permeation of Great Tradition classical ideals can be discerned. The primary expression of classical influence upon New England Larges in Michigan is that the traditional New England floor plan was modified. While the room arrangement was basically the same, the central chimney was displaced by a central hallway, and symmetrical end chimneys or variously placed flues were incorporated into the design. With the change in chimney location, the kitchen was no longer invariably located in the center of the rear rank of rooms (fig. 4).

It appears that most conservative pre-Civil War farmers, who preferred the traditional two story rectangular farmhouse oriented broadside to the road, could afford to build a full-scale New England Large rather than the one room deep I-house. Although Washtenaw County's New England Large dwellings are more numerous than the I-houses, they are representative of a residual tradition that was perceived by most settlers at the time as no longer meeting their domestic needs and aspirations.[25]

Robin Haynes

Figure 4. Michigan New England Large house type.

The Gable-Fronter

The gable-fronter is a one, one-and-a-half, or two-story dwelling with a gable roof in which the front-facing entry is located in the gable-end of the structure (fig. 5). It originated in New England and upstate New York at the turn of the nineteenth century where both Great Tradition and little tradition examples are plentiful.

The gable-fronter arose as a response to the Greek Revival movement. In English and American building traditions the long side of a building faced the front except where the narrow frontage of urban lots precluded such an orientation. Even then the roof was constructed so that the eave rather than a gable comprised the upper element of the facade. Despite embracing the Greek Revival architectural vocabulary, the New England one-and-a-half cottage, the I-house, and the New England Large maintained this tradition. Academically trained American architects realized at the beginning of the nineteenth century, however, that a true realization of the Greek temple form required that the gable should face the front, and

31

Robin Haynes

Figure 5. Gable-fronter house type.

ideally, project over a raised porch supported by columns designed
to accord with one of the classical orders. The first gable-front
buildings were public structures, then high style houses. They represented a Great Tradition assimilation and interpretation of the classical Greek architectural heritage.

In New England and New York use of the Greek Revival architectural vocabulary, especially the gable-front orientation, penetrated further down the socioeconomic ladder than elsewhere in the
country. Reorienting the gable to the front and shaping the gable as
a pediment became a general Yankee response. Whether colonnaded
or simply utilizing a pedimented gable, these "temple houses"
became a hallmark of the New England culture region and a statement of ardent belief in the efficacy of democratic institutions. The
gable-fronter represents a fundamental break with the New England
folk culture tradition. It does not have colonial roots, and therefore,
is not truly a folkhouse. As employed in rural areas of the New
England culture region, most examples are not really high style

houses either, but the type nevertheless is a regionally expressed adaptation of a nationally fashionable style and consequently an artifact of New England culture.[26]

Reorientation of the house necessitated a relocation of the front entry, and more fundamentally, a restructuring of interior space. Insufficient focused study of the gable-front house type has been carried out, particularly of little tradition representatives, to generalize about floor plans although it is apparent that some gable-fronters made use of row house side-passage plans. While both large- and small-scale gable-fronters are common in upstate New York, and although they are a common urban house type in southern Michigan,[27] examples of Greek Revival gable fronters built as farmhouses are not numerous in Washtenaw County.[28] It can be speculated that a large gable-fronter was too demanding in construction time and economic resources, consequently, the one-and-a-half cottage was preferred. The most popular large-scale farmhouse form in pre-Civil War Washtenaw County, judging by surviving period houses, was the upright-and-wing. Basically, the latter type is composed of the conjoining of a gable-fronter and a one-and-a-half cottage. To the farm family aspiring to endorse the success of its homesteading endeavor, building the one-and-a-half first would present the least economic challenge and would not predetermine the ultimate scale of the upright-and-wing house. Because the upright or gable-front unit must have larger proportions than the wing, building the gable-fronter prematurely, before the family's economic means allowed for ample proportions, would result in an undersized house.

The Upright-and-Wing House

The upright-and-wing dwelling is a compound farmhouse made up of a one-and-a-half to two-story gable-front unit called the "upright", and a lateral wing, which during the period of Greek Revival popularity was almost invariably of a somewhat lower height than its companion unit. Together the two units form a tee-shape, although in its formative stage of development in New England and New York, some examples can be observed in which either the front or back wall of the wing is flush with the equivalent wall of the upright, thereby assuming an ell shape. Like the gable-fronter, the upright-and-wing is a postcolonial dwelling type. Generally an open porch is attached to or recessed into the wing (fig. 6).

Robin Haynes

Figure 6. Upright-and-wing house type.

Scholars have surmised that the first upright-and-wing houses came about by adding a gable-fronter to a preexisting one-and-a-half cottage and vice versa. Many instances of such accretion have been documented in the Northeast as well as in Michigan.[29] It has also been suggested that the Greek Revival fashion was responsible for the upright-and-wing house displacing the earlier New England Large as the big farmhouse in the New England repertoire of house types.[30] The upright provided a facade eminently suitable for displaying all the elements of a Greek temple front while the wing cornice could be fashioned as an entablature and, with the addition of an open or recessed porch, could even accommodate a miniaturized colonnade.

In New England and New York extensive experimentation in the massing and proportions of the two component units took place during the formative period of the upright-and-wing house type. While variety is found among Michigan representatives, expression of the form during their period of construction was much more standardized than had been the case with their eastern predecessors. Nevertheless, stages in the evolution of the Michigan upright-and-wing can be discerned. In early examples (1830–1840) the length of the wing varied from one to three rooms, but by about 1850 a one-room and passage or two-room length had become the norm. The kitchen was usually located within the wing. During the period in which the Greek Revival style was employed, the upright unit went through two stages of development. In the earlier type the upright was one and a half to two stories high and generally three bays wide. Most diagnostic of this stage of development was the fact that the main entry was located in the facade of the upright segment of the house. This location of the door, as well as the three bay width of the upright, directly links the ancestry of the upright-and-wing house to the gable-fronter. A 1983 survey of upright-and-wing houses in Oakland, Livingston, and Jackson counties found that all the dwellings with the main entry located in the upright, for which construction dates could be determined, were built between 1840 and 1865.[31] In the second stage of development, the upright relinquished the front door to the side wing, while generally shrinking in width to two bays. The wing also tended to gain in height. Dates of construction for this type, as established in the 1983 survey, ranged from about 1830 to the early twentieth century.[32] The earliest of these may be surmised to be one-and-a-half cottages subsequently expanded into upright-and-wings, thereby accounting for the door being in the wing, while the post-1870 dwellings are Victorian-era structures. It might be noted that some of the most vernacular upright-and-wings constructed in Washtenaw County in the 1870s and 1880s, while bearing the vertical proportions characteristic of the period, possessed ornamentive details limited to shaped lintels over windows and narrow cornices with very abbreviated returns or merely simple frieze boards under the roof eave. It is apparent that by this time the simplest elements of the Greek Revival idiom had become incorporated into the basic fabric of the little tradition.

A common variation of the upright-and-wing in southern Michigan has a room projecting forward from the far end of the wing. Frequently the front wall projects to the same plane as the facade of the upright. The gabled roof of the wing extends to the front to incorporate the protruding end unit, thereby creating a recessed or umbrage porch between the upright and the end room. In Greek Revival examples of this type, classical columns *in antis* characterize the porch entry. The prevalence of square columns testifies to a pervading provincial interpretation.

Only the wing portion of the upright-and-wing house has direct colonial folk roots in New England. The gable-front segment exemplifies a Great Tradition interpretation of the Grecian past, but before being capable of being used as a component of the upright-and-wing house it had to go through the gable-fronter evolutionary stage of being recast in a simpler New England middle-class mold. As was the case with the one-and-a-half cottage and the gable-fronter, the use of Greek Revival decorative elements on Michiganian upright-and-wings was more restrained than in New York and northeastern Ohio. The Michigan houses were built one to four decades after the height of Greek Revival popularity and hence were further removed in time and space from the original sources of Great Tradition inspiration than their eastern prototypes. Of all the Greek Revival types in southern Michigan, the upright-and-wing was the most popular choice of New England settlers.[33]

Upright-and-Doublewing

The upright-and-doublewing dwelling possesses a one-and-a-half to two-story upright with the gable facing the front and has a wing, of lower height, on each side of the upright (fig. 7). The Greek Revival upright-and-doublewing is not a common house type in Michigan. Local examples have two derivations—one Great Tradition, the other, little tradition. The high style derivation can be traced to Palladio and it was popularized by Thomas Jefferson, particularly in the South, as an appropriate house type for the gentry. High style examples are symmetrical in arrangement and classical in their proportions, although those constructed by provincial master builders sometimes reflect that freedom has been taken with classical rules of proportion and interpretation of decorative motifs. However, in the New England culture region some dwellings have attained an upright-and-doublewing form by means of expanding an upright-and-wing house. Sometimes the wing addition is constructed in an appropriate manner, although this does not always entail a symmetrical match with the original wing. More frequently, in the case of farmhouses, the construction materials and/or the stylistic vocabulary comprise a mismatch with the rest of the house.

Robin Haynes

Figure 7. Upright-and-doublewing house type.

The Hen-and-Chicks House

Of all the Greek Revival farmhouse types in southern Michigan, the hen-and-chicks dwelling is perhaps the most unique to Michigan. Long ago Talbot Hamlin noted its prevalence and possible uniqueness to southeastern Michigan.[34] The type consists of a centrally located gable-front block complemented on each flank by matching wings of lower elevation. Unlike the cross-axial orientation of the gable roofed wings of the upright-and-doublewing house, the axial orientation of the wings on hen-and-chicks dwellings parallel the axis of the central upright, and the roof form of the wings is either half-hip or leanto (fig. 8). Because of the roof form and the fact that it is the narrow ends of the wing blocks that comprise part of the facade, the total profile of the facade gives the impression of a mother hen with her wings hovering protectively over her brood of chicks gathered around her feet. A subtype, the one-half hen-and-chicks house, with only one wing, is also prevalent in southern Michigan (fig. 9).

Figure 8. Michigan hen-and-chicks house type

Figure 9. Michigan one-half hen-and chicks house type

In more formal terms, the massing appears to be that of a basilica, a spatial grouping of building components more commonly
employed for religious and public buildings than for domestic structures. Some of the larger examples in Michigan actually do employ a
basilica plan in the interior. However, a modified New England plan
is an alternative ground floor arrangement commonly concealed
within the basilica profile. Most hen-and-chicks houses in
Washtenaw County have two full-scaled front rooms separated by a
central passage leading back to a kitchen and a mix of bedrooms,
pantrys, and utility rooms in the rear. Only the central upright is
two stories high and in the non-basilica plan the second story exterior walls do not penetrate into the ground floor space or play a role
in the division of that space. Many hen-and-chicks houses also vio-
late the ornamentive restraint so characteristic of the other types of
Greek Revival farmhouses. Some southern Michigan examples are
exuberant in their use of door surrounds, pediments, entablatures,
and pilasters. More than with any of the other types, use is made of
colonnaded porches, although this practice seems to be less the case
in Washtenaw County than in other localities in southern
Michigan.

The hen-and-chicks house in southern Michigan exemplifies the
ideal solution to synthesizing the nationally fashionable Greek
Revival style with traditional New England arrangements of interior
domestic space. Of all the local Greek Revival house types in
Washtenaw County, the hen-and-chicks dwelling is the most successful in conveying an exterior impression of Great Tradition cos-
mopolitanism, yet the arrangement of interior space frequently is
entirely folk-derived. The New England Large and the New England
one-and-a-half cottage, while adopting elements of the classical
idiom, sacrificed the use of a temple-front gable in order to perpetuate traditional interior spatial arrangements. The gable-fronter made
the opposite tradeoff. While the upright-and-wing house represents
a compromise, it is one achieved by forgoing the symmetry of the
facade. Only the hen-and-chicks house combines a happy symmetry
of appearance with a familiar interior spatial arrangement.

Hen-and-chicks houses in southern Michigan are fully associated in exterior form and in decorative vocabulary with the pre-
Civil War national landscape as dictated by Great Tradition taste.
Nevertheless, these dwellings were designed and constructed by
master builders, and despite their stylistic exuberance, the craftsmanship (the frequent use of square columns and other forms of free

interpretation of classical motifs) reveals them to be a product of rural middle-class culture. This middle-class Yankee culture was open to the intellectual currents of national fashion, but it also felt free not to slavishly copy, but rather to reinterpret the classical idiom into forms with which it felt comfortable. The commonplace use of the basilica massing with the New England floor plan appears to have been a uniquely Michigan development giving rise to a distinctly Michigan regional house type.[35]

Cobblestone Construction

Some of the classically styled houses of southern Michigan are of cobblestone construction. Use of this form of masonry material originated as a folk practice in upstate New York, and comprises still another culture trait in Michigan's cultural landscape which links the state to the New England culture region. Cobblestone buildings are, perhaps, most numerous in Oakland and Washtenaw counties, where several fine Federal and Greek Revival examples can be found.

Conclusion

The United States is composed of a mosaic of physical and cultural landscapes. In regard to the latter, cultural geographers have identified three colonial-era cultural hearths—southern New England, the Delaware River Valley, and the Tidewater South—where distinctive regional cultural landscapes took form.[36] Each of these regions has been characterized by a unique amalgam of land divisions, road networks, settlement patterns, crop assemblages, and building types comprising a composite landscape. Emigrants from each of these cultural hearths carried with them their traditional heritage of material culture and strategies of land occupance to other areas of the country. In many areas new regional landscapes came into being made up of two or more of the cultural hearths.[37]

In Michigan, however, the pioneer stock in the initial years of cultural landscape formation came primarily from a New England cultural background.[38] Modifications to the regional landscape heritage in Michigan were effected primarily by newly emerging national landscape institutions.

The idea of a distinction between national and regional landscape elements is complemented by Redfield's Great Tradition-little tradition dichotomy. Redfield's model emphasizes that regional traditions are not exotic in regard to national tradition but rather are vernacular or common folk interpretations of the Great Tradition.

Michigan, even in the nineteenth century, was not isolated and its population was not illiterate. Consequently, as helpful as Redfield's model is in making the point that folk traditions and "cultured" traditions are not mutually exclusive, in analyzing rural Greek Revival house types in Michigan we have struggled under the constraints of a dichotomous model. Although early New Englanders were not peasants, they were the bearers of viable folk-housing traditions. The nineteenth-century Michigan house types just discussed, on the other hand, do not easily fit categorization either as folkhouses or as high style architecture.

Another model, one that is specific to architecture and that conceptually parallels those already discussed, accommodates the Michigan circumstances. William Pierson, Jr. argues that in seventeenth-century England "a wholly new level of architecture" came into being with the emergence of a powerful middle class. This middle-class architecture, which he calls "low style," was directly derived from the high style or Great Tradition architecture of the aristocracy.[39] In a vein similar to Redfield, Pierson evokes the process of "permeation" of style downward through the fabric of society.[40] Ultimately, even folkhouses absorb elements derived from the high style idiom. Low style buildings, however, reflect a much more direct and intimate relationship with Great Tradition fashion than folk-houses. In seventeenth-century England low style house possessed almost no connectivity with folk tradition, but on a more modest economic scale slavishly copied upper-class houses. Such was not the case in the more open society of nineteenth-century America. Low style architecture in the New England culture region, which includes Michigan, drew inspiration from both folk tradition and national fashion.

Nineteenth-century rural Greek Revival house types in Michigan were representative of a low style architectural tradition that was well on its way to displacing folkhousing as the embodiment of vernacular architecture. The New England one-and-a-half cottage was the most folk-derivative of the Greek Revival house types erected in Michigan. It still adhered to the New England colonial tradition of the roof eave facing the front, a height of one-and-a-half stories, a width of two rooms and a depth of one to one-and-a-half rooms. Only the roof slope and chimney locations deviated from New England folk tradition. Greek Revival fashion was expressed largely in terms of ornamental garnish. The few New England Large houses found in Michigan, in terms of morphology, represent the culmination of the New England folk tradition, but their scale reveals them to be middle-class farmhouses and the symmetrical spatial arrangement of window, door, and chimney placements testify to the absorption of an earlier generation of classical influences. Greek Revival gable-fronters originated in the East as a solution of the urban elite to the problem of imitating the aesthetic purity and form of the ancient Greek temple while adapting it to the needs of a functional domicile. The far more numerous modest versions of the gable-fronter, which took considerable freedom with the classical architectural idiom, were expressions of low style interpretation. The upright-and-wing, with its off-balance massing and its use of a medieval-derivative additive principle, was a low style house type right from conception. The hen-and-chicks house represented an attempt by middle-class builders to use not only Greek Revival ornamental detailing and symmetrical massing but also to emulate classical concepts of interior spatial organization associated with the basilica plan. However, except in the very large-scaled examples, the rooms located in the wings were too small for comfortable living, and therefore, many resorted to the familiar New England plan.

Although the Greek Revival fashion was a national movement and can be identified as a diagnostic element of the national landscape, this study attempts to demonstrate that regional cultural traditions achieved their own individual interpretations of the Greek Revival style. In rural Michigan the Greek Revival house types that have been identified were associated with the middle class and an emerging "low style" architectural tradition which partook of both national and regional elements. Although the Greek Revival fashion was responsible for the morphology of some of the house types, several of the new morphological forms persisted in Michigan once other styles became fashionable. In sum, the rural population of Michigan and adjacent states fashioned new house types early in the nineteenth century which, despite subsequent superficial decorative changes, became traditional for the remainder of the century.

Acknowledgments: The author is grateful for the illustrations provided by Robin Haynes.

1. The notion that culture groups, by means of their occupance strategies, forge distinctive cultural landscapes and thereby endow culture regions with a characteristic sense of place originated with the geographer Carl Sauer. See "The Morphology of Landscape," in *Land and Life; A Selection from the Writings of Carl Ortwin Sauer,* ed. John Leighly (Berkeley and Los Angeles: University of California Press, 1967), 315–50. See also Marvin W. Mikesell, "Landscape," in *Man, Space, and Environment,* ed. Paul Ward English and Robert C. Mayfield (New York: Oxford University Press, 1972), 9–15; and D. W. Meinig, ed., *The Interpretation of Ordinary Landscapes* (New York: Oxford University Press, 1979), especially the paper by Peirce Lewis, "Axioms for Reading the Landscape, Some Guides to the American Scene," 11–32. Another central figure in the study of American cultural landscapes is John B. Jackson, former editor and longtime contributor to *Landscape.* For a review of Jackson's influence upon American landscape studies, see Meinig, "Reading the Landscape; An Appreciation of W. G. Hoskins and J. B. Jackson," 195–244.

2. The distinction between local or regional landscape elements and national design components is made explicit in John R. Stilgoe, *Common Landscape of America, 1580 to 1845* (New Haven: Yale University Press, 1982).

3. Hildegard Binder Johnson, *Order upon the Land* (New York: Oxford University Press, 1976), 40–46; John Fraser Hart, *The Look of the Land* (Englewood Cliffs, N.J.: Prentice-Hall, 1975), 55–59.

4. Raymond E. Murphy, "Town Structure and Urban Concepts in New England," *Professional Geographer* 16 (March 1964): 1–6.

5. For examples of the myth, see Edna Scofield, "The Origin of Settlement Patterns in Rural New England," *Geographical Review* 28 (1938): 652–63; and Glenn T. Trewartha, "Types of Rural Settlement in Colonial America," *Geographical Review* 36 (1946): 568–96. For the defrocking of the myth, refer to Joseph Sutherland Wood, "The Origin of the New England Village" (Ph.D. diss., Pennsylvania State University, 1978). Wood does point out that some "linear" agricultural villages did exist in colonial New England, mostly in the Connecticut River Valley and in southwestern Connecticut (see p. 148).

6. Initially the Puritans did not believe in "a house of God," and religious services were held in the meetinghouse, an all-purpose community building.

7. Wood, 203–85.

8. The crossroad hamlet is identified as a settlement type by Glenn T. Trewartha, "The Unincorporated Hamlet: One Element of the American Settlement Fabric," *Annals of the Association of American Geographers* 33 (1943): 32–81.

9. In size and function, incorporated villages in Michigan are what past generations called "market" or "country" towns. It should be noted, however, that many nucleated villages, past and present, which serve the same economic functions as their incorporated counterparts have never incorporated and thus have remained an integral part of the township. In this respect they parallel their nineteenth-century prototypes in New England.

10. Edward T. Price, "The Central Courthouse Square in the American County Seat," *Geographical Review* 58 (1968): 29–60.

11. Fred B. Kniffen, "Louisiana House Types," *Annals of the Association of American Geographers* 26 (1936): 179.

12. The cultural geographer who pioneered "house type" studies is Fred B. Kniffen. The two studies by Kniffen that form the foundation for subsequent research are "Louisiana House Types," and "Folk Housing: Key to Diffusion," *Annals of the Association of American Geographers* 55 (1965): 549–77. Two recent studies of methodological interest, which use morphological elements to identify house types, are John A. Jakle, *The Testing of a House Typing System in Two Middle Western Counties: A Comparative Analysis of Rural Houses,* University of Illinois, Department of Geography Occasional Publication no. 11 (Urbana: University of Illinois, 1976); and James R. Shortridge, "Traditional Rural Houses Along the Missouri-Kansas Border," *Journal of Cultural Geography* 1 (1980): 105–37.

13. Peirce F. Lewis, "Common Houses, Cultural Spoor," *Landscape* 19 (January 1975): 20–22.

14. The trailblazer of the material culture approach to the study of dwellings is Henry Glassie. See *Pattern in the Material Folk Culture of the Eastern United States* (Philadelphia: University of Pennsylvania Press, 1968); and *Folk Housing in Middle Virginia: Structural Analysis of Historic Artifacts* (Knoxville: University of Tennessee Press, 1975). A recent excellent study by a former

student of Glassie is Howard Wright Marshall, *Folk Architecture in Little Dixie* (Columbia: University of Missouri Press, 1981). Although trained as an architectural historian, Dell Upton, in "Vernacular Domestic Architecture in Eighteenth-Century Virginia," *Winterthur Portfolio* 17 (1982): 95–119, also approaches the regional dwelling as a product of cultural process.

15. Michael Southern, "The I-House as a Carrier of Style in Three Counties of the Northeastern Piedmont,"in *Carolina Dwelling*, North Carolina State University, School of Design, ed. Doug Swaim (Raleigh: North Carolina State University, 1978), 70.

16. Ibid.

17. Robert Redfield, "The Social Organization of Tradition," *Peasant Society and Culture* (Chicago: University of Chicago Press, 1956), 40–59.

18. Alan Gowans, *Images of American Living* (New York: Harper and Row, 1976), 71. The essentially medieval folk core of seventeenth century New England is discussed by Gowans, 64–78.

19. Ibid., 72.

20. Wilbur Zelinsky, "Classical Town Names in the United States: The Historical Geography of an American Idea," *Geographical Review* 57 (1967): 463–95.

21. The New England one-and-a-half cottage is also found in upstate New York, northern Ohio, especially the Western Reserve, northern Indiana and Illinois, and Wisconsin, as well as in New England itself. This house type was first identified in the culturogeographic literature by Richard Pillsbury and Andrew Kardos, *A Field Guide to the Folk Architecture of the Northeastern United States*, Geography Publications at Dartmouth [College], no. 8 (Hanover, N.H.: Dartmouth, 1970), although they called it a "New England enlarged cottage." See also Lewis, 148–50; and Allen G. Noble, *Wood, Brick,and Stone; The North American Settlement Landscape*, vol. 1, *Houses* (Amherst: University of Massachusetts Press, 1984), 104–6.

22. A plan specifically identified as the "New England floor plan" is my own suggestion. This plan, utilized by the Cape Cod cottage, the New England large, and the saltbox house types, is one and a half rooms deep. The plan is characterized by hall and parlor rooms separated by a central chimney in the front section of the house and a narrow file of two or three rooms, with the kitchen centered behind the chimney in the rear. The front door enters upon an interior vestibule which also contains an elbow stairway located directly in front of the chimney structure leading to the upstairs. This floor plan appears to represent the New England folk ideal much as the Georgia plan represents the fulfillment of the classical ideal in the Delaware River Valley.

23. Marshall McLennan, project director, "Washtenaw County Rural Building Survey," 1981–82. The survey was carried out with funding from the Historic Preservation Fund of the U.S. Department of Interior. The Michigan Bureau of History of the Michigan Department of State acted as grant administrator.

24. The term "bay" is used here to refer to the number of window and door openings, normally symmetrically placed, found in the ground floor level of the facade.

25. Of the 506 Greek Revival houses identified in rural Washtenaw County in 1981–82, only 20 were of the New England Large type.

26. The term "popular house" has emerged in the literature to refer to houses that represent a midpoint between little tradition folk dwellings and the high style houses of the Great Tradition. The emergence of popular houses is associated with the rise of the national landscape. The term applies not only to houses representing a synthesis of the Great Tradition and the little tradition but also to modern period bungalows, ranches, bilevels, etc., which comprise housing for the masses rather than design for an individual client. A term that embraces both the concepts of folk and popular house types is "common house types"; see Lewis, "Common Houses, Cultural Spoor." In recent years the term "vernacular houses" has come to be used in the same all-embracing vein as "common houses," but in the past was used by English architectural historians as synonymous with folk housing and by many American architectural historians to refer to houses lacking stylistic vocabulary. The gable-fronter originated as a Great Tradition design but found regional vernacular expression by being "co-opted" into the fabric of New England culture.

27. The gable-front orientation is well suited to narrow urban lots.

28. Of 506 Greek Revival structures identified in rural Washtenaw County in 1981–82, only 29 were gable-fronters.

29. Pillsbury and Kardos, 29.

30. Lewis, "Common Houses, Cultural Spoor," 24–27; and Kniffen, "Folk Housing," 559.

31. Thomas D. Mackie, Jr., "Go West, Old House: New England Influences in Southern Michigan Folk Housing" (Research paper for GEO 548 American Folk Architecture, Eastern Michigan University, April 1983), 11–12.

32. Although some of the later type can be given an earlier date of construction than any among the earlier type, the latter is conceptually older. Examples of the three bay with front door type can be found in upstate New York from the 1820s. For another approach to subdividing the upright-and-wing house, see Robert W. Bastian, "Indiana Folk Architecture: A Lower Midwest Index," *Pioneer America* 9 (December 1977): 116–17.

33. Of the 506 Greek Revival structures identified in rural Washtenaw County during the 1981–82 survey, 221 are upright-and-wing dwellings.

34. Talbot Hamlin, *Greek Revival Architecture in America* (New York: Dover, 1945/1965), 294–96.

35. The author has observed some examples of the hen-and-chicks house in the hinterlands of Madison, Wisconsin, and one example each in Medina County, Ohio, and in upstate New York. The floor plans of these houses are not known.

36. Kniffen, "Folk Housing"; Wilbur Zelinsky, *The Cultural Geography of the United States* (Englewood Cliffs, N.J.: Prentice-Hall, 1973), 117–28; Pillsbury and Kardos; Lewis, "Common Houses, Cultural Spoor." Glassie, *Pattern in the Material Folk Culture*, aggregates two southern hearths for discussion purposes, 36–152.

37. Robert Mitchell, "The Foundation of Early American Cultural Regions," in *European Settlement and Development in North America*, ed. James R. Gibson (Toronto: University of Toronto Press, 1978), 66–90.

38. For New England migration patterns, see Louis (Kimball) Mathews Rosenbury, *The Expansion of New England: The Spread of New England Settlement and Institutions to the Mississippi River, 1620–1865* (Boston: Houghton, Mifflin Company, 1909).

39. *American Buildings and Their Architects; The Colonial and Neo-Classical Styles* (Garden City, N.Y.: Doubleday, 1976), 15.

40. Pierson, 12.

A Fantastic Tradition: Cedar Fan Carving in Michigan

C. Kurt Dewhurst and Marsha MacDowell

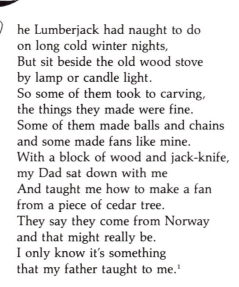

he Lumberjack had naught to do
on long cold winter nights,
But sit beside the old wood stove
by lamp or candle light.
So some of them took to carving,
the things they made were fine.
Some of them made balls and chains
and some made fans like mine.
With a block of wood and jack-knife,
my Dad sat down with me
And taught me how to make a fan
from a piece of cedar tree.
They say they come from Norway
and that might really be.
I only know it's something
that my father taught to me.[1]

Until his death in 1983, John Smedley—author of the above poem, son of a Michigan lumberjack, former tool and die shop laborer, ex-World War II Army infantryman—spent his time manning a CB radio (handle, "Merry-go-round"), writing poetry, and carrying on his father's tradition of carving fans out of cedar. Smedley learned this whittler's trick of carving a fan from a single block of wood from his father when he was a young man, but did little with his skill until a serious back injury forced him into an early retirement. "I couldn't just sit in a wheelchair and watch the world go by. . . . I remember how my Dad had taught me to carve those cedar fans. . .and so one day I picked up a piece of cedar kindling and started carving [again]."[2]

The technique of carving looks difficult to the novice, but is, however, relatively simple. All one needs is a block of wood, a sharp knife, perhaps some water, a little skill, and a lot of patience. The technique is so simple, in fact, that with a couple of demonstrations anyone can learn it, and for the seasoned whittler the technique is a snap (fig. 1). Illustrations and instructions for making fans have been published in several sources, including one of the whittler's standard reference books, E.J. Tangerman's *Whittling and Woodcarving* and the National Woodcarvers Association's periodical *Chips and Chats*. Tangerman devotes eight pages to various fan designs, acknowledging that "whittling fans, usually very ornate, from a single block, has always been considered quite a stunt."[3] A quick scan of woodcarving how-to manuals and popular publications reveals that they often include illustrations of fan carvings. For instance, *Woodcarving: Yesterday and Today in America*, pictures a

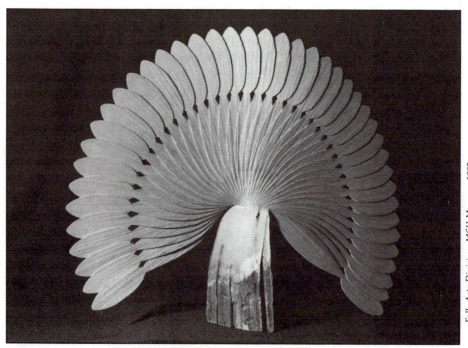

Folk Arts Division, MSU Museum 1982

Figure 1. Cedar fan made by Glen Van Antwerp.

couple of fans with the caption "Unique WATSHALYCALITS by Samuel L. Newswenger. The wings are split and fanned out from a single piece of wood!"[4]

Cedar fan carving first came to the attention of the staff of the Folk Arts Division at the Michigan State University Museum during the preparation for an exhibition of twentieth-century folk arts in Michigan. A press release issued through the Michigan State University Information Services announced a state-wide call for information on carvers. Stan Van Antwerp of Hudsonville read that notice and called the Folk Arts Division office (a state center for research on Michigan folklife traditions). "Say, if you just walk across the street and meet my son, you'll see some real nice carvings. I carve fans out of cedar and taught him how to do it. He works in data processing at Michigan State University."[5] A meeting with Glen resulted in the introduction to a traditional carved form—wooden fans. Discovery of Stan and Glen's work led to Smedley and the eventual identification of numerous other carvers in Michigan as well as in other parts of the country and the world. This in turn led to a recognition of makers and objects as part of a regional folk tradition that had undergone changes in both function and symbolism as it evolved from an ethnic to an occupational/regional to a more personal form of expression in both its countries of origin and in the United States.

Historical Ethnic Background

Some type of fan carving has long been a part of the folk tradition of several countries in the world, but it was especially popular as part of a "splint bird," a traditional form found in Scandinavia. In her book, *Swedish Handcraft*, Anna-Maja Nylen commented that

> Similar forms of 'splint-birds' are found on the Continent also; and there is no reason to suppose that this type of wooden sculpture originated there. . ..
>
> Technically, the conditions for 'splint-bird' manufacture were especially favorable wherever there was manufacture of molded, bent-wood boxes, as well as white coopering. Thus, 'splint-bird' making was more widespread in woodworking areas such as northern Skane and Smaland, which have produced several 'splint-bird' carvers.[6]

Nylen also described the specific religious function which the bird served: "The whittled splint bird, created under influence from Christian symbolism. . .[includes] the Holy Ghost in the form of a dove and Christ as the pelican, pecking its breast bloody to feed its young."[7] Finnish and Russian folk museum curators speculate that the form was introduced into Scandinavia by Russian soldiers.[8]

At Christmas time in Finland, the farmers decorated the ceilings of their homes with woven strips of wood. Over a table laid with festive food was hung the wooden dove or *joululintu*, symbol of the Holy Ghost. In older farmhomes, the Christmas season was one of the few times in the year when the dark, smoke-blackened interior was enlivened with embroidered hangings, painted cloths, and carved items. In Sweden the Christmas season was historically a time to decorate the farmer's home with wall paintings and textiles, and the finest linens and utensils were used on the tables. There too, wooden doves or crowns of straw were suspended over the table.[9] Nowadays, farmsteads have heating systems that do not thrust wall-blackening smoke inside the rooms, thus eliminating the need to disguise the room with an effusion of decorations. While in contemporary times the Christmas season is still a period for engaging in symbolic decorating, some of the traditional handmade items, such as the wooden birds, have been replaced by manufactured paper models. Therefore, while the bird form is maintained as a traditional religious symbol for some Scandinavians, for others the form exists only as a decorative symbol associated with a past history.

However, as Nylen has noted, the carving of pliable wood into fan shapes has not been an activity restricted to Scandinavia. Museums in Russia, Yugoslavia and Czechoslovakia have included historical and contemporary examples of cedar fans and other objects decorated with this splint-wood technique in their collections. In addition, craftsmen from the Philippines have been exporting a variety of objects incorporating the wooden fan technique.[10] So, a single point of origin cannot now be pinpointed though it is obvious that the use of this fan carving technique arose and became popular in areas where pliable wood, such as cedar, was available.

Fan Carving in America: A Lumberman's Art

The lumbering boom in the United States—notably in Maine, the upper Great Lakes and the upper Northwest—enabled an influx of Scandinavian immigrants to find work in the lumber camps. Whether seeking geographic locations with environments similar to their homelands or recruited by lumber companies, immigrants from Scandinavia quickly found employment logging off the virgin pines and hardwoods. In the United States, lumber camps provided a new context for wooden fan production. In *Between the Iron and the Pine*, a 1951 reminiscence of pioneer days in Iron River, Michigan, author Lewis C. Reimann recalled, "Lumberjacks were great whittlers. . ... In their leisure time, evenings and on Sundays, some whittled on soft pine, fashioning chains inside blocks of wood, wooden fans with notched edges for souvenirs for girl friends, toys, and figures of big-hipped and heavy-breasted women."[11] Michigan resident Stan Van Antwerp recalls his father telling him that "the making of cedar fans was one of the folk arts that the lumberjacks worked on in the evenings in the lumber camps. . .there were many variations of designs." Van Antwerp, by occupation an electrical engineer, continues to make what he calls "a Swedish folk art." Of his carving, he claims, "This is nothing. You should've seen my uncle's fans. He could carve a large fan with a smaller fan on each blade."[12] Another carver of fans, John Smedley, said "My father was a lumberjack, he taught me to make the fans. Dad said they carved them to pass the time."[13] In Michigan, other fan carvers claim they learned their skill through lumberjacks and reports from Maine, Vermont and Oregon have indicated that most fan carving activity is related to the lumbering industry.[14] This finding is not too surprising, for after all, the loggers certainly had on hand the materials necessary to make fans. The loggers also had time in the evening to spend whittling, time that was known to have been filled with singing, dancing, telling tales and playing fiddles and dulcimers.

The few examples of old wooden birds using the fan technique that have been found in Michigan, have either come from inactive logging areas or regions heavily populated by Swedes and Finns. It is in these same geographic pockets of Scandinavian population that woodcarving has been continued by numerous practitioners. In the exhibition catalogue, *Norwegian-American Wood Carving of the Upper Midwest*, Marion Nelson suggests that, "among possible explanations for the survival of woodcarving in America as opposed to other traditional Norwegian crafts is the position which woodcarving held in the economic structure of rural Norway and which it continued to hold for a short while [here]."[15] For them and other Scandinavian groups, certainly the continued availability of wood and the occupational setting provided by lumbering made possible the continuity of production of folk objects in wood.

Contemporary Fan Carving

Carving wood blocks into fanlike shapes continues to be practiced in Scandinavia, the United States, and other parts of the world. In Sweden and Finland the traditional wooden doves are made for marketing through the *hemslojd* or homecraft associations. The 'splint-birds' are even imported to the United States and marketed as traditional "Swedish folk arts" in places ranging from the Flint (Michigan) International Institutes' annual Folk Arts Fair to the Swedish-American Institute in Minneapolis, Minnesota. Like the familiar "Dala horse" they are available as authentic Swedish folk art for the tourist trade. Ina-Marie Greverus in "Nothing But a Dala Horse or: How to Decode a 'Folk' Symbol," describes these brightly painted wooden horses:

> The symbols of the encoded message are the colorful and bright artifacts and socio-facts of old-fashioned people, maintained as their culture. . . . The little red Dalecarlian horse is the symbol for Dalarna's natural beauty, rich cultural tradition and modern comfort for leisure. . . . In this text, the Dala-horse is featured as a symbol for tourist expectations: attractive landscape, health, leisure, and traditional culture. The Dalecarlian horse belongs among the so-called traditional handicrafts that are supported today by the regional home industry organizations and sold as Swedish souvenirs in gift and curio shops. Its survival depends on communicative mobility.[16]

Today there is no mention of the making of the doves for symbolic holiday decorating—perhaps since in many private homes, the paper rather than wooden ones are used.

A recent issue of *A Look at Finland* carried an article, entitled "The Birdmaker," about a contemporary Finnish carver, Joel Nokelainen. However, in Nokelainen's case, the art is not produced in the hemslojd structure nor is it described as a traditional folk art. As Nokelainen himself explains, the emphasis is on being an artist, "I grab a piece of wood—carefully selected and matured though it is—take one look, and feel an urge from inside to make my bird. And make it good."[17] Nowhere in this article is mention made of the traditional symbolic characteristics that the bird had in Finland, Sweden or elsewhere.

Glen Van Antwerp, son of carver Stan, is well aware of the historical, ethnic, occupational, and family origins of his own carving skills. According to Glen, "As a child, Pa taught me to make cedar fans. I rather think Pa learned it from Grandpa Van. I don't remember for sure, but I rather think that Grandpa Van learned it from his dad too, who was a Michigan lumberjack."[18] Glen and his son Jeremy not only continue the family tradition of making cedar fans, but also market their fans in art fairs around Michigan (fig. 2). The brochure handed out with each purchase proclaims "Folk art of the Michigan lumberjack" and "each piece handcrafted." Glen Van Antwerp goes on to say in his brochure "I have made hundreds of these fans, continually expanding and refining my style to keep alive this beautiful but nearly forgotten art."[19] While Glen is aware of the roots of this form, he also delights in the artistic challenge that a good block of cedar holds for him and he has fashioned, among other things, peacocks, woodcocks and flying birds.

At one time John Smedley marketed his fans at art fairs in northern Michigan and through a business called "Northwood Fans" that he and his wife Arlene operated out of their home in Kewadin, Michigan. At first Smedley simply replicated the simple forms his father had taught him. But as Smedley continued to find personal satisfaction in, as well as public attention to, his art he began to experiment with more complex or variant forms. Encouraged and further challenged by his wife, Smedley created a wide repertoire of

Folk Arts Division, MSU Museum 1982

Figure 2. Stan, Glen, and Jeremy Van Antwerp—three generations of Michigan cedar fan carvers.

cedar fan forms—from angels to Indian heads to butterflies. He even perfected a process of making miniature fans which were embedded in plastic resin then fashioned into earrings and necklaces. He delighted not only in meeting the challenge of combining his knowledge of technique and medium with the idea of a new form but in sharing the resulting forms with appreciative audiences. His son, John Jr., is now taking up where his father left off. John Smedley and Glen Van Antwerp, like other tradition bearers who no longer operated within a tightly defined folk group, began to explore new directions with the skills they originally acquired within that folk tradition.

There also exists another group of fan carvers who did not learn how to carve through any of the above traditional avenues. These are of course the hobbyists who by reading articles in the various popular woodcarver's manuals, periodicals or sourcebooks, have discovered for themselves how to master this whittler's trick. In an article entitled " The Folk Technics of Chain Carving," Simon Bronner has made the following observation regarding the production of a similar woodcarver's trick: "Whether as a form of play, a learning model, an expression of love and friendship, a demonstration of creativity and artifice, or a reinforcement of identity and self-worth—the technics of chain carving has displayed some pronounced continuities over time and space."[20] The work of such carvers, be they hobbyists or traditionally trained artists, must be considered in terms other than the ethnic, familial, regional or occupational classifications already cited. For them, the act of carving fans out of a block of cedar can be best understood by exploring the more personal motivations of the artist. Roger Welsch has written of this type of motivation of carvers who were in an exhibition of Norwegian-American woodcarving. Welsch notes that "carvers love their wood. . .these carvers have pride in their art of course, and perhaps love it, but their feeling for wood—its colors, grain and texture—is unmistakably love."[21] Some carvers—like Nokelainen, Smedley, and Van Antwerp—might also be best understood to be artists in wood as they continue to expand upon the traditional skills they learned from family members or fellow carvers. Such carvers, who produce objects originally made in a folk tradition find themselves working without a definable folk group. This results in a type of carving which relies on the motivations and aesthetic sensibilities of the individual artist and not on conventional traditional patterning.

Conclusion

While it appears that knowledge of the technique of carving the fans and its symbolic function attached to holiday tradition was very likely one of the ethnic folk traditions brought to America by the Scandinavians, its clear ethnic identity was short-lived in the New World. In its place, an association with an occupation—that of lumbering—temporarily emerged. That more examples of old fans do not exist in public or private collections is not surprising. As Smedley's father told him, "Most of the fans went for kindling."[22] That the fans were regarded as trinkets for friends, kindling for fires, or simply as products of an activity designed to while away the time, meant they were not intended as valued items requiring careful safekeeping. In addition, the fans were inherently delicate when first made and with age became more brittle and susceptible to breaking. Unlike the many songs and tales in the oral traditions associated with lumbering which have been recorded, the material folk tradition of fan carving is less well documented and thus less well known. Due to the activity of a handful of tradition bearers, the skill has been retained long after the woods have been logged off. As for the artists themselves, whether bearers of an ethnic or familial tradition, practitioners of a pastime once linked to an occupational setting found in certain regions of the United States, or simply leisure time whittlers, these makers of fans will continue to share a skill and delight in the challenge that a block of wood holds and invest new meaning in a long-standing folk tradition.

Note: A version of this paper was first presented at the American Folklore Society meeting in Pittsburgh, 1980. This research led to the development of an exhibition of fan carving which was held at the Michigan State University Museum in 1981.

1. John H. Smedley, unpublished poem, 1981.
2. Larry Wakefield, "Carving of Cedar Fans is Not Lost Yet," *The Grand Rapids Press*, 8 February 1981, 13a.
3. E. J. Tangerman, *Whittling and Woodcarving* (New York: Dover Publications, 1962), 92.
4. Elmer L. Smith and Melvin J. Horst, eds., *Woodcarving: Yesterday and Today in America* (Lebanon, Penn.: Applied Arts Publishers, 1976), 23.
5. Telephone conversation with Stan Van Antwerp, 1977.
6. Anna-Maja Nylen, *Swedish Handcraft* (New York: Van Nostrand Reinhold Company, 1977), 359.
7. Ibid.
8. Based on discussions with curators from the Norsk Folkemuseum, (Norway); the Bergen (Norway) Historical Museum; The Hermitage (Russia); and the National Museum of Finland during a Smithsonian (National Museum Act) Grant in 1978.
9. Albert Eskerod, *Swedish Folk Art* (Stockholm, Sweden: Nordiska Museet, 1964), 56–59.
10. Fans from the Philippines have been found in ethnic gift shops in New Orleans (1980) and New York (1981). In addition, friends have given Glen Van Antwerp several items made in the Philippines.

11. Lewis C. Reimann, *Between the Iron and the Pines* (Ann Arbor, MI: Edwards Brothers, Inc., 1951), 37.
12. Interview with Stan Van Antwerp, 1978.
13. Interview with John Smedley, 1980.
14. Personal correspondence with carvers, collectors and folklorists who have studied carvers has revealed repeated relationships between lumbering and fan carving.
15. Marion Nelson, "Norwegian-American Wood Carving: Historic and Aesthetic Context," in *Norwegian-American Wood Carving of the Upper Midwest*, exhibition catalogue (Decorah, Iowa: Vesterheim Publication, 1978), 13–14.
16. Ina-Maria Greverus, "Nothing But a Dala Horse or: How to Decode a 'Folk' Symbol," in *Folklore Today*, ed. Linda Degh, et. al. (Bloomington: Indiana University Press, 1976), 183.
17. Erkki Savolainen, "The Birdmaker," in *Look at Finland* Vol. 4, no. 1 (1980), 34–35.
18. Glen Van Antwerp, 1978.
19. Glen Van Antwerp, *Cedar Fans*, brochure (n.d., n.p.).
20. Simon Bronner, "The Folk Technics of Chain Carving," *Studies in Traditional American Crafts* Vol. 4 (1981), 3.
21. Roger Welsch, "The Wood Carver," in *Norwegian-American Wood Carving of the Upper Midwest*, exhibition catalogue (Decorah, Iowa: Vesterheim Publication, 1978), 21.
22. John Smedley, 1980.

Michigan Hmong Textiles

C. Kurt Dewhurst, Yvonne Lockwood and Marsha MacDowell

s in countless other communities across America, one of the most highly visible clues to the existence of a new group of refugees in Michigan has been the appearance of their brilliant, jewel-like, embroidered and appliqued textiles in church bazaars, museum gift shops, art fairs, and art galleries. Called *paj ntaub* and pronounced "pan dau" (literally translated as flower cloth, but more accurately meaning embroidered or decorated cloth), these textiles, produced by Michigan-Hmong refugees and their relatives from Indochina, provide a visual testament to the powerful ability of traditional life to sustain cultural practices during a period of upheaval and change.

Events in the lives of Hmong over the last twenty years have drastically affected all aspects of *paj ntaub* production and use. Eric Crystal believes that "the tribal Lao textile tradition is part and parcel of an integral culture, often pregnant with symbolic meaning, intimately linked to ethnic identity, reflective of ancient mythological and contemporary historical traditions of the Hmong people. . .and yet the [recent American] appreciation, valuation, and inevitable commercialization of craft skills have necessarily altered traditional orientations towards production and meaning."[1]

Reprinted with permission from *Michigan Hmong Arts*, MSU Museum Folk Culture Series, 3, no. 2 (December 1983): 15–26.

The recruitment of Hmong farmers as soldiers in the Vietnam war years, the exodus of Hmong from their villages to southern Laos and then to Thai refugee camps, and the resettlement of Hmong in communities scattered across the United States have signaled turning points in the way *paj ntaub* has been produced and used. This study of the production of *paj ntaub* in Lansing, which houses one of Michigan's largest Indochinese communities, has provided an opportunity to observe and document some of those subtle changes, as well as the emergence of new forms of textile expression. As our society increasingly depends on standardized, mass-produced objects, traditional ethnic art meets the demand for handmade objects and for distinctiveness in an otherwise plastic world. Ethnic arts also symbolize a heterogeneous society and, thus, rich cultural diversity. Hmong *paj ntaub* contributes to the wide range of varied traditional cultural expression in the United States and is but one example of the nation's cultural wealth.

A Hmong legend tells of a time long ago when the Chinese threatened to kill anyone who spoke the Hmong language. The legend tells how women then hid their alphabet in the embroidered stitches and batiked designs of their skirts, sashes, and hats.[2] It was not until the 1950s that missionary workers in Laos began to write down in the Western alphabet the sounds which the Hmong had until that time written only in pictorial form. Although the "original alphabet" has been lost, the designs remained and have been handed down from generation to generation.[3]

It was the Chinese, too, who divided the original Hmong kingdoms into subgroups and forced them to wear particular clothing. From the predominant colors of these imposed costumes have come the various names of the Hmong today: (1) Green (blue), (2) White, and (3) Striped. Over the years various other tribal names have been ascribed to the Hmong subgroups.[4] These include Flowery Hmong, Chocolate Hmong, Red Hmong, and Black Hmong. The traditional costumes of each subgroup included skirts, hats, trousers, sashes, jewelry, and hair styles, and the distinctions between the costumes persist to the present time and are readily described by Michigan Hmong. For example, the cultural show at the 1982 New Year's party in Lansing (fig. 1) contained a fashion parade in which various types of Green Hmong and White Hmong costumes were modeled and described.

In daily life today, Hmong in Michigan tend to wear clothes that somewhat conform to rather than distinguish them from their neighbors. Children and teens especially are dressed in the

Figure 1. Hmong-American New Year's celebration.

"uniform" of other Americans their age. Performing recently at an East Lansing park, Hmong rock group members were dressed no differently than any other typical junior or senior high girls. However, while some of the older women have adapted to Western dress, others continue to wear sarong-like, wrap-around Lao skirts and head-scarves. Only on special occasions, such as weddings, parties, or funerals, are the elaborate traditional clothes and jewelry unwrapped and put on. Young Hmong women spent several hours dressing for a Lansing New Year's celebration. Even on these occasions, not everyone wears complete or even parts of traditional costumes. Some Hmong teenagers in Lansing were observed dressed in Hmong clothes for the Hmong cultural show at the New Year's party, but they changed to Western dress for the latter portion of the evening which was devoted to Western popular music and dance.

Only ten years ago the standard dress of the Hmong was what we call traditional costume or Hmong clothes. In Laos at that time, the production and use of these elaborate costumes were an integral part of Hmong life. Of the many ethnic tribes in Southeast Asia, the Hmong have long been perhaps best known for their independence (Hmong even refer to themselves as "free people"[5]) and for their folk arts. According to one ethnographic study, they also called themselves *M'peo* or "embroidery people."[6] The identification with their textiles has endured over the years in Laos and Thailand and now is continuing in the United States.

The distinctive *paj ntaub* was used in the production of many of the clothes that adorned both young and old. Babies wore hats to protect their heads from both the weather and evil spirits; young women proclaimed their availability for marriage through the display of their handiwork and the wearing of certain decorations; married women announced their status by wearing particular costume items; and the deceased were buried in special burial pieces. As of 1983 Lansing-area Hmong continued, albeit inconsistently, to place hats on their young infants and wear traditional clothes at weddings. When a leader in the community died this year his traditional funeral garb was replete with an elaborate *paj ntaub* square.[7]

The amount of *paj ntaub* produced depended on the demands of the daily and yearly work cycles, as well as the daily and ritual needs of the maker and her family. Women worked in the fields and cared for their home and children. When there was time to sit, women (sometimes in groups and sometimes alone) would sew and socialize. As major ceremonial events approached, it was customary to have new or fresh costumes. In the pre-refugee period, almost the entire output was intended for personal or family use.

In their homeland, Hmong women began learning the techniques and designs of *paj ntaub* when they were very young. Most of the women interviewed in Lansing and Detroit said that they started learning at about 8 to 10 years of age and the majority learned the traditional designs from their mothers or grandmothers. For instance, Paj Yang, the 13-year old daughter of the prolific Lansing *paj ntaub* artist, Sue Vue, has already begun to market her own work.[8] In America, Hmong children can sell their work, whereas formerly in Laos and Thailand their practice pieces were used for everyday work clothes in the same spirit that an American mother displays and encourages her child's first artistic products. Even though most of the instruction passed from one female generation to the next, the designs may also have been well known to men. At least two men in Lansing were able to name and even execute some of the embroidered designs.[9]

Hundreds of traditional basic designs are memorized by the Hmong textile artist. When questioned about the ability to remember all these designs, one artist replied, "I learned these just like you learned the alphabet. It is a language for me."[10] However, the art of the Hmong has never been static. Subtle innovation has been accepted as part of their needlework tradition. Routinely, a young Hmong woman in Laos provides evidence of her proficiency in needlework by expressing herself in creative or derivative ways.

The Green Hmong are known especially for their batik work. Detroit area resident Mao Hang is among the few Hmong in Michigan who continues to use her skills in producing the carefully marked and dyed pieces. Complex geometric designs are drawn freehand in wax on undyed cotton. The fabric is then dipped into an indigo dye bath. After dyeing, the wax is removed and small strips or squares of fabric are applied onto the design. The fabric design then may be used as a prepared background for appliqued and embroidered stitches. This fabric provides the base for the circular skirts and baby carriers used by both Green and White Hmong. Batik is done in only one color and is considered only a foundation for further sewing, although individual patterns have names.

The White Hmong are especially noted for their reverse applique created by folding a piece of cloth and then cutting designs, much as American children make paper snowflakes. By layering two pieces of cloth of contrasting colors, and sometimes inserting additional pieces, the artist is able to create very complex appliqued designs. Lansing artist Cha Vang spends nearly all her spare moments executing intricate reverse appliqued designs. In Figure 2 she holds in her hands an example of her work that shows the graphically striking results that can be achieved using this technique. Like the Green Hmong, the White Hmong also embroider designs using cotton, metallic, or silk threads. It should be noted that the Lansing community is primarily White Hmong and the Detroit community is roughly half Green and half White Hmong and that other Hmong interpretations and methods of executing *paj ntaub* exist.

The exodus from highland to lowland villages in Laos and the resettlement in Thai refugee camps created a set of circumstances that had an immediate impact on all aspects of Hmong life. All that was familiar had been replaced by social uncertainty, economic deprivation, and cultural disruption. In the camps the new rhythm of life had a direct effect on *paj ntaub* production. The enforced

Figure 2. Cha Vang with *paj ntaub*.

Folk Arts Division, MSU Museum 1982

mingling of Hmong subgroups meant that designs and techniques began to be shared. One White Hmong woman interviewed recently in Lansing freely admits that she prefers to make Green Hmong clothes now, because the colors are "so much prettier."[11] Had she still lived in her former all White Hmong village in Laos, such free adaptation probably would not have occurred. In the camps, freed from the demands of soldiering and farming, both men and women had significantly increased amounts of time on their hands. Women devoted more time to fabricating textiles and some men even began to fill their hours by creating *paj ntaub*.

The initial war-induced transfer of Hmong from the hills to the lowlands of Laos brought about a significant change in the artists' motivation for producing textiles. Whereas traditional textiles had not been a commercial commodity before, women now in need of money began to sell textile pieces on the streets and in the market places of Laotian urban centers. Visitors from the West, and even Laotians, were their customers. However, the commercialization and economic importance of textiles developed more fully in the refugee camps of Thailand.

Perhaps one of the most influential factors in the camp affecting *paj ntaub* production is a type of assistance program set up by refugee resettlement workers. During the mid-1970s, under the direction of Jean Adrianoff, a program called CAMA-Craft (Christian and Missionary Alliance) was set up "in order to alleviate boredom, provide a small amount of money for the women, promote leadership among the women and to encourage teaching and passing on of the Hmong embroidery skills."[12] For the first time, Hmong traditional art was being formally coordinated, standardized, taught, and marketed. Women were supplied with materials at cost, given instructions on dimensions of textiles and colors to use, and their finished products were scrutinized under a quality-control system. If the finished *paj ntaub* passed the quality-control inspection, the program purchased the piece and marketed it in Japan, Germany, the Netherlands, or Bangkok (at ethnic festivals). Pieces were inspected for sloppy placement of design, poor needlework, dirt, tears and other flaws, and poor quality. If necessary, a piece was returned to its maker for repair. The program involved both men and women. Whereas the women created the textiles, Hmong men were in charge of selling raw materials to the women and keeping the books. However, in the camp other Hmong men not associated with the formal craft program operated a small sales booth and other women sold *paj ntaub* to tourists. Among the pieces these enterpreneurs acquired for resale were pieces rejected by the craft program. Refugee camp workers assisted in bookkeeping, served as quality-control inspectors, and handled the sales to overseas markets.

The CAMA-Craft program closely monitors the types of items that are produced in an effort to produce products that appeal to a Western market. Because of this regulated production system, Hmong women for the first time in their lives were producing nontraditional items expressly for non-Hmong. Aprons, children's bean bags, dolls, coasters, potholders, pillowcases, wall hangings, placemats, and bookmarks were produced along with more traditional squares, belts, purses, and bed coverings. Even the bright colors traditionally used by Hmong were softened and neutralized in order to appeal to Western taste. It was also the first time that Hmong women had produced large-scale *paj ntaub*.

The camp programs and the camp environment itself, however, helped to sustain textile production both for Hmong cultural needs and for the newly developing audience of non-Hmongs. In the camps women documented visually the life they had just left and the dramatic events that they had so recently experienced. Previously, Hmong textiles were nonfigurative, but in the camps embroidered panels depicting Hmong activities ranging from farming to courtship games began to be created by textile artists.[13] Even such nontraditional events as refugees fleeing across the Mekong River or Hmong soldiers shooting down communist bombers have been recorded in stitchery.[14]

The migration of Hmong to American communities caused even more drastic changes in Hmong life than the resettlement in Thai camps. In the refugee camps, Hmong still were able to maintain aspects of their traditional life. But the minute they stepped aboard the jets that carried them to new homes, their traditional ways were challenged. Acquisition of a new language and adoption of new apparel are perhaps the most visible changes to outsiders, but every aspect of Hmong life, including *paj ntaub* production, has been tested in this period of resettlement.

Textile artists were faced with the immediate problems of acquiring a new language, a new home, a new costume, and in some cases, a new occupation. *Paj ntaub* was not needed immediately in Hmong daily life to the extent it was in either their Laotian homeland or the Thai refugee camps. Nor were there, in the beginning months of American resettlement, any craft assistance programs such as CAMA-Craft to help market the textiles. Yet the marketing, and consequent commercialization, of *paj ntaub* has greatly accelerated as more Hmong have established residency in the United States and other countries. When more Americans became aware of the Hmong about marketing, and to enable refugees to support themselves and to foster confidence in a new environment.

two groups plus an unknown number of individuals participate in the selling of this art work in the United States. Much of the activity is through local cooperatives and businesses organized specifically to market Hmong (and other Southeast Asian) textiles. Many are established, supported, and often managed by volunteers representing refugee organizations, church groups, individual sponsors, and teachers of English language. A number of regional groups have received assistance from federal and state agencies in their efforts to develop textile art cooperative businesses. As cooperatives, the profits are shared by everyone who participates: Hmong women receive anywhere from 60 to 90 percent of the money from the sale of their work. The textiles are marketed in a variety of ways: craft stores, museum and art gallery gift shops, church bazaars, arts and crafts festivals, Tupperware-type parties in private homes, individuals, etc. Sales are also promoted by local professionals and business establishments that offer free advice and services, provide display space, and donate materials. The motivation for Americans to volunteer to help market *paj ntaub* has been primarily based on the American ideology of helping refugees to help themselves. Like those of the refugee camp workers, the stated goals of American participants in these marketing activities are to encourage the tradition of *paj ntaub*, to acquaint Americans with Hmong art, to teach Hmong about marketing, and to enable refugees to support themselves and to foster confidence in a new environment.

Nationally, the marketing of *paj ntaub* has been generally successful. Despite the fluctuation in numbers of participating Hmong women and attrition of volunteers, a number of groups reported a notable increase in the volume of sales for 1987. The same is true for individual artists. In addition to income generation, groups also report success in preparing refugee women to assume responsibility for marketing and instructing others in traditional needlework, applique, and batiking techniques. However, the future marketability of any single ethnic traditional textile is unpredictable. The American public is noted for following rapidly changing decorative trends, and what may have been prestigious and desirable one year may not have the same appeal the next. To protect the future, cooperative groups and individual sellers have started campaigns to convince the public that *paj ntaub* is an art and to seek new ways of using *paj ntaub*.

On the local scene, marketing of *paj ntaub* has met with mixed success. Modest selling began in the Lansing region in the late 1970s, shortly after the Hmong began arriving. Appreciation of the intricate and colorful textiles and a wish to help Indochinese refugees led teachers and sponsors of the Hmong to assist in marketing Hmong textiles. Hmong brought a few examples of their work to English language classes. These pieces were subsequently sold informally to American friends and relatives and at church social events and local events, such as the Multi-Cultural Arts Festival, The East Lansing Arts Fair, and the Michigan State University Union Christmas Sale. Teacher David Bunch invited a group of Hmong women and their textiles to the first annual Looking Glass River Festival. For Cha Vang and Blia Vue, this was one of the first public occasions for them to market textiles in Lansing. With the aid of one volunteer, Susan Julian, a method of numbering and inventory was also devised to help keep track of sales.

With the support of the Catholic Refugee Services Center and teachers from Lansing Community College's Refugee Program, a volunteer cooperative marketing project was established in 1982. Some fifty people of the Lansing area participated in the project. On designated days they brought pieces to the Refugee Center where volunteers handled the bookkeeping, finances, and sales. Textiles were stored in an unused closet and lists of monthly sales were posted on the wall. Some of the other similar marketing groups in the United States had as a goal the establishment of a retail shop, but the cooperative efforts in Lansing never had this as a stated goal. Despite the positive response of the Hmong community to this marketing activity, most of the *paj ntaub* makers left the sales and management to the American volunteers; consequently, few women learned the skills necessary to market their work on their own.

The cooperative marketing project lasted one year. Burdened by a waning inventory of locally produced *paj ntaub* and a declining number of volunteers, the cooperative efforts as originally envisioned ceased, and *paj ntaub* is once again available from individual Americans who attend public events such as fairs and otherwise sell from their homes and to other retail establishments. Elsewhere in Michigan, efforts to market *paj ntaub* have also fared with mixed results. However, when an established Detroit area art gallery held an exhibition of Hmong textiles, the gallery owner, Eva Boicourt, reported that sales were slow and that she thought there really wasn't an art market for *paj ntaub*.[15] Susan Julian continues to work closely with Detroit area women and has had considerable success in marketing their sewing skills.

In Michigan, a Hmong system of marketing remains intact. It existed before the *paj ntaub* marketing effort of the Lansing Refugee Services Center and it persists after the center's demise. Hmong women in Laos and Thailand or even other parts of the United States send *paj ntaub* to a trusted relative who believes that she has a good sales opportunity. If it is not sold at that location, it may be sent to another relative. This can lead to confusion for Americans dealing with Hmong as to the ownership and authorship of individual *paj ntaub*, but to Hmong this system is considered an extension of family and clan linkages and mutual support systems.

As in the Thai refugee camps, the people inevitably exerted an influence on the form, colors, techniques, and designs of Hmong *paj ntaub*. Yet this outside influence by non-Hmong has often been overrated, and the truth is that adaptation is less organized and substantially more complicated. Hmong women ask each other what sells and copy readily. Overheard comments at sales, advice from relatives in different states, availability of cloth in the customary shopping place, and receipt of pieces from relatives in Thai refugee camps all strongly influence what is produced. Hmong across the United States maintain close contact by phone or by tape cassette, and one community's production must be considered in the light of what is produced elsewhere.

Textile artists have been encouraged to use "American decorator" colors, to spend less time on intricate designs, and to use larger patterns in order to speed up production. Textile artists have also been discouraged from creating items such as *baht* bags that are traditionally Hmong. New product lines are also being developed to protect the future of *paj ntaub* marketability in the United States. Few limit their sales to only traditional *paj ntaub*; many have success with fashion accessories and home furnishings. One of the more innovative undertakings has been an attempt to apply *paj ntaub* to designer gowns and other high-fashioned clothing. Of course, the artists have been bombarded with Western culture and some themselves have added new designs, colors, fabrics, and uses to their work. For instance, Lansing artist Nang Vue designed a *paj ntaub* that might have been inspired by the top of a Whitman candy sampler box. Another artist, Mai (May) Xiong, has used embroidery to practice spelling English words. Tzer Vang has incorporated in her pillow cover pieces some stitched crosses. Christian symbols frequently appear in deference to refugee camp missionary influence, church sponsorship, or in some cases personal involvement in a new religion. Yet another artist, Yer Vang, makes highly decorated guitar straps for the young Hmong musicians who have adapted quickly to Western music and who have formed competitive rock bands.

Upon being asked to see their *paj ntaub*, textile artists in Lansing inevitably first bring out items that have been produced to sell to non-Hmong. When pressed further about items made for their families, women usually bring out small bundles tied up in pieces of cotton cloth. Untying the wrapping, they reveal far more carefully executed and intricately designed pieces. They were not produced for American use or taste but for specific Hmong purposes in traditional Hmong colors. The differences between the colors, forms, fabric, and execution employed in the pieces produced for Hmong and those produced for non-Hmong are considerable.

The effect of marketing and exhibiting of *paj ntaub* on the Hmong community cannot yet be measured. On the one hand, successful marketing might mediate negative aspects of acculturation experienced by the Hmong. For example, when the textiles are in demand and praised, as *paj ntaub* is, they bring pride and encouragement to maintain the tradition. Continuity of this traditional art form also contributes credibility to other older cultural forms, which in turn can slow the process of acculturation and reinforce the role of *paj ntaub* in differentiating Hmong from other ethnic groups. On the other hand, however, we need look only to other cultures for possible marketing effects. In Japan, traditional artists have been acknowledged and have received considerable official attention for many decades, but artists have become very competitive. Rather than attempt to maintain a tradition as it is known within a region or group, artists emulate the art of those acknowledged as successful.

Despite the number of skilled artists in the Lansing area, the present picture of *paj ntaub* production is not altogether promising. As has already been pointed out, the cultural disruption these tribal people have undergone over the past twenty years has affected all aspects of their lives. Among the observed changes that are now directly affecting the amount of *paj ntaub* produced in Michigan are the following: (1) a relatively small rate of financial return on the amount of labor invested in producing *paj ntaub* as compared with minimum-wage occupations; (2) the loss of the traditional extended family household and the concurrent increased home and child care demands on the female in the single-family household; (3) the amount of time spent in English classes; (4) the uncertainty about the availability of and access to marketing outlets; and (5) pressure from children to relinquish Old World ways in favor of more American practices. As these pressures are exerted on a woman's time and energy, they will undoubtedly continue to shape the future of Hmong textile work in Michigan.

Only time will tell what the future of *paj ntaub* is in Hmong and non-Hmong communities in the United States. In some respects, it appears as though American praise of the art is for those pieces that meet American aesthetic values rather than the values of the Hmong. This situation has played an important role in the kind of changes that are taking place in *paj ntaub*. Clearly, however, the future of *paj ntaub* marketability also depends on a semblance of tradition being maintained; *paj ntaub* must retain a degree of distinctiveness that outsiders will recognize as "Hmongness."

Being in a state of flux and without a country of their own, Hmong and Hmong culture inevitably will reflect accommodation to a majority people, a situation all too familiar among Fourth World peoples.[16] However, change is not the issue. Culture is always changing; societies in contact exchange materials and ideas. Rather, it is the nature in which change is introduced by the majority—i.e., by instruction or advice on American preferences—and not through informal and random contact and observation. However, not all change is destructive. For example, as Hmong textiles are produced both for the use of others as well as for Hmong, the art begins to express more than one symbolic and aesthetic system. Change, then, merely reflects a new reality.

In an interview, Neng Vang realistically yet poignantly commented. "Our cultures are so different. . .it is difficult for us since we are not Americans."[17] As time passes, it is likely that the recently transplanted Laotian-Hmong will feel more a part of their new homelands. The acculturation process was already in place the moment they stepped onto foreign soil. For better or for worse, their lives and their art have been and will continue to be subject to change. The Hmong people have already been acknowledged as survivors; time will only tell how much of their traditional cultural life will survive.

69

The authors gratefully acknowledge the helpful suggestions of Susan Julian in the preparation of this essay.

1. Eric Crystal, "Lao Hmong Textiles in the Crucible of Social Change," *Michigan Hmong Arts,* Michigan State University Museum Folk Culture Series 3, no. 2 (December 1983): 5–13.
2. Jane Hamilton Merritt, *Hmong and Lao: Mountain Peoples of Southeast Asia (privately printed, 1982), 3.*
3. See C. Kurt Dewhurst, Yvonne Lockwood, and Marsha MacDowell, *Michigan Hmong Arts,* Michigan State University Museum Folk Culture Series 3, no. 2 (December 1983): 70–71.
4. For example, see *Minority Groups in Thailand,* Ethnographic Study Series, Headquarters, Department of the Army (February 1970): 573; and William P. Geddes, *Migrants of the Mountains: The Cultural Ecology of the Blue Miao (Hmong Njua) of Thailand* (Oxford: Clarendon Press, 1976), 16, 38–39.
5. Amy R. Catlin and Sam Beck, *The Hmong From Asia to Providence* (Providence, R.I.: Center for Hmong Lore, Roger Williams Park Museum, 1983), 5.
6. *Minority Groups in Thailand,* 573.
7. This practice was observed in Lansing in July 1983. Deceased male elder Mao Yang was given a Hmong funeral ceremony one day and a Baptist one the following day before burial.
8. Interview with Blia Vue, Sue Vue, and Paj Yang, 13 July 1983.
9. Interview with Tong Her and Mai Lue, 8 July 1983; interview with Ny Her, 4 August 1983; and conversation with Helen Jones, 6 August 1983.
10. Interview with Mao Hang and Song Yang, 31 January 1983.
11. Interview with Blia Vue, Sue Vue, and Paj Yang, 13 July 1983.
12. From typescript notes prepared by Susan Julian after meeting the CAMA Craft volunteer Sandy Nelson, n.d.
13. For a brief discussion of corresponding allusions to culture elements in Hmong folk literature, see Charles R. Johnson, "Hmong Myths, Legends and Folk Tales: A Resource for Cultural Understanding," in *The Hmong in the West: Observations and Reports,* ed. Bruce T. Downing and Douglas P. Olney (Minneapolis: University of Minnesota, 1982), 90–96.
14. The incorporation of nontraditional elements in traditional textiles has also occurred among other groups who have had contact with outsiders. A prime example is the molas produced by the Cuna Indians of Panama. See Mari Lyn Salvador, "The Clothing Arts of the Cuna of the San Blas, Panama," in *Ethnic and Tourist Arts: Cultural Expressions from the Fourth World,* ed. Nelson H. H. Graburn (Berkeley: University of California Press, 1976), 165–82.
15. Interview with Eva Boicourt, 7 July 1983.
16. Nelson H. H. Graburn, ed., "Introduction," *Ethnic and Tourist Arts: Cultural Expressions from the Fourth World* (Berkeley: University of California Press, 1976), 1–32.
17. Interview with Neng Vang, 20 July 1983.

Museums for the People: Museum Bars

C. Kurt Dewhurst and Marsha MacDowell

Sprinkled across northern Wisconsin and the upper peninusla of Michigan are a number of drinking or eating establishments which either include the word "museum" in their business name or are called "museums" by local citizens.[1] Like the more conventional community historical museums, these places house extensive assemblages of artifacts which are on public display. During more than a decade of fieldwork on material culture in this region, we have often been directed by locals to these places as good sources of regional material and information. It was through visits to such places as Tom Gamache's "Museum Bar" in Hurley, Wisconsin, Bildo's "Museum Bar" in Daggett, Michigan and Walter Kinney Jr.'s "Antler's Bar" in Sault Ste. Marie, Michigan that it became evident that not only was it worth examining more closely the individual materials within the bars but also the bars themselves. In particular, we began to investigate how these community-oriented depositories were formed, how they reflected community history and values, and how this form of museum was related to other historical and contemporary museums. What we discovered was that not only did this form of museum have a clear link to the historical development of museums themselves, but also that an understanding of the content, formation and audience for each museum bar was integrally tied to its cultural and

Reprinted with permission from *Material Culture* 18, no. 1 (1986): 37-50.

social setting. In this paper, we will briefly describe selected museum bars from the Upper Midwest, then examine how they fit into the historical notion of museums, how the museum itself is an artifact and how these museums reflect and present community history and values.

Museum Bars in the Upper Midwest

Hurley, Wisconsin lies just across the Wisconsin-Michigan border from Ironwood, Michigan. Unwitting travellers on the main business route between these two points might not even know they've passed from one town to the other for there are no "Welcome to Wisconsin" or "Welcome to Hurley" signs marking the political boundaries. However, the traveler soon senses what most long-time area residents have known all along—that the primary business activities of Hurley's bar-lined main street are not quite the same as those of Ironwood. Indeed, according to one retired Michigan furniture company worker, Hurley was known among woodworkers throughout the Upper Great Lakes as "the last wide-open town in the Midwest."[2] At the height of the lumbering boom and for many years after, Hurley was the town in which lumbermen and miners were able to let off steam due to Wisconsin's more lenient alcohol regulations. Hurley has in more recent years gained a more reputable kind of fame since it serves as the home of the Paavo Nurmi Race (named for the famous Finnish Olympic marathon runner). It was at the finish line of this marathon that for about fifty years a museum bar was operated. As late as 1981, a person in search of a good 25-cent draft beer as well as an art gallery could find both at Tom Gamache's Museum Bar on Silver Street. Inside the premises were housed over a hundred carvings done by August Jackson who lived in a shed behind the tavern. According to Gamache, "Jackson traded these carvings to the previous owner in exchange for room, board and booze. . . he carved at a workbench in front of the bar."[3] According to other local residents, Jackson was a loner and even his surviving daughter knows little about her father. In addition to such whittler's tricks as balls-in-cages, ships-in-bottles, wooden chains, and miniature carved lumberjack tools, Jackson created numerous figures reflecting local social or occupational life or his own political views. For instance, he carved lumbermen sawing down trees, a barroom scene with a girl waiting on a table, and an Uncle Sam depicted as a "he-man" pounding the head of Hitler with a carnival hammer. In another grouping, Jackson carved an American eagle in whose claws hung the figures of Tojo and Hitler. These items were carefully displayed inside a three-shelved shallow glass case that ran for about twenty feet along one wall of the tavern's interior. Other artifacts from the local logging and mining days were hung above the cases or from the ceiling. When asked about the carvings, Gamache said, "Many older residents like to come in and look at the carvings and reminisce and relive their past which Jackson preserved in the old-time figures and scenes. They come in after the tourists have all fled in their campers and cars."[4]

Edward Nelson came to Ontonogan, Michigan, in 1932 and founded Stubb's Bar which later was renamed Stubb's Museum Bar. Known to his friends as "Stubb" because of the loss of one hand in an accident, Nelson created a remarkable landmark in the western Upper Peninsula. The bar displays a vast collection of "donations" and items taken in trade for a favorite beverage. The walls, ceilings and every conceivable open space are filled with stuffed animal mounts, wood carvings, lumbering tools, guns, ice skates, Indian artifacts, photographs and an endless array of oddities. A Wurlitzer juke box still plays in the corner and a stuffed bear (supported by a pool cue) stands by the door to welcome visitors to Stubb's Museum Bar. The wooden bar is covered with stamped log marks and chiseled nicknames of lumbermen who worked the many logging camps in the area. "Single Eye Johnson," "Handle Bar Hank," and "Snuff Box John," are but a few of the names scratched into its surface, providing a visual documentation of Michigan's lumbering heritage.[5] The term "museum" was first used by Nelson to informally describe the collection, then more formally, when he added a neon sign which spelled out M-U-S-E-U-M. The flashing sign continues to operate today, drawing curious travelers as well as some old timers who sit and reminisce about many a fight and hard-drinking celebration that occurred when lumberjacks came into town (fig. 1).

Daggett, Michigan is a ghost of the town it once was in prime logging days. Now, like so many other small upper Midwest towns, among the remnants of its heydays are its crossroads corner bar. Seated at the counter of Bildo's Museum Bar, one can still be served a 25-cent beer and have the opportunity to slowly take in all of this museum's collections. Hundreds of matchbooks, all kinds of paper money, washer wringers, irons and many other items hang from the ceiling, line the walls and fill a small showcase. According to local workers who come in for morning coffee breaks, the former

Figure 1. Museum bar sign in Ontonagon, Michigan, 1983.

tavernkeeper, William Leipart, carved many of the wooden items. Totems, Indians, and wooden chains were fashioned by Leipart using a saw, chisels, awls and a jackknife (fig. 2).

When the Mackinaw Bridge spanning Michigan's upper and lower peninsula at the Mackinac Straits was being built, the population of the small town of Mackinaw City was suddenly greatly increased by the presence of the bridge construction workers. During the years the "Mighty Mac" (as the bridge is known locally) took shape, the community of workers began to socialize at off hours at Sofie's Tavern, a bar owned by Sofie Reise and her husband Mike Hornick, who was a bridge construction worker (Local #25). Because of her own interest in collecting bridge memorabilia and in an effort to personalize the bar, Sofie decorated the interior of her establishment with items directly related to the bridge construction workers. The workers themselves donated many items, most notably their hard hats, which were decorated with their names, pictures and their union numbers. When the bridge was completed in 1957,

Figure 2. Bildo's Museum Bar in Daggett, Michigan, 1982.

most of the construction workers moved out of the region and the bar's clientele became mostly tourists. The bar continued to function as a living museum for those workers who remained, as well as an interesting exhibit for visitors. When Sofie and Mike died, J.C. Stilwell, a retired ironworker, bought the bridge items that they had displayed in their tavern and installed them in a separate room above a pizza parlor he opened.[6] Now advertised as the Mama Mia Pizzeria and Bridge Museum, this facility has become the headquarters of an annual "Ironworker's Festival."

When Otto Rindlisbacher, a well-known northern Wisconsin violin maker and tavern owner died, his obituary carried the following information about the Buckhorn tavern which he and his brothers at one time ran: "Famed for the collection of stuffed animals and curios collected by the brothers over a 50-year period moved two doors south on Main (Rice Lake, Wisconsin) about two years ago when Otto had an opportunity to buy a building—'To give these things a permanent home,' he said, according to his daughter. . . . Fame came [to Rindlisbacher] when the Buckhorn was given national coverage on television for its curios and atmosphere."[7]

When visitors to the Locks at Sault Ste. Marie ask a local where they can get a really good meal, they will inevitably be directed to Antler's Bar. If, on seeing the exterior of the tavern, Mom, Dad and kids are somewhat dubious about this recommendation, they are in for more of a surprise when they enter this popular establishment. Every square inch of wall and ceiling space is covered by objects— from birchbark canoes to carved diaramas of logging scenes, six-foot stuffed snakes to steam whistles from Great Lakes ore carriers— the place is packed. According to the information provided on their printed placemats:

> The story (false) is that the Kinneys acquired all the junk that hangs from the ceiling by barter. Local wags point out to visitors that the Antlers had a policy of exchanging money for material goods; thereby operating one of the few "bar" gaining economies in the world.
>
> Anyone who ran out of money on a good binge, so the tale goes, could trade a rifle or another antique for enough loot to get stoned for a while. In a town that has its share of habitual drinkers who also happen to be broke, it seems to be a good story.
>
> The truth is that when the Kinneys took over in 1948, there was little ornamentation on the walls, and most of that is not reprintable. Harold and Walt Kinney, enterprising former Detroit policemen, then took over and "steaked" out the place. That is, they added prime steak to beer and booze, and they have had a meaty business ever since.

One story persists, however, that one of the chief patrons, Tiny T., was one of the chief contributors to Antlers Museum. According to some local tourist guides, Tiny, while on a two-week toot, traded a moose head, his pistol, his watch, his cousin and his Pontiac. All of the stuff now adorns the upper atmosphere of the bar, they point out, except for the cousin and the car. The cousin sits stuffed on one of the stools, and Tiny's car is parked nearby, next to a huge log that was left there by a drunken lumberjack, who thought he could get a case of Jack Daniels for a stick of pulp.[8]

And if the collection of artifacts didn't provide enough stimulation visually, an aural stimulation also awaits the Antler's initiate. Whenever any ore carrier glides by in the Locks across the street, the bartender marks the occasion by blowing the whistles, ringing bells and otherwise creating a noisy ruckus. In this bar where the Detroit Red Wings were once known to hang out and where episodes of Gunsmoke were once filmed, the explosion of noise only adds to the lively character of the place. Walt Kinney, Jr., present owner of the bar, has felt so strongly that the collection of artifacts and noisemakers were important to the atmosphere of the bar that he once refused loaning one of the carvings to a regular museum's temporary exhibition.

Museum Bars in Historical Perspective

In their book, *Lock, Stock and Barrel: The Story of Collecting*, Douglas and Elizabeth Rigby provide a good introduction to the historical development of collections, both private and public, from the initial assemblages of curiosities for home curio cabinets to the systematically collected groups of study specimens. As they trace the evolution of the formation of and audience for these assemblages, they note the transition from more private to a more public oriented collection.

By the beginning of the eighteenth century 'museums' had actually become a form of popular amusement. It was no longer merely a question of tourists coming to private homes to see collections which had gained repute among the well informed. Now enterprising proprietors of coffeehouses, remembering the crowds that had flocked to South Lambeth, set up 'repositories of curiousities' in their establishments, much as modern restaurants employ orchestras and floor shows. . . . American museums in the early nineteenth century for the most part were patterned after the popular museums of Britain. For instance in New York City in 1810, itinerant organ grinder John Scudder opened

"The American Museum of John Scudder" which contained all manner of curiousities and for which he charged customers 25 cents admission. Showman Phineas T. Barnum took over this collection in 1841–1842 to open 'Barnum's American Museum,' which contained over 500,000 curiosities.[9]

The Rigbys were not the first to take note of such establishments and in their book they reprinted the description given by another observer of a nineteenth century barber shop museum in Cambridge, Massachusetts:

The walls were covered with curious old Dutch prints, beaks of albatross and penguins, and whales' teeth fantastically engraved. Suspended over the fireplace, with the curling-tongs, were an Indian bow and arrows, and in the corners of the room stood New Zealand paddles and war-clubs, quaintly carved. The model of a ship in glass we variously estimated to be worth from a hundred to a thousand dollars. . . . Among these wonders, the only suspicious one was an Indian tomahawk, which had too much the peaceful look of a shingling hatchet . . . did any rarity enter the town it gravitated naturally to these walls, to the very nail that waited to receive it.[10]

The presentation of an engaging environment for patrons continued into the twentieth century. The Rigbys noted the success of an enterprising restauranteur who, with a museum-like decor, lured customers to his urban restaurant:

In the tradition of 'museums' in barber shops, coffee houses and inns is Bill Hardy's 'Gay nineties' collection of shaving mugs, wooden phonograph records, gold-trimmed spittoons, barroom nudes and other relics of that droll era, all used to embellish his New York City restaurant. In addition, to the customers on pleasure bent, the exhibit attracts outsiders of every sort from milliners to museum workers, who go to Bill Hardy's to do research, and who tarry, we suppose to revive the inner man.[11]

Unlike some of the museum bars profiled earlier that relied on local patronage and cooperative community curatorial efforts in building up the exhibits found in the museum bar, Bill Hardy clearly set out to attract "outsiders" who were only consumers, not creators, in the museum restaurant enterprise.

Community museum bars are dramatic examples of a locale where exhibitions of artifacts are offered in contemporary public eating or drinking establishments. Today numerous owner-operated bars or restaurants maintain at least small areas devoted to displays of artifacts. For example, common are bowling trophies earned by a bar sponsored team, souvenirs or materials reflecting the restaurant's ethnic orientation, or photographs of famous people who have visited the establishment. Such exhibitions generally create a more personalized working environment for the owner while at the same time creating a source of decorative distinction for patrons.

The use of displays of artifacts to create a certain ambience in a restaurant is by no means restricted to owner-operated places. The use of displays of nostalgia-evoking items is a marketing ploy being successfully used in other restaurants. If living in any metropolitan area, one doesn't have to search far to find an eating place that uses "old things" as a decorative theme. Some restaurant chains have even hired designers or interior decorators to create predictably nostalgic looks for all of their stores. For example, every new Bennigan's Restaurant that opens is chock-full of old photographs, brass railings, stained glass, and other "old" items. One Bennigan's manager recently recounted how one designer does all of the national franchises.[12] The objects in these places, however, have little direct meaning to the experience of a community but rather are chosen to evoke a general feeling of a time past.

Museum Bars and Their Community Audiences

All of the above are examples of museums, that like the more traditional local historical museums, have become repositories for regionally produced, used or collected items. The museum bar collections have also been formed in ways mirroring the local historical museum. Generally, the collections have been created through donations, trade (in the bar's case, for liquor — in the regular museum's case, for other artifacts) or as a direct result of an owner/curator's or patron's collection interest.

As in a regular museum, a museum bar's collection is carefully, even artfully, arranged and displayed for public viewing. Glass or distance separates the object from the viewer. Objects are accorded a place of respect and are meant to be viewed with appreciation. Groupings may be made of business cards or bowling trophies, deer heads lined up along one wall, or lucky dollar bills tacked behind the register.

Neil Harris, in his article, "Museums, Merchandising and the Popular Taste: The Struggle for Influence," has written perceptively on the public fascination with museum exhibitions:

The museum enterprise is a public mood which is difficult to define but pervasive in its effects and which demands a total immersion in nostalgic evocation. The roots and directions of contemporary nostalgia are still unclear, but they include an affection for physical objects and details that is quite astonishing in its inclusiveness and perhaps in its lack of discrimination. Public absorption with mementos of a past that is continually recorded and yet recedes into memory as styles change can only be satisfied ultimately by total environments. The museum alone has the stock of objects to permit total immersion."[13]

The museum bar, like the regular museum, has an abundant collection of artifacts that collectively create a powerful feeling of immersion that clearly affects the patron of this cultural experience.

These collections of objects by virtue of being located in a bar, are more closely associated with the daily lives of people. Unlike the hushed galleries of an art museum or a curator monitored exhibition hall, museum bar collections are in the mainstream of community experience. The objects elicit memories from old-timers and questions for newcomers—in short, they foster communication among the bar's clientele. While in none of the above cases was the collection formed as a direct advertising or marketing ploy, the museum aspect of each bar has served to attract new customers. Some bars, like Daggett's or Stubb's or Hurley's have even changed their name to museum bars and lit their new names up in lights.

While at first glance, Stubb's Museum Bar and Bennigan's tavern might have much in common, a closer analysis reveals major differences in such aspects as origination, and development, function, audience participation/response, type of clientele, and ownership. By studying these public exhibition spaces, one could explore community history, community values and the very essence of the relationship between the individual and the objects. The museum bar can perhaps best be understood by investigating more thoroughly the community response to the various museum bars. In an article entitled, "Interpreting Material Culture: A View from the Other Side of the Glass," Harold Skramstad, Jr. has observed:

An exhibition, whatever its content, is a complex artifact with a life of its own. If successful, it becomes a work of art itself which often transcends the value of the objects or insights, or historical information it may contain and which reflects the culture that created it. I suggest that we spend less time examining individual artifacts, reading into them personal visions and idiosyncracies, and instead spend more time expanding exhibitions, which may be artifacts of a higher order and which require important and serious critical analysis.[14]

This suggestion can be readily applied to the museum bar exhibitions as they are more significant as a collective exhibit experience than noteworthy as a random series of objects. There is a local communal life that surrounds these environments that can be revealed through the eyes of the customer/informants that participate in these cultural meeting places.

Another extremely profitable course of inquiry focused on the customer/informant of the museum bars would delve into the psychological response of the individual to the museum bar exhibition. To term the response simply nostalgia is to minimize the depth of meaning that the setting may provide for the patron. The language, behavioral patterns, and the unconscious visual affinity of the museum bar customers all deserve attention as they comprise the essence of cultural life of the museum bar. This premise has been put forth in an important study by Mihaly Csikszentmihalyi and Eugene Rochberg-Halton entitled, *The Meanings of Things*. Psychoanalytically oriented psychologists claim, in effect, that it is not the instincts that determine the way we deal with "objects," it is our relationship with objects that brings about instinctual needs. In other words, children do not get attached to their parents because they have a need for attachment; it is the interaction with the parents that create such a need.[15] They go on to conclude that:

> Objects affect what a person can do, either by expanding or restricting the scope of that person's actions and thoughts. And because what a person does is largely what he or she is, objects have a determining effect on the development of self, which is why understanding the type of the relationship that exists between people and things is so crucial.[16]

Museums and Community Conservation

Museum bars can be understood to be directly related to the experience of the community. As a gathering place, the museum bar provides an opportunity for the objects assembled there to be invested with new meanings as well as convey a connectedness to past traditions. Usually developed through community participation, rather than through the efforts of a single curatorial vision, the collection of objects and the related folklore can provide a rich index of community life. In a recent essay, Alan Jabbour pointed out the value of documenting and analyzing types of museums seldom thought of as important sources of regional history and folklore.

Community participation in collecting, documenting and present-ing cultural traditions is certainly a fact of life in the twentieth-century America. It is striking how deeply that phenomenon is intertwined with the new technological developments that characterize the cen-tury. . . . Museums are another means of documenting and preserving folk traditions. As a class, museums function in our civilization to provide for "the increase and diffusion of knowledge" (to cite the Smithsonian's memorable charge), as well as to preserve and present objects and artifacts which embody that knowledge. They may once have been preserves where the scholarly and the initiated could study and reflect on culture and history, but the rise of home museums as a widespread American phenomenon suggests that the idea of museums has been fully internalized by local communities across the land. . . . Midway between the home museum and the larger metropolitan, regional and state museums stands an important third category: the community museum. . . . In a community museum individuals make significant statements about what they value and what they want the community to value in the future. For the insider, they represent important statements about what is culturally significant in the community—what ought to be preserved and reflected upon now and in the future. . . . Folklorists and other researchers owe it to them-selves, and to the communities they visit, to take community self-documentation and self-presentation into account. To ignore it is to ignore the single most cogent guide to community values.[17]

Understanding the cultural life of a museum bar therefore begins with fieldwork within the closed circle of museum bar patrons. Only then can the objects be properly considered as part of the expressive local culture that deserves consideration.

Conclusion

Museum bars offer rich potential for fieldworkers who are seeking to explore the transaction between objects (or assemblages of objects) and the object maker or object user. Objects are invested with meaning by people and serve a function whether it be generally to give order to a situation or to inspire disorder.[18] Museum bars should not be thought of as mere collection centers for odds and ends; rather they operate as living community museums that not only reflect community culture, but conserve and contribute to community life in an active way. Perhaps the museum bars reflect most accurately the notion of public "living museums." For within these taverns walls, the museums collections function as part of the ordinary experience of the community.

1. A version of this paper was originally presented at the Popular Culture Association meeting in Toronto, Canada, in March 1984.
2. Conversation with George MacDowell, July 1975. MacDowell was a retired pattern maker from the Grand Ledge (Michigan) Chair Factory.
3. *Upbeat*, 6 August 1976.
4. Ibid.
5. C. Kurt Dewhurst and Marsha MacDowell, *Rainbows in the Sky: Folk Art of Michigan in the Twentieth Century* (East Lansing: Michigan State University, 1978), 99.
6. Val Berryman, Curator of Historical Artifacts at the Michigan State University Museum was particularly helpful in gathering information on this museum bar.
7. James P. Leary, *A Beginning Fieldworker's Guide to European Ethnic Music in Northern Wisconsin* (Ironwood, MI: North Country Press, 1981).
8. Paul Ripley, *The Antlers* placemat.
9. Douglas Rigby and Elizabeth Rigby. *Lock, Stock and Barrel: The Story of Collecting* (Philadelphia: J. B. Lippincott Company, 1944).
10. Ibid., 217.
11. Ibid., 463.
12. Conversation with Bennigan's manager, East Lansing, Michigan, 1984.
13. Neil Harris, "Museums, Merchandising and the Popular Taste: The Struggle for Influence," in *Material Culture and the Study of American Life*, ed. Ian M. G. Quimby (New York: W. W. Norton & Company, Inc., 1978), 140–74.
14. Harold K. Skramstad, Jr., "Interpreting Material Culture: A View from the Other Side of the Glass," in *Material Culture and the Study of American Life*, ed. Ian M. G. Quimby (New York: W. W. Norton & Company, Inc., 1978), 175–200.
15. Mihaly Csikszentmihalyi and Eugene Rochberg-Halton, *The Meaning of Things: Domestic Symbols and Self* (Cambridge, MA: Cambridge University Press, 1981).
16. Ibid., 53.
17. Alan Jabbour, "Keeping Track of Culture: Grassroots Conservation," in *Passing Time and Traditions: Contemporary Iowa Folk Artists*, ed. Steven Ohrn (Ames: Iowa State University Press, 1984), 149–59.
18. Two recent publications highlighting unusual contemporary collections or enviorments are examples of the rising attention to these assemblages as sources of information on collecting and local history: Ellen Land-Weber, *The Passionate Collector* (New York: Simon and Schuster, 1980), and Daniel Franklin Ward, ed., *Personal Places: Perspectives on Informal Art Enviornments* (Bowling Green, Ohio: Bowling Green State University Popular Press, 1984).

Storytelling and Meaning

Commercial Fishermen & Isle Royale

Urban Legends

Paul Bunyan & Hiawatha

Black Legends of Calvin

eople the world over love to tell

and listen to stories. Most of us tell stories at one time or another, even if we do not regard ourselves as storytellers. When was the last time you heard yourself telling about a recent personal experience or repeating an incident that involved someone else? You thought it was just talk, just conversation. But conversation is, in fact, one context in which people tell stories, especially jokes, anecdotes, and legends. The subject matter is appropriate to what is being discussed, so you tell your story.

Raconteurs, however, are a different case. They tell stories consciously and purposefully, sometimes informally among friends and even formally on stage. Sometimes an "expert" storyteller is known as the local "liar," i.e., someone who can "spin a good yarn" or "tell a good one." Other locally recognized individuals like to talk about the past and are able to make local past events and individuals come alive in stories. This type of storyteller is seldom called such, but rather a local or folk historian; regardless, the history is told in narrative.

The range of traditional prose narratives in oral circulation is great, but the basic types include folktales (which are considered fictional), legends (which are usually secular truth), and myths (which are sacred truths). These categories can be divided into smaller groups of even more specific types, such as anecdotes, jokes, tall tales, personal reminiscences, and family stories.

All folk narratives reveal something of the interests, values, and attitudes of the people who tell them. In this respect, stories and storytelling are a form of communication. Tim Cochrane explores how the commercial fishermen of Isle Royale feel and think about their environs. Their culture is intimately involved with Lake Superior, which is a creative stimulus to the folk culture of the island. Their traditional narratives communicate a sense of the fishermen's relationship to the island and to the lake.

Detroit is also the subject of traditional narratives, which communicate a sense of the city's relationship to its inhabitants. With its multi-ethnic population, industry, and varying neighborhoods, Detroit is a city of many faces. Janet Langlois surveys Detroit historical and place-names legends still in oral circulation and compares this legacy with the modern urban legends of today. The result is a greater awareness and appreciation for the city and its people.

Two popular misconceptions about Michigan folklore are that Paul Bunyan figured large in the pantheon of lumberjack folk heroes and that Hiawatha was a great Indian hero. Neither, in fact, is the case. Eliot Singer tackles this issue by examining the relationship between folklore heroes for mass consumption and true folklore in order to recover the authentic traditions behind the figures of Paul Bunyan and Hiawatha. The result is that truth *is* greater than fiction.

Mary Richardson was a marvelous teller of traditional tales, with whom Richard Dorson spent many hours in her Calvin Township home in 1952. Her stories mix the historical, strange and macabre; regardless of what skeptical listeners thought, she regarded her tales as true. "Negro Tales of Mary Richardson" is a classic collection of Afro-American narrative in Michigan.

The articles in this section illustrate various types of narratives, some told directly to the author by the storyteller, others obtained from secondary sources. The authors apply different methods of dealing with folklore in order to understand both the stories and the people who tell them. This selection only begins to introduce the reader to the range of traditional narratives associated with Michiganders.

Commercial Fishermen and Isle Royale: A Folk Group's Unique Association with Place

Timothy Cochrane

group's folklore is highly revealing of the interests and attitudes of its members. Favorite stories, customs, and material culture are built
upon and project commonly held values. For example, an Isle
Royale fisherman's story about navigating in "heavy seas" is built
upon group-wide assumptions that Lake Superior is powerful,
unpredictable, dangerous, and to be respected—even feared. From
this, and other examples which follow, we can see that folk expressions are particularly sensitive to and reflective of local sentiment.
Folklore directly reflects local interests and attitudes for another reason. Because stories, pastimes, and artifacts are produced and used
by the same group there is little pressure to "touch-up" their folklore
for an outside audience or authority. For example, fishermen's
doubts and prejudices concerning Michigan Department of Natural
Resource fishery biologists are frankly depicted in their stories.[1]
However, fishermen are not likely to tell these stories to biologists;
they keep them to themselves. In sum, folklore is a sensitive baro-
meter which gauges people's attitudes, beliefs, and actions.

Many people associate folklore with a group having a special—
and usually long-standing—relationship to a locality. Often these
groups are said to be tied or rooted to a place. So if what we have
said is true, then folklore should tell us what a group feels and
thinks about their home and neighborhood. Here we explore how
Isle Royale commercial fishermen feel and think about their

immediate environs,[2] and suggest how fishermen became "attached" to Isle Royale. To do this, we must first review Isle Royale fishing history and then examine "modern" fishermen's folk expressions.[3]

Isle Royale is the geologic twin of Michigan's Keweenaw Peninsula. Its surface and subsurface topography (important for fish habitat) resembles a series of breaking waves, gently sloping upward on one side and crashing down on the other. "The Island," as it is known regionally, is actually an archipelago in Lake Superior. Its numerous bays and reefs are excellent habitat and spawning grounds for lake trout, whitefish, and herring. Lake Superior isolates Isle Royale from mainland activities and produces climatic conditions which affect all quarters of life on the island. The fury of the "big lake"—its cold and turbulent waters—can threaten any unwary mariner.

The commercial fishing story on Isle Royale is old, rich, and largely untold.[4] No one can definitely say when net fishing first began. It is likely, however, that the prehistoric Native American copper miners and sugar mapling Ojibwa set gill nets in island waters prior to Anglo-discovery of Lake Superior. These early fishermen took fish only for their own diets. The first commercial fishing enterprises on Isle Royale were operated by the famous fur companies—first the North West Company (circa 1800) and then the American Fur Company in the 1830s. The American Fur Company, the largest fishing operation on Lake Superior in the 1800s, shipped salted "fat trout" (or siskiwits) in barrels via sailing schooners to Detroit and other midwestern market cities.[5] The financial panic of 1837 crushed the ailing American Fur Company operations[6] which was then succeeded by a host of small trading post operations which sent out laborers to fish Isle Royale seasonally.

By the 1880s and 1890s startling changes forged a new fishing era on Isle Royale and elsewhere. This modern fishing era is of particular interest to us. It can be characterized by six changes. First, a rapid influx of Scandinavians changed the ethnic make-up of island fishermen. Norwegians, especially from Lofoten Island and the north of Norway, and some Swedes and Finns flocked to island fisheries. Second, advances in fishing technology improved throughout the modern era when engines for power boats and net-lifters, radios, and new net materials were adopted. Third, new markets were opened up with the invention of refrigerated railroad cars. Fourth, large fish companies dominated and, in the case of A. Booth and Sons, monopolized the early modern fish trade. Booth's grip on the trade was such that he could stake immigrant fishermen on Isle Royale, lending them credit, supplies, and equipment. These fishermen worked for "the company" until they paid their debts, then became independent fishermen who sold fish to the A. Booth and Co. steamer circumnavigating Isle Royale. Fifth, tourism, along with fishing, became an important Isle Royale industry. And sixth, people began to prefer fresh "lean" trout and herring, thus making regular shipments necessary to get fresh fish to market. Today, only a shadow of the modern fishing continues.

Island fishermen were more homogeneous than most American folk groups. They shared a potentially dangerous occupation, a unique and insular home, and often family and/or ethnic allegiances. Some island fishermen considered their occupation and island home the most important entities in their lives.

Most important for our discussion, fishermen were intimately involved with the Lake Superior environment. Fishing success depended upon the understanding and adapting of the Scandinavian fishermen to fresh water conditions and fish. Their preoccupation with the island's coastal zone was so consuming that they knew little about the island's interior. Ingeborg Holte summed up the fishermen's perspective when she said, "We loved the island from the lake."[7]

Isle Royale fisheries were relatively tiny settlements surrounded and dwarfed by pristine land and seascapes (fig. 1). Fishermen did not feel threatened by this wilderness; they felt little need to erect

National Park Service

Figure 1. Sivertson Fishhouse and dock, Isle Royale.

symbolic or actual barriers to hold off the encroachment of wild lands, animals, or plants. Order, predictability, and domesticity prevailed only inside homes or in the small domestic flower and vegetable gardens. Outside the borders of gardens and houses, fishermen lived in two disparate landscapes—one littered with old rusty or moldy equipment and the other unmistakably wild. Island residences were built with a clear view of the harbor, and if possible, on a knoll to improve the view as well as water runoff. From a rise, a fisherwoman could spot her husband coming off the lake, gauge the bustle of activity in the fishhouse, or watch moose grazing for submerged aquatic plants. Fishermen lived in a functional landscape situated in an untrampled environment.[8] Their fisheries might seem unkempt to outsiders, but since the fishery landscape fulfilled its function for fishermen, it was not judged esthetically objectionable. Fishermen appreciated both the utility of an area dotted with machine parts, old boats, and fishery equipment and the esthetic qualities of a wilderness neighborhood.

Successful island fisheries were located where environmental conditions were favorable. A successful fishery was dependent on a "good harbor" with (1) deep enough water at the dock and out to the fishing grounds to keep the boats from scraping, and water for maneuverability inside the harbor; (2) a gradual slope to the lake bottom so crib docks could be easily constructed and a water depth not exceeding ten feet where the dock cribs were sunk; (3) shelter from heavy seas; and (4) close proximity to fishing grounds. "Onshore" criteria for locating a successful fishery included adequate space for fishery buildings; high, dry ground to minimize the numbers of mosquitoes, black flies, and "no-see-ums" for residences, yet shelter from cold off-shore winds, if possible.

One location rarely fit all these criteria, so tradeoffs were made in choosing a fishery site. However, the first three criteria for harbor location were musts. Fishery location is predicated on environmental constraints. In this case, the cultural landscape (the fishery) is intimately related to, and dependent on, the physical environs (island geology, geography, limnology, and biology). While noting this relationship we must be careful with our interpretation. Not all fishery structures, let alone folk culture, is predicated on environmental givens—a form of environmental determinism.[9] More often, the environment is a creative influence on folk culture, not a determinant. For example, fishermen devised special cantilevered docks in shallow harbors to overcome the "deep water" criterion mentioned above. It is crucial to note that fishermen accepted environmental limits and reacted creatively to make the best of their situation.[10]

Perhaps one of the most creative solutions island fishermen devised was the opportune use of "pulp sticks" in crib dock construction.[11] Cribs made of a rectangular log framework were the foundation on which dock planking was built. A crib would be built on the shoreline out of shallowly notched pulp sticks spiked together. The interstices between pulp sticks were purposely left open. After the crib was built at the right height (the height from the lake bottom to twelve to eighteen inches above the waterline), logs were inserted to form a floor. The crib was then pushed or pulled into the water and filled with boulders until it was barely buoyant. While still afloat the crib was towed into position and sunk with the addition of more rocks. Positioning and sinking the crib in the right location was the tricky part (fig. 2). The crib had to settle in line with other cribs and at the right depth. Fishermen not only preferred crib docks because the logs were free and near-at-hand, but they also appreciated the ability of crib docks to withstand winter ice. Other types of docks did not withstand the tremendous pressure of

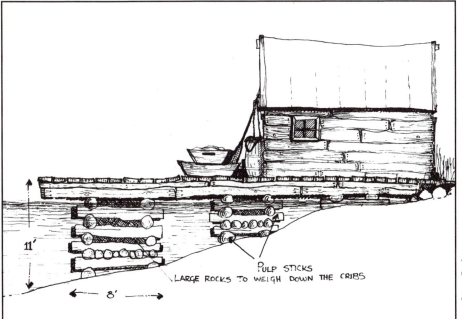

Figure 2. Pulp stick dock.

winter ice, thus requiring annual repairs—a luxury fishermen did not have time for.

The discussion of crib docks naturally leads us to the lake, where fishermen's skills and knowledge were most expansive and practical. Fishermen developed a "strategy"—though never put into words—for fishing success and safety. In reality their strategy was a complex system, a diagnostic and belief system, that insured success and safety. The "system" helped fishermen make countless daily judgments, read and react to weather and lake conditions, and find good fishing "sets" for each season and species. Since the system worked, conventions were developed to insure its continued existence and use. For example, conventions about fishing grounds—really aquatic territory—were resolved through widely recognized agreements.

A fishing enterprise is filled with uncertainty and even mystery. After all, fish live in an unseen realm where the fisherman cannot go. Boat navigation is fraught with danger and uncertainty. One way island fishermen minimized navigational problems was to hone their sensory skills as a natural response to a harsh and unforgiving resource—Lake Superior. One observer has commented on similar situations: "People can develop exceptional perceptual acuity in the course of adapting successfully to the challenges of a harsh environment."[12]

Fishermen learned to recognize orienting stimuli while on the lake: if sunlight conditions were right, a fisherman could tell where he was, and if he was in danger, by the color of the water; green water in the spring meant shallow water and fishermen should be wary. The most common navigational technique was a timed compass course. To reach a destination a compass course would be taken at a preset speed and time. For instance, a fisherman would run south at 1400 rpm for fifteen minutes, but many did not have tachometers in their boats so they would run a compass course at a motor speed "that sounded right" for an allocated period of time.[13]

If a fisherman became disoriented on the lake in a fog he would stop his boat, turn off the motor and listen. While momentarily adrift all kinds of stimuli, but especially sounds, would become noticeable, and from these clues he could reorient himself. Sounds, such as waves breaking on shore or a reef, or bird cries (including sounds distinguishing the bird species or number), helped the fisherman become reoriented. For example, warbler songs told the fisherman he was dangerously close to a shoreline. On extremely rare occasions two other means of "dead reckoning" were used, namely, the fragrance of plant life and echo of sounds from the shoreline.

In another phase of fishing, fishermen were so alert to underwater conditions that they had mental maps of the lake bottom and lake currents. Stan Sivertson knew the subsurface conditions off McCormick's Rocks well enough to set the exact length of anchor ropes on his nets at his fishery before going out. Setting a gill net up horizontally with the anchors down hundreds of feet on a steeply pitched bottom requires intimate knowledge and memory of the lake bottom (fig. 3). Fishermen knew more than the contours of the bottom; they knew what it was made of (sand, mud, rock), which fish favored these conditions, and how the highly variable lake currents would affect fishing at that location.

Weather and lake-lore are yet another part of the diagnostic and belief system that helped fishermen to be successful and fish safely. Weather and lake-lore were useful to make volatile phenomena more predictable. The importance of weather and lake-lore in a fisherman's life is witnessed by how commonly they were told and sought out. Yet the form of Isle Royale weather and lake-lore is surprising. The lore was extremely empirical and conversational rather than superstitious, lyrical, or said in rhymed couplets. Fishermen's

National Archives

Figure 3. 1890s style gill net fishing on Lake Superior.

discriminating observations and desire to learn produced highly localized weather and lake-lore.

A commonly held belief that "the island makes its own weather" best expresses this localization tendency. Some weather and lake-lore was very site specific such as for Wright Island or McCormick's Reef. Ingeborg Holte could tell the approximate wind direction by the temperature inside her island home. She understood how the surrounding trees, outer islands, the main island, and the length of sweep across open water affected the temperature by knowing which winds were likely to be cold, moderate, or warm.

Curiously, the weather and lake-lore was devoid of directly stated magical beliefs, omens, or good luck devices. This lack of magical or superstitious beliefs runs counter to the accepted inter-pretation that extremely risky occupations (rodeo, gambling, fish-ing) usually develop magical beliefs.[14] It had been thought that the physically threatening and unpredictable character of marine envi-ronment provides a strong drive for ritual magic. Not so with Isle Royale fishermen; instead their diagnostic and belief system empha-sized empirical observations and judgments.

Island fishing ways were maintained through various occupa-tional customs. Informal conventions about fishing territory rights permitted fishermen to concentrate on fishing rather than fighting for or defending their fishing sets. The fishing sets of "old-timers" (the veteran members of the first generation of Scandinavian fisher-men) were recognized and respected. However, in instances where fishing competition was acute, claims might be challenged from one year to the next. For most island fishermen (except the old-timers) fishing ground claims were established twice a year—one claim for hookline fishing and another for gill net fishing. Once a fishing ground was claimed by setting a net, it was recognized as belonging to that fisherman for the duration of the season for that method of fishing.

Island fishing grounds were a form of occupational territory. Many of the characteristics of human territoriality are applicable to the island situation. Thus, fishing grounds were personalized, evoked feelings of familiarity and belonging, were defended, and had distinct boundaries recognized by others. One example illus-trates the degree of personalization a fisherman had toward his fish-ing grounds. Ingeborg Holte observes: "My father never got over the fact [laughing] that 'that boat' [the steamer *Glenlyon*] went down there [off his fishing grounds near Menagerie Island]. Sometimes you would think from listening to him that it had done it on pur-pose."[15] Fishing grounds were also defended. Mrs. Holte mentioned a "bop in the nose" was the most extreme way a fisherman would defend his claim. Fishermen's fishing grounds were identified by onshore and submerged landmarks. If possible two or three land-marks were used to mentally triangulate a point in a fishing ground. The "green bunch" or "the landslide" are two examples of onshore landmarks used to locate grounds. Submerged landmarks such as shipwrecks, reef, or dropoffs also helped fishermen apportion fish-ing grounds.

Onshore customs provided a satisfying and secure counterpart to the dangers, unpredictability and rigors of lake fishing. Fishermen thoroughly enjoyed social folk customs, especially since they inter-rupted the tedium of isolation and long workdays. These were times of fun, relaxation, social stimulation, education (catching up on mainland news and island gossip), and always informality. "Coffee" was one of the most common and yet spontaneous of island folk customs. During coffee, island fishermen welcomed unexpected strangers and fellow fishermen into their homes. Upon arrival at a fishery the guests would be escorted to the house, warmed by a stove and conversation, and feted with homemade baked goods and strong coffee. Rolls, pies, breads, cake, and jellies—made from island berries—were offered in generous quantities. Besides eating, conversation and storytelling were common activities. Great care was taken to make sure guests who were often wet and chilled were made comfortable, both physically and socially.

Scandinavian in origin, coffee satisfied guest and host alike on Isle Royale. Among its many functions, coffee allowed the fisherwo-man to demonstrate her cooking skills. Great pride was taken in the quality of the baked goods offered. These very rich foods tasted especially good to lake travelers and fishermen who burned up tre-mendous amounts of calories in the course of the day. Elaborately made baked goods also demonstrated the civility of island society by showing that a fisherwoman could rise above her primitive cook-ing equipment and limited supplies to make "elegant" foods.

The conversational component of coffee was also vital. Con-versation played a much larger and more important role among island people than among many Michiganders. The island was pre-eminently a verbal community that depended on conversation for news of the outside world, intra-island events, education, and enter-tainment. During coffee, guests and hosts exchanged news freely, with widely ranging topics. A great deal of latitude was tolerated and even encouraged in conversation.

The common experience of crossing Lake Superior helped to provide a group feeling and was frequently discussed. Crossing the lake tended to produce respect for its size and hint at its power. Fishermen were all but too familiar with the size and power of Lake Superior and enjoyed hearing other people trying to understand it. Visitors and fishermen personally identified with the island whose limited size was seen as personable, less awesome or abstract than a continent or a geographical abstraction such as the "north woods." As a limited resource with naturally defined borders, it could be more easily identified and appreciated. Thus the group feeling of coffee participants was augmented by the camaraderie of lake travelers and the personal identification most visitors have for Isle Royale.

Coffee honored the fishermen hosts and homes and island friendships but did so, uncharacteristically, indoors. Coffee was carefully cultivated in a warm, secure, and domestic atmosphere which contrasted sharply with the natural environment—the fishermen's workplace. The immediate context of coffee, inside a snug and well-used living room and kitchen, emphasized feelings of shelter from an otherwise wild, cold, and rocky archipelago. Ultimately, coffee welcomed people into the stability and calm of a fisherman's home. If this is so, if coffee took people away from the natural environment and celebrated social amenities, how does that square with our question of a group's relationship to place? First, we must note that coffee—though an indoor phenomenon—was complementary, not antithetical, to fishermen's sense of place. Fishermen, like all other people, needed customs which provide a respite from venturing out in a harsh environment. Because it occurred inside and was primarily social does not mean it was irrelevant to fishermen's feelings and thoughts of the island. In short, it was not a rejection of their place; rather coffee conversations with guests helped fishermen articulate their feelings about the island. Furthermore, memories of social encounters were intermeshed in fishermen's views of the island. Coffee enhanced their appreciation of their homes, workplace, and wild places. The warm, snug feeling of island homes allowed fishermen to relax, digest, and reflect on their own and other's feelings and actions toward Isle Royale. The domestic harbor of the house was as necessary a condition for environmental appreciation as all the knowledge and skill it took to "lift a gang of nets" on a choppy and bucking "sea."

The most creative folk expressions—stories and art—made the most dramatic statements of island fishermen's attachment to Isle Royale. For example, Ingeborg Holte found it difficult to paint any other subject than her Wright Island home. Other folk art, such as Greenstone jewelry, underscored the uniqueness of the island. Folk narratives, too, can tell us much about fishermen's thoughts and feelings toward Isle Royale. However, while the stories make dramatic statements about fishermen's affinity for the island, these statements are often indirect or symbolic.

Island fishermen's stories put a premium on humor. Stories which blend humor, insight, and surprise were highly esteemed. Fishermen's narratives had a strong first person perspective, hence they related personal experiences of the narrator or a friend. Storytellers often cited story characters by names which helped to add credibility to the story, acknowledge where the story originated, and personalize the story.

The storyteller and audience placed a strong emphasis on the veracity of most stories. However, island narratives also gravitated toward unusual and remarkable experiences of daily life. Fishermen-storytellers took much delight in telling tales that had dramatic tension between truth and incredibility, believability and amazement. Yet these remarkable events rarely had a supernatural component. Like their tendency toward empirical beliefs, fishermen prized plausible stories about supernormal events.

Fishermen's stories revered the past on Island Royale, but not always solemnly. Their stories asserted that Isle Royale has changed through the years. For example, Buddie Sivertson told a story in which fishermen were depicted as being so frugal in the "old days" that each season they transported their large cook stoves to and from the island.

> Oh, one little . . . anecdote about what the fishermen used to have to do in the fall, when the *America* came. They only had one cook stove that they used all winter in Duluth. And they used it in the summer at Isle Royale. This was one of those huge cook ranges, you know, one of those big Monarchs.
>
> Must have weighed a thousand or two thousand pounds. But they had to keep those functioning because they never knew when the boat was going to come and pick them up in the fall, you know. So they used that stove all the time to cook their meals, heat their house and everything like that. So when the whistle blew out there . . . they would dump the ashes out of the stove . . . put wooden handles, you know, put wooden logs underneath the corners and carried that stove. Maybe four guys carried that stove down to the dock, into the boat,

Maybe four guys carried that stove down to the dock, into the boat, and rowed it out where the *America* was. And hoisted it aboard the *America*—that hot stove.[16]

Buddie's story is an excellent example of a legend that dramatically contrasts truth with the unusual. It is also an example of an "immigrant story" that stresses the hardships of the immigrants' early days in America.

Buddie's story illustrates another characteristic theme of island storytelling: the primitive and yet perfectly functional fishing technology. A common Isle Royale folk belief reinforced this theme, namely, you can get by with what is on hand. Other examples of island ingenuity included beating wrenches on empty 55-gallon gas barrels as fog horns, using half an upturned mackinaw boat for an outhouse frame, and keeping perishable food in the fishhouse near the cool lake water.

Fishermen told stories in a variety of settings—out on the lake, while "dressing" fish, at coffee, during the Fourth of July, and whenever an audience was assembled. Fishermen who worked in pairs (the most common work arrangement) told stories throughout their workday. Narratives that were short and unstructured, such as jokes and legends, were told in almost any environment. Visual jokes, rather than stories, were also exchanged among fishermen out on the lake. Hand signals, gestures, and an occasional shout were all there were to these jokes. They were told, in Buddie's words, "to screw the others up a bit" by making a competitor believe that your boat made a particularly heavy or unsuccessful haul.

Fishermen did not tell many stories about fish encountered while commercial fishing. There were no "fish stories" about fish that got away or fish of amazing size in the context of their workday. Fishermen told fish stories only in the context of recreational fishing. Their preference for animals and not fish as storytelling subjects is interesting. Animals that were peripheral to fishing operation were favorite subjects of verbal art, while animals that were crucial to their livelihood, e.g., fish, were discussed in a conversational or non-artistic manner.

"Moose stories" were the fishermen's favorite. They were told often enough to be recognized as a category of stories by the fishermen. The fact that moose stories became so popular reveals a great deal about fishermen's ideas of Isle Royale. For example, they preferred wild animal stories. There were a few stories about dairy cows swimming from island to island and family pets smuggled on Isle

Royale against National Park Service regulations, but they were the exceptions rather than the rule. There was also a preference for "wild" animal stories in which these animals befriended or grew comfortable with their fishermen neighbors.

The following two stories illustrate the moose story category and, incidentally, contrast two very different storytelling styles. Buddie Sivertson related:

> They [the moose] were just all over. If you had to walk down the path at night, if you didn't have a flashlight, you carried a stick in front of you. Like a blind man. . . .
>
> My Uncle Gus ran right into one one night. . . . He was coming around the corner of a building and he was coming, you know it was dark. You're visiting somebody and you forgot your flashlight and it turns dark. So you have to go home in the dark. . . . He went around the corner of the house and ran right smack into this hairy thing. I mean ran his face right into the side of the moose.[17]

And Stan Sivertson told the following tale:

> It was in the fall of the year and he [a moose] was swimming from Booth Island to Singer's Island. And I was up at our fishhouse. [I] happened to be out washing nets. And I thought, gee, if I can get a picture . . . if I ran down the path there and chased him out into the lake I could get a good picture because of his big horns. By the time I got the camera and got down there he had already come up the path. There he was. I hollered like a wolf and went around. He turned and ran down the path. He stopped where the trees hadn't been cut. When I came around the path he was there. I chased him again. I chased him four times. Finally I got him down on the point where he came out. And he ran out in the water.
>
> Anyway, when I got him back in the water and looked in the camera. My gosh, his head was this way, huge, and it was supposed to be. . . . Then he chased me and came out of the water. Finally he got to snorting! Then he calmed down. I started sneaking up on him, he was in a dark background on land and it would have made a poor picture. That's why I wanted him out in the water. I really thought his eyes were turning red. He was so mad!
>
> So this chase went on. And he was snorting again. I was worried. . . . Finally he ran straight at me, then turned and veered around the house and crashed into the woods.[18]

These stories that Buddy and Stan told were humorous in intent, although Stan's made inferences about moose—and human—behavior. Less commonly, moose stories, like animal stories in medieval bestiaries, made moralistic points. Most, like the ones above, stressed that moose were highly unusual, even comical, animals that acted as foils for fishermen. For example, moose were described as being gangly in shape and uncoordinated yet perfectly suited for the island environment, like the fishermen's belief in the "primitive" yet effective fishing technology. Some moose were thought to have very expressive facial expressions, while their actions were depicted as puzzling. Indeed, some stories have their actions running counter to their facial expressions. While moose were sometimes portrayed as threatening, a moose-human confrontation never ended in injury. Fishermen's stories outline how moose that attack were often unwittingly drawn into aggressive behavior by human actions, as in Stan's story.

Why did moose become the fishermen's favorite wildlife subject? First, their unusual shape and visibility made them "natural" storytelling subjects; and second, they were more common on Isle Royale than on the mainland, and so represented a unique island resource. However, there are more complex reasons for their popularity. Fishermen saw moose as symbols of their conception of Isle Royale as unusual, wild, and separate from mainland life. Like their own primitive, yet effective, technology, moose were appreciated for their struggle to survive and for their homely appearance.

Scandinavian fishermen felt kindly toward moose because they both migrated to Isle Royale near the turn-of-the-century. Their tenure coincided decades before the island became a national park or wolves arrived. Finally, fishermen symbolically identified with moose because they behaved properly—that is, they were peaceful, independent creatures—not predators. Since fishermen considered themselves harvesters of a renewable crop (like farmers) they could identify with an animal that lived similarly.

Fishermen had other favored story subjects, such as family members, notable characters and places, and shipwrecks—which is no surprise since there have been over 325 wrecks on Lake Superior in recorded history.[19] There have been three major shipwrecks on the southwestern corner of Isle Royale alone. Dense fogs of spring and fierce fall storms have contributed to the loss of many ships. A number of Isle Royale shipwrecks occurred in undramatic stages: the ship would run aground, stay aground on a reef for hours or days, and then be pushed from the rocks by storm waves, wind, or currents.

Many shipwreck narratives are humorous and focus on lost or seized opportunities to salvage materials. The aftermath of the sinking of the *America* is well remembered by Washington Harbor fishermen. Buddie Sivertson recalls that so much fruit floated out of the sinking *America* that "whenever you wanted fruit you just stuck your pike pole down the dip hole . . . and there was bound to be a banana bunch going by at the time."[20] Anecdotes about all the fruit eaten are legion. There was rejoicing, at first, at the surprising appearance of free fresh fruit, but many overindulged and there were subsequent stories about fishermen not being able "to look at a banana."

Buddie told another story about what occurred after the *Cox* was abandoned on "Nut Shell Reef."

> Seeing Nels Wick, an old fisherman, you know, who wore the baggy pants and dirty clothes, you know. And that was kind of raggedy and patched and all this kind of thing. Nels Wick had gotten up on the main deck of the *Cox*. You know, they could climb up because the *Cox* was right down in the water. They could walk right up the deck. Everything was at an extreme angle, of course, and the ship had been abandoned so everything aboard was fair game, you know.
>
> So Nels Wick went in this cabin. No one was paying much attention; everyone was grabbing, getting what they can. And some people started missing Nels Wick. Saying, what happened to him. And he came out of this cabin. He came out a dapper gentleman, with a brand new white suit and ah . . . and a straw hat and cane and all that. And he rode home in those clothes in the old fish boat.[21]

Besides its obvious humor, Buddie's story demonstrates a common attitude expressed in most shipwreck stories—a deep respect for the law. Fishermen rarely salvaged any material from a wrecked ship before it was officially declared abandoned; afterwards, however, it was plundered for any useful materials. From various wrecks, fishermen gathered dishes, furniture, fire extinguishers, murals, lumber, clothing, and other detachable items. Buddie's story exhibits another characteristic of island shipwreck stories: fishermen rarely were aboard a ship before it went down, so their stories emphasize what happened after the ship was found in their midst rather than the wreck itself.

Shipwrecks were startling places for fishermen even if the ship was no longer visible from the surface because they were reminders that they, too, could go down in Lake Superior. No one was immune from shipwrecks and swampings; the stories remind listeners that even freighters can and do sink. However, the stories reveal that fishermen were not overly apprehensive. Salvaging materials from a wreck was looked upon only as a somewhat spooky and special opportunity to recover costly goods.

The sinking of the *America* had an importance to island fishermen beyond that of other shipwrecks. The *America*, with its style and size, was and remains the symbol of the halcyon days of commercial fishing on Isle Royale. Ingeborg Holte tells that her mother made a new dress for her for each trip they took on the *America*. The heyday of commercial fishing sank with the *America*. Its demise was important enough to island fishermen that they developed a cluster of stories about her fine captain (who was not at the helm at the time of the wreck), her value, and her unfortunate and suspicious wrecking.

Although tourists prefer wolf stories, fishermen favor stories about moose, the *America*, and notable characters—symbols of the unusual, exotic, grand, and independent character of Isle Royale. They are, in one observer's words, "a particular component of the landscape [which] stands for a place"[22]—the fishermen's storytelling snapshot of what Isle Royale means to them.

I must thank three Isle Royale fishermen who were particularly helpful with this study: Mrs. Ingeborg Holte, Stanley Sivertson, and Buddie Sivertson. Also, Steve Cochrane's sketch and Jean Cochrane's helpful comments are much appreciated.

1. I have adopted the fishermen's definition of themselves. A person is recognized as a "fisherman" if he or she grew up or was employed at an Isle Royale fishery, regardless of sex.
2. This article is condensed and modified from Timothy Cochrane, "The Folklife Expressions of Three Isle Royale Fishermen: A Sense of Place Examination" (M.A. thesis, Western Kentucky University, 1982).
3. What follows is only a brief survey of fishermen's folk expressions. I hope that what is discussed will suggest the complexity and sophistication of fishing folk culture.
4. For more information on Isle Royale and Lake Superior history see Grace Lee Nute, *Lake Superior* (New York: Bobbs-Merrill, 1944).
5. The original papers of the American Fur Company are housed at the New York Historical Society, New York, N.Y.
6. Grace Lee Nute, "The American Fur Company's Fishing Enterprises on Lake Superior," *Mississippi Valley Historical Review* 12 (1926): 486.
7. Taped interview with Mrs. Ingeborg Holte, 17 August 1980. For more information on Mrs. Holte's Isle Royale experience consult her recently published book, *Ingeborg's Isle Royale* (Grand Marais, Minn.: Women's Times, 1984).
8. David Lowenthal, "The American Scene," *The Geographical Review* 58 (1968): 73.
9. Environmental determinism is now a largely discredited theory which asserted that nature always had a direct causal effect on culture.
10. Indeed, most fishermen did not accept environmental limits and left fishing for other employment.

11. Pulp sticks were eight-foot long logs intended to be made into pulp wood products. At the time they were rafted in great and slow-moving log booms across Lake Superior to paper mills. Often a storm would burst open a log boom and scatter pulp sticks. Fishermen used this free resource opportunely, adapting some of their structures—including crib docks—to accommodate the eight-foot long logs.

12. Yi-Fu Tuan, *Topophilia: A Study of Environmental Perception, Attitudes, and Values* (Englewood Cliffs, N.J.: Prentice-Hall, Inc., 1974), 55.

13. Taped interview with Mr. Buddie Sivertson, 14 February 1980.

14. John J. Poggie, Jr. and Carl Gersuny, "Risk and Ritual: An Interpretation of Fishermen's Folklore in a New England Community," *Journal of American Folklore* 85 (1972): 66.

15. Taped interview with Mrs. Ingeborg Holte, 5 August 1980.

16. Buddie Sivertson interview, 14 February 1980.

17. Taped interview with Mr. Buddie Sivertson, 14 April 1980.

18. Taped interview with Mr. Stanley Sivertson, 10 July 1980.

19. Ryck Lydecker, *The Edge of the Arrowhead* (Duluth: University of Minnesota Sea Grant, 1976), 21.

20. Buddie Sivertson interview, 15 April 1980.

21. Ibid.

22. David E. Sopher, "The Landscape of Home," in *The Interpretation of Ordinary Landscapes,* ed. D. W. Meinig (New York: Oxford University Press, 1979), 138.

Urban Legends and the Faces of Detroit

Janet Langlois

 everal years ago, the *Detroit Free Press* ran a feature called "Mental Maps of Detroit: The City is All in Your Head." Reporter Tom Fox asked Detroiters of different ages, ethnic backgrounds, and neighborhoods to draw maps of the city. Because each map was quite distinct, he wrote: "People see Detroit in strikingly different ways. . . . Images are often only vaguely tied to reality—as determined by the world's official mapmakers. Detroiters consider the city from peculiar vantage points—often a place of work, a house, a restaurant or park."[1] Stories of the city, often labeled "urban legends," are verbal counterparts of those individualistic maps for they also focus on just those city places which are significant to their tellers and listeners. These stories have as many distinctive variations and unofficial versions as the maps.

Take, for instance, some place-name legends for Detroit-area points of interest. Most Detroiters know the official story of how Detroit got its name: Antoine Laumet de la Mothe Cadillac and his company entered what is now the Detroit River from Lake Huron via Lake St. Clair on July 23, 1701. On the following day, July 24, Cadillac chose as the site of the future city the place where the river connecting Lake Erie to Lake St. Clair was narrowest and called the place "Detroit" or "the Strait."[2] The naming of Lake St. Clair is not so clear. Some say the lake was named after St. Clair, on whose feast day, August 12, 1679, Robert Cavelier, Sieur de La Salle, sailed into

the lake on the ill-fated *Griffin,* which was destined to be the first
ship lost on the Great Lakes. And others say, with official sanction,
that it was named after General Arthur St. Clair, American
Governor of the Northwest Territory, 1787–1805.[3]

The origin of the name of Belle Isle, the island park in the
Detroit River, is also disputed. Detroiters interviewed in recent years
say that the name "Belle Isle" dates from the early French settlement
because it means "Beautiful Island" in that language. Still others,
again with official sanction, see its American connections for they
say it was named after Governor Lewis Cass's daughter Belle on July
4, 1845, just nine years after Michigan became a state.[4] The different
etymologies for Lake St. Clair and Belle Isle contrast the French past
of Detroit, which lasted from 1701 until the British took possession
of the city in 1760, with its American heritage which began in 1796.

Two legends about Belle Isle are good starting points for discussion because they show, in microcosm, the many contrasting faces
of Detroit. They encapsulate differences between ethnic groups in
the city's history as well as differences between the old and the new
Detroit. The first legend concerns Belle Isle's earlier names. Some
say that it was once called "Rattlesnake Island" because it was
infested with snakes. That name was supplanted by the French *Isle
Aux Cochons* (Hog Island) when *habitants* put hogs there to eat the
snakes and to grow fat on acorns.[5] Others, however, preferring a less
prosaic explanation, look to "The Snake God of Belle Isle," an
Indian or pseudo-Indian legend that Charles M. Skinner, a
nineteenth-century compiler of anthologies on American myths and
legends, included in one of his volumes. Skinner tells his readers that
an Indian demi-god kept his beautiful daughter hidden in a bark
boat on the Detroit River, yet the Winds fought to possess her, and
ultimately smashed her boat into what is now called Belle Isle. Skinner adds, "Here Manitou placed the girl, and set a girdle of vicious
snakes around the shore to guard her and to put a stop to further
contests."[6]

Skinner further notes that Michigan Indians erected and wor-
shipped a natural stone idol on Belle Isle which, when smashed and
thrown into the Detroit River in 1670 by two French priest-
explorers, reunited as a monster serpent to protect the Native
Americans from the white man. M. C. W. Hamlin, in her rendering
of "The Cross and the Manitou: A Legend of Belle Isle," writes,
"Each stone was converted into a rattlesnake which should be as a
sentinel to guard the sacredness of his [Manitou's] domain from the

profaning foot of the white man."[7] Historians Frank and Arthur Woodford write that the report by Francois Dollier de Casson and Renée Brehant de Galinée is vague concerning the exact location of the heathen object that so offended them. The Woodfords place it near the mouth of the River Rouge and continue: "Legend says that unregenerate Indians fished the pieces out of the river and set them up on the lower end of Belle Isle."[8] Although it is not clear whose legend this is—Indian, French, or American—or which version is "more correct," it is clear that the story highlights the confrontation between Native American and French religious views in seventeenth-century Michigan.

Another confrontation occurred on Belle Island almost three hundred years later and is contained in a legend said to have begun the Detroit race riots of 1943.[9] The story is really two stories: one told by black residents who lived in an area of the city east of Woodward Avenue known as "Paradise Valley," its southern tip known as "Black Bottom," and one told by white residents who lived west of Woodward Avenue in "Cass Corridors." The black version tells of whites throwing a black baby, or a black woman and her baby, off the bridge connecting Belle Isle to the city, officially named the MacArthur Bridge, but more popularly known as the Belle Isle Bridge. Mrs. Everlee Watson, who came to Detroit from Georgia in 1935, remembers: "I heard someone said that this fellow came into the club where they had this dance, and said that a white man had just thrown a Negro woman and her baby into the Detroit River."[10] The white version tells the reverse—of blacks throwing a white woman—sometimes a white woman and her baby—off the bridge. Jay McCormick, a *Detroit News* reporter, recalled that "when they later sorted out the riot, they found that the same rumor had been spread in each community."[11]

Although no babies, black or white, were found in the Detroit River, the legend versions pinpoint the wartime tension between the two groups recently arrived from the South to work in the war plants who faced similar housing shortages and discrimination from other residents. Yet the differences in the two groups, reflected in the different official responses to the two versions of the story, show the specific racial discrimination underlying the riot. The white version of the legend was suppressed and the version in which the blacks were victims was highlighted in the official riot report given to the governor. Although most experts agree that rumors, in and of themselves, cannot cause riots, the report of the Committee to Investigate the Detroit Race Riot concluded that the black version of the story "excited passions and must be cited as the principal cause of the tragedy that followed."[12] Perhaps this story can be a parable for the late twentieth century in which power and powerlessness are major issues.

"The Snake God of Belle Isle" and "The Belle Island Bridge Incident" confirm the findings of Wayne State University graduate student Elizabeth Meese who interviewed residents about their legends of Detroit in 1966 in order to determine how these stories functioned for their tellers and listeners. Meese found a nostalgic emphasis in stories about "Old Detroit," the Detroit that existed before 1940. Residents remembered how the city used to be; those memories were expressed in stories that pictured the city in an essentially romantic light. Skinner's "Snake God" captures the romance of Detroit's frontier period, for example. Meese found that the major function of stories about "New Detroit," the post-1940 Detroit, however, was an expression of and method for dealing with tensions and fears generated by urban life.[13] "The Bell Isle Bridge Incident" exemplifies how stories and urban conflicts can be intertwined. The distinction between "Old Detroit" and "New Detroit," then, forms the structure of the following survey of Detroit legends.

Old Detroit

Perhaps no book has done more to enhance the romance of French Detroit than M. C. W. Hamlin's *Legends of le Detroit*, originally printed in 1884, but reprinted by Singing Tree Press in 1968.[14] Hamlin, who claims to have heard these tales from the "aged lips of those ancestors whose memories extend back into the last century,"[15] shows that French residents in the first half of the eighteenth century not only had to deal with the British, their Indian allies and the Americans, but also with an occult world shared in common with the French in Quebec and in Normandy. *Habitants* contended with *la chasse galerie*, a phantom canoe portending death, and *le feu follet*, a phosphorescent swamp light that could entice the unwary, and an array of ghosts and supernatural occurrences. Two legends in particular epitomize the Detroit experience and are as much the city's legacy as the vestiges of the French ribbon farms in street names such as St. Antoine and Beaubien or the circular layout of downtown Detroit. They are the stories of *le Nain Rouge* and *le Loup Garou de Grosse Pointe*.

Le Nain Rouge, or the Red Dwarf, was a small impish creature who brought disaster to anyone who crossed its path. Despite warnings, Cadillac struck the dwarf with his walking cane, and so lost his claim to fortune in the city he had founded. The story begins in a Quebec banquet hall where Cadillac and his officers were celebrating his recent return from France with a royal grant for fifteen acres of land to set up a fort and colony along the Detroit River. A fortuneteller read the officers' fortunes as part of the night's entertainment. She told Cadillac that he would found a great city and a family line, but that he must appease *le Nain Rouge* so that his descendants would inherit his Detroit properties. Cadillac scoffed at this omen and disregarded it. According to the legend, when he and his wife finally met the dwarf in 1707 in Detroit, Cadillac hit the creature. Not long afterwards, in 1710, he was removed from office and appointed governor of Louisiana Territory. He returned to France in 1720 to take the governorship of a small town near his birthplace where he died in 1730.[16]

Other residents, less illustrious than Cadillac, suffered misfortune whenever the red imp was sighted. It was seen on stable roofs, on mill wheels, and in the woods heralding neighbors' quarrels and family feuding. Its influence extended past the period of French rule, for it was seen at the Battle of Bloody Run with Pontiac in 1763 when Detroit was under British control; in the streets when Detroit, as an American city, burned in 1805; and when the American general, William Hull, surrendered the city to the British in the War of 1812.[17] Contemporary sightings were reported before the riots of 1967, before a 1976 ice storm, and prior to a 1981 thunderstorm.[18] There has even been a recent suggestion that the Red Dwarf might be seen romping on Detroit's People Mover.[19]

Le Loup Garou, or werewolf, of Grosse Pointe has none of the humor or prophetic quality of *le Nain Rouge.* It is, instead, an awful figure of a wolf-man intent on ravishment. In one legend, Jacques Morand, a *coureur de bois,* or lumberjack, had been rejected as a suitor by Genevieve Parent, who planned to become a nun in Quebec City. While waiting for a reply from the convent, she built a shrine to the Blessed Virgin on the shores of Lake St. Clair. Jacques Morand, who had become a werewolf with the help of a local witch, tried to accost Genevieve at her prayers and was turned into stone just as he reached her kneeling figure.[20] In another legend, Archange Simonet was seized by a werewolf while dancing at her own wedding. Her bridegroom spent a year searching for her and finally traced the werewolf to the edge of Lake St. Clair, but it eluded his grasp by jumping into the water and down the throat of a catfish, leaving its footprint on a boulder along the shore.[21]

It is said that the stone werewolf and the werewolf's footprint were observed for some years by residents of the lakeshore. No contemporary sightings of werewolves have been recorded, but stories of *le Loup Garou* are still told in the popular press, such as *The Werewolf of Grosse Pointe and Other Stories*, and are in oral circulation, especially among younger Grosse Pointe residents.[22] Charles Skinner, who almost certainly drew his material from Hamlin's work, connects *le Nain Rouge* and *le Loup Garou* to "The Snake God of Belle Isle" by suggesting both creatures were the Snake God's progeny in Detroit.[23]

The latter half of the eighteenth century was a tempestuous one for Detroit. French residents had to make the transition to British rule in 1760 and British residents had to make the transition to American rule in 1796. A romantic legend, a tragic love story set at the beginning of British rule in Detroit, condenses some of the social and political ferment of the time for later residents. A mill run by a French-Canadian family stood at the site of what is now the base of the Ambassador Bridge at the foot of 24th Street. The miller adopted an Ottawa Indian girl who loved a British officer, a Colonel Campbell, and was loved by Wasson, a Saginaw warrior fighting with Pontiac. Because of the discord between the French and British, and between the British and Indians, the girl and Colonel Campbell could only meet secretly when the miller was away on business. To this end, they worked out a system where the girl would signal to her lover with a lighted candle in the window that the coast was clear. Wasson decoded the signal, went to the mill, confronted the girl with her tribal disloyalty, then stabbed her to death. He then killed Colonel Campbell when the British officer was taken prisoner at Pontiac's camp after the Battle of Bloody Run in 1763.[24]

For some years afterwards it was said that one could see a lighted candle moving in the window at dusk. The mill was avoided because of the girl's ghostly presence. Skinner noted that it was torn down in 1775, just when British and American antagonisms ushered in the Revolutionary War which ultimately changed the face of Detroit from British to American. According to Hamlin, it was still standing but deserted in 1795 as the Americans prepared to take over the city.[25]

During the nineteenth century Detroit developed into an urban center in the midst of broader state and national concerns.

Statehood, the Civil War, the coming of the railroad and heavy industry, all played a part in creating the city's progressive image. That image's underside, however, is revealed in accounts of haunted parts of the city reported in Detroit newspapers by the century's end. Two such accounts are particularly instructive. One appeared in the *Detroit Journal* on June 11, 1893:

> There is a superstition among the people who live in the neighborhood of Gratiot and Russell streets that the Eastern Market is haunted. It is said that dim and shadowy figures have been seen hovering about in dark corners of the buildings at night. When the wind blows, the building strains and tugs at its moorings, and it is said that one can hear strange noises, muffled cries, squeaking and gibbering as of someone in distress.[26]

The hauntings appeared connected to the construction of Eastern Market three years before in 1890. Workmen preparing the grounds for construction disturbed a cemetery once in use during the mid-nineteenth century. As Mary Solomon Smyka put it in a 1982 *Detroit Monthly* article, "Spirits of Detroit": "Square sixteen, shed four, and the adjoining parking area of the market are built upon a graveyard violated in the name of Victorian progress."[27]

The other account appeared in the *Detroit Free Press* on September 20, 1874. The reporter began his article, "Startling Statements: A Haunted House on Jefferson," by saying: "There are comparatively few persons in this age of the world's progress who will admit a belief in supernatural manifestations of the sort usually understood in connection with so-called haunted houses." The reporter refined the contrast between progress and the supernatural by comparing Jefferson Avenue with the city's less desirable areas: "Detroit has its haunted house and instead of being stealthily hidden on a back street, in some lonely part of the city, it stands prominently on Jefferson Avenue." The house in question had undergone a structural change: once a single-family home on an avenue that housed Detroit's elite families, "of late it has been and still is a boarding house." This change indicated a change in the city's social structure itself.

One of the boarders interviewed by the reporter recalled his otherworldly experiences. "Mr. G." had just settled in his bed for the night when he "heard close at hand a noise like that made by an old-fashioned spinning wheel in motion" and "heard a woman walk across my room from the direction of the hall door, and go into my clothes press. She seemed to have on a silk dress. At least it rustled like that." The haunting contrasted another Detroit—the Detroit that was pre-industrial and elite—with the 1874 present through references to the old-fashioned spinning wheel and the silk dress of the lady who had perhaps once lived in that very house before its gracious rooms were divided up into sleeping units for boarders.[28]

The Jefferson Avenue haunted house story hints at the major social and ethnic changes the railroads and heavy industry brought to Detroit. The boarders might have been some of the thousands of immigrants and migrants who came to work in the city at the turn-of-the-century. The Woodfords wrote:

> Between 1870 and 1930 Detroit became truly cosmopolitan—a city of many tongues. Immigrants from almost every corner of the world showed up, with the result that ethnic groups from Albanians to Ukrainians were firmly planted here. So numerous were these people that in 1900 twelve percent of the city's population spoke no English. No other major American city could make that claim.[29]

Ethnic neighborhoods created a complex patchwork across the city. Their folk names, each with its own story, are another part of Detroit's multifaceted landscape. There was "Corktown" on the lower near west side named after Irish immigrants from County Cork—although some suggest the name refers to the stereotypical Gaelic penchant for drink. The Woodfords wrote:

> Corktown existed almost as much in sentiment as in geography and its borders are rather vaguely defined. Some place it between Lafayette and Myrtle with its eastern boundary at First Street and its western limit at Brooklyn or even beyond. But many an Irish-Detroiter born outside these boundaries claimed Corktown as his native hearth—and there were few to dispute him. Even today to have sprung from Corktown is a badge of honor and a distinct political asset, although it became pretty well depopulated of Irish by 1920.[30]

There were Hamtramck and "Poletown" where Polish immigrants once settled; there was "Greektown" where early Greek residents congregated around Annunciation Church on Monroe Street; "Delray," in the southwest part of the city, was home to Hungarians; while Detroiters of Italian descent laugh at an early name for the Italian district in the northeast part of the city. It was situated at the point where the interurban trolley car looped back south, so was called by its residents *Cacalupo (car loop)—as far out as the wolf (lupo) defecates (caca).*[31]

The black community lived on the east side in the area known as "Paradise Valley," its southern tip called "Black Bottom" as discussed earlier in connection with "The Belle Isle Bridge Incident." Most Detroiters assume "Black Bottom" refers to the ethnic composition of residents who lived along Congress and Larned Streets from Randolph Street east, perhaps because other cities, such as Chicago, have "Black Bottoms" with Afro-American residents. A recently interviewed resident of the area gave another interpretation: "Black Bottom" historically refers to the richest, black earth in the bottom lands near a river and is the most desirable for farming. The name is an agricultural, not an ethnic, allusion to the area near the Detroit River.[32] "Cass Corridors," also referred to earlier, was home to southern Appalachian migrants to the city, so that adjacent streets Third and Hamilton were called "Little Kentucky" and "Little Tennessee" through the 1950s.[33]

Overlaying the memories of ethnic communities are the memories of Prohibition days when people said Detroit bootleggers received illegal shipments of alcohol via underwater tunnels connecting Hiram Walker's distillery in Windsor to Detroit wharves, and when the Purple Gang held sway in the neighborhood of Twelfth Street. Memories of Vernor's ice cream parlor at the base of Woodward Avenue and the Belle Isle ferry rides on summer afternoons vie with memories of the huge Michigan stove on Jefferson Avenue and stories about Reginald Scott, the notorious gambler who gave the fountain bearing his name to Belle Isle.[34] All these stories and more confirm their tellers' and listeners' nostalgia for a Detroit that, like Corktown, now exists more in sentiment than in geography.

New Detroit

Although "New Detroit" seems startlingly different to those remembering the "Old Detroit," it has much in common with the remembered city. As a 1971 map of urban ethnic groups shows, Detroit is still a crazyquilt, although specific patterns have changed. Black and Maltese families live in old Corktown; black and Macedonian residents live in Hamtramck; Jewish and southern Appalachian communities have moved to the northwest suburbs; East Indian, Filipino and Hmong families have come as well. Southwest Detroit is home for an Arab community said to be one of the largest outside the Middle East.[35]

Although Detroiters have lived in relative tolerance of each other given the number of different languages, life styles, and traditional customs practiced here, ethnic and racial conflicts do occur. The 1943 race riot with the reciprocal stories of babies thrown in the Detroit River has been noted. The 1967 riot widened the split between inner-city and suburban Detroit. Stories told of the second riot are remarkably similar to those told twenty-four years earlier. Suburban white residents heard that a white child had been castrated in a public restroom by members of a black gang while his mother waited for him outside. Inner-city black residents heard the same story with the race of the victim and the gang members reversed. Social psychologist Marilyn Rosenthal suggests that these two versions of an event that did not happen were aftershocks of the earlier riot.[36]

Folklorists have traced the story of "The Castrated Child" to quite ancient sources as well as forward to every shopping mall in every major city in the United States.[37] Detroiters in subsequent years have heard this atrocity was committed in Northland, Eastland and Fairlane Mall restrooms. One recent variation of this story, also with national circulation, has been exchanged by Detroit shoppers. A child, this time a girl, is kidnapped from a public restroom while her mother waits outside. The kidnappers are said to have cut and dyed the child's hair and dressed her in boy's clothes so that she was spirited away without her mother recognizing her. This story too has overtones of white-slave narratives told of cities both ancient and modern.[38]

Another Detroit shopping mall story is a recent variation of a legend also widespread in the United States. The first story, dubbed "The Killer in the Back Seat" by folklorists, has a young woman driving alone on the expressway. A large truck bears down on her, shining its bright lights and almost blinding her in the mirror. She finally comes to a gas station and pulls in. The trucker pulls in also, jumps out of his cab and grabs a man from the back seat of her car who was trying to kill her with a knife or hatchet.[39] The shopping mall variation has a shopper come to her car in the parking lot, only to find an old woman sitting in the back seat. The elderly lady tells the car's owner that she was so tired that she just sat down to rest for a moment. The shopper makes some excuse, contacts a mall security guard, and finds that the old woman is actually a man dressed in drag and waiting to kill her with a hatchet.[40] These stories, though in the strictest sense untrue, do highlight very real concerns in urban life and serve at least as warnings to watch children in malls, to check one's backseat, and to lock one's car doors—all sensible advice.

Other stories about Detroit shopping malls and department stores range from the humorous to the tragic. Perhaps the downtown J. L. Hudson's store has so many legends attached to it because of its landmark status. The Woodfords wrote that by 1946 "Hudson's became the third largest department store in the United States, running close behind Macy's in New York and Marshall Field's in Chicago."[41] And it is in just these three stores that folklorist Richard M. Dorson placed variations of the following anecdote:

> Other stories go the round from Macy's in New York to Hudson's in Detroit to Marshall Field's in Chicago. A well-dressed dowager pays for a small purchase with a hundred-dollar bill. The clerk takes it to the cashier to be checked, and the dowager screams her indignation. The bill is good, and milady stalks off in a huff. Next day she returns to the same counter, presents another hundred-dollar bill for a trinket, and this time is promptly given her change by the abashed clerk. But this bill is counterfeit.[42]

Dorson also discusses versions of a tragic story, graphically labeled "The Elevator Decapitation," which circulated about Hudson's in the 1950s but has since been connected with other elevators in other buildings. In this story, a woman is caught in a moving elevator with only her head inside the car while her body hangs outside. She is decapitated and the head falls into the car. All the women in the elevator faint. One version has the blame fall on a careless elevator operator, a situation no longer a problem although the impersonality of highly-mechanized modern elevators may make present-day shoppers even more nervous.[43]

Shopping malls depend on shoppers' mobility; therefore, the automobile is the first prerequisite for success. As Robert Conot shows in his *American Odyssey*, the growth of the automobile industry and the growth of Detroit are intertwined and connect the nineteenth-century city to the twentieth.[44] Legends about and by the industry range from stories about Henry Ford, Henry Ford II, Lee Iacocca, and other executives to the guy on the line who outwits the bosses. Perhaps the most famous story, again widespread across the United States, is the one about the "Magic Carburetor," in which the Big Three, in league with OPEC nations, suppress information about a car that can run 100, 200 or more miles per gallon. In the most extreme versions, the inventor of the car, and even some of its drivers, are liquidated.[45] As folklorist Gary Alan Fine has pointed out, these stories highlight the sense of powerlessness most consumers feel in the face of multi-national corporate structures.[46]

Two legends, fairly well confined to the Detroit Metropolitan area and usually shared by teenagers, highlight both the power and the powerlessness associated with the automobile. The first is usually called "Knock-Knock Street" and has been circulating since the late 1940s. Dorson's account in his 1959 *American Folklore* summarizes a number of versions:

> In recent years a street in Detroit has gained the reputation of being haunted. Different streets in several sections of the city are named and the details vary, but all accounts agree that a little girl was struck and killed by a hit-and-run driver, and that ever since cars driving over that street hear bumps from the child's body dragging behind the fender. Some say that one of her arms was cut off and that the arm is thumping against the doors of passing cars. Other ascribe the bumping noise to a curse placed on the road by the mother (or the father). In several versions the girl was riding a bicycle when the speeder ran her down, and she knocked vainly on his door to attract his attention, before losing her balance and falling under the wheels of the car. So many drivers heard the knocks that complaints reached the Detroit Department of Roads, who tore up and repaved the street, but the knock continued. The legend reached the Detroit papers, and curious drivers thronged the street, causing so much traffic that a policeman had to be stationed there.[47]

Recent studies of "Knock-Knock Street" suggest that Strasburg Street in Grosse Pointe is the place where the tragic accident occurred. Young drivers still take their cars down it to hear the ghostly thumps despite the more rational opinions that uneven pavement or air pockets beneath the road are the cause of the noise.[48] Young drivers also go to Tanglewood Drive on Belle Isle—a traditional lover's lane—after football games or school dances. Once there, they tell each other about "The White Lady of Tanglewood Drive." Some say that she was killed in a car accident while hitchhiking years before, a Detroit version of "The Vanishing Hitchhiker." Others say that she was a bride, deliberately run over by her husband in a jealous rage, or that she was a girl raped and murdered on Tanglewood's bridge. Drivers can see her white form if they shut off the lights and honk the horn three times.[49] Although the element of good fun cannot be ruled out in both these stories, their victims killed by speeding cars speak to humans' vulnerability in the machine age. The drivers' interest in coming to the spot where the tragedy was said to occur shows, on the other hand, the power of adventure and risk-taking that an automobile affords. Both aspects of car culture, the vulnerability and the thrill, are caught in these Detroit legends.

Conclusion

This brief excursion into legendary Detroit can only highlight the most visible stories. Countless others have been, are, and will be told in family kitchens, local barrooms, downtown and suburban restaurants, workplaces, and perhaps even on the freeways connecting one part of the city to another. These stories, as much as the industry, the buildings, and the neighborhoods, hold the place together.

1. Tom Fox, "Mental Maps of Detroit: The City is All in Your Head," *Detroit Free Press*, Sunday Magazine Section, 7 May 1978. Geographer Kevin Lynch's influential book, *Image of the City* (Cambridge: MIT Press, 1960), was one of the first to note individual residents' "cognitive maps" of their cities.
2. Walter Romig, *Michigan Place Names* (Grosse Pointe, Mich.: Walter Romig, 1972), 154–55; Frank B. Woodford and Arthur M. Woodford, *All Our Yesterdays: A Brief History of Detroit* (Detroit: Wayne State University Press, 1969), 35–37.
3. Wayne State University Folklore Archive, *Dorson Collection of Michigan Folklore*, 1946–1953, file; ed. Kelsie K. Harder, *Illustrated Dictionary of Place Names* (New York: Van Nostrand Reinhold, 1976), 477.
4. Elizabeth Meese, "A Preliminary Investigation of Urban Local Place Legends," unpublished paper, Wayne State University Folklore Archive, Accession Number 1969 (50), 6; Romig, 53; Marie Caroline Watson Hamlin, *Legends of le Detroit* (Detroit: Thorndike Nourse, 1884), 7.
5. Hamlin, 7; Romig, 53.
6. Charles Montgomery Skinner, *Myths and Legends of Our Own Land*, vol. 2 (Philadelphia: The Lippincott Co., 1896), 136–37.
7. Skinner, 138; Hamlin, 1–7.
8. Woodford, 24–25.
9. Janet L. Langlois, "The Belle Isle Bridge Incident: Legend Dialectic and Semiotic System in the 1943 Detroit Race Riots," *Journal of American Folklore* 96, no. 380 (April-May 1983): 183–99 for summary of materials related to the legend.
10. Ibid., 193–94.
11. Ibid., 188.
12. Ibid., 190–91.
13. Meese, 10–18.
14. Hamlin.
15. Ibid., 17.
16. Ibid., 22–39.
17. Ibid.
18. Mary Solomon Smyka, "Spirits of Detroit," *Monthly Detroit*, October 1982, 50.
19. Janet Langlois and Robert MacDonald, "Folklore: The Nain Rouge," *The Royal Oak Daily Tribune*, 1 October 1986.
20. Hamlin, 17–21.
21. Ibid., 113–21.
22. As quoted in Smyka, 50, see also Ron DiCicco, "The Werewolf of Grosse Pointe," unpublished collection, Wayne State University Folklore Archive, Accession Number R1978 (142).

23. Skinner, 146.
24. Hamlin, 122–27; Skinner, 149–51.
25. Skinner, 150; Hamlin, 127. Anthropologist Arnold Pilling, Wayne State University, states that the land at the base of 24th Street was given to the Potawatomis by treaty in the 1770s; a contemporary map and historical archaeology confirm this.
26. Smyka, p. 50.
27. Ibid.
28. The author thanks writer and producer Todd Hissong for information on Detroit legends appearing in local newspapers catalogued in the Burton Historical Collection, Detroit Public Library.
29. Woodford and Woodford, 244–45.
30. Ibid., 247–48.
31. Leonard Moss and Vittorio Re, "Early Immigration," papers delivered at "Italians in Michigan," a conference co-sponsored by the Italian Cultural Center and Wayne State University, 6–8 November 1981.
32. Ines Marie Bridges, "Paradise Valley—Detroit's Black Bottom," unpublished collection, Wayne State University Folklore Archive, Accession Number 1979 (55).
33. David W. Hartman, "The Development of Detroit's Cass Corridor: 1850–1975," Ethnic Studies Occasional Paper no. 3 (Detroit: Wayne State University, Center for Urban Studies, 1975).
34. Meese.
35. Ethnic map of Detroit prepared under the supervision of Bryan Thompson, Department of Geography and Urban Planning, Wayne State University.
36. Marilynn Rosenthal, "Where Rumor Raged," Transition 2, no. 4 (1971): 34–43.
37. Jan Harold Brunvand, The Choking Doberman and Other "New" Urban Legends (New York: W. W. Norton & Co., 1984), 78–92.
38. Ibid.
39. Ibid., 214; Jan Harold Brunvand, The Vanishing Hitchhiker: American Urban Legends & Their Meanings (New York: W. W. Norton & Co., 1981), 52–53; Jan Harold Brunvand The Mexican Pet: More "New" Urban Legends and Some Old Favorites (New York: W. W. Norton & Co., 1986), 58–59.
40. Personal communication from students in English 260 Introduction to Folklore, and English 360 Survey of American Folklore, courses taught at Wayne State University.
41. Woodford and Woodford, 222.
42. Richard M. Dorson, American Folklore (Cambridge: Harvard University Press, 1959), 253.
43. Ibid., 254.
44. Robert Conot, American Odyssey (New York: William Morrow,1974).
45. Brunvand, The Vanishing Hitchhiker, 175–78 and The Mexican Pet, 161–63.
46. Gary Alan Fine, "The Goliath Effect: Corporate Dominance and Mercantile Legends," Journal of American Folklore 98 (1985): 63–84 and "Redemption Rumors: Mercantile Legends and Corporate Beneficence," Journal of American Folklore 99 (1986): 208–22.
47. Dorson, 252.
48. Raymond Kettel, "Knock-Knock Street: The Ghost of Strasburg," unpublished field research collection, Wayne State Univrsity Folklore Archive, Accession Number 1980 (115).
49. Susan Lukasiewicz, "The White Lady of Tanglewood Drive," unpublished field research collection, Wayne State University Folklore Archive, Accession Number R1977 (24).

Paul Bunyan and Hiawatha

Eliot A. Singer

he only enduring sagas thus far mothered by America—the Paul Bunyan and Hiawatha tales—are grounded in large part in Michigan's Upper Peninsula.

Stan Newton[1]

In all the dreams and hopes of my years of hard labor in camps and mills, Paul Bunyan had no part.

James Stevens[2]

[Longfellow] caused great confusion by adapting to [the myth of Manabozho] the name of the Iroquois hero, Hiawatha. . . . The court-ship of Hiawatha and Minnehaha, the least "Indian" of any of the events in "Hiawatha," has come for many readers to stand as the typi-cal American Indian tale.

Stith Thompson[3]

Folklore or Fakelore?

Paul Bunyan and Hiawatha are Michigan's two favorite native heroes. Elementary school textbooks tell how Paul Bunyan invented logging and how he dug the Great Lakes as a water trough for his Blue Ox, Babe. Among the first poetry many children hear is the verse:

By the shores of Gitchee Gumee,
By the shining Big-Sea-Water,
Stood the wigwam of Nokomis,
Daughter of the Moon, Nokomis.[4]

Michigan has Paul Bunyan festivals, Paul Bunyan statues, Paul Bunyan pasties (and RV park), Paul Bunyan postcards, Paul Bunyan breakfasts, and Blue Ox steaks (fig. 1); the Mackinac Bridge is firmly anchored on Paul Bunyan's doughnuts. Michigan has a Hiawatha County, a town of Hiawatha, a Hiawatha National Forest, a Hiawatha Music Festival, a Hiawatha drive-in, Hiawatha motels, Hiawatha restaurants, Hiawatha gift shops, a Hiawatha miniature golf course, and myriad streams, lakes and waterfalls named for the likes of Iagoo, Nokomis, Winona, Onaway, Keewayden, or Minnehaha.[5] Paul Bunyan and Hiawatha are as integral to Michigan's self-image as is Henry Ford and his Tin Lizzie—the Indian hero paddling along the Lake Superior shore in his birch bark canoe, the mighty lumberjack towering over the trees brandishing his ax.

As literature, public relations, tourist attraction, and source of state pride, Paul Bunyan and Hiawatha are characters of immense proportion. But what about as folklore, that is to say, as products of the oral traditions of the Aniishinaabe (Chippewa Indians) and the Michigan lumberjacks by whom they were supposedly spawned?

Was Paul Bunyan truly a legendary hero of the lumberjacks? This question remains an unresolved and controversial one among scholars. It is definitely not true that, as one Paul Bunyan author put it, "Students of folklore and legend recognize Paul Bunyan as one of American's few myths."[6] The late Richard Dorson, an eminent folklorist who collected from Michigan lumberjacks in the late 1940s, went so far as to state bluntly that "Lumberjacks did not tell Paul Bunyan stories."[7] Other highly respected folklorists, however, have collected examples of Paul Bunyan stories from former lumberjacks. Unfortunately, by the time they started running around with tape recorders trying to obtain stories in their natural context, the "shanties" with their "deacon seats" and raconteurs had long since disappeared, so it may never be possible to establish with certainty the role Paul Bunyan played in lumbercamp narrations. Anyway, the real issues are not whether lumberjacks told any Paul Bunyan stories, but when, in relation to his emergence as a pop culture figure, they told them, how prominent he was as a lumberjack character, and to what extent the stories lumberjacks actually told resemble the stories now found in children's books, cartoons, and other mass media.

Folk Arts Division, MSU Museum

Figure 1. Paul Bunyan carving from miniature carved lumber camp by William Monigal, c. 1930. Iron County Museum.

The voice of reason must admit that some lumberjacks did tell some Paul Bunyan stories, but the evidence suggests that Paul Bunyan was, at most, a minor figure in lumberjack tradition, and that the kind of stories which have now become grist for the children's literature mill were not popular in the lumbercamps. There are several undisputable examples of stories about Paul Bunyan collected directly from former lumberjacks by reputable scholars, including Michigan field recordings of Perry Allen.[8] However, since serious collecting from lumberjacks did not begin until the 1930s, long after the popularization of Paul Bunyan had begun, most of these examples may well have been influenced by published accounts. In some cases, this may simply have involved substituting the name of Paul Bunyan in stories told earlier about other characters; in others, the story may have been taken directly from a published source, as Daniel Hoffman shows in his excellent book, *Paul Bunyan*, from Perry Allen's telling of "The Round River Drive."[9] Nonetheless, there are a few examples that cannot be explained away as post-popularization creations: several lumberjacks, including Perry Allen, insisted that they had heard stories about Paul Bunyan prior to the turn of the century,[10] and no less a scholar than Stith Thompson, father of American folklore studies, has provided documented proof of hearing Paul Bunyan stories when he worked briefly in a lumbercamp before the first Paul Bunyan book was published.[11] It is also hard to dismiss as spurious claims by the prominent Canadian folklorist, Edith Fowke, that the Paul Bunyan stories she has collected are genuine, although she did not obtain them until a late date.[12]

Still, it is clear that Paul Bunyan was not a great lumberjack hero. Given the enormous amount of material collected from lumberjacks, the proportion devoted to Paul Bunyan, including that influenced by pop culture, is relatively small. Much more common are anecdotes, however exaggerated, that the lumberjacks told about themselves or about real life characters—camp bosses, tough guys, tricksters, etc.—whom they knew about first or second hand. So, for instance, Stewart Holbrook was told by lumberjacks about the life and times of Jigger Jones,[13] Lewis Reimann about Silver Jack Driscoll,[14] and Richard Dorson about Con Culhane,[15] but none of them about Paul Bunyan.

The case is much clearer for Longfellow's *Song of Hiawatha* which supposedly was based primarily on Henry Rowe Schoolcraft's collection of Ojibwa legends from Michigan's Upper Peninsula. The real Hiawatha, however, was an Onondaga leader from upstate New York who probably lived in the late 1500s and was instrumental in creating the famous League of the Iroquois. Longfellow chose to use Hiawatha instead of the Ojibwa Manabozho partly for euphonic reasons and partly because his East Coast audience was more likely to be familiar with the Iroquois name. More importantly, Longfellow's Hiawatha bears no resemblance whatever to Manabozho as a character. The great romantic Indian hero is entirely the product of the poet's imagination.

So, neither Paul Bunyan nor Hiawatha, as most Michiganders know them, are truly the product of Michigan folklore. But it is too simple to dismiss them, as Dorson does when he labels them "fake-lore," as literature, commercialism, and chauvinism passed off as genuine tradition on a gullible public; for the relationship between folklore heroes for mass consumption and true folklore is more subtle and more interesting than mere charlatanry. And by looking at this relationship it often becomes possible to recover authentic traditions.

The Folk Process vs Processed Folk

Folklore is inherently local: it exists in, by, and for communities. What is often called the "folk process," a term not particularly well-liked by folklorists, occurs when an item of tradition, say a story or a song, moves from one community to another; the new community then adapts and shapes the item according to its own standards, values, needs, and knowledge—often changing it almost beyond recognition. That is, each community takes folklore and localizes it. Take, for example, the Michigan lumberjack song, "Jack Haggerty," which includes such verses as:

> I'm a heartbroken raftsman, from Greenville I came.
> My virtue's departed, and also my fame.
> From Six Lakes to Shelby, I'm very well known,
> And they call me Jack Haggerty, the pride of the town. . .
>
> So farewell to Flat River, for me there's no rest.
> I will shoulder my peavey, and I will go west.
> I will go to Muskegon, some pleasure to find,
> And I'll leave my fair Annie and the Flat River behind.[16]

When the song was adapted by cowboys, the equivalent verses became:

> I am a bold cowboy, from Salt Creek I came,
> While virtue's departed, alas I'm profane.
> In the cold ports of Cuba I'm very well known
> As a roving young cowboy, and Beeville's my home. . .
>
> It's down on Salt Creek for me there's no rest;
> I'll saddle Old Joe, and I'll push further west.
> I'll go through Muskogee some good times to find,
> And I'll leave my old sweetheart with another behind.[17]

Notice how not only place names and occupations change (Muskegon to Muskogee, Greenville to Salt Creek, etc.), but also the tools of the trade (shoulder my peavey to saddle Old Joe), yet both form and sentiment remain the same. This kind of change in detail to fit the location is what folklorists call "oicotypification," something analogous to ecotype adaptation in evolution.[18] In the "folk process" each community extracts from a piece of folklore what is relevant to it, discards what is irrelevant, and then adds those elements necessary to make it its own.

The introduction of folklore from a local to a mass audience, however, involves something else altogether. Instead of a "folk process" what occurs is what may be called "processed folk."[19] Processing folk entails fitting what is inherently a local product, one that often requires esoteric knowledge and particular aesthetic standards, into mass sensibility and taste. When, for instance, "Jack Haggerty" was recently resurrected and turned into a popular folk revival song by the band Touchstone, it not only livened up the tune and jazzed up the accompaniment, it discarded the verse about Muskegon—a favorite lumberjack's hangout for whoring and drinking—since the reference is lost on a mass audience unfamiliar with lumbering history. (The cowboys, who picked up the song directly from lumberjacks, however, retained the verse about "good times.")[20] "Processed folk," then, involves removing as much of the esoterica as possible from folklore, and making it fit into whatever are the prevailing mass social norms.

Paul Bunyan and Hiawatha, as most of us know them, are "processed folk": they have lost all of the local element that made tall tales popular among lumberjacks and myths among Indian groups. And, although both Hiawatha, as written by Longfellow in 1855, and Paul Bunyan, as developed by James MacGillivray, W. G. Laughead, Esther Shephard, James Stevens, and others in the teens and 1920s, were intended for and enjoyed by adult audiences, they have now been relegated to the status of children's books; this would not have happened to the original stories.[21]

True vs New Episodes

"Processing folk" involves one or more of several specific kinds of changes. One of the most important of these is the addition to and deletion of stories from the traditional repertoire. Consider Hiawatha. If we take, as Longfellow would have us do, the Aniishinaabe mythical figure of Manabozho as a model, then only three, possibly five, out of twenty-two episodes in the poem derive directly from the original: the story of Hiawatha's birth, the story of Hiawatha being swallowed by a sturgeon, the story of his fight with Pearl Feather, and two episodes about fasting and canoe construction, in which Longfellow took very brief references from Schoolcraft and elaborated them into entire chapters. The best known of Longfellow's episodes, those involving Hiawatha's love for Minnehaha, or Laughing Water, were invented by the poet almost out of whole cloth. (Manabozho was anything but a romantic lover: among the well-known traditional Ojibwa tales, his only "romantic" encounters are one in which he pretends to be a woman by fashioning a vagina out of a liver and one where he pretends to be dead in order to seduce his sister. In many stories he does have a wife, but she is primarily there to nag and scold him.) Other chapters are very loosely based on other Aniishinaabe, Dakota, and Iroquois legends and on Indian songs, history, and ethnography.[22]

At least as important are Longfellow's deletions. The sturgeon and the Pearl Feather episodes are just about the only ones from Ojibwa mythology in which Manabozho appears to behave heroically in the simple European sense; and the birth episode, an immaculate conception (by the wind), resembles the miraculous births so typical for Indo-European heroes. Most of Manabozho's adventures, or better, misadventures, are funny, not romantic or heroic, and are often what westerners regard as obscene.

A typical story, one which remains popular today, tells how Nanabooshoo (Manabozho) breaks the necks of the dancing geese. The following text is a reformatted abridgement and translation of William Jones' transcription of a story told by Wasaagoonashgank.[23]

NANABOOSHOO BREAKS THE NECKS OF
THE DANCING GEESE

(I)

1.   Once he is walking about. He saw a lake; he saw somebody there.
"I wonder who?" he thought.

2.   And so he approached there. Lo and behold: geese!
"I wonder what I should do?" he thought.
Then he discovered what he would do.
"'Come!' this, I will say," he thought.
"'Come! Dance with me!' I will say," he thought.

3.   And so, now he begins canoeing.
"Hey, it is Nanabooshoo! He will not be silent!
"So go out into the lake!" said the goslings.
Then Nanabooshoo sees them.
"I wonder why you do that whenever I see you? Truly, I am greatly disappointed. Behold, there is an event where I come from. Truly, they are partying; a great blast they are having where I come from. Oh, my! what a great dance! Behold! Come here!"
Why, truly, they come.
"Younger brothers! a dance I bring.
"So these songs I pack. Look! I will make you a dance. Make it ready, that I may make you a dance."
Why, truly, out of the water came the goslings.

4.   And so, then they make it ready where there will be made a dance.
Why he teaches them how to make it ready.
By and by it is made so.
"Why, so, then you must enter."

So, now they fill it.
By and by he taught them what they should do.
"So, as I shall dance, you must do likewise.
"So you must do. Listen! I shall show you how I shall dance.
"So you must do likewise," he said to the goslings.
"Why continue to obey me when I reach out with my hands. I shall leap to my feet.
"So I will be doing it, when I reach out with my hands."
"Why, so I will be moving about there; as I reach out with my hands, I will be moving about, again and again."

Why, so, then he starts to dance with the goslings. Truly they make a dance.
"Why, probably, then I should kill them," he thought.

5.   And so he sings, "A one legged dance I bring, my younger brothers!"
Why, so truly a one legged dance make the goslings.
Why they make it so.

(II)

6.   Once again he starts.

7.   And so he calls, "A dance with the eyes almost closed, I bring, my younger brothers!"

8.   And so they make it, those goslings.
Already he begins, "A dance with the eyes closed, I bring, my younger brothers."

Why, so truly, now they close their eyes.
Already, again he renames the song, "All the geese here, once more group together, my younger brothers, my younger brothers."

Why so truly they did it, those goslings.
Thus, they are bunched together in a group.

9.   Why, and so, here he said, "So, here, I will stand up; also I will be moving about," he said.

10.   And so, truly he stood up.

So he butchers them grouped together.
Now he breaks their necks.

Why, so at the same time he sings, he goes by breaking their necks.

(III)

11.   Why, so then Nanobooshoo wanted to cook until well done those goslings of his.
Now he makes a great fire.

12.   And so, why he buries in hot ashes those goslings of his.

13.   And so, why those feet of theirs are sticking out.
"Truly greatly I want to sleep," says Nanabooshoo.
"Well, I will sleep," he said.

14.   And so, to that ass hole of his, he said, "Come! Watch for strangers coming around the point," he says to that ass hole of his.

So he slept.
So he lay with his ass sticking up; he loved those goslings of his.
Why some people are paddling by where Nanabooshoo lies with his ass sticking up.
"Nanabooshoo is there. Something, probably he has killed," say those people.
Why, then it watches, that ass.
Then truly it sees some strangers coming around the point.
"Strangers are coming around the point," says that ass.
Now Nanabooshoo stands up, troubled.
Why who could he see?
"Already they have turned back," says that ass.

15.   And so, again, now he lies with his ass sticking up.
"Probably, then he was asleep," say those people.
"Probably he was asleep," they say.
"Come! Again let us go around the point."
Now they go around the point.
Again, now they turn back.
Then, again he is told by that ass hole of his, "Strangers are coming around the point."

So Nanabooshoo awakes.
Again says that ass hole of his, "Always they turn back," says that ass hole of his.
"Wretch," he says to that ass hole of his.
Now he scratches it; constantly he scrapes it.

So he leaves it alone.
"Truly not again will I tell him," said that ass hole of his.
Again, now around the point come those people.
"And so he was asleep," they said.
"Ah! come let us look around. Something he has killed."

16.   And so, truly, now they disembark; truly his kindled fire was there.

17.   And so, now they steal all those goslings of his.
Why they cut them off.
Why those feet are sticking out where they dug up those goslings.
Then Nanabooshoo wakes up.
"Ah! I have overslept. Probably burnt are those goslings of mine. Well, they may be dried out."
Why he pulls out those feet of theirs.

So, now they crumble.
"Why, so truly burnt are those goslings of mine."
Again one in vain he pulls out.

So still, now, they crumble.
"So, truly burnt are those goslings of mine."

18. And so, why all of them he pulls out.
"Perhaps I was robbed?" he thinks.

19. And so he says to that ass hole of his, "You will suffer if I have been robbed," he said to that ass hole of his.

20. And so in vain he searches.

So not a single one does he find.
"Wretch!" he says.
"What caused it? You must tell me," he says. Truly he is angered by that ass hole of his.

So, now he fetches firewood; high he stacks the firewood.
Now he kindles a great fire.
By and by a great fire will be kindled.
Now in the middle of the fire,
Why it burns. For nothing, "Shi," utters that ass hole of his,
Until it is cleansed by the fire, fully cleansed by the fire.

21. Why, and so he says to that ass hole of his, "Yes, 'Shi, shi, shi' is what you will say for letting me be robbed of my goslings," he says to that ass hole of his.
It makes a sound.
"Probably it is burnt," he thought.

22. And so he stepped aside.
Already, in vain, he wants to start.

So, now he is unable in vain to start.

So, now he is bow-legged.
Why he is not able to walk.
"What is the matter with me?" he thinks.

So he is unable, though in vain he wants to walk.

23. And so he thought, "I don't know why I am unable in vain to walk."

24. And so he sought somewhere a big cliff.
Then he slid down the cliff. Falling, he looks back; everywhere he lands are those scabs of his.

25. And so he said, "Lichens the people will call them till the end of the world."

Most of the other Manabozho stories are similar. In one he tries to imitate how a woodpecker obtains its food and injures his nose. In another he gets stuck inside a moose head. In yet another he is frightened by his own farting. Hardly the stuff of which romantic heroes are made, and Longfellow found it necessary to systematically delete these episodes, already censored by Schoolcraft, from his *Song of Hiawatha.*

With Paul Bunyan the same basic process is at work: the popularizers took from the lumberjack repertoire those tales that fit their conception of an American superhero, discarded those that did not, and invented new episodes to fill out the corpus. However, establishing which stories are genuine lumbercamp tales can be done with far less confidence than for Hiawatha and the Manabozho myths. Many of the authors whose works provided the basis for later Paul Bunyan books—Esther Shephard, W. B. Laughead, Ida Turney, and Stan Newton—both rewrote tales they picked up directly or indirectly from oral sources and invented their own stories, without bothering to distinguish between the two. Since most Paul Bunyan stories were collected from actual lumberjacks only after literary versions were already available (i.e., after Laughead's first pamphlet in 1914), these collections cannot be taken as definitive in deciding which stories were told in the lumbercamps, although they do provide evidence of the kind of stories lumberjacks considered worth telling. To a large extent, then, it is necessary to conjecture which stories are genuine and which are spurious based on common sense considerations and a knowledge of other tall tale traditions. It must be remembered that when lumberjacks told tales on the "deacon seat" in the lumbercamps, grown men were telling stories to other grown men, and the stories they told were unlikely to be those that any ten-year-old now finds silly.

Folklorists make a somewhat technical, but necessary, distinction between tall tales and legends. Tall tales merely bend the truth, and are clearly based in reality. Myths or heroic legends require powers that are truly supernatural. Tall tales are always basically mundane. The lumberjacks told tall tales usually about themselves or about well-known real people. They were exaggerations of things that really happened (like big fights), activities they regularly engaged in (like hunting or eating), conditions they lived under (like cold weather or mosquitoes), and unusual characters with whom they were familiar. Paul Bunyan, on the other hand, is, as one author put it, "America's own legend."[24]

Much is made in popular images of Paul Bunyan's bigness and that of his Blue Ox, Babe. Shephard describes how they had to fit Babe with a new yoke:

> He measured forty-two ax-handles between the eyes—and a tobacco box—you could easily fit a Star tobacco box after the last ax-handle. That tobacco box was lost and we couldn't never take the measurements again, but I remember that's what it was. And he weighed accordin'. Though he was never weighed that I know of, for there was never any scales made that would of been big enough.[25]

While there are no documented early oral sources for this emphasis on bigness, E. C. Beck did obtain later examples, including this description of Paul:

> From the soles of his feet to the root of his hair he split the atmosphere exactly 12 feet 11 inches. His weight he told me—and I don't doubt his word—was 888 pounds. . . . When he opened his mouth in one of his prodigious yawns, you could have inserted a ten-quart pail.[26]

Unlike big obstacles or adversaries (e.g., big fish that got away), big people or big animal helpers are not common tall tale motifs. While it seems possible that some lumberjacks may have told tales about a particularly big man or a particularly big ox, much like they might have told about a cold day or a gigantic tree, what seems untenable is that they would then have turned such creatures into heroes. After all, basic to any adventure is an element of achievement or risk, and it's no big deal for someone of superhuman proportions to accomplish superhuman tasks; the only thing that keeps Superman honest is kryptonite. More common in legitimate lumberjack lore are motifs celebrating the accomplishments of lesser beings. One of the most popular of the shanty ballads, for instance, tells of the triumph of "the little brown bulls" over the much larger "big spotted steers" in a log skidding contest.[27] And many stories tell of fights between little and big men, such as the one collected by Dorson about the time tiny Pikey Johnson bested big Black Tom McCann.[28] Like most of us, lumberjacks preferred the underdog, and Paul Bunyan was too big to be an underdog.

Another set of well-known Paul Bunyan stories involves geographic creations: the Soo Canal, Hudson Bay, Puget Sound, the Rocky Mountains, the Great Lakes, etc. Again there is little evidence for an oral tradition of these stories, although Stith Thompson did report an early telling; of the creation of Puget Sound,[29] and, as with big men, these motifs are not standard among tall tales. It hardly seems likely that men who could work sixteen hours a day at forty degrees below and who battled mosquitoes, log jams, mud, snow, and giant trees would find it necessary to invent heroes to engage in Herculean tasks. Even in oral mythology—the Manabozho stories, for instance—etiological motifs play an ancillary rather than primary role in the telling; usually they are tacked on at the end of the story, and the myth is never "about" origins. Geographical origins are especially rare; of all the Michigan places for which there are supposed "Indian" myths, only those for Sleeping Bear Dunes are probably genuine.[30] The belief that "folk" groups systematically tell stories in order to explain how geographical features came into being is nonsense.

In light of this, Perry Allen's retelling of the "Round River Drive" is instructive. This story, which often shows up in Paul Bunyan books, does resemble many traditional tall tales, especially as a slight exaggeration on real log drives which, with all the bends and curves and jams, really did seem to take place on round rivers. As Perry Allen tells it:

> We cut our logs and stacked 'em on the river. And in the spring when the ice and snow was off, we started a spring drive of logs. We drove those logs down stream for a couple of weeks. And we come to a set of camps that looked just like Old Paul's camps. So we drove for a couple of weeks more, and we come to another set of camps that looked just like Old Paul's, so we started for a third week, and we begin to think there might be something wrong. So when two weeks is up and we come to the set of camps again, we went ashore, and sure enough, it was Old Paul's camp! And there we'd been draggin' those logs around and round, around and round, around and round the river all that time and never knowd the difference. Didn't know that river didn't have no beginnin' and no end.[31]

Perry Allen poses no solution. In most of the literary versions, however, Paul Bunyan, like the hero he is made to be, must succeed against nature at all costs, so he is made to straighten out the river, with or without the help of Babe, to create some great river (often identified as the Muskegon).

At least as dominant themes, bigness and the creation of geographical features probably stem from literary rather than folklore sources. This is also probably true of virtually all of the derivative stories. As a consequence of Paul and Babe's bigness, for instance, various difficulties arise: the infant Paul falls into the ocean, swamping the royal navy, Babe's prodigious appetite creates an enormous thirst that must be satisfied, etc. The humor of these—the sense in which they mock the easy accomplishments of a great hero—may well be that of the lumberjacks, but in that case these stories were a reaction to, not a precedent for, the popularization of Paul Bunyan. Other stories—cute childish ones like the popcorn blizzard, and political ones like Paul Bunyan's espousal of capital- ism, communism, or Christianity—are clearly of literary origin.

On the other hand, most of the Paul Bunyan books, both those intended for children and those for adults, do contain stories which are common tall tales found well outside the lumberjack canon: hunting tall tales, mosquito tall tales, eating tall tales, weather tall tales, and exaggerations of the true difficulties in logging. Many of these tales are still in oral circulation and can readily be heard here in Michigan. However, it makes much more sense that lumberjacks told these stories about ordinary men than about a giant, and Paul Bunyan author James Stevens, himself, complained about how giv- ing these stories Paul Bunyan's name was corrupting his attempt to create an epic hero.[32]

As with Hiawatha, pop culture also censored much from the lumberjack tall tale repertoire. Shephard quite readily admitted to her editing:

> The stories in this volume have been selected from a great number and do not include stories which are too technical or too closely tied with some small geographical detail to be of general interest, and stories which in my opinion seemed to be too new or too outside the pale really to belong to the Paul Bunyan cycle. Many of the Paul Bunyan stories are very vulgar and obscene and obviously cannot be included in a volume of this kind.[33]

Almost invariably the literary versions eliminate many of the lesser achievements and the one-liners that are so common in true tall tales. Typical lumberjack tall tales tell, for instance, how a lumber- jack riding a log down a slide is going so fast he goes right through a tree, or how a tree is so big two lumberjacks are sawing at it for three days before they discover two other guys sawing at it from the other side. These stories are simply too short and too ordinary in their extraordinariness to fit with the giant lumberjack hero of litera- ture. Other stories are too esoteric for the pop audience. Take, for instance, a brief comment such as, "That winter it was eighty below, and there was a foot between each degree." In order to understand this line you have to know something about how old-fashioned thermometers measured temperature. Many of the other lumbering tales require some knowledge of lumbering in order to understand them. Finally, many of the favorite stories among real lumberjacks, as with most of us in our own lives, concerned fights—often dirty fights—strange characters, and practical jokes. Dorson tells about one well-known character, P. K. Small, who would "pick up a big dried-up slab of manure and eat it, for a drink."[34] And one of the favorite tales from Seney tells of the time a woman reporter visited to investigate rumors that innocent women were being forced into stockades as sporting girls for the lumberjacks. Sure enough, when she got there, she found a stockade full of women. Seems the local prostitutes and the men got together to fabricate the scene, but it made the national papers, and Seney's reputation as a bad town was assured. These stories are, of course, beneath the dignity of America's national legend, and so they have not been attached to the Paul Bunyan "cycle."

Literary Models of Plot and Character

In addition to adding and deleting episodes, processing folk often involves incorporating folk narrative forms into the literary conventions of plot and character. One important aspect of this is what I call "the singularization of character." By this I mean that instead of there being a series of stories about many different characters which are only loosely connected, as is the case for stories we tell in conversation, the authors and popularizers of processed folk systematically bring stories together around a single hero and a coterie of associates, as is the aesthetic for modern literature, and connect these stories into a single work of fiction. Often, in order to do this it is necessary to invent new stories or significantly transform old ones in order to fit an idealized character.

The singularization of character is an old process in trying to create national heroes. Finland's famous Kalevala, which Longfellow used as a model for Hiawatha, took many unconnected narratives and fashioned them into a single epic in the pursuit of nationalism.[35] Hiawatha was intended to serve the same purpose in this country. Longfellow took historical events from the life of the Iroquois leader, Hiawatha, stories from the Dakotas, and ethnography from other tribes, as well as Ojibwa stories not about Manabozho, and put them all into one long poem, thereby inventing a hero who bears no resemblance to any of the sources. Like most of us, lumberjacks told stories about themselves, about people they knew, or about people they had heard about from others, and while it is common practice to tell several stories about a single character, most people are not sufficiently interesting to have more than a half dozen stories—most of them very brief—produced about them. (Even Silver Jack Driscoll, who had many scandals laid upon him, is involved in no more than a dozen.) But, in order to write an entire book about Paul Bunyan, it is necessary to have many stories to work with, and this requires the authors to give Paul Bunyan's name to stories which may have been told about others. More importantly, since different characters have different personalities, these stories need to be adapted to the personality of the hero. For example, lumberjacks told many stories about fights, usually involving feisty characters of small size who were forever brawling and did not fight particularly "fair." But when Paul Bunyan is made by the fiction writers to battle with Hels Helstrom, the two characters are of equally giant proportion and the fight is conducted without benefit of eye gouging or stomping, and neither combatant ends up with "lumberjack pock marks" on his face.

Folk narratives rarely tell much about a character's childhood, family, or other background, but the processed folk versions of both Hiawatha and Paul Bunyan follow the nineteenth century literary convention of providing the reader with an entire life history of the hero. So Longfellow gives long descriptions of Hiawatha's childhood: how he learns to hunt, and fasts for knowledge (both of which are aspects of Indian ethnography but not of myth), delineates his parentage, tells of his courtship, and even of his departure in deference to the coming of the white man. And various books tell about Paul Bunyan's infancy, his family, his schooling, his wife, his daughter, etc., and provide at least suggestions of his "last stand" against modernity.

Even when folk narrative does contain a cycle of stories about a single "hero," such as Manabozho, it does not sustain other characters who associate with him. But processed folk, again following literary convention, finds it necessary to develop other characters to go with the main hero. So Longfellow gives Hiawatha friends, Chiabos and Kwasind; a rival, Pau-Puk-Kiwis; and, of course, a lover, Minnehaha—Laughing Water. And most books about Paul Bunyan include not only his Blue Ox companion, but Sourdough Sam, the cook; Big Ole, the blacksmith; and Johnny Inkslinger, the bookkeeper.

One important aspect, then, of processing folk narratives into a book is stringing together stories into a plot that follows the hero's life story, with side adventures of his friends. But it is not only the entire plot that undergoes processing; in many cases the plot of individual episodes is changed. (I have already noted some examples of this, as when Longfellow takes a single mention of Manabozho fasting and turns it into an entire chapter, or when Paul Bunyan authors make him defeat the round river.) Most of the Manabozho myths follow some variation or combination of the following sequences: Manabozho's attention is attracted by something, he provides misinformation to trick it, then he kills or otherwise hurts it; or Manabozho is attracted by something, he misunderstands what it is, acts inappropriately toward it, harms himself, then correctly understands it, and identifies it with a name. The "Dancing Geese" story, for instance, consists essentially of the first sequence followed by the second.

Many of Longfellow's episodes have almost no plot at all: the wooing of Minnehaha, for instance, involves nothing more than the giving of a gift to obtain a beautiful bride from an enemy tribe. (It is hard to imagine even a European folk plot that did not require its hero to accomplish some task or defeat some enemy to gain his love.) Longfellow's reworkings of the Manabozho plots are even more instructive. In the Aniishinaabe version, Manabozho gets purposefully swallowed by the sturgeon (i.e., he tricks it) so as to kill it from inside where it is vulnerable; in Longfellow, the sturgeon, an inherently evil monster against whom Hiawatha must revenge himself, unfairly attacks and swallows the hero. In the Aniishinaabe version, Manabozho seeks out Pearl Feather for illegitimate reasons, lies to him in order to obtain the secret of his vulnerability, and in consequence brings death to the world. In Hiawatha, the hero is motivated by vengeance, wins the battle thanks to the secret of vulnerability given him by a woodpecker, and the net result is the benefit of humanity.

Many, though not all, of the Paul Bunyan stories are also plotted differently than folk tall tales. Many oral tall tales simply consist of one-liners with the basic formula: "he (or it) was so. . .that. . .," where the second part of the formula is a clever exaggeration. For example, a tall tale teller might simply say, "The mosquitoes were so thick, you could leave a path just walking through the woods," or "He could shoot a buck so far away, he had to salt his bullets so the meat wouldn't spoil before he could get to it," or "The land was so fertile, the vines grew so fast they wore out the pumpkins as they dragged them along." Another standard tall tale formula is to tell a lie, then exaggerate it even more: "It was ninety below, and there was a foot between each degree;" "He was walking along when he heard two mosquitoes talking. 'Well,' said one, 'should we eat him here, or should we take him back to the swamp and eat him there.' 'We'd better eat him here,' said the other. 'If we take him back to the swamp the big mosquitoes might take him away from us.'" Yet another formula involves an impossible solution to a basically mundane problem, often told as a series with cumulative exaggeration. Simple examples include how one time the tall tale hunter is about to shoot at a buck when it takes off around a bend, so he twists the barrel of his rifle in order to shoot around the curve. Or the hunter has only one bullet when he encounters two bucks, so he puts his hunting knife on a rock in between them and aims at the knife, splitting the bullet in two and killing both bucks. A more cumulative example tells how the mosquitoes were so big that the hero had to hide under a huge iron cauldron to escape, but when he looks up the mosquitoes are drilling through the top of the kettle. So he took his sledge hammer and clenched those stickers, just like you'd clench a nail. Next thing you know, there's a loud humming sound, and those mosquitoes flew off with that kettle.

Now there are two key aspects of all these tall tale formulae: they are humorous—usually with punch lines—and they always involve some kind of clever twist. It never suffices to say, "Paul Bunyan was eight feet tall." Most of the Paul Bunyan children's books do contain many of these kinds of tales, but the emphasis is different. Instead of the clever twist being an end in itself, what counts is the triumph of the hero. In the traditional tall tales, as often as not the protagonist is not a victor over nature: Perry Allen's Round River keeps flowing around and around; a cold day is just a cold day. In the literary versions, almost inevitably some solution is posed: Paul Bunyan defeats nature or solves some problem, even if it is of his own making: he straightens rivers, builds canals, logs off North Dakota.

One important requirement of written literature of quality is character motivation. Characters must have a reason for doing what they do, and with heroes it had better be a good reason. But this is mush less true for oral stories. Traditional tall tales, for instance, rarely bother to explain why the character goes out hunting, why he is attacked by mosquitoes, or even why he took up logging in the first place; it is precisely because tall tale situations are presented as ordinary—they occur in the context of everyday life—that there is no necessity to motivate them. The Paul Bunyan books vary considerably in discussing motivation. Some, especially the adult ones, dwell on various ideological factors, including what amounts to simple greed (i.e., capitalism). Even in the children's books, though, there is usually some necessity that motivates the individual feats— the need to feed the men, or the need to get logs to market.

In the Manabozho stories motivation is very rare, and, with the exception of one act of vengeance (which leads to the great flood), is limited to hunger and desire. For the most part, Manabozho's adventures are things he just happens upon, as is made clear by the favorite opening formula (the equivalent of "once upon a time"): "Manabozho was wandering about." (In the Aniishinaabe language, the verb used is specifically that for unmotivated rather than purposeful walking.) In Hiawatha, however, every episode is predicated on some higher motive—quest for knowledge, love, or the needs of humanity.

Thus, processing folk leads to the entire transformation of plot and character. The Aniishinaabe told "trickster tales" about Manabozho; the lumberjacks told "tall tales." But both the Paul Bunyan and the Hiawatha of literature are epic heroes.

Oral vs Written Style

Oral myths, legends, and tall tales are told out loud; written myths, legends, and tall tales are written. This observation may not seem profound but its consequences are enormous. "Processed folk" involves changing the style and language of presentation from the conventions of oral narrations to the canons of literature.

Most individual tall tales are very short; storytelling is sustained by stringing them together and, less often, by repetition of a single event (like each trip around the round river, or a series of ducks popping their heads out of the water and being shot in turn). Literary convention insists that stories be of chapter length so that in a children's Paul Bunyan book the Round River Drive may take three to four pages (plus pictures), instead of the single paragraph in the oral telling. This lengthening is even greater for Paul Bunyan books intended for adult audiences such as those of James Stevens.

Indian myths are quite variable in length. Aniishinaabe narration is generally more laconic than that of most other Indian groups, but many of the stories remain quite brief. As with oral tall tales, most longer stories involve considerable repetition of events or the stringing together of episodes. Nonetheless, there are numerous Aniishinaabe myths of sufficient length for chapters in children's, if not adult, literature.

However, in writing chapters, authors have their own ways of creating length. The most important is description. Most oral narrative traditions make little use of long descriptive passages. A single sentence will usually suffice, and that only when necessary to the plot. In telling the "Round River Drive," for instance, Perry Allen simply says, "And so we come to a set of camps that looked just like Old Paul's camps." In writing the same tale, however, Esther Shephard engages in a lengthy description:

> There was the same cook house pretty near like in our own camp, with the stove pipe and the smoke comin' out of it, and there was the barns for the cattle and the manure piles and everythin', and the stacks of wood that the bull-cooks had got in, behind the cook-shanty, and the blacksmith shop and all just exactly like we had in our camp. . ..[36]

Aniishinaabe myths are also almost entirely devoid of elaborate description or sustained metaphor. But "Hiawatha" contains little else. The following passage, chosen at random from the poem, is typical.

> On the dam stood Pau-Pau-Keewis
> O'er his ankles flowed the streamlet,
> Spouted through the chinks below him,
> Dashed upon the stones beneath him,
> Spread serene and calm before him,
> And the sunshine and the shadows,
> Fell in flecks and gleams upon him,
> Fell in shining little patches,
> Through the waving, rustling branches.[37]

At the same time description is added, written versions systematically eliminate the colloquial expressions and specialized jargon which are so important to oral narrative traditions. So, for instance, a Paul Bunyan author might substitute an ax for a crosscut saw, or refer to chewing tobacco instead of "Peerless," on the assumption the wider audience would be unfamiliar with the terms. In other cases a "native" term is used, but the author then finds it necessary to explain what it means, perhaps with a simple translation ("Gichee Gumee" means "Big Sea Water"), sometimes by engaging in a lengthy discussion of a related custom. But remember, it is precisely that local esoteric element that creates the in-group identity which is the basis for true folklore.

Written literature usually insists on such conventions as complete sentences, good grammar, coherent paragraphs, and so on; when Paul Bunyan authors use "bad" English deliberately, it sounds very forced. Oral narration usually has its share of false starts, mistakes, incomplete sentences, and so on. Both the tall tales and Manabozho myths usually have short clauses and simple or compound sentences; literary versions eschew "choppy sentences" by complex embedding. The oral equivalent of paragraphs tend to be highly variable in length—anywhere from a single clause to dozens of sentences; written paragraphs are of relatively consistent duration.

Probably the most subtle, but most important, change between oral and written language is the way in which text is organized. Written Paul Bunyan stories have sentences, paragraphs, and punctuation. Oral tall tales, at least those of sufficient length to warrant organizational markers, rely on pauses and on words such as "and" or "so" to punctuate the telling.

The difference between "Hiawatha" and the Manabozho myths is far more extreme. The former is in poetry, the latter are in prose. Moreover, it has been clearly shown that Longfellow based his poetic rhythm on that of the Finnish Kalevala and not on anything Indian.[38] The meter is called trochaic tetrameter, and there is frequent use of parallelism to create a very lyrical and rhythmic poetic form. Needless to say, the Aniishinaabe myths are not in trochaic tetrameter. However, looking at native language texts and careful translations, the Manabozho myths can be seen to have a clear and systematic narrative, though not poetic, organization. As with the tall tales, instead of marking off parts of the story through rhythmical devices, as in poetry, or punctuation and paragraphing, as in written prose, these stories make considerable use of initial particles—and then, then, and so, when, thus, later, etc.—to indicate when things are happening in the story. These particles are highly repetitive, as are such expressions as "he said," but in oral storytelling, which lacks visual punctuation, such particles are absolutely necessary for teller and hearer to follow the story line, and in that sense they are no more repetitious than are commas and periods. When these stories are rewritten, however, as in the many children's books of Indian tales, this kind of repetition is systematically eliminated. One can always tell when a professional storyteller has learned her repertoire from written sources, because these particles are virtually absent, making the telling sound like a library story hour.

Heroes, Tricksters, and Lies

Probably all these changes that occur when folklore is processed for the mass market would not matter if it weren't that their net result is to misrepresent the nature—the ethos, the sensibility, the "vibes"—of the story traditions from which they are claimed to derive. As characters who are supposed to express something about the beliefs and attitudes of the people from whom they have come, Paul Bunyan and Hiawatha are inauthentic.

Paul Bunyan, as he survives in children's literature, is a superhero. As Shephard, whose work has had more of an enduring influence than other early authors, describes it:

> The Paul Bunyan legend centers around a mythical hero of the woods, a kind of super-lumberjack, who is noted for his wonderful deeds of cleverness and skill and for the extraordinary size of his logging operations. Paul is never "stumped" and no job is ever too big or too hard for him and his Big Blue Ox to handle. The story of his deeds is really epic in its sweep and immensity.[39]

Paul Bunyan is a good giant who can fell forests with a single stroke, straighten rivers, and harness the wilderness. Bigger, stronger, and better than all the obstacles in his way, he is a symbol of America's manifest destiny, of the unconquerable power of hard work and resolve.

Hiawatha is a typical and classic romantic hero: he slays monsters, creates important things, and woos and marries an unobtainable girl of his dreams. All he does produces goodness for the world, albeit, like other classical heroes, "as the epic approaches its end [his] world retreats into shadows and darkness."[40] Hiawatha represents the pristine time before the white man's step spoiled the balance of nature.

For nearly half a century, between the Civil and First World Wars, Michigan was shaped, literally and figuratively, by its lumberjacks. Cities—Saginaw, Manistee, Ludington, Alpena, Muskegon, and others—grew to mill the logs they felled and to provide the whores and bars to satisfy their appetites. Primeval forests fell swiftly to their axes, leaving behind a barren landscape. Today, they are remembered with great fondness and nostalgia, and their memorabilia fuels the museum and tourist trades. Their ballads remain one of America's finest original cultural heritages.

In retrospect the lumberjacks are all Paul Bunyans. But, in their day, they were more scourge than paragon of society. They were treated as second class citizens: exploited by their bosses and by the townsfolk, merchants, and prostitutes who benefited from their labor. They were rough and coarse men for whom brawling and drinking were honorable activities. They were strong, tough, and self reliant; they had to be to survive—those who did—the cold and wet, the mosquitoes and lice, the falling trees, log jams, and unsafe tools. They were proud and competitive, always ready for a contest or a boast. "The typical lumberjack was the most independent man on earth," Richard Dorson was told by Moonlight Harry Schmidt. "No law touched him, not even smallpox caught him. He didn't fear man, beast, nor devil."[41] The characters they told about represented this toughness and independence. Jigger Jones "would walk a felled spruce, barefoot, and kick off every knot from butt to top."[42] "'Stuttering' Jim Gallagher left his mark—mostly with the nails of his hobnail driving shoes on the faces of those who found his speech amusing."[43] The truly legendary Silver Jack Driscoll spent much of his life in jail for various petty and not-so-petty crimes. Drinking, fighting, logging, surviving—that was the stuff of which their stories were made. Their good humored lies exaggerated their own accomplishments and the hardships they had to endure. Theirs was a world of earthy reality with little need for gigantic mythic heroes.

The Aniishinaabe (Chippewa, Ojibwa) were, and are, one of America's most prominent native peoples. Like all native cultures, theirs has a complex and sophisticated system of beliefs, and their literature and mythology is extraordinarily rich. Manabozho, one of their most important mythical and religious figures, should be treated with respect, but to take that to mean with solemnity would be to fail to understand his depth and, in many ways, his very modern significance. For Manabozho is what is known as a trickster.

Tricksters can be found in literature from throughout the world. Anasi, the African spider, Krishna the Hindu diety, Hermes and Loki from classical and Norse mythology are just a few among the many familiar examples. Most of the tricksters to whom we have frequent exposure—Road Runner, Woody Woodpecker, and Bugs Bunny of cartoon fame, for instance, or Brer Rabbit—are pure fun, usually defeating more powerful opponents through clever dealings, although sometimes, as in the "Tar Baby" story, getting themselves in trouble first. Sacred tricksters are far more difficult for most westerners to accept; indeed, many westernized Indians are embarrassed by them. The dominant religions—Judaism, Christianity, Islam—have become, over the centuries, deadly serious. In them the exemplary dieties, prophets, saints, and leaders are all incessantly moral and spiritual. From this perspective, while tricksters may be acceptable in the realm of the profane, they must be expunged from all that is holy. Yet, in many traditional religions, tricksters are not only part of the pantheon, they are the most important creators and most prominent figures in the sacred literature and mythology.

How can someone like Manabozho, whose main aspirations are for food and sex, who lies, cheats, and steals, who defecates on baby birds for the fun of it, and who, almost literally, can't tell his ass from his elbow, be the sacred Aniishinaabe mythical figure responsible for giving the Indians the most holy of religious symbols and ceremonies? The answer is that Manabozho, like other sacred tricksters, represents not what is essentially godly, but what is quintessentially human. Manabozho presents not an ideal of what we should be, but a model of what, in actuality, we are. Unlike other animals, humans are relatively lacking in both instincts and natural abilities. We survive through our wits and our manufacture—our culture. Key to this is our capacity to communicate and to lie through language and other sign systems, and to interpret the ambiguities of the signs around us. While, oversimplifying somewhat, other creatures react automatically to stimuli—food, sex, danger— humans must learn how to tell what signs mean. We can gain the upper hand on other creatures by falsifying signs (i.e., by lying), as when we bait a trap or a fishhook, but we can also get into great trouble by misreading what signs mean. Having the ability to do nothing, and the potential to do everything, it is this non-automatic response to signs—technically the independence of signifier and signified—which is the power that enables humans to survive and conquer; but it is also the liability that threatens our destruction. For as a species we must learn when to lie and when not to, when to believe signs and when not to. This is the significance, and a very deep significance it is, of Manabozho. It is his role as a literary and sacred figure to make his way through a labyrinth of signs, lying, reading, and misreading, to provide signposts for the humanity that is to follow him, and to remind us—through laughter—of the precariousness of our interpretations of the world around us.

Former Michigan governor Chase S. Osborn, praised "Hiawatha" for giving "to the maze of stories a beginning and an end, and a direction."[44] "Longfellow separated the predominating goodness of Manabozho from his inconsistent mischievousness."[45] But in doing so, Longfellow deprived the Indian myths of their essential character, of their tragicomic profundity, and has left us a legacy of "Indian" legends of lovers' leaps. Under the pen of the popularizers, Paul Bunyan became a national symbol; what remains are a few children's books, a decaying statue in Oscoda, and assorted nick-nacks.

When folklore is processed to make it acceptable to a wider audience—its language smoothed out, its earthiness and violence censored—the ultimate result is to weaken it. Making it pretty takes all the guts out of it. It is little wonder that both Hiawatha and Paul Bunyan, and, indeed, storytelling in general, are now seen as something for children. Longfellow's poem has been reduced to picture books, sometimes with the storyline gone altogether; Paul Bunyan lives on in the elementary classroom, his last mighty task to teach literacy. Both are wooden, one-dimensional, wholly positive characters—certainly boring in comparison to all the sex and violence on television. But listen to the original lumberjack tall tales and the original Manabozho stories. Here we find the true excitement, cleverness, fun, and even poignancy, that explain why people have loved to tell and listen to stories since the beginning of time.

---

1. Stan Newton, *Paul Bunyan of the Great Lakes* (Au Train, Mich.: Avery, 1946, 1985), 15.
2. Quoted in Richard Dorson, "Folklore, Academe, and the Marketplace," *Folklore and Fakelore* (Cambridge: Harvard University Press, 1976), 7. James Stevens was author of the early and influential *Paul Bunyan* (New York: Alfred A. Knopf, 1925) and *The Saginaw Paul Bunyan* (New York: Alfred A. Knopf, 1932).
3. Stith Thompson, *Tales of the North American Indians* (Bloomington: Indiana University Press, 1929), xv. Thompson actually blames Henry Rowe Schoolcraft for this confusion, a scholarly fallacy which has become widely accepted as true and needs to be corrected. The confusion, although he himself was never confused, can be placed squarely on Longfellow's shoulders. At no point in his collections of myths did Schoolcraft call Manabozho "Hiawatha." He did entitle one late collection *The Myth of Hiawatha*, but this did not appear until 1856, one year after Longfellow's *Song of Hiawatha*, and the book, which was dedicated to Longfellow, was clearly intended to take commercial advantage of the enormous popularity of the poem. In Schoolcraft's earlier books, which Longfellow used for inspiration, Manabozho was always called by his Ojibwa name.
4. Henry Wadsworth Longfellow, *The Song of Hiawatha* (New York: Bounty Books, 1968), 27.
5. For a complete list of Michigan place names derived from "Hiawatha" and other literary sources, see Virgil J. Vogel, *Indian Names in Michigan* (Ann Arbor: University of Michigan Press, 1986), 67–80.
6. Dell McCormick, *Paul Bunyan Swings His Axe* (Caldwell, Ohio: Caxton, 1977), 7.
7. Richard Dorson, *Bloodstoppers and Bearwalkers* (Cambridge: Harvard University Press, 1952), vii.

8. Library of Congress Recordings Nos. 2264-B2, 2265-B2, and 2266-B2. Excerpts from the tapes are quoted in Daniel Hoffman, *Paul Bunyan: Last of the Frontier Demigods* (Lincoln: University of Nebraska Press, 1982), 37–38. See also E. C. Beck, *They Knew Paul Bunyan* (Ann Arbor: University of Michigan Press, 1956), 1–27, especially 20–23.

9. Hoffman, *Paul Bunyan*, 37–38. It is not my intention to review the ground covered by Hoffman's book, which I highly recommend, especially his discussion of the popular and literary works Paul Bunyan spawned. Readers interested in tracing the history of written and mass media presentations of Paul Bunyan should avail themselves of both Hoffman and Richard Dorson's articles, "Paul Bunyan in the News" and "Folklore, Academe, and the Marketplace," both reprinted in his *Folklore and Fakelore*, and his earlier article, "Folklore and Fakelore," *American Mercury* 70 (1950): 335–43.

10. See Hoffman, *Paul Bunyan*, 23–62, and his bibliography, 193–94 for information about Paul Bunyan stories collected directly from lumberjacks.

11. Edward O. Tabor and Stith Thompson, "Paul Bunyan in 1910," *Journal of American Folklore, 59* (1946): 134–35.

12. Edith Fowke, "In Defence of Paul Bunyan," in *Explorations in Canadian Folklore*, ed. Edith Fowke and Carole Carpenter (Toronto: McClelland and Stewart, 1985), 189–99.

13. Stewart Holbrook, *Holy Old Mackinaw* (New York: Macmillan, 1938), 1–13.

14. Lewis Reimann, *Incredible Seney* (Au Train, MI: Avery, 1982), 111–22. See also Reimann's *When Pine Was King* (Au Train, MI: Avery, 1981).

15. Dorson, *Bloodstoppers and Bearwalkers*, 197–99.

16. E. C. Beck, *Songs of the Michigan Lumberjacks* (Ann Arbor: University of Michigan Press, 1941), 131.

17. Ibid., 143.

18. C. W. Von Sydow, "Folktale Studies and Philology," in *The Study of Folklore*, ed. Alan Dundes (Englewood Cliffs, NJ: Prentice Hall, 1965), 219–45.

19. To the best of my knowledge, "processed folk" is an original term, for which my wife actually deserves the credit. It is a term for which I, and I suspect many folklorists, have been looking for years to describe the way in which popular culture takes the flavor out of folklore in order to make it palatable to a mass audience.

20. The lumberjack version can be found on the album, "Songs of the Michigan Lumberjacks," Library of Congress Recording AAFS L56. Hear also Touchstone, "The New Land" (Canaan, CT: Green Linnet, 1982).

21. For references to these and other popularized and children's Paul Bunyan books, see Hoffman, *Paul Bunyan*, 194–95.

22. For details on Longfellow's sources in Henry Rowe Schoolcraft's many books, see Chase S. Osborn and Stellanova Osborn, *Schoolcraft-Longfellow-Hiawatha* (Lancaster, Penn.: Jaques Cattell Press, 1942). Most of Schoolcraft's stories are available in his *Myth of Hiawatha*. The reader must remember, however, that Schoolcraft, himself, took great liberty with the Indian myths, and some, like the legend of Leelanau, were probably his own invention.

23. William Jones, *Ojibwa Texts*, Publications in the American Ethnological Society 7 (1917), 101–13.

24. McCormick, *Paul Bunyan Swings His Axe*, 2.

25. Esther Shephard, *Paul Bunyan* (New York: Harcourt, Brace and World, 1924), 35.

26. Beck, *They Knew Paul Bunyan*, 2.

27. From the album "Songs of the Michigan Lumberjacks."

28. Dorson, *Bloodstoppers and Bearwalkers*, 190–91.

29. Tabor and Thompson, "Paul Bunyan in 1910."

30. Such well known "Indian" place-name myths as those for "Big Spring" and for the many beauty spots of Mackinac Island were fabricated by local poets and businessfolk. When Dorson asked about such Munising place names as "Bridal Wreath Falls," "Caves of the Bloody Chiefs," etc., the Chamber of Commerce Secretary admitted, "They're just some Indian legends we had to make up for the tourists." See *Bloodstoppers and Bearwalkers*, 15–16.

31. The transcription is taken from Hoffman, *Paul Bunyan*, 37–38.

32. Quoted in Dorson, "Folklore, Academe, and the Marketplace," 7.

33. Shephard, *Paul Bunyan*, x.

34. Dorson, *Bloodstoppers and Bearwalkers*, 194.

35. The extent of Longfellow's indebtedness to the *Kalevala* has been subject to a long debate since *The Song of Hiawatha* was first published. I hope the final word on the subject will be that of Ernest J.

Moyne, *Hiawatha and Kalevala*, F. F. C. Communications No. 192 (Helsinki: Suomalainen Tiedeakatemia, 1963).
36. Shephard, *Paul Bunyan*, 52.
37. Longfellow, *The Song of Hiawatha*, 173.
38. Moyne, *Hiawatha and Kalevala*, 61–71.
39. Shephard, *Paul Bunyan*, v-vi.
40. Douglas DeShield, "Foreword" to Longfellow, *The Song of Hiawatha*, viii.
41. Dorson, *Bloodstoppers and Bearwalkers*, 186.
42. Holbrook, *Holy Old Mackinaw*, 1.
43. Reimann, *Incredible Seney*, 6.
44. Osborn and Osborn, *Schoolcraft-Longfellow-Hiawatha*, 102.
45. Ibid.

Black Legends of Calvin

by Richard M. Dorson*

fragile old lady pained with "arthuritis," and conscious of her flat nose corroded by hoodoo poison, Mary Richardson contained in her frail body an indomitable spirit and verve. She spoke about witches and hants when I first met her in Calvin Township, Michigan, in June 1952[1] and on later visits I spent rich evenings in her two room shack writing down and recording her tales. In the end she contributed twenty-three stories to my *Negro Folktales in Michigan*, the second largest number of any informant, next to Suggs. In addition she gave me fourteen variants to other texts published in that collection,[2] and some seventeen additional narratives, plus sayings, signs, beliefs, and one song text, "The Frog Went Courting," which she recited rather than sang.

Mary Richardson was born in North Carolina between Wilson and Selma, on an eighty acre farm owned by her father, who was part Creek. "I'd have to go back to the Bible to get the date," she says, but believes that she turned seventy-one on March 18, 1953. However her family moved to Clarksdale, Cohoma County, in northern Mississippi in March 1881, when she was seven, which would make her seventy-nine in 1953. "My father read in the paper where Mississippi land was so rich you didn't have to manure it; so he sold out and emigrated."

Reprinted with permission from the Hoosier Folklife Society, *Midwest Folklore* 6, no. 1 (1956). Originally published as "Negro Tales of Mary Richardson."

*Richard M. Dorson was on the faculty of the history department at Michigan State University when this article was first published.

Mary only went to school for a day here and there. "I don't know as I got one year of school if all the days was put together. I went one day in North Carolina, and I stood up and cried all day; it was a mean teacher, and I was afraid of him. He crocked me up and down the head with a lead pencil. It was the longest day God ever made, that first day I went to school. I was hungry, tired, sick, and had a headache where he struck me up and down the forehead with that lead pencil and hollered 'E'. When it come to 'rithmetic and subtracting I'd get lost, like the dog on the rabbit's tracks. But for a piece or a speech I'd be right up there with the good scholars."

Mississippi proved disappointing to Mary. "I didn't like the situation in the South. A person should be judged on what they is, not make angels out of white and devils out of black. I got tired picking such big crops for so little, on halves." So she began moving north, along the route of many other Deep South Negroes, farming in Arkansas and Missouri with her first husband. She married Mose Hale in 1922—"no license"—and moved to Chicago with him and their four children in 1930. "We got divorced about a year after. I got tired him drinking, th'owing away the money. I decided I could live better in a breshpile than with him hunting me." In Chicago she earned her living sewing and doing housework, and married Eddie Richardson from Mobile, Alabama, in 1943. The next year they bought a little farm in Calvin, where Mary could live "near the earth, like the rabbit. I'd rather stay here and fry frogs." One son, Nathan Hale, lives on the hill close by her and works at Studebaker in South Bend, two others are in Chicago, and a fourth is a preacher in Decatur, Illinois. She cannot join them as she loses her old age pension if she leaves Michigan. Eddie was severely crippled in one arm and one leg, and Mary did all the chores, planting and pulling the corn, feeding the hog and chickens and dogs and cats, when I met them. Still she kept her tiny home spick and span. On my last visit to Calvin, in September 1955, we found her living alone. Eddie had been taken to a hospital in Chicago with a serious kidney ailment, and she despaired of seeing him again. She had given up her livestock, but still tended her cornfield. At dusk she "barred up" the house, and kept it dark to appear deserted, sleeping with a gun under the bed. "I'll stay here as long as I can burn bread," she told us. "Then I'll go up to the red house on the hill [the old folks' home] and get acquainted with those folks."

A marvelous narrator of realistic occurrences, Mary excels at the supernatural belief tale rather than the humorous fiction. She thoroughly credits witchcraft and hoodooism, and will tell for true, as specific localized events, folktales that other informants relate for amusement. Her repertoire thus contrasts with that of John Blackamore[3] whose twenty-eight texts, which run to the animal and Old Marster tale and the racial jest, correspond with hers in only two instances. Mary Richardson specializes in the strange and macabre experience, and sometimes the listener cannot be sure whether she relates fact or fiction.

None of the following stories appear in *Negro Folktales in Michigan*, nor in "Collecting Negro Tales in Pine Bluff, Arkansas."[4]

I. ANIMAL & BIRD STORIES

1. RABBIT & TURTLE[5] _____

The rabbit was in the garden eating the cabbage. And the turtle come 'cross him, going to the creek. So the rabbit said, "Where you goin, short-legs?" The turtle says, "I can outrun you." So he said, "Well, we'll have a race then. You come down tomorrow." So the turtle took his wife with him to the garden. He place her at one end of the rows, and he went to the other end. So the turtle asked the rabbit, "Are you ready for the race?" The rabbit says, "Yes." So they start to counting. So they both started to running when they counted three: "One-two-three." So the turtle and the rabbit started off, left the end together. But when the rabbit got to the end he looked up, so there was the turtle. So he says, "Let's try it again." So they tried it a third time. But the turtle always beat the rabbit to the other end. When the rabbit got to the end of the row the turtle would say, "Here I am." But the rabbit had never discovered that there was two turtles, and neither one never left the end, he just started and stayed there. And the other popped up his head when the rabbit got there.

2. NORTHERN & SOUTHERN BUZZARD[6] _____

The Northern and Southern buzzard met up, and the Northern buzzard went south with the Southern one. The Northern buzzard didn't like the hot weather, even though there was plenty to eat, because anything died when th'owed in the woods, in the South. (Up here they make fertilizer out of it.) So they both started to fly north. The Southern buzzard got tired and the Northern buzzard tole him, said, "Get on my back, I'll carry you." So he got alongs with him. While he was on his back he was so contented he started him a song:

> I'm going back where the living don't bury the dead.
> O Lordy Lordy.

But he had to catch birds, he didn't get anything th'owed out in the North.

3. BUZZARD & CROW[7]

The buzzard and the crow was across the ocean. The crow couldn't fly as far as the buzzard, so he told the crow, "Get on my back, and we'll go where the living don't bury the dead, O Lordy Lordy."

(When we were picking cotton, Doc Wadlow would say, "Do you want to hear that old song about 'Let's go back where the living don't bury the dead.'" I called it an old ragtime song; it never appealed to me, but it sounded good when he did it. I don't know where he got it from.)

They don't bury nothing down South—they drag it off in the woods—nothing but a mad dog, they'll bury him.

4. HOW THE BUZZARD GOT HIS BALD HEAD[8]

Old poor horse laying down. Buzzard and the crow saw him. Buzzard asked the crow, "Is he dead?" Crow said he didn't know. "Try him, try him." [high] Buzzard stuck his head under the horse's tail, the horse tucked his tail down on the buzzard's head, and jumped and ran. (Anything that a buzzard find, a horse or dog or cow, he enters from behind and pulls his entrails out, get him to be a carcass, then he can stay up in him, gnaw the bones. Next thing he pulls out the eyes.) Buzzard pulls out, and skins his head, and that's why buzzards are bald-headed now.

5. THE FROGS & THE ELEPHANT[9]

Elephant came to the creek to get a drink of water and the baby frog saw him. So the baby frog told the mother when she come, said, "We saw something today it was so big, it came down here and dranked; it was the biggest thing I ever saw in my life." The mother frog asked the babies, "It wasn't no bigger than I am, was it?" "Oh yes, mother, much bigger." So she swelled out her sides and then asked the little frogs, "It wasn't no bigger than I am now, was it?" And they told their mother, "Yes, much bigger." So she swelled again, and busted her sides, she busted open.

And the next day the elephant came to get a drink, he sit there and let the elephant step on him. So the elephant asked the frog, "Am I very heavy?" This frog says, "No, not so heavy, but you're so hard on my eyes."

He was busting him open, just like the other.

6. THE JACKAL & THE CAMEL [10]

The jackal and the camel would go across the creek every evening to eat sorghum. The camel didn't get enough as quick as the jackal did, because it took more to fill him up. So the jackal would get tired of waiting on him and he'd holler so the farmers would hear, come down and chase them out. The jackal got on the camel's back to swim back, and the camel asked him, "Why do you holler every evening?" And he told him, "Oh, it's just a habit I have."

So the camel turned over in the water (the jackal couldn't swim), and ducked him good fashion. The jackal asked him, "Why did you do that?" "Oh, it's just a habit I have. Every evening when I eat I turn over."

(I heard that in Mississippi. It was supposed to be an old true story we was told in the sorghum, the cane patch. They'd strip the leaves off the stalk, press the juice out and make molasses out of it.)

7. THE INCHWORM & THE HOPPERGRASS [11]

I'm slow, like the inchworm. (It's a pa'able of the fast, big man.) The hoppergrass and the inchworm met, had a conversation. Hoppergrass says, "I don't see how you make your living, you get around so slow. You would never get to heaven." Inchworm says, "Yes I would." (Just a inch long, and just walks on two ends of him, stretches up his head and pulls up his tail, measures an inch at a time.) So they 'cided they'd start to heaven. So the hoppergrass walked along with him a while. Then he told the inchworm he was too slow: "I'll go on to heaven and tell the angels you coming." So he riz and flew. When he got there, the gates was close, and he couldn't get in. So he had to stay in the yards of heaven outside. After a long time he saw the inchworm coming down the road. And when he crawls to the gate, the angel opened the gate and told him to come in, "For I knowed you had a hard time getting here." The hopper-grass didn't get in heaven at all, so he said, "The easy way is not the best way after all."

Gab'l told the inchworm he knowed he come through hard trials and great tribulations.

8. PREACHER & THE FOWLS [12]

—A—

When the preacher would come to the sister's house for dinner they'd always kill a chicken. They'd act as if he wasn't fed unless he had chicken—you didn't honor him with a delicious dinner unless you killed a chicken. So the chickens would all leave the yard and go down to the woods all day, until about sundown time to go to roost. Then the rooster would get up on the stump, or bush, or log, and flop his wings and crow:

> I wonder is the preacher go-o-o-o-ne.
> I wonder is the preacher go-o-o-o-ne. [*high*]

And the turkey gobbler would say:

> It's doub'ful, doub'ful. [*deep, rapid*]

—B—

The preacher come to the sister's house for dinner. And the sisters didn't know nothing but cook chicken for the preacher—every preacher come to the house he must have chicken. So the chickens learnt when the preacher comes somebody had to die, a chicken had to be killed. So they all left the yard and went to the woods, when they saw him coming in the yard with his handgrip. So, late in the evening, when it was about time to come up to roost, the rooster flew up on the fence, and flopped his wings, "Floppity—floppity—flop" and said:

> I wonder is the preacher go-o-o-n-e.

And the turkey says:

> It's doub'ful, doub'ful, doub'ful.

9. PARROT & SOW [13]

Way we heard it, the cook was cooking and Old Missus was going to church. She cooked them tea-cakes for herself, to carry to her little hut, not for Mistress' dinner. She slips them under the cushion of the chair, to hide them, because Old Mistress come back before she had them ready to carry off. So Old Mist'ss was going to sit down, and the parrot said, "No, no Mist'ss, hot cakes burn ya' ass." She got up and looked under the cushion and found them. The cook got a whipping for using Old Mistress' stuff.

Then she (the cook) baptized the parrot for telling it, dipped him in a tub of water, dirty washwater—she aimed to drown him. And later the old sow come down the road, and she was muddy, had been in a mud hole. The parrot told the sow, "Poor old sow, you been telling lies too."

II. SPIRITS & HANTS

10. BORN WITH A VEIL [14]

I've heard say that people born with a veil over their face can see spirits just like they see living people. They can see them even before they can talk; they'll talk with them when they gets so they can talk. They'd walk along and talk with the dead (I calls them) and ask them anything: "How is you?" A woman I knowed born with a veil was named Marthy. I said, "I'll never go with you then," because they say if you look over their left shoulder you can see what they can see. They'll say, "See that man over there?" and you say, "No," and they say, "Look over my left shoulder."

I never talked with but one spirit and that was in a dream. That was my brother. I saw him on a creek bank. He said, "It's lonesome this evening, ain't it?" And I said, "Maybe you came out too early this evening." Spirits aren't supposed to come out till after dusk, sundown. He'd been out around the creek bank for the longest.

11. SPIRIT OF GRANDMOTHER [15]

I seen the spirit of my grandmother, my father's mother, Grandma Edney. I wasn't more than five year old. I remember it because it was something new to me. I was out in the yard, and I saw her go out the gate, to my other grandmother, and I ran after her, to go with her. In running I couldn't look down the road and keep running in the hot dust, and when I looked up I didn't see her nowhere. So I thought she'd hid side of the rail fence (a "worm" type fence) to keep me from going with her, and I had passed her I thought. So I looked the fence carefully as I went back, and I didn't never see her till I got back to the house.

She was sitting in her chair she loved to sit in and I asked her, "Grandma, *where* have you been?" She said, "Nowhere, honey." I repeated again. I saw her going out that gate. She said she hadn't been out the house today. She was old, she didn't get out the house like mother.

Only thing I could figure it was her death. She died in six months, or less than a year. It was her spirit I saw. People see a sign or dream of the death before it happens. There's a spirit that's in a live person, and looks just like him. And when he dies he changes his clothes. When a person is going to leave you you can see his spirit, or hear him call you, and maybe you answer it. Sometimes it won't say a thing, just call you by your name, and you look and never find nothing. I've had my name called and answered, run to the door and look and see nobody. You'd lose somebody in the family, a friend or a neighbor, pretty soon. Right in the daytime.

12. GYPSIES IN HANTED HOUSE [16]

I heard about some gypsies was traveling in covered wagons—now they travel in cars. And they came to this old 'lapidated house, which was hanted. They went in to sleep, and the house was so hanted they couldn't sleep. Doors opening and closing, stomping and walking through the house. So they asked the hants, what did they want. They told 'em, "Get up and put on your clothes, get your shovel and follow me." Two or three men did it. They went down to an apple tree in the orchard, and the hant stomped his foot and said, "Dig here." They found a pot of money, silver and gold. But this hant left them when he stomped his foot, quite bothering them.

They took the money to the bank and had it changed, because it was old money. They had to take a discount on it. There was thousands of dollars in that pot, an old iron pot. They didn't sleep no more that night, they worked the balance of the night.

The hants looked like shadows, but they walked and talked like men. Colored folks is scared of hants you know—they don't like to have nothing to do with the dead.

That was before they had banks—people would bury their money. The Bible speaks against burying your money.

13. TREASURE GONE [17]

This was in Hayti, Missouri. We had got through picking cotton on our crop, and turned our kiddies loose to make them some money on their own. So they was working for their auntie, Sally, my husband's sister, picking cotton. It rained one day so they went to hunting pecans [pronounced *puckawns*]. And there was an empty house on the place, and two pecan trees not far apart, something like fifteen or twenty yards I guess. And Joseph says to Sammy, "I bet there's some money buried at this old house, between these two trees." Nathan says, "No, no money buried there."

So the next time they went to hunt pecans, they saw the hole where someone had dug the money up, and took the pot away. They saw the hole with the crown where the pot had sit—a number seven stove pot.

I said, "Yes, the hants would have put you in the hole."

III. HORRORS

14. GRANDMOTHER WHIPPED [18]

That was way back yonder in old slavery times. I heard my grandparents talk about it—I wouldn't took all they took, I'd a took the grave. My grandmother was working in a field (in North Carolina). They grubbed up all the ground instead of plowing it, they dug it up with grubhoes. And she couldn't keep her breat' up, she couldn't keep up with the gang, because she was pregnant. (They ought a left her at home.) And Marster took her hoe and dug a hole in the ground and laid her face foremost in the hole, and whipped her with a cat-o'-nine tails (a piece of leather split in nine parts, and every time they hit they hit you nine times).

He dug the hole so he wouldn't lose his little nigger. He didn't want to damage her but he wanted her to keep up with the gang. But she couldn't keep up; they had to help her at each end.

15. MEAN HUSBAND [19]

There's some people so mean, they carry Michigan rocks in their body.

On Richland plantation, three miles north of Clarksdale, Mississippi, there was a man too mean to wear pants. He'd lock his wife up in the house (sharecropper tworoom house) and put the key in his pocket, and take ashes from the fireplace and sprinkle it in front of the window. And he'd trot all the way to town—two mile— and when he come back he'd say, "Someone been here and come in this house at the window. Lavinia, I see a track here." She said, "I didn't see nobody nor hear nobody." Then he'd unlock the door and let her out and say, "He's a bigfoot nigger," and put his foot in the track, but his heel back of the print to make it look bigger. And then he'd whip her and beat her half to death, like she was a mule, knock her around there like she was a mad dog.

I'd hear her there crying—I stayed three houses away—till I'd want to go down there with my husband's Winchester and shoot him. Starks was his name—a goodsized, wellstocked man—she was medium size.

She run away and stayed gone long enough to marry, and when he found her he was going to make her come back home. And her husband killed him, shot him. He had to go stand trial, but he told how it was done.

16. PANTHER-FIGHTING MARY [20]

Down on Asack Plantation, owned by a big Jew, five miles from Clarksdale, Mississippi, this woman Mary lived next to me. She told me an awful tale, it was true though. She was going through the woods to a dance at a sawmill with a couple of fellows. It was about two mile through the woods. So they outwalked her, so that kept her behind them. And a panter jumped out the tree down on her and split her shoulder down the back; he just stroked her down with his claws, like you ketch at somebody and don't get a good hold. And she squalled, and the men ran and left her. And she reached down and got a piece of board off the track. (There was a tram track that the car ran off, it took logs to the mill on that tram.) And she pulled a plank off and it had a nail on it. When she struck him with it he lay down, and that give her time to get further while he's fixing to make the next spring. (A panter has to get down, like a cat, before he can jump.) Then he run around her and come back to the edge of the woods and cut her off. She had to fight him again, but by hollering to the mill the people heard her and come to her rescue. They shot and killed the panter, and stretched his hide on the mill shed. And they gave her $75 or $80 for being so brave.

I saw the scar myself, three streaks right together, on her shoulder. After that they called her "Panter-Fighting Mary." They took her and the panter's picture.

IV. CURIOSITIES

17. PROFESSIONAL ROUGE [21]

This really happened, on the next plantation cross a couple of miles from where I stayed, a mile out of Clarksdale. Bob Dixie was a professional rogue (colored feller). He would go and steal the hogs out the lot, scald them, cut them up and salt them down before day. So the Marster hired a fellow to watch him, 'cause he couldn't catch that rogue. The fellow was watching for the rogue, with the Marster's Winchester. And he fell asleep, so Bob tiptoed up and took the gun from him and hid it. Then he waked up and asked him, "What you doing sitting in this lot this time of night?" He told him, "Somebody has been stealing Mr. Doll's hogs, and he hired me to ketch him. And somebody stole my gun." So Bob Dixie went around with him to help him find it. The watchman said, "The gun is worth more than the hog; I'll give $10 to get it back." They walked around the lot with Bob Dixie. The watchman gave him the $10, so Bob didn't take any hog that night.

After that Bob went and told Mr. Doll he was going to get a hog outa that lot, and kill it and salt it and bring him a piece for breakfast, and the watchman wouldn't see it. And Mr. Doll said, "If you do it again I'll kill you." He told Mr. Doll, "You can put all the men you want to watch me." He told Mr. Doll that at the store Saturday evening, with two or three men sitting there. And he did it. This here rogue tiptoed past the two watchmen when he'd catch them nodding, and then he'd hit the hog so hard it wouldn't squeal. And he brought Mr. Doll a piece for breakfast.

So they chased him out of that neighborhood, he was such a slick rogue. The white folks run him out the country.

I used to see him every Sunday, a heavyset man, dark; he could pick a two hundred pound hog just like it was a stick you put on your shoulder. He was a good worker, but he was a better rogue.

18. BOBO IN THE WELL [22]

Bob Bobo was going to see his girl friend Liza. That was down in Mississippi, at the Richland Plantation. He stayed until it was dark—it was dark when he left. He couldn't see the well side of the road, and he walked in it, fell in it. He thought he was going to drown, to die in there, so he started to sing a prayer:

> "O Lord just deliver me
> From the bottom of this well,
> I'll serve you the balance of my days."

And the people that lived at the house heard him, and went out and seed him in the well. And Liza's father got a rope and let it down to him.

He prayed so long, with such a long tune, it seemed like a song—he was singing his prayer.

19. MERMAIDS [23]

It used to be six months for the ship to cross the ocean or the sea. (That's the way they used to steal the coloreds out of the country, brought 'em over here and sold 'em for slaves.) The mermaids would upset the ship if they didn't throw them something out there. They would ask for a name if they heard a name called. So ships would take empty barrels with them, to keep from throwing over a little Negro child, and they'd call the child "Barrel." So when the mermaid asked for a name, they'd pitch him a barrel. They'd say, "You barrel you." They was just using a substitute till they got across the water.

They followed the ship like a school of fish, they wanted something to eat, they was hungry. They'd eat up the people was thrown over. They couldn't eat the barrel, but it would take them time to search it.

I went to the Ringling Brothers Circus and saw pictures of mermaids, but no live ones. I don't believe such a thing as that grows, it's only an old fairy tale I think, something they printed and made up. I've been to the Chicago zoo several times; they say they got every kind of animal, sea-cow and sea-lion and hippopotamint, but I didn't see no mermaid.

20. SNAKE & BABY [24]

I heard of a woman working in the field, and left her baby at the house. Down in the South. When she came back she found the snake in the crib with the baby. The snake was laying with the baby to lick its mouth, they decided; it liked the smell of breast milk. She killed the snake, and the baby got poor and sick and weak, and dried up—wasn't nothing they could do for it.

The snake had been coming there every day—they could see signs of it. It would crawl out and hide when he heard the mother walking on the porch. He'd crawl out the crib from the baby. Oh, the baby was about six or seven months old.

They must have been partners. The snake took up with the baby. They should have let them grow up together, until the baby outgrowed the snake.

21. DEAD MAN SITS UP [25]

Down in Mississippi round where I lived was a man died and they swowded him and laid him out. They give him a bath and put the clothes on him what was to be put in the coffin—they didn't have an undertaker then. (Now they'd bury them the third day; then if they'd get offensive they'd put salt on their breasts, so they wouldn't purge, foam at the mouth.) His family and friends sat around and sing and pray and drink coffee and talk until day; some of them get drowsy and go home, so there was just a few left, all gone to sleep, nodding around. So when they did wake up, the man was sitting up on the cooling board and he said, "What am I doing here?" The men sitting there they practically tore the door down getting out.

He was just in a trance. If they had buried him just a little bit quicker, when they thought he was dead, he would have been dead.

22. PO' THING [26]

The old lady never saw a train. Her daughters took her to the depot and bought her a ticket, and they were sitting around waiting for the train to come. The train blew about a half a mile from the station. Everybody went out on the platform, to get on the train when she ran up. They all got on when she stopped. It puffed, "Pheeeew."

The old lady said: "It's too tired. Po' thing. Look at the way it's huffing and puffing; it's a sin." She said, "There's too many on it already; they've overloaded it." And she wouldn't get on it. So the daughter had to take her back home; she didn't go.

V. THE LORD

23. *SAM PRAYS TO THE LORD* [27]

Sam work hard and at night he was so tired before going to bed he would say his prayers. He prayed for the good Lord to come get him: "O Lord please come take me out of this troublesome world." So some fellows, boys, heard him saying these prayers, so they come by and called him, as if they were Death.

"Oh-h Sam, oh-h Sam, your soul is acquired at the bar of God tonight." [*high*]

And Sam heard it and told his wife Millie to hush, so he could understand what Death was telling. And he crawled under the bed and told his wife to tell Death, I am not here. "Sam been gone three long days ago."

Millie tells him, "Sam, you come out from under that bed and go with the good Lord, 'cause Millie ain't studying him."

(She wasn't bothered about Death, she wasn't going nowhere, hadn't been begging him to come.)

Well you know this world, you don't know that other one yet.

24. *CROPPED ANGEL* [28]

The angels all take a circle, the holy angels would fly over heaven. And that one come in newly, he didn't know how to act, he wouldn't fly with the gang. He'd stop and meddle things along the way. So old Saint Peter cropped his wing to make him fly even with the gang you know—he flied too fast and meddled things, so they slowed him down. So then he couldn't keep up, made him stay always behind them. So he never got to the throne in time, he'd come up behind all the time. He'd come in on a wing and a piece, flop flop. So he was a cropped-wing angel, a crippled angel.

(I've seen children that way, overspeeding, they're so happy to be along with you.)

25. *LORD, IS THIS HEAVEN?* [29]

Old colored woman lived in the country all her life, and she had a chance to go to Memphis. And she went in a store where there wasn't anything but ribbons and lace and dressing for Christmas, and it glittered and shined in there. So she got so happy to know she had made it to heaven she went to slapping her hands:

> Lord, is this heaven
> And am I here?
> Lord, is this heaven
> And am I here!

And she just went to jumping around and standing on the counter and grabbing the ribbons and the lace and tearing up the store and shouting. So they put her in the jailhouse for tearing up and stomping and tangling and damaging the store.

Now that was told for the truth.

26. *WHY JEWS WON'T EAT HOG* [30]

The way I heard it, there was peoples in Christ's time who had 'ligion of the devils, the devil was in them. And Christ demanded them to come out of those people, and go in those swines. Then he told the swines to go in the river. And they did so, and was drowned. That's why Christ told Peter, "What have I cleaned, call it not unclean." That didn't mean the rest of the hogs was still of the devils.

27. *PETER & THE ROCK* [31]

When Moses was leading the Jews out of Egypt to the Promised Land, and they got hungry on the journey, Christ told Moses to demand the children get 'em some stones, pile up some stones. Moses told the children to bring some stones and pile 'em here side of the road. Luke and Matthews and Mark, they got good sized stones, big stones. Peter he was so trifling he picked up a little bitty stone, and brought it and laid it down. Then Christ come and turned each man's stone to bread. Peter's loaf of bread was the smallest one of 'em. Jesus said, "You reap what you sow." The others had bread to leave.

VI. FAIRY TALES

28. THE DEVIL'S DAUGHTER [32] _____

Jack wanted the Devil's daughter—he courted the Devil's daughter. So the Devil told him if he'd work for him seven years he'd let him marry his daughter. He'd give him his daughter. And Jack hired to the Devil. First thing the Devil set him out to do was to go out and clear up a piece of land, and plant it in corn, and bring him some roasting ears back for dinner. (That was raising 'em fast I guess.) So Jack took his axe and went out to clear the land up. And his daughter come and brought Jack's breakfast. So Jack sits down on the log he'd cut, with Sally—the Devil's daughter was named Sally—to eat his breakfast. Sally told him, said, "I'll plant your corn while you eat your breakfast." And Sally didn't take the axe like Jack did. She told the trees, "Fall down." And they fell. And she told the trees, "Huddle up." And they piled up. And then she told them to burn up. That was to clear the brush and the ground so he could plant the corn. And the trees burnt up. Instead of plowing the land she told it to turn over, and the ground turned over, like when a plow turns it. Then she say, "Corn, be planted. Come up and make roasting ears for dinner." So that was done. Jack carried an arm of roasting ears in for dinner.

So that ended that story, and the Devil gave him another job. He told him to go out and ketch his horses—one was named Baldy, other was named—I forget—Jerry, I believe. And nobody never had caught or bridled those horses except the Devil; he knew nobody was going to get a bridle on neither one of them. So Sally knowed them horses was going to kill Jack, because they never had been bridled by nobody but the Devil. So Sally gets up and goes out to the stable, told Jack, "Get your stick and knock the Devil out of the horse." Then he could put the bridle on him. So Jack caught the horse and put the saddle on him. Hitched him to the Devil's hitch post and told him, "Your horse is bridled and saddled."

So Jack had done about everything the Devil had told him to. So it was time for the Devil to give Sally up, to let 'em marry. So Sally told Jack, said "Papa ain't never going to give me up. So let's us run off." So they decided they would run off the next night. So they saddled the same horse Jack saddled for the Devil, for himself and Sally, and that night him and Sally got on it. So they rode down the road, and was gone about an hour. So the old rooster was on the yard, he saw what they were doing, he began to crow:

Sally and Jack's gone,
Sally and Jack's gone.

The Devil got up and began looking for them. So the Devil caught the other horse, knowing he couldn't travel as fast as Baldy, and aimed to overtake them. So Sally she throwed down an egg, and it made a creek in the road, and when her daddy got there he couldn't cross it, 'cause that horse couldn't swim. Then he rode that horse back home and caught an ox. And when he got to the same creek he told his ox:

Drink my big bull,
Drink.

Forty gallons a swallow, that's what his ox would drink. He was going to drink the creek dry. And the ox waded across the creek, and went on uptown. Sally and Jack had got to the courthouse, and the judge was saying "Salute the bride" when they walked in. So they beat the Devil.

That's the way I heard that old tale, from North Carolina people in Mississippi.

29. THE THREE FOOLS [33]

There was a fellow once courting a girl—he asked privilege from the mother and father to court their daughter. So they went in, prepared dinner for the family. And after the mother and daughter had cooked dinner and put it on the table, they told the daughter to go draw a cool pitcher of water, so they would have cool water for dinner. And she took the pitcher and went to the well and sit down. She stayed so long the mother went to the well to see what had happened. And when the mother got there she said, "How come you didn't bring the water home? They're all waiting to eat their dinner."

And the daughter told her mother, said, "Mother, I was just thinking, if I married that man, what would we name the first child?"

The mother said, "That is something to think about," and she sit down there with her. So they stayed till the husband come to see what was the matter with the wife and the daughter. And he stayed until the boy that was courting the girl said, "I'll see what's the matter with the whole family." (All gone to the well and none had come back, had left him in the house by himself.) And they told the story to him when they didn't come back to the house, what they was thinking about.

And the man told them, said, "Well sir, I'll go and if I'll find three more fools like you are, I'll come back and marry your daughter."

And whiles going down the road he saw a man had plowed his ox until twelve o'clock. And he had a rope around the ox's horn trying to lead him up to the top of the house for his dinner (let the ox graze on top of the house).

And the next thing he saw down the road was a man had his pants hung up the side of a tree and was running and trying to jump in them. He told him to take 'em down and put one foot in at a time, that was the way to put his trousers on.

That was two of them fools he found. The next thing, he found a woman that had scrubbed her floor and she had a wheelbarrow and was rolling the sunshine in the house to dry the floor. He told her to open the door, and the sun would shine in the house.

He said, "That's three fools." He had to marry that daughter.

He found his three fools, so he was entitled to marry the girl.

VII. NURSERY SONG

30. *THE FROG WENT COURTING* [34] _____

Mother made us hush that mess. I wasn't no Christian—I liked those jumped up songs. We sang that thing till it was a pity.

1. The Frog went courting and he did ride, ahm, ahm, ahm,
   With a sword and pistol by his side, ahm, ahm, ahm.
2. Soon Lady Mouse came stepping down
   In her silk and satin gown.
3. - - - - - - - - - - - - - - - -
   Says to Lady Mouse, Will you marry me?
4. She says, Not without Uncle Rat's consent
   I wouldn't marry the president.
5. Where shall the wedding be?
   Way down yonder in a holler big tree.
6. What shall the wedding be?
   Two big beans and a blackeyed pea.
7. About the middle of that fray
   The cat and the kitten come astray.
8. The frog come hopping side the wall,
   Says "The Devil's 'mongst you all."
9. The duck come swallowed the frog down her crook,
   And that was the last of the history book.

VIII. BELIEFS & SAYINGS [35]

1.   A mojo is the right back foot of a rabbit. You carry it in your pocket for luck, say when a fellow is courting a girl. I seen fellows with them old things in their pockets. Or they'd use love powder, little brown powder, and when they was talking to her they would sprinkle it on her—calling it "controlling her mind." Anything they asked her for she would agree to it. Looked like face powder. That's all foolishness. Old people would teach the girls, "Now never drink any whiskey or eat any candy a man brings you, he might fix it, control your mind and ruin you." That's fifty year old stuff. I don't think anybody ever tried it on me, but I couldn't prove it.

2.   If a rooster comes to your door and crow, sign of a stranger coming to your house. If your right hand itches, you're going to get money, if your left hand itches you'll spend it. Old folks used to teach that. My mother'd spank us if we swept dirt out after sundown. Combing your hair after night makes you forgetful. After I got grown I just wore off from some of those old sayings.

3.   When somebody dies they cover the mirror up or turn it around. They tell me you can see death in the mirror.

4.   The bluejay carries a grain of sand to hell every day. I thought the bluejay was the prettiest bird there was—I wondered how he come back from hell.

5.   When they build the bridge across the Mississippi from Memphis, they wouldn't let a cat cross it till it was finished, because they were afraid it would shake it. A cat can shake a house, the way he steps—he got a rock in his trot.

6.   This place is so poor two I'shmen couldn't raise a fuss on it with a jug of whiskey.

7.   Mississippi isn't poor, it's lowdown.

8.   Old Job had a turkey and he didn't feed him. The turkey got so po' until when he went to gobble he had to lean against the fence.

9.   The boys used to have an old saying, "Is you a setting dove or a flying lark?" (Was she married or single.) That's what a boy asked a girl when he wanted to know could he 'company her.

1. See Richard M. Dorson, "Negro Witch Stories on Tape," and "A Negro Storytelling Session on Tape," *Midwest Folklore* 2 (Winter 1952): 229–41; and 3 (Winter 1953): 201–12.

2. One of these variants is printed in *Southern Folklore Quarterly* 18, "King Beast of the Forest Meets Man" (June 1954): 126–27, "Panther and Bear."

3. *Western Folklore* 13 (1954): 77–97, 160–69, 256–59.

4. Richard M. Dorson, *Negro Folktales in Michigan* (Cambridge: Harvard University Press, 1956), hereafter referred to as *NFIM*.

5. This is Type 1074, "Race," and Motif K11.1, "Race won by deception: relative helpers." Mary Richardson uses the "hogshead" in place of the turtle in her similar text in *NFIM*, 37–38, "Rabbit and Hogshead have a Race," which is close to Julia Courtney's variant in *NFIM*, no. 6, "Rabbit and Hedgehod." See also Richard M. Dorson, "Negro Tales from Bolivar County, Mississippi," *Southern Folklore Quarterly* 19 (June 1955): 106, "Tapin and the Deer."

6. "Why the Buzzard Went South" is in *NFIM*, 42, from Jefferson Haire, and see note 10, pp. 206–7. I have four more Michigan Negro texts explaining the absence of buzzards and carrion up North. This variant is unusual in having a Northern buzzard who tries the South.

7. In *NFIM*, "The Buzzard goes to Europe" by J. D. Suggs, p. 43, the preceding plot is given a transatlantic twist, evident in the fragment here.

8. The parallel text in *NFIM* is "Crow, Buzzard, and Mule" by John Blackamore, 43–44, and note 12, p. 207. Only the final aetiological motif in the present tale explaining the baldness of the buzzard unites it with Sarah Hall's "The Reason the Buzzard is got a Bald Head" in *NFIM*, 41–42 and note 9, p. 206, a tale-type involving a separate trickster situation.

9. See Motif J955.1, "Frog tries in vain to be as big as ox," and *NFIM*, no. 12, "Bullfrog and Terrapin," by Sally Courtney, which are joined in the present tale of the swelling and the crushed frogs.

10. A close variant is told on "Elephant and Jackal" by Harold Lee in *NFIM*, no. 14.

11. Motif L148, "Slowness surpasses haste," applies here.

12. See the texts of "The Preacher and the Guinea" by J. D. Suggs in *NFIM*, 47–48, and note 17, p. 208, and of "Preacher and Fowls" by Rev. J. H. Lee in Dorson, "Negro Tales from Bolivar County, Mississippi," *Southern Folklore Quarterly* 19 (June 1955): 107–8. E. W. Baughman in *A Comparative Study of the Folktales of England and North America*, 3 vols. (Ph.D. dissertation, Indiana University, 1953), assigns the motif number X459.2*(b), "Fowls hide when preacher comes to visit." I have seven other variants from Michigan Negroes. The A and B texts are two tellings of the same tale.

13. Related texts are in *NFIM*, 48, "Poll Parrot and Biscuits" by Johnny Hampton, and "The Poll Parrot, the Hawk and Jim" by James Schacklefore, and see notes 18 and 19, pp. 208–09; and *NFIM*, no. 17, "Poll Parrot," where five variants are given. This widely traveled jest is cited under Motif J2211.1, "Why the sow was muddy."

14. Newbell N. Puckett, *Folk Beliefs of the Southern Negro* (Chapel Hill, N.C., 1926), discusses "'Double-sighted' Folks," 137–39, and mentions the Southern Negro belief that only a person born with a caul can see ghosts, but that other persons can look over the left shoulder or under the upraised right arm of one with the power to see the ghost. Suggs told me that he was born with a caul and could see spirits when he was younger. Cf. *Drums and Shadows*, by the Georgia Writers' Project (Athens, Georgia, 1940), 192, for a similar statement.

15. There is a good deal about spirits in Puckett, e.g., 97–98, "Troublesome Spirits," and in *Drums and Shadows*, but the present account is unusual in that Mrs. Richardson saw the spirit before the death of its owner.

16. The idea of friendly spirits pointing the way to buried treasure is well known to Southern Negroes. See *NFIM*, "The Spirit and the Treasure," by Katy Pointer, 132–33, and "The Horse and the Money," by Sarah Jackson, and note 91, p. 221; and *NFIM*, no. 37, "Treasure Dream," by John Courtney.

17. The obverse idea is presented here, and hants frighten away colored people who dig for treasure. Mary Richardson gives another such account in *NFIM*, "Buried Treasure and Hants," 133–34 and note 92, p. 221. Cf. the comments in *Drums and Shadows*, 15, 41, 97, 124.

18. Cruel whippings of slavery times are rife in Negro tradition. See *Lay My Burden Down*, ed. B. A. Botkin (Chicago, 1945), especially 163 ff., "Praying to the Right Man."

19. Mary Richardson gives an even more vicious narrative of a mean husband in *NFIM*, "The Man who Sold his Wife for Beef," 95–96.

20. This avowedly true tale bears a close resemblance to the fantastic exploits of "Doughty Dames" who conquer wild beasts, in the Crockett almanacs, assembled in *Davy Crockett, American Comic Legend*, ed. R. M. Dorson, (New York, 1939), 47–56.

21. There are suggestions here of Type 1525, "The Master Thief," whose A form has been collected among several ethnic groups in the United States. I have a Polish text, with references to other American examples, in "Polish Wonder Tales of Joe Woods," *Western Folklore* 8 (January 1949): 39–47.

22. Noteworthy here is the characteristic device in Negro storytelling of the inserted chant. At a church service in Calvin I heard E. L. Smith in response to the preacher's request for a prayer improvise a lovely chant. Later I tried to record it, but he laughingly said I had caught him off base, and he could only give forth when the spirit moved him.

23. Comparable texts are in *NFIM*, "The Mermaid," by J. D. Suggs, 147–48 and note 98, p. 223, and *NFIM*, no. 39, by Silas Altheimer. Here for once Mrs. Richardson shows skepticism, alone among my eight informants of this previously unreported legend.

24. This is Type 285, "The Child and the Snake," and Motif B765.6, "Snake eats milk and bread with child." See *NFIM*, 149, "Snake and Baby," by Mrs. E. L. Smith, and note 101, p. 224.

25. Suggs tells a similar story in *NFIM*, "Embalming a Live Man," 96, and note 60, pp. 217–18. The circumstances of Southern Negro burials made cooling-board tales poular, and Tobe, John, and Julia Courtney each gave me different humorous specimens; see *NFIM*, no. 43abc, "On the Cooling Board."

26. *NFIM*, no. 74, "Po' Thing" by John Courtney, is a variant, and I have two other Michigan Negro texts. Related tales will vary the objects misunderstood by the country Negro or the noodle Irishman.

27. A version by Suggs of this popular Negro tale is in *NFIM*, "Efan Prays," 6, and note 31, p. 212. The text in *NFIM*, no. 22, "John Praying," by Harrison Stanfill, is a related type, of God-in-the-praying-tree rather than God-at-the-door. Baughman assigns Motif J217.0.1.1 for "Tricksters overhears man praying for death to overtake him."

28. In *NFIM* Tommy Carter gives an extended treatment of this plot, pp. 79–81, "Colored Man in Heaven," and see note 48, p. 216. I have five other variants from Michigan Negroes.

29. This appears to be a localized adaptation of the preceding theme. The unfamiliarity of the country Negro woman with city life also appears in no. 22, "Po' Thing,"

30. Suggs gives two versions of "Why the Jews don't eat Hog" in *NFIM*, 160–61, of which the first text is Biblical like the present, and the second a folktale about Christ. See note 115, p. 226.

31. This follows Suggs's text in *NFIM*, "St. Peter and the Stone," 158–59 and note 112, p. 225, save that the tag is missing, where Peter the second day carries a great big stone, and Christ tells him to build His church upon that rock.

32. This follows the structure of the tale by Suggs with the same title in *NFIM*, 189–91, and see note 153, p. 231. Both Southern Negro and mountain white tradition contain robust examples of this plot, Type 313A, "The Girl as Helper in the Hero's Flight," reported by Richard Chase, Zora Neale Hurston, Elsie Clews Parsons, Vance Randolph, and Leonard Roberts.

33. See the text and references in *NFIM*, no. 56, "Three More Bigger Fools," by Julia Courtney. The present narrative combines tale-types often found together, and all reported by Baughman as extremely popular in America: Type 1450, "Clever Elsie"; 1348, "The Husband Hunts Three Persons as Stupid as His Wife"; 1210, "The Cow is Taken to the Roof to Graze"; 1245, "Sunlight Carried in a Bag into the Windowless House"; and 1286, "Jumping into the Breeches."

34. Unlike other star storytellers in Calvin, Suggs and the E. L. Smiths, Mrs. Richardson did not sing. One of her hoodoo tales in *NFIM*, 104, refers to "a little old song" sung by her hoodooed grandmother, about "The old grey horse come out the wilderness," which is known as a Negro lullaby; see *The Frank C. Brown Collection of North Carolina Folklore*, vol. 3 (Durham, NC, 1952), no. 174, p. 216. The only independent song text she gave me is this example of "The Frog's Courtship" which she recited. It falls into the nasal grunt or hum refrain form, in texts D–W of no. 120 in the *Brown Collection*, 3, pp. 157–64. The first line in stanza three is missing, and would probably read, "He took Lady Mouse upon his knee."

35. For data on Negro love powders (1), see Puckett, 264–66, "Negro Love Charms," and Vance Randolph, *Ozark Superstitions*, (New York, 1947), 170. I have similar accounts of Ojibwa and Sioux love powders in *Bloodstoppers and Bearwalkers* (Cambridge, 1952), 34–37. Negro, Irish and German love potions are given in H. M. Hyatt, *Folk-Lore from Adams County, Illinois* (New York, 1935), 498–515. Puckett describes the mojo (1), 19.

A rooster crowing (2) means a preacher or a stranger is coming, Puckett, 485. If you sweep after sundown (2), "you'll sho' sweep out some member uv de family," Puckett, 395. For Negro beliefs that mirrors hold the image of the dead (3), see Puckett, 81–82. Two of Puckett's informants share Mary Richardson's notions about itching hands (2), 451.

The jaybird (4) makes a trip to hell every third day to tell the devil about the people's sins, according to Puckett, 550. Job's turkey (8) is matched by pigs so poor they fell over in plucking a spear of grass; see Dorson, *Jonathan Draws the Long Bow* (Cambridge, 1946), 127. The courtship query about the setting dove and the flying lark (9) is found in Puckett, 77.

Folk Music and Song

Folk Singing on
Beaver Island

Fiddling &
Instrumental Folk
Music

Art Moilanen's
Musical Tradition

House Parties &
Shanty Boys

o some the term "folk music" is synonymous with folklore. This form of traditional expressive culture has high public visibility, and it may be the only example of folklore that many people recognize. Folk music is, however, just one form of folklore. Some traditional music of the Michigan population originally from Kentucky might have a country sound, and country and western music influences are obvious in the repertoires of some local musicians, but this music does not predominate in the state, except on the radio. Ideas of what folk music is and is not need clarification.

Folk song comprises poetry. Like other forms of traditional culture, folk music and song are perpetuated by oral tradition. Even when literate, the traditional singer usually learned and remembered the songs by hearing them. If traditional musicians read music to learn a piece, as many have taught themselves to do, they rarely refer back to that source to "correct" their rendition. Not all folk songs and music originate in oral tradition. The important distinction of folk music is not origin, but rather transmission, i.e., the manner in which the song and music is passed on to others and perpetuated.

Music and songs current in the repertoire of a *traditional* musician and musical group should be considered traditional. Musicians are exposed to much extraneous materials and are subject to influences of varying intensity. These outside materials, however, are not merely imitated; rather, a creative reshaping takes place. Folk music and song are manifestations of culture; thus, "foreign" musical influences are transformed, reshaped, and reworded to meet the demands and expectations of both the traditional musicians and singers and their audience.

Traditional music and song exists throughout the state. Common public settings are local bars, taverns, fraternal halls, picnics, and church-sponsored dances. Private affairs—anniversaries, weddings, birthdays, christenings, and homecomings—are often celebratory. In multi-ethnic regions, such as the Upper Peninsula, the musician often plays an intermediary role between the different ethnic patrons of a bar. Although every ethnic group shares a common regional U.P. culture, and thus some traditional music in common, ethnic-specific music and songs also exist. The popular traditional musician's repertoire often includes some music from other ethnic cultures that has moved into the public domain, and is performed in appropriate contexts. Music and song are media of communication that cross group boundary lines.

The following articles address the issues of influence, historical role, social meaning, and cultural implication of traditional music and song in Michigan.

Ivan Walton's enthusiasm for sailors' songs and traditions of the Great Lakes began while he was still a teenager and became the impelling force in his work and life. He began collecting data on these topics in 1938; one result is his essay "Folksinging on Beaver Island," which provides a sample of the richness of this folklore and insight into Walton's extensive knowledge of it.

To date very little has been written about Michigan fiddling style, however, it is a vital form of musical expression in the state. Fostered and maintained by the Original Michigan Fiddlers' Association, one finds fiddle music at local dances and music festivals throughout the state. Drawing from years of fieldwork and observations, Paul Gifford identifies the characteristics that distinguish a Michigan fiddling style from those of other regions. In addition to a discussion of music itself, he examines the role of fiddling in rural communities, attitudes toward music, dissemination of tunes and the influence of popular dance music and the music of European immigrants, and the formation of a common, shared repertoire in Michigan.

James Leary introduces the reader to Finnish-American accordion player and 1986 Michigan Heritage Award recipient, Art

Moilanen. Despite his unique characteristics, Art is typical of other Finnish-American (and possibly other ethnic) dance musicians raised in a close bilingual rural community, accustomed to physical labor, fond of social activities, and imbued with a strong sense of Finnishness. His eclectic musical repertoire is a product of multi-ethnic America. It consists of immigrant Finnish folk music, popular Finnish-American dance tunes, country and western hits from the 1940s and 1950s, and pan-ethnic polka music of professionals such as Frankie Yankovic. Through the medium of music we gain a sense of Upper Peninsula life and especially of one of its traditional musicians.

From the music of Woodlands Native Americans to the revival of the house party at the Port Huron Museum, "House Parties and Shanty Boys: Michigan's Musical Traditions" is a historical look at the music and musical instruments in the state. Stephen Williams outlines the origins and functions of the house party in rural Michigan, and introduces us to the many influences that have shaped the configuration of traditional Michigan music.

Folk Singing on Beaver Island

Ivan H. Walton

olk singing on Beaver Island is of special interest because of its variety and extensiveness and because of the important place it has held in the social and cultural life of the limited but highly homogeneous people living on the Island, who for nearly a century have been quite isolated from the mainland, state, and outside world. Folk singing became one of their chief sources of entertainment, and it preserved their group consciousness and many of their dominating attitudes.

The Island, the *Ile d'Castor* of the 16th and 17th century French fur-traders, is approximately sixteen miles long and from two to six wide, and it is located in northern Lake Michigan about twenty miles off the northwest corner of the Lower Peninsula of the state of Michigan. Its long axis is in a north-south direction. It is of glacial formation, and its soil is mostly of a gravelly nature and not very productive. It has some sand dunes along the west side, a half dozen small inland lakes, and an excellent and spacious landlocked harbor on the northeast corner. To the north and west are about a dozen other islands ranging in area from about five square miles to an acre or less. Together they comprise the Beaver group of Lake Michigan islands. Big Beaver, as it is known locally, is the only one that has had a continuing white or even Indian occupation.

Reprinted with permission of the Hoosier Folklore Society from *Midwest Folklore* 2, no. 4 (Winter 1952): 243–50.

The immediate forebears of the present dominant group of inhabitants, the Irish, came mostly from County Donegal in the extreme northwest of Ireland during the decade following the expulsion from the Island of James Jesse Strang's Mormon colony in 1856. In that year Irish fishermen and their friends from the north side of Beaver Harbor and from the Michigan mainland, and from as far away as Mackinac Island, who had suffered real or fancied wrongs at the hands of the Mormons, swooped down upon the helpless colonists after the assassination of their leader Strang, and drove them property-less aboard the awaiting vessels which took them to Milwaukee and other ports south to Chicago.

Letters to economically hard-pressed relatives in sea-indented, barren Donegal soon brought fisher and farmer folk from there in considerable numbers to this northern island already fabled for its timber and furs and especially for the seemingly inexhaustible supply of marketable lake trout in its surrounding waters. Most of these early immigrants made only brief stopovers in New York City or Montreal before continuing on by water or overland to their island destination, and a few still living in their island homes at the time of the writer's first visit there in 1932 conversed in their native Gaelic. Land was cheap. The Mormons who had lived there earlier in comparative isolation had cleared farms and constructed roads and log buildings, and had made their village of St. James, named for their leader, the seat of government not only of the island, but of a considerable section of the mainland as well.

The new inhabitants established a "little Ireland" that was not without some characteristics of their native Donegal. The land was rolling and relatively unproductive; the climate was much the same; and always near at hand was the ever-dominating sea, the source of much of their livelihood and no small number of their tragedies. The newcomers bore such names as Bonnar, Connelly, Dunlevy, Gallagher, Green, Kelly, Kilty, Malloy, Martin, O'Donnell, McCann, McCarthy, McCauley, McDonough, and Roddy. Some families became so numerous that their friends resorted to an intriguing system of line nicknames to distinguish the individuals. They brought with them from Ireland their religion; their occupations of fishing, sea-faring, and farming; and their characteristic Gaelic nature, sociability, and folklore. A limited number of residents of other north-European stock were among them and also a limited and varying number of Ojibway Indians. The latter group, however, were on the far side of a strict color-line and generally ignored. Sailor captain Manus Bonnar, who was born on the Island in 1858 of parents who had arrived but a short time earlier, stated characteristically that in his youth, "the Island was known as a home of tame Indians and wild Irishmen."

No reliable statistics of Island population seem to be available. Several of the older inhabitants, however, estimate that at the turn of the century there were all told about one thousand people living there, but the source of their livelihood—fishing, lumbering, schooner-sailing, and farming—was already declining; and in the next decades many of them, especially the young, sought their fortunes in the industrial areas of the mainland. In 1940 there were less than half of the peak number, and today probably not more than three hundred have their year-around home on the Island.

In numbers and industry the Beaver Island Irish have never equalled their Mormon predecessors, but in sociability and especially in the singing of folksongs, it is doubtful that any equal area of their adopted country has surpassed them.

Living conditions on the Island have been particularly favorable to the preservation and creation of songs. First, as already noted, the people there have to a large extent a common racial, geographical, and occupational background. Second, they have had a high degree of isolation, and as a result little or no tendency to disparateness. Until recently they have been completely shut off from the mainland and the outside world each year during the four winter months when navigation was closed on the Upper Lakes except for irregular mail delivery by dog sled or other messenger when the twenty mile stretch of intervening lake was covered with a dependable thickness of ice. During the other eight months communication was only by sailing vessel or steamer. In recent years the telephone, airplane, and radio have changed the situation considerably. This long comparative isolation made them quite self-sufficient for entertainment. Third, the average Irishman seems to be blessed with a strong penchant for sociability; and drinking, dancing, and singing seem to have been their chief source of enjoyment. These activities suffered but little diminution during the prohibition Era. They liked songs that are concerned with the sea. They also brought home songs from the mainland winter lumber camps; and like most other normal people, they enjoyed traditional songs and ballads that came to them from a wide variety of sources, particularly those from Old Ireland.

Many of the middle-aged or older people on the Island will, with an appropriate opening, or even without one, still tell of the song competitions that a while back used to take place between groups in rival saloons across the harbor from each other, and "by next daylight neither had sung the other down." During the long winter months frequent dances were held in the village of St. James and in the farm homes, and, while the fiddler rested, or when the others got danced out, they would frequently spend the remainder of the night singing. Some individuals sang at their work or wherever they were—in a lumbercamp bunkhouse, at the wheel of a Great Lakes schooner, in their fields, in their homes, or in any of the numerous gathering places.

The songs mentioned below were collected in manuscript and on disc recordings during several visits to the Island between the years 1932 and 1940 and a few by correspondence since then. Some of these manuscripts and recordings are duplicates—the same song recorded by different singers or by the same singer at different times—and some are in varying stages of completeness, but altogether they comprise a considerable collection.

Ireland's young men, especially those from north coastal Donegal, have been fishermen and seafaring men for long ages, and those who came over to Beaver Island and their descendants have fished and sailed the Great Lakes for nearly a century, and part of their harvest has been the numerous songs they brought to the Island annually at the close of navigation. Some of these originated among Lakesmen, but more were learned from salt-water men who drifted inland to the Lakes for temporary sojourns. Some of the Island songs which originated on the Lakes include such well-known ones as "The Red Iron Ore," "The Timber Drover (Drogher) Bigler," "The *Persian's* Crew," "The Steam Tug *Olsen*," "The Smugglers of Buffalo," "The Drunken Captain," and others. The original of the last-named is, of course, an ocean song which begins, "Off Canso Strait our schooner lay," but an Island singer localized the events narrated on Lake Erie, and began it, "Off Cedar Point our schooner lay."

Ocean songs sung on the island include the "Stately Southerner," "The Lowlands" (Child 286), "The New (High) Barbaree," "The Lady Leroy," "The *Cumberland's* Crew," "The Bold *Princess Royal*," "The Gallant Brigantine," "The *Beaver* Brig," "The *Flying Cloud*," "Paul Jones," "The Banks of Newfoundland," "The

Stowaway," "The Ship that Never Returned," "The Schooner *Hesperus*," and others. The last mentioned will be recognized as Longfellow's poem of that name. Fragments of capstan shanties such as "Away Rio," "The Banks of the Sacramento," "Shenandoah," and "Highland Laddie," were also obtained. A stanza of the latter was paraphrased to:

> Were you ever in Marquette (Quebec)?
> Sailor laddie, bully laddie,
> Red ore cover'n all the deck,
> My bully sailor laddie.

In addition to these songs acquired from shipmates and sailor friends, the Islanders have also kept alive some songs that originated on the Island and are concerned with marine events. In the late sailing season of 1873, three boys in their late teens left the Island in a small sailboat for the mainland for needed winter supplies. On their return they were overtaken by a severe squall, and, although their boat drifted upon the south shore of the Island, the boys, two Gallagher brothers and a friend Tommy Boyle, were never seen again. The event gave rise to at least two songs that are still current; one entitled by some "Crossing Lake Michigan," and by others, "The Gallagher Boys," opens with the lines,

> It was in October of Seventy-three,
> They left Beaver Harbor upon a calm sea
> Bound for Traverse City, their destination to go,
> They were crossing Lake Michigan where the stormy winds blow.

The other is entitled "The Gallant Tommy Boyle," and relates his virtues and the grief of his parents and friends.

Another local song, "The Ill-fated *Vernon*," tells of the loss of the new passenger and freight propellor in a night storm in October in 1877 in northwestern Lake Michigan with all on board including six Island crewmen. A later song entitled "In Honor of Captain Kilty," is concerned with the loss of the car ferry *Pere Marquette 18* which foundered and sank twenty miles off Cheboygan, Wisconsin, in September, 1910, with her Beaver Island captain and twenty-eight crewmen. Still another, "The *Clifton's* Crew," tells of the loss of the freighter *Clifton* in Lake Huron in a storm in the late season of 1924, with all hands including Captain Emmet Gallagher and others from the Island. In the middle thirties, the Steamer *Merold*, after completing her regular round-trip between Charlevoix and Beaver Harbor

(St. James), attempted to salvage some gasoline from a tanker stranded on a reef north of the Island and suffered a violent explosion which wrecked and sank the vessel and took the lives of all on board. A recorded song describes the event.

There are two others of a less tragic nature. "The *Light Ship 98*," written by a Beaver Islander, describes good-naturedly life aboard the lightship anchored on the Eleven-Foot Shoal off Manistique on the North Shore. The other is entitled, "The Fisher Yankee Brown." According to the song the "Yankee's" accomplishments didn't entirely live up to his accounts of them.

> Once when beating down the Lake, he had to come about,
> He heeled the Mattie o'er so far he scooped up thirty trout.

During the last half of the last century, when Michigan's superb white-pine forests were being riotously and wastefully exploited by the invading lumber barons, young men from Beaver Island as from many other places, spent their winters in lumber camps, and, when they returned home in the spring, brought with them the songs they had learned in the bunk house. For three quarters of a century Beaver Islanders have remembered and sung "The Shantyman's Alphabet," "The Foreman Young Munroe," ("Jam on Gerry's Rock"), "Harry Dale," "The Falling of the Pine," "The Little Eau Pleine," (one singer calls it "The Lill' U Plain"), "Jack Haggerty's Flat River Girl," and others. "Johnnie" Green, an Islander, with a most phenomenal repertoire of songs, as will be pointed out later, recalled that he had learned many of his non-lumbercamp songs from fellow workmen in the lumbercamps in the Manistique region.

By far the larger group of songs obtained on the Island originated far from there, and a considerable portion long before the ancestors of the present occupants crossed the Atlantic. These for convenience can be divided into three loosely-formed groups: those originating in the United States, those from England and Scotland, and, most numerous and seemingly most cherished, those from Old Ireland. The variety and number in each group are quite surprising.

In the American group are some with a war background such as "Captain Molly Pitcher," "The Last Fierce Charge," and "James Bird"; some of "love gone wrong" such as "The Flower of Albany," "The Lily of the Lake," "The Creole Girl of Lake Ponchartrain," "Fair (Young) Charlotte," and "Fair Fanny More"; and some immigrant songs including "Lament of an Irish Immigrant," "My Parents Lived in Connaught," "In Wild Americay"; "Patrick Sheehan," and such others as "The Indian's Lament," the highwayman song, "Cole Younger," the well-known Virginia railroad song, "The Old 97," "The Chatworth Wreck," and "The Roaming Gambler."

A large group came from across the North Channel and the Irish Sea. From Scotland came "Robin Thompson's Daughter," "The Bonnie Highland Soldier," "The Pride of Glencoe," and Burns' "Highland Mary." From England came a dozen or more including fragments of "The Derby Ram," and "The Frog That Went A'Courtin," and versions of "Captain Wedderbourne's Courtship," "Barbara Allen," and "The House Carpenter" (Child Nos. 46, 84, and 242, respectively), "Brennan on the Moor," "Mary of the Wild Moor," "The Rich Merchant," "The Middlesex Flora," "The Banks of Claudy," "Bloody Waterloo," "Bengin on the Rhine," and others. The "Liverpool Girls," became among lake sailors the "Buffalo Girls," and on the Island, "The Beaver Island Girls," and it describes in part the cruise of the fishing boats—all under sail—straining canvas to get back into Beaver Harbor from their annual July 4th race around Garden Island so as to be there when the Beaver Island girls arrived for the big evening dance.

Songs from or about Ireland and the Irish are the most numerous. Such pro-Irish, anti-British songs as "Sentenced to Death" and "Skibbereen" are sung with much feeling as are those of a nostalgic nature, such as "Old Erin," "Dear Old Ireland," "The County Tyrone," "Sweet Raquale," "Gra Gal McCree," "Hibernia's Lovely Jean," "Bonny Kathleen," "The Wexford Girl," the stirring song of the Irish chieftain, "O'Donnell Oboo," and many others.

Still another group, all very Irish, express their love of wit and good fun. These include such songs as "The Hat Me Father Wore," "The Irish Barber," "Kelly Have You No Shame At All?" "Mrs. McLaughlin's Party," "Mrs. McSorley's Twins," "The Widow's Pig," "The Old Leather Breeches," "Casey and O'Donnell," "Shamus O'Brien, Why Don't You Come Home?" and "Kathleen Mavourneen, Won't You Let Me In?"

I cannot close this account of folk singing on Beaver Island without at least brief mention of a few Island singers. One inquiring about the origin of island songs will repeatedly be told, "I learned that one from old Captain Rody, and how he would sing it!" I unfortunately arrived on the Island too late to hear him, but the memory of his singing is still very vivid among many of those with whom I talked. He was a big muscular man weighing around 250 pounds, and he had a big powerful bass voice. He acted out his songs, and seemingly had an unending supply of them. He owned and sailed several "lumber hookers" on Lake Michigan during the late 1800s. Several men who did their first sailing with him told of his leaving them aboard to watch ship while the lumber was being unloaded in Chicago while he spent the time in sailor hangout saloons or "free-and-easy shows," where there was much singing; and at his trick at the wheel on their way back down the Lake—he always stood the captain's watch himself—he would start humming and singing bits of the songs he heard, and "soon he'd be singin' 'em all." His son, Frank, or "Francie" as he is called in the Island, who sang many old songs himself, said of his father, "He never had to buy no drinks himself." He was referring to the custom in shore saloons which catered to sailors of giving free drinks to anyone who would sing a song or provide some other form of entertainment. Francie added that his father "Never had no schoolin' at all, but he could sing any god-damn song that ever was," and other Islanders agreed with him.

Tall, stately, white-haired, tenor-voiced, and genial Dominick Gallagher, a retired lighthouse keeper, who himself recorded a score or more songs, paid high tribute to his Ireland born father, who, he said, sang old songs at parties all over the Island almost to the day he died. "With a few drinks he'd sing all night." He seems to be the one who brought a good share of the current Irish songs to the Island.

Unassuming, diminutive, sailor, farmer, and Island fiddler, Pat Bonnar has not only supplied the music for Island dances for the last several decades on his "Stradivarius" violin—a faded label on the inside proves it—but he also composed and sang at least one song, "The *Clifton's* Crew." He is, no doubt, a better fiddler than poet, but he sang and dictated more than a dozen old songs.

And how can one describe "Johnnie" Green!—sailor, lumber-jack, farmer, and singer par excellence. His father, several uncles, and grandfather were all good singers. In his middle seventies when I last saw him, his former rich, baritone voice had become badly cracked; and his health and memory had deteriorated, probably as a result of the unusually rugged life he had lived, but he dictated and recorded several score of songs and fragments. In answer to a question of how many songs he knew he replied in an entirely off-hand manner, "Probably about a hundred." Recordings made by him and mention of titles, lines, and subjects of others that came from him continually, and a list of titles of his songs compiled by his daughter over a several-months period gave pretty good evidence that he knew or had known probably many more than twice that number. He knew practically all the songs recorded or dictated by others on the Island, and he recognized a good share of a long list of others mentioned to him. He stated somewhat apologetically, in answer to a question about how he learned songs, that frequently he had to hear a song twice and sometimes three times before he could sing it himself. It is most unfortunate that some collector did not come across him twenty years earlier. He probably could have sung a much larger proportion of the Island's extensive folk songs than is available now.

Fiddling and Instrumental Folk Music in Michigan

Paul M. Gifford

hile watching television one often sees a commercial advertising beer, instant lemonade mix, or breakfast sausage, which includes the happy faces of folks dancing to fiddle music. More than likely, the actors in the commercial are wearing overalls and straw hats and speaking in some cornball Southern accent. "Country!" says that fiddle in contemporary popular culture, whether it be in television commercials or in Nashville-originated commercial music. Like the cowboy hat, blue jeans, and other American symbols, the fiddle evokes a powerful image in the minds of the general American public. The fiddle, the Southern Appalachians, the Old West—these popular images are closely associated. Yet for all the popular association of the fiddle and square dance music with the South and, to a lesser extent, with the West, fiddling has played a role in community life throughout North America. In Michigan, as in other states, people have passed down a distinct tradition of fiddling and instrumental folk music.

The fiddle is the same instrument as the violin, but to define fiddling in terms of technique is not adequate, because one can find too many exceptions to the frequently made observation of the fiddler holding and playing his instrument in ways obsolete to the classical school. The individualistic technique of the fiddler is merely part of a larger characteristic of fiddling—its self-taught, aural, traditional nature.

Tradition preserves older tunes and carries with it a core repertoire. In Michigan, as elsewhere in North America, that core consists largely of tunes derived from Anglo-Celtic tradition. Such commonly played tunes as "Turkey in the Straw" and "Rickett's Hornpipe" identify the tradition as part of a larger North American tradition; other tunes, such as "Money Musk" and "Haste to the Wedding," place it within that of the northern United States and Canada. But fiddling, in general, is eclectic. American society is too ethnically and socially diverse to have permitted a distinct, self-sustaining, peasant musical culture. Yet fiddling, which has always synthesized music of diverse origins, has indeed maintained a close connection with rural society.

Michigan's fiddling tradition has been shaped by particular local developments. Settlement patterns, geography, and individuals themselves have each contributed to the formation of a reasonably unified style. This article attempts to identify and explain those developments, as well as the mechanisms by which diverse musical sources have become integrated into a regional repertoire and style.

The fiddler was an important figure in community life on the southern Michigan frontier. Many county histories published in the years following the nation's centennial mention their own county's first Fourth of July ball. This holiday allowed the new settlers to relax from their work in the woods and meet one another. Patriotic fervor mixed with social pleasures created the first sense of community in the new settlements. It is of no small significance that the fiddler at the first Independence Day balls in Ann Arbor was none other than the city's founder, speculator John Allen.[1] Like oil in the gears of a machine, Allen's fiddling eased relations among newcomers. It was as much a political as a musical act. By promoting community solidarity, it strengthened the foundations of the fragile settlement.

Within fifty years of the opening of the Erie Canal in 1824, nearly all the Lower Peninsula's tillable land was occupied. Most of the original settlers came from western New York and descended from colonial New England stock, as Gregory S. Rose has recently shown.[2] Most settlers in the Thumb and along the Lake Huron shore were of Canadian origin, probably from the St. Lawrence River region.[3] Dutch immigrants dominated the settlement of Ottawa County, and Germans predominated in some rural areas near Saginaw Bay. Irish and British families settled throughout the state, especially in the Canadian areas. Despite this variety, later immigrants accommodated and conformed to the musical dialect of the original Yankee settlers, which all but displaced the earlier French-Canadian musical style and established the particular regional identity the music has today.

Not until the early nineteenth century do sources allow us to form a picture of fiddling among the French in Michigan. All agree on the fondness of the habitants and voyageurs for dancing and merrymaking. At Mackinac Island[4] and Sault Ste. Marie it was customary for fur traders and their employees to sponsor dances during the annual idle period when traders hired their employees and waited to collect their trade goods. Despite the fact that the fiddler played "always the same tunes, and that is by jerks," he was obviously in great demand at these remote outposts during the slack summer season.[5] Among the French of the Detroit River region, one or two fiddlers usually provided the music for "reels" and contradances such as the French Four.[6] To this ensemble might be added a jew's harp *(bombarde)*[7]. Clarence M. Burton remarked that if those instruments were lacking, "flying feet might keep time to cleverly manipulated bone clappers *(castagnettes)*."[8] In the early 1820s, French-Canadian musicians played regularly at dances for Detroit's Anglo-American elite.[9] By that time, their repertoire must have been compatible with the requirements of the dances brought by the new settlers to Michigan. This Yankee flood overwhelmed the culture of the native French.

Certain distinctive elements of the early French-Canadian fiddling style, nevertheless, have survived. The strongest evidence comes from the playing of certain Indian and non-Indian fiddlers living in the eastern Upper Peninsula and in the northernmost Lower Peninsula. Their foot-tapping tends to be more pronounced than that of fiddlers elsewhere in the state. Although not the intricate double-footed tapping of the Quebecois fiddler, the prominence accorded it by fiddlers in this area might derive from an earlier style brought by voyageurs from Quebec. Also distinctive in the repertoire is the presence of a number of reels with a modal harmonic structure, for example, "Devil Shake the Half-Breed," in the dominant key of A major with G major as its secondary chord. This characteristic probably results from a strong, early Scottish influence.[10] "Devil Shake the Half-Breed" was probably derived from the well-known strathspey "Miss Drummond of Perth."[11] Finally, many fiddlers in this area play tunes with "tails."[12] Most dance tunes are divided into equal parts of four, eight, or sixteen measures. Dancers, especially square dancers and callers, are aided by this regularity. A "tail," however, adds from one-half to two measures or more to one of the tune's parts. Elsewhere, fiddlers with a poor sense of rhythm may play tunes like this occasionally. But the consistency with which these eastern Upper Peninsula musicians play this type of tune indicates that solo step-dancing has been more common in this area than in other parts of the state.

Virtually the only dances known in the new agricultural settlements were contradances, called "country dances."[13] All of these dances required tunes in a duple meter (2/4 or 6/8) and in a similar tempo. Music was provided, when possible, by a lead and a second fiddler. It was not long, however, before the number and types of dances increased and the textures of dance music grew more complex. The 1850s witnessed major changes: not only had cotillions (ancestors of modern square dances) replaced contradances as the dominant type of dance, but round dances, mainly the polka and schottische, came on the scene. With these new dances came new tunes and rhythms.

In 1852 Ingham Township, Ingham County, was introduced to the cotillion. That fall, James Swan played his fiddle for a dance at an Ingham Township tavern and taught the figures of cotillions to the dancers, who until then had only known country dances.[14] Swan's claim that he was the first person in Michigan west of Detroit to "call off" a cotillion is unlikely, but the fact that he could make the claim indicates that by 1852 a disparity had already developed between rural and urban fashions. Given the fluidity of the population, however, that disparity could not have been great.

Music for the new cotillions combined the desire to preserve the older jigs and reels used for contradances with the need to incorporate currently popular parlor and minstrel songs and operatic airs. Fiddler Henry P. Smith, of Schoolcraft, arranging music for the cotillions he was to teach the "noisy imps" and "little girls" at a local hotel in 1853, included all of these kinds of tunes.[15] This variety reflected musical influences on Smith and his community—the traveling circus and minstrel shows, parlor music played on the piano and guitar by young ladies of well-to-do families, and especially weekly "fiddling bees."[16] Schoolcraft and other communities included residents of varying levels of education and income and, hence, musical taste, but social distance between these levels was not as great as it would be later in the century.

Cosmopolitan tastes in dances and dance music spread rather

rapidly into rural Michigan. Just as New Yorkers looked to Europe for the latest fashions in clothing and dances, Detroiters looked to New York City. Allen Dodworth, New York's leading dancing master, introduced the polka to his pupils in 1845,[17] probably using as music "The Jenny Lind Polka," which he arranged and published in 1846.[18] By 1849 fiddler Henry P. Smith was familiar with the dance.[19] We can assume that the tune traveled with the dance, since it is still widely known by fiddlers in Michigan. The schottische, introduced in Dodworth's school in 1849, probably was being taught soon afterwards by Adam Couse, the leading dancing master and music dealer of Detroit. In 1854 Couse wrote "The Detroit Schottisch," which sold over 100,000 copies.[20] Fiddlers still play this "hit" at dances in Michigan, albeit in an abbreviated version whose origin is unknown to them.[21] Dances like the schottische reached outlying communities through the efforts of itinerant dancing masters such as J. K. Goodale of Detroit, who in 1857 rented a room in a hotel in Monroe and advertised that his dancing school would consist of a series of twelve lessons.[22]

By 1850, instrumentation in dance "bands," as they were known, was becoming more complex. With the growth of community military bands before and after the Civil War, wind instruments became more common. A phenomenon of the 1850s was the introduction to many communities of the "cotillion band," known at the end of the decade (as cotillions evolved into quadrilles) as the "quadrille band." The instrumentation of the quadrille band, which continued into the early years of the present century, varied. Its leader, however, was always a fiddler, who also called the figures of the quadrille. A second fiddler, generally playing an accompaniment to the melody in the form of one note on the downbeat and double stops on the upbeat, was customary. Three or four other instruments, commonly the clarinet, cornet, trombone, and bass viol, usually filled out the ensemble.

The career of Hull and Arnold's Quadrille Band, although better known and longer-lived than other such organizations, resembled those of other Michigan quadrille bands. In 1837, fiddler John Hull (1816–1884) came to Florence Township, St. Joseph County, from Sandy Hook, New York, and organized the band the following year. Its original members, all local farmers, included brothers Daniel Arnold, clarinet; Oliver P. Arnold, cornet; and Morris I. Arnold, trombone. The band played by note, much of its music being manuscript arrangements of published piano scores of popular songs. Hull, who called at the dances, also invented many new quadrilles. Traveling exclusively by wagon until 1852, the band developed a wide following; over the span of its fifty-year career, it played in an area encompassed by Cleveland, Fort Wayne, and Grand Rapids.[23] Hull and Arnold's Quadrille Band did not restrict itself to formal balls in county seats, however. Fiddlers from rural areas might go to a dance in a village hotel to hear the band play its arrangements of the latest tunes, as Henry P. Smith did in 1853, when he heard its "sweet music" at the hotel in Schoolcraft.[24]

These trends closely mirrored national and even international fashions in dance music, yet there were local variations that influenced the development of rural fiddling. Orange Fame ("Cub") Berdan, whom many Michigan fiddlers still hold in high regard, published collections of dance music in Adrian and Detroit in the 1870s and 1880s, many in the series *One Night in a Ball-room*. He was able to respond to the demand for music to dances such as the "ripple," devised by local dancing masters and only locally popular.[25] William Harmon, fiddler and leader of a popular four- and five-piece orchestra in Plymouth, bought music needed for locally devised dances such as the "Detroit" and the "dutchess" from Berdan's Detroit store for the winter season of 1892.[26] Other fiddlers learned Berdan's compositions by ear from note readers like Harmon. By the 1970s, oral versions of the first "change," or figure, of Berdan's "Pacific Quadrille" were still being played by Michigan fiddlers.

By the end of the century, leading quadrille bands like that of Hull and Arnold had evolved into fully professional "orchestras." Although such prominent groups as Charles Fischer's Orchestra of Kalamazoo and Theodore Finney's Orchestra of Detroit, the latter composed of blacks, were led by violinists and included quadrilles in their repertoires, these orchestras were dominated by wind instruments and a repertoire of round dances such as waltzes, schottisches, mazurkas, and two-steps.[27] As the Gilded Age reached towns in Michigan as small as Otsego, local elites demanded such touring orchestras at formal dances.[28] Eventually, these professional orchestras evolved into the "big bands" common at mid-twentieth century in hotel ballrooms and fraternal-order dinner-dances. Such was one development of nineteenth-century fiddling in Michigan.

Although dance music heard at urban and rural hotels carried prestige, hotel dances lost favor as the century wore on. Dancing had always been opposed by certain religious segments. In some areas, especially in heavily Dutch Ottawa County, that segment was a majority.[29] Some of the opposition resulted from the introduction of new dances, like the waltz in the 1870s.[30] A few held the fiddle, because of its associations, to be the "favorite instrument of the Devil."[31] But public dances at hotels appear to have incurred the greatest wrath. The combination of liquor and young men led to drunkenness; jealousy over young women led to fights; and sometimes the fights ended in murder. At the turn of the century, house parties, which had always been widespread, carried more respectability.[32]

Public and domestic traditions of dance music followed different lines of development, yet inevitably there was much overlap. Music families hosted regular dancing parties in their homes or barns, as the Bovays of Chippewa Township, Mecosta County, did about 1900.[33] When Jasper Bisbee, his wife and two sons played for dances at a hall he owned near their home in Paris,[34] both domestic and public traditions came into play. At the turn of the century, agricultural towns with one to two thousand people supported touring dance orchestras which mimicked and probably rivaled any in New York City. Such influences did affect musical fashions on the farms. Still, older dances and dance music held sway at house parties outside those towns. Stewart Carmichael recalls, for example, that around 1920 people still danced the Virginia Reel, but strictly at house parties.[35] The Money Musk, Opera Reel, and Irish Trot were popular dances at the West Crockery Township Grange Hall (Ottawa County), where Claus Borchers played his dulcimer with a fiddler in 1919.[36] Dancers in towns by that time had long abandoned contradances, although quadrilles, now generally called square dances, remained popular.

Related to the dichotomy between public and domestic traditions is the dance music of communities dominated by nineteenth-century immigrants from Europe. In most areas, immigrants were probably exposed to native dances soon after their arrival. At bowery dances in Ludington in the 1880s, which were accompanied by one or two fiddles and an organ playing tunes such as "Money Musk" and "Turkey in the Straw," some girls came wearing Scandinavian national costumes.[37] Commenting on dances in Iron River in the 1890s, Lewis C. Reimann remarked that public dances such as these brought "our mixed nationalities into common touch and helped to unite us in a feeling of belonging in the community."[38]

Most immigrant communities, even if they dominated several

contiguous townships, did not close themselves off to the Anglo-Americans around them. Immigrant musicians and their children learned square dance tunes. Peter Seba recalled that when German immigrants of his father's generation got together at parties in rural Ravenna about 1890, they would have a keg of beer, sing, and dance to waltzes like "O du lieber Augustin" played by a violin. But Seba and other second- and third-generation German-Americans living near him adopted the Anglo-American dulcimer, and, with the fiddle, were playing at square dances in barns and community halls before the turn of the century. Although they retained German waltzes, by 1980 they did not identify them as German.[39] A similar process occurred with the Danes in Montcalm County and the Poles in the Thumb.

Although the general trend has been immigrants accommodating to a locally existing repertoire, some native-born, "non-ethnic" fiddlers have learned the odd traditional Swedish schottische or Polish oberek. The exceptions to this musical assimilation have been in the western Upper Peninsula, dominated by Finns but including myriad other nationalities, and to a lesser extent in overwhelmingly Polish Presque Isle County, where immigrants settled on virgin territory ignored by native-born settlers. Consequently, traditional fiddlers and accordionists in these areas, while retaining Finnish and Polish dance tunes into the second and third generations, generally have a meager repertoire of square dance tunes.

Another difference in the public and domestic traditions has been in instrumental combinations. At house parties these combinations tended to be simpler than those at hotel and other public dances. The solo fiddler, common during the pioneer era, was rare thereafter.[40] A typical ensemble consisted of two fiddlers, one playing the melody and the other playing "second," as was customary in Columbia Township, Jackson County, and, as late as 1920, in Trowbridge Township, Allegan County.[41] The bass viol, used earlier in the nineteenth century to accompany congregational singing, frequently was added to the two fiddles. Volney Gunning bowed his bass with two fiddlers and called the dances at house parties around Plymouth ten or twenty times each winter in the early 1880s.[42] A cello might substitute for the bass viol.[43]

The [hammered] dulcimer was often used to accompany the fiddle. Such a combination provided the usual music at inns in northern Oakland County in the 1850s and 1860s.[44] In the 1860s dulcimer makers such as William Thurston of Farmington,

Mortimer DeLano of Oxford, Ezra Durand and William Vogel of Chelsea, and Jarvis Stocking of Otisco, were filling the demand for the instrument. Until about 1900, in much of central and western Michigan, it appears to have been the leading accompanying instrument. This instrument, currently undergoing a large revival, seems to have had greater popularity in Michigan than in other states.

The guitar and five-string banjo enjoyed great popularity between 1880 and 1920. Minstrel shows undoubtedly were greatly responsible for the introduction of the banjo to Michigan. The earliest references to its use that I have found indicate that players used banjo to accompany songs.[45] Indeed, one banjoist, Ed Klingen (born about 1870) of Mancelona, referred to his playing style as the "nigger rap."[46] By the turn of the century the banjo was often used to accompany the fiddle. The guitar, which like the piano and harp had been a genteel, lady's instrument earlier in the century, gained steel strings and became a man's instrument. It might be added to the earlier ensembles such as lead and second fiddle, the instrumentation of the group which plays for the homecoming party in Della Lutes's *Home Grown*.[47] Both five-string banjo and guitar were replaced in popularity in the 1910s and 1920s by the tenor banjo.

The accordion and harmonica, or "mouth organ" as it is still generally known in rural areas, had considerable appeal at the turn of the century. Even more than the dulcimer, banjo, and guitar, both free-reed instruments were confined to informal situations. Accordion and banjo accompanied stag dances at the hotel in Sharon about 1905 on the days the lumberjacks received their pay.[48] Volney Gunning played both the bass viol and the accordion, but he used the latter instrument strictly for informal playing, as he did with members of his family in 1883.[49] The portable and versatile mouth organ might appear anywhere. It could substitute for, yet not replace, a fiddle at a lumber camp stag dance, or it could add to the fiddler's music at a house party.[50]

Reed organs appeared everywhere in the 1880s. Possessing a certain religious and middle-class respectability, the instrument became the first to enter many homes. One writer believed that it "finally broke the taboo" against musical instruments.[51] Many families purchased reed organs primarily as instruments to accompany the fiddle. The girls of the family might take a few lessons on it, then learn to "chord" by ear.[52] The mass introduction of the reed organ in some ways was revolutionary. Belonging to an older, domestic tradition, it was acceptable for women to play. Nevertheless, it also adapted well to the demands of the oral dance-music tradition. Women now had a secure place as dance musicians,[53] although men still dominated the activity.

Older fiddlers alive today grew up in a musical environment undergoing rapid change. This change, of course, was part of larger changes in society. Between 1910 and 1920 the balance of population in Michigan, and that of the United States as well, shifted from the farms to the cities. Technological change led to many unforeseen developments. Pianos replaced reed organs in popularity, bringing with them a secular repertoire of Tin Pan Alley hits. In the 1910s phonographs introduced new music to accompany first the one-step and then the fox trot, more complex than the marches and other tunes used for the two-step, which had entered rural Michigan about 1900. Automobiles allowed farmers to ride into towns more easily, even if they still relied on sleighs in the winter. This development both facilitated the attendance of rural people at dances in towns and lessened their need for homemade entertainment. By 1920 house parties were a thing of the past in some neighborhoods,[54] although they lingered on until the 1940s in other places. What attracted popular attention in the 1920s was not what went on in rural areas, however, but what was happening in the cities. And in urban ballrooms dance bands were playing jazz for a succession of dance fads.

Ironically, the popular hero who bore much responsibility for the changes in society, both indirectly and directly, was a fiddler who detested these changes. Henry Ford, who had played "Sally Waters" and other tunes as a young man,[55] began a campaign of sorts in 1925 to "replace the jazz dances popular in the cities with the more graceful steps" of the square dance and other dances popular in the 1880s.[56] Ford's interest in dancing and fiddling had been rekindled by a visit with Thomas A. Edison to the home of fiddler Jep Bisbee of Paris, Michigan, in the summer of 1923. Thrilled by Bisbee's music, the manufacturer that winter hosted a party and sleigh ride at his brother-in-law's home in Traverse City with Bisbee and his wife providing the music for dancing.[57] Within two years, Ford hired a permanent dancing master, Benjamin B. Lovett, and an orchestra consisting of violin, dulcimer, cimbalom, and sousaphone. Newspapers around the country publicized Ford's new activity extensively. Fiddlers from Michigan, such as Seymour Thompson of Victory, Billy Nolan of Sugar Island, Henry Thorne of Sault Ste. Marie, and George Pariseau of Bad Axe, played for him.

The highly publicized visit of Mellie Dunham of Norway, Maine, led to a spate of fiddling contests in the Midwest, upper South, and Northeast. This flurry of activity died down after 1926. Until Ford's death, Lovett and the Ford Orchestra continued to play for dances and classes at Detroit-area schools, private Ford functions, Greenfield Village, and the Michigan State Fair.[58]

Ford's interest in old-fashioned dancing had several favorable results in Michigan. At least ten regional fiddling contests were held on short notice in different cities in the state, sponsored independently by fraternal orders, theaters, and newspapers. The state championship was held in Detroit on January 19, 1926. Five thousand people, including Ford and judge Mischa Elman, watched Jep Bisbee win with his renditions of "Money Musk" and "Opera Reel."[59] Workers in the Ford Music Department copied down tunes and probably dance calls from fiddlers.[60] Presumably, Lovett incorporated some of the dances, like the Scotch Reel and the French Four, into his manual, *Good Morning*, and the Ford Orchestra played tunes which had been learned from the visitors. Edison produced three records by Bisbee, the earliest-born American fiddler known to record. One preserves an example of simultaneous calling and fiddling, which had generally disappeared by 1900.[61] Other fiddlers went to commercial studios to make recordings. Frank Woods of Detroit, runner-up in the state contest, went to the Okeh studios in New York, and George Pariseau's six-piece family orchestra recorded several sides for Gennett.[62] Pariseau's orchestra also went regularly from Bad Axe to Detroit to play at the Grande Ballroom for square dances one night a week and for fox trots twice a week.[63] Even the aged Bisbee was touring western Michigan with an "up-to-date" nine-piece fox trot orchestra.[64]

The verdict was clear. People would still dance square dances. They preferred, however, to dance fox trots to the latest hits played by a "jazz orchestra." Fiddles started to take a back seat to saxophones in the 1920s. In small-town dance halls, such as Grange halls, Oddfellows halls, and the like, the typical ensemble consisted of four or five pieces , generally violin, saxophone, piano, and drums; tenor banjo, trumpet, or trombone might be added. Except for the saxophone, which replaced the earlier clarinet, none of the instruments were new to dance orchestras. What was new was that the fiddle now started to fade from many of them. Like earlier ensembles, dance orchestras of the 1920s and 1930s assimilated new dances and tunes, but now the result was that the saxophonist tended to lead on the round dances (waltzes, two-steps, and fox trots), and those were the dances which predominated. Yet square dances demanded a fiddle, and young fiddlers still had many occasions to play, both at dance halls and at house parties.

Traditional dances with square dances as a regular feature have gradually declined since the 1930s. In some areas fiddlers and other musicians have died, leaving no one to take their places. In other areas, however, dances are as healthy as ever. At the Barnard Grange near Charlevoix, tenor banjoist and fiddler Jasper Warner leads several other musicians for regular dances on holidays. All ages attend and different Grange members take turns calling. Similar in the range of attendance are dances at halls in Dimondale and Onondaga where the Wranglers, a six-piece group headed by fiddler Bud Sebastian and caller Guy Lincoln, play regularly. Frank Matteson's orchestra (Fig. 1) was still playing for dances in Trufant every other week at the time of his death, at the age of 92, in 1986. Other fiddlers play at occasional dances, often called "senior citizen" dances.

The main new developments since the 1930s have been country-western music, polka bands, and rock-and-roll. Although it grew partly out of a southern dance musical tradition and has used the fiddle extensively, country-western is essentially a vocal genre. Its influence was strongest about 1940, when radio shows, especially the "National Barn Dance" on WLS in Chicago, broadcast the music. The impact of country-western on Michigan fiddlers has been mainly in repertoire rather than in style. Certain songs with a danceable two-step beat, like "Your Cheatin' Heart" and "Honky Tonky Angel," or waltzes, such as "Waltz Across Texas" and "Kentucky Waltz," have been added with little difficulty. But country-western appears to have had much less influence in Michigan than, for example, in Canada, where fiddlers who grew up in the 1940s and 1950s can routinely improvise accompaniments to a singer.

Polka music, typified by that of Frankie Yankovic, added "Blue Skirt Waltz" and music for the new, faster polkas such as "Helena Polka," "Clarinet Polka," and "Beer Barrel Polka." These tunes, despite their Czech, Slovene, and Polish origins, were readily adopted by Michigan fiddlers because their ABAC form was similar to those of nineteenth-century quadrilles and schottisches already in their repertoires. Finally, rock-and-roll, immensely popular since the 1950s, has made virtually no headway into the repertoire. Rock-and-roll, instead, has drawn the universal ire of traditional fiddlers. It is

Figure 1. Frank Matteson, traditional fiddler and 1985 Michigan Award recipient.

199

the rare square dance band, like the Wranglers, that has an electric guitar player who can play enough boogie to satisfy those fifty and under.

The repertoire of the Michigan fiddler today is an eclectic mix of tunes comprising virtually the entire history of popular and folk music in the northern United States. At the core are jigs and reels of eighteenth-century British derivation, which, after all, are the *raison d'etre* of fiddling. These tunes may be well known, such as "Irish Washerwoman," or they may be totally obscure, like "Mother, O Mother, My Toes Are Sore From Dancing So Long on Your Sandy Floor" and countless nameless tunes. Minstrelsy added "Oh Dem Golden Slippers," "Climbin' Up the Golden Stairs," and other tunes to the square dance repertoire. Nineteenth-century schottisches, polkas, and quadrilles, such as those in Berdan's collections and those in *Gems of the Ballroom*,[65] form a substantial part. Others are waltzes from the late nineteenth century like "Over the Waves" and "After the Ball"; marches like "Repasz Band"; and ragtime-era two-steps like "Whistling Rufus" and "Red Wing." Later Tin Pan Alley waltzes and fox trots, such as "Darktown Strutters' Ball" and "Five Foot Two" are a large staple. Besides the country-western and polka tunes, fairly recent pop hits like "Paper Roses" and "Somewhere My Love" appear occasionally.

The repertoire listed here is, of course, a generalization. Since 1970 I have met and heard fiddlers who played virtually nothing but jigs and reels and a few waltzes; however, they were mostly men born in the 1880s whose active playing years were before 1920. Even fiddlers who learned most of their tunes from their fathers and have not played at dances to any extent have learned at least a few new fox trots, waltzes, or polkas. Some regional differences are worthy of mention. Canadian fiddle tunes, such as "St. Anne's Reel" and "Little Burnt Potato" are known in those parts of the state—mainly the Thumb and the eastern Upper Peninsula—that lie within the range of Canadian radio stations which broadcast the influential fiddling of Don Messer in the 1940s and 1950s.[66] Another regional variation is the presence of Polish tunes in the repertoire of some fiddlers in the Thumb and northern Lower Peninsula. But enough consistency exists so that it is possible to speak of a common repertoire and, hence, style in Michigan.

This commonality, especially of old, nameless square dance tunes, was largely unknown to the fiddlers and other musicians who, in 1976, began attending "jamborees" in different locations around the state that were held under the aegis of the Michigan Fiddlers Association. Many had learned a body of tunes, many or most lacking names, from their fathers or other relatives and assumed, since they had never heard them on records, radio, or television, that no one else knew them. Often that was true. Sometimes a tune had undergone enough permutation orally that it was no longer recognizable to someone who knew another version of that tune. But eventually fiddlers recognized other versions. They also learned or relearned tunes they had heard before but had forgotten or never practiced. Aided immensely by the cassette tape recorder, old tunes were saved from oblivion. This process was just one of the benefits of the jamborees.

The major development in fiddling and traditional instrumental folk music in the last twenty years has been the growth of new public forums for the music. The Original Dulcimer Players Club was organized by several elderly players at Barryton in 1963. Meetings, held twice a year, were open to the public and attracted fiddlers and other musicians. The organization has sponsored a "Funfest" at Evart since 1973, which annually draws thousands of visitors. The Michigan Fiddlers Association grew out of a series of jamborees, consisting of an afternoon program featuring individual fiddlers and an evening dance, which began in 1976 with a core of members from the Original Dulcimer Players Club. Since 1978 two organizations have sponsored jamborees in many towns around the state: the Original Michigan Fiddlers Association[67] and the Michigan Fiddlers Association. The Port Huron Museum of Arts and History also holds regular "rap 'n' jam sessions." These events, although they probably do not have the public appeal of contests, which have not been too successful in the state[69], nevertheless draw faithful crowds. Because of their noncompetitive nature, the jamborees seem to foster more harmony among musicians than contests.

These trends portend well for the future of the tradition. Young people are learning tunes from people their grandfather's age. Even if three-piece electrified bands with repertoires of rock, country, and polka standards are now filling most of the local demand for dance music in bars and at weddings, young fiddlers and their friends are preserving and adding something to the musical tradition for the future.

1. O. W. Stephenson, *Ann Arbor: The First Hundred Years* (Ann Arbor: Chamber of Commerce, 1927), 75–76.
2. Gregory S. Rose, "South Central Michigan Yankees," *Michigan History* 70 (March-April 1986): 32–39.
3. John C. Hudson, "Cultural Geography and the Upper Great Lakes Region," *Journal of Cultural Geography* 5 (Fall-Winter 1984): 25–31.
4. *The Autobiography of Gurdon Saltonstall Hubbard* (Chicago: Lakeside Press, 1911), 20.
5. William Johnston, "Letters on the Fur Trade 1833," *Michigan Pioneer and Historical Collections* 37 (1909, 1910): 139 (hereafter cited as MPHC).
6. Friend Palmer, *Early Days in Detroit* (Detroit: Hunt & June, 1906), 374; Charles Lanman, *Adventures in the Wilds of the United States and British American Provinces* (Philadelphia: John W. Moore, 1856), 1:140.
7. Clarence M. Burton, "Amusements in Detroit in Colonial Days," *MPHC* 38 (1912): 333. The *bombarde* was certainly known to the voyageurs of the previous century. Archeologists have excavated scores of them in the Straits of Mackinac region, merchants having brought them there as trade goods.
8. Ibid., 333 (author's translation, based on contemporary Quebecois usage).
9. In card index (source not specified), Burton Historical Collection, Detroit Public Library, there is a reference to a ball at Woodworth's Hotel in 1821 sponsored by the military officers of Detroit, the musicians for which were Pierre Griffard, Joseph Laurence [sic], and Henry Hanson. The instruments that this trio played might be the "violin and jewsharp or clarinet" which, according to a newspaper article published sixty years later and kept in the Frank Woodford Scrapbooks in the same repository, accompanied Detroit Bar Association dances at Woodworth's Hotel.
10. A good example of early Scottish influence is shown by Archibald Lyons, a trapper on the Tittabawassee River who was married to a "French half-breed." Probably of Scottish origin, as his name indicates, he died about 1819 while skating down the river to play for a "dancing party" in Saginaw. *History of Saginaw County, Michigan* (Chicago: Chapman, 1881), 143.
11. "Devil Shake the Half-Breed" as played by the late Bill Cameron of Brimley and by Elmer House of Sault Ste. Marie.
12. Pete Keller of Cross Village uses this term to describe this phenomenon. This characteristic can be heard regularly in Quebecois fiddling and the fiddling of the Metis in Manitoba.
13. The best known, or at least the most frequently mentioned in later sources, was the Money Musk. Others were French Four, Scotch Reel or Eight-hand Reel, and the Opera Reel. Henry P. Smith's dance call book, in the Stanley Barney Smith Family Papers, University Archives and Regional History Collections, Western Michigan University, includes Lady Washington's Reel, Virginia Reel, Hull's Victory, Speed the Plow, and Irish Trot. The Yankee settlers, like the French, also indulged in "jigging," a strenuous activity which one couple would begin, only to be "cut out" by other couples and individuals. The jig would stop only when the musician quit playing. See Albert Baxter, *History of Grand Rapids, Michigan* (New York: Munsell, 1891), 565–66; *History of Hillsdale County, Michigan* (Philadelphia: Everts & Abbott, 1879), 145; and *History of Washtenaw County, Michigan* (Chicago: Chapman, 1881), 139.
14. Mrs. Franc L. Adams, *Pioneer History of Ingham County* (Lansing: Wynkoop Hallenbeck Crawford, 1923), 1:405, 408.
15. Book containing dance calls, Stanley Barney Smith Family Papers, University Archives and Regional History Collections, Western Michigan University.
16. Diaries, 12 September 1848; 20 December 1848; 28–29 August 1849; 18 August 1852; 6 January 1853; 15 January 1853; Henry Parker Smith Papers, Michigan Historical Collections, Bentley Historical Library, University of Michigan (hereafter cited as Smith Diaries).
17. Allen Dodworth, *Dancing and Its Relations to Education and Social Life* (New York: Harper, 1885), 52.
18. Allen Dodworth, arranger, *The Jenny Lind Polka: as Played by Dodworth's Cornet Band* (New York: Firth, Pond, 1846).
19. Smith Diaries, 26 March 1849.
20. Farmer, *History of Detroit*, 1:356.
21. Much of the rest of the country, however, knows "The Detroit Schottisch" as "Flop-Eared Mule," played as a reel.
22. John M. Bulkley, *History of Monroe County, Michigan* (Chicago: Lewis, 1913), 1:336.
23. "Hull and Arnold Quadrille Band One of First of Kind in Country," *Kalamazoo Gazette*, 17 September 1939; *The One Hundredth Anniversary of Constantine, 1828–1928* (Constantine,

Mich.: Advertiser Record, n.d.), unpaginated.

24. Smith Diaries, 1 July 1853.

25. O. F. Berdan, *Berdan's Medley: Galop and Telephone, Ripple, Heel and Toe Polka* (Philadelphia: T. A. Bacher, printer, 1880). Benjamin Lovett and Henry Ford's Orchestra revived the "ripple" in 1924, a dance for which the Massachusetts dancing master had trouble finding the steps.

26. Volney A. Gunning Diaries, 12 April 1892; dance ticket in 1892 diary. I wish to thank Elmer and Edson Whipple for their generosity in allowing me access to these very useful diaries.

27. "Music Aplenty," *Kalamazoo Telegraph*, 12 October 1901; Tom Shea, "Finney's Orchestra," *Newsletter of the Ragtime Society* 4 (July-August 1965): 35; W. Scott Munn, *The Only Eaton Rapids on Earth: The Pioneer History of Eaton Rapids and Hamlin Township, with Reminiscences* (Ann Arbor: Edwards Bros., n.d.), 284, 287.

28. Archie P. Nevins and Dorothy Dalrymple, *As It Was in Otsego* (Otsego, Mich.: Bicentennial Committee, 1975), 21.

29. The staunchly Calvinist Seceders there never countenanced dances or dance music. Although there have been fiddlers and dulcimer players of Dutch descent, I have not found any dance tunes of probable Dutch origin in western Michigan.

30. J. S. Morton, *Reminiscences of the Lower St. Joseph River Valley* (Benton Harbor: Federation of Women's Clubs, n.d.), 46. Mrs. Martha Gray, in "Reminiscences of Grand Traverse Region," *MPHC* 38 (1912): 308-9, attributes Methodist camp meetings to this change in attitudes.

31. Eugene Davenport, *Timberland Times* (Urbana: University of Illinois Press, 1950), 193. This association, frequently mentioned by writers referring to attitudes in the upper South, seems not to have been widely held in Michigan, since this is the only such Michigan reference I have been able to find.

32. Daniel Abbey, *Reminiscences* (Corunna, Mich.: Louis N. Sheardy, 1903), 116-19; *The History of Iosco County, Michigan* (East Tawas, Mich.: Iosco County Historical Society, n.d.), 132; Prosper G. Bernard, *Years Gone By: An Illustrated Account of Life in Prairieville, Barry, Hope and Orangeville Townships of Barry County, Michigan in the 19th and Early 20th Centuries* (N.p.: 1967), 54-55.

33. Stewart Carmichael, interview with author at Evart, Mich., 19 July 1986.

34. "Fame for a Fiddler," *Detroit News*, 5 January 1926.

35. Carmichael interview, 19 July 1986.

36. Claus Borchers, interview with author at Spring Lake, Michigan, 22 September 1985.

37. Luman W. Goodenough, *Lumber, Lath and Shingles* (Detroit: Daniel W. Goodenough, 1954), 115.

38. Lewis C. Reimann, *Between the Iron and the Pine: A Biography of a Pioneer Family and a Pioneer Town* (Ann Arbor: Edwards Bros., 1951), 100f. Differences in dances, after all, were not as great as one might imagine. Both North Americans and northern and western Europeans shared variations of the waltz, polka, schottische, varsovienne, and even quadrille.

39. Peter Seba, interview with author at Coopersville, Michigan, 4 September 1981; Albert Hober, interview with author at Pewamo, Michigan, 28 September 1980.

40. However, as late as the 1930s, Bill Bigford was playing by himself at house parties around Marion and getting paid for it.

41. E. W. Kiebler, *Contributions to the History of Columbia Township, Jackson County, Michigan* (Lansing: E. W. Kiebler, 1957), 35; Leslie Raber, interview with author, Evart, Michigan, 19 July 1986.

42. Gunning Diaries, 1881, 1882, 1883, passim.

43. A photograph of an 1890s trio consisting of violin, guitar, and cello is in *Vernon: Yesterday and Today* (Vernon, Mich.: Historical Committee of the Vernon Area Centennial Corp., 1971), 10.

44. "Reminiscences of Mortimer A. Leggett," *MPHC* 35 (1907): 689f.

45. Gunning Diaries, 30 March 1881; Archie Barnes, oral history for Okemos history project, 1965, describes it being used with two guitars in 1892 to accompany "comic songs"; Camille Ferri-Pisani, *Lettres sur les Etats-Unis d'Amerique* (Paris: Hachette, 1862), 251, describes, however, a black steward playing one for a dance on a Lake Huron steamer in 1861.

46. Robert Spinner, telephone conversation with author, 6 January 1986. Spinner says he played both accompaniment and melody (one tune being "Shortenin' Bread") in a frailing style.

47. Della T. Lutes, *Home Grown* (Boston: Little, Brown, 1937), 253.

48. Rex J. Dye, *Lumber Camp Life in Michigan* (Hicksville, N.Y.: Exposition Press, 1975), 43.

49. Gunning Diaries, 7 June 1883.

50. John W. Fitzmaurice, *The Shanty Boy; or Life in a Lumbercamp* (1889; reprint, Upper Saddle River, N.J.: Literature House/Gregg Press, 1970), 222.
51. *Timberland Times*, 193.
52. Jennie O'Henley Minnick, "Rapson: Area Development Through More Than a Century," in *A Wind Gone Down: Fire and Ice* (Lansing: Michigan History Division, 1978), 55.
53. Although women fiddlers were rare, they did play at dances occasionally, such as those in Kalamazoo during the winter of 1834–1835 "to the inspiring tones of the Whitlock fiddles, none the less inspiring because two of them were scraped by rosy girls." *History of Kalamazoo County, Michigan* (Philadelphia: Everts & Abbott, 1880), 217.
54. Mary Lockwood Boening, *Webberville Yesterday and Today* (Fowlerville, Mich.: Rudnicki, 1970), 81.
55. Margaret Ford Ruddiman, "Memories of My Brother Henry Ford," *Michigan History* 37 (September 1953): 261. I mention "Sally Waters" partly because it was a widespread couple dance accompanied by a tune of the same name. This dance may not be known widely outside of Michigan.
56. *Detroit Free Press*, 2 July 1925.
57. "Ford Kicks His Heels," *Detroit News*, 5 January 1924.
58. The best account of this phenomenon is in David L. Lewis, *The Public Image of Henry Ford: An American Folk Hero and His Company* (Detroit: Wayne State University Press, 1976), 226–28.
59. "Jep Saws His Way to Victory," *Detroit News*, 20 January 1926.
60. Henry Ford, in collaboration with Samuel Crowther, *Today and Tomorrow* (Garden City, N.Y.: Doubleday, Page, 1926), 223. Manuscripts of this unusually early "field" collecting have unfortunately become lost.
61. Bisbee was born 29 July 1843 in Allegany County, New York, and came to Michigan in 1858; "Opera Reel" (Edison 51278, 9264-A) has his calling. The second earliest-born fiddler known to have made recordings was also a Michigander, "Col." John A. Pattee, born 5 June 1844 in Huron Township, Wayne County. Leader of a vaudeville troupe called the "Old Soldier Fiddlers," Pattee recorded two sides for Columbia in 1924, the year of his death.
62. I am grateful to Guthrie Meade for this information.
63. Ford Pariseau, telephone conversation with the author, February 1985. See also "Thumbnail Sketch: The Pariseau Family," *Houseparty* 3 (September 1985): 2–5.
64. Bisbee to Henry Ford, 2 March 1924, Correspondence Series, Acc. 572, Box 7, Archives and Library, The Edison Institute.
65. D. S. McCosh et al., *Gems of the Ballroom* (Chicago: E. T. Root, n.d.). This series of dance music was arranged in parts for dance orchestras of varying sizes and sold through Sears & Roebuck. Its influence was strong in an area stretching at least from New York State to Nebraska.
66. The repertoire of the British settlers from Ontario, who were the dominant settlers in these areas, was probably not too different from that of the Yankee settlers, since there had been earlier migration from New York and New England into Ontario. The main noticeable difference would be the greater Irish and Scottish influence in the Canadian tradition. Messer popularized many new jigs and reels not known to the original Canadian settlers in Michigan.
67. A good profile of this organization and an excellent source for information about contemporary Michigan fiddlers is in Original Michigan Fiddlers Association, *Old Time Music & Dances of Yester-year* (N.p.: The Original Michigan Fiddlers Association, 1986).
68. Fiddling contests have been held sporadically since the 1920s, including some at Ubly in the late 1960s, and at Hastings, East Lansing, New Boston, and elsewhere, within the last ten years.

Reading the "Newspaper Dress": An Exposé of Art Moilanen's Musical Tradition

James Leary

t was a pristine July Saturday, 1983, at the Aura Town Hall near L'Anse, Michigan. More than one hundred patrons of the annual "Aura Fiddler's Jamboree"—most of them second, third, even fourth generation Finnish-Americans—crowded into chairs or stood jostling in aisles, waiting, heads cocked toward a small stage. Art Moilanen adjusted his microphone, hitched up his piano accordion, and, with brief words of introduction and a nod to guitarist Tom Hiltanen, began the "Newspaper Dress." A young lady, clad in "comic strips from her knees to her hips," collided with a careless smoker, and her gown—"front page, sports section, and all"—was reduced to ashes in 3/4 time. After final notes and applause, Art reckoned he was bound for Finland to present "traditional immigrant music" to a national folk festival.

I wondered if the festival's organizers would applaud "Newspaper Dress" with comparable enthusiasm; it was, after all, neither an old folk dance like "Kiikuri Kaakuri," nor an echo of the Kalevala, but an English language parody of Pee Wee King and Redd Stewart's late 1940s country music classic, "Tennessee Waltz." Perhaps Art had similar misgivings. Later that afternoon he told me that the invitation from Finland had been unexpected, even intimidating: "I don't quite know what they want me to do." Yet knowing "what they want me to do" had been no trouble in Aura on Art's home ground.

My speculation and Art's uneasiness owed plenty, I believe, to contradictory meanings implicit in the phrase "traditional immigrant music." "Tradition" can suggest a relatively fixed body of venerable cultural traits or lore transmitted and enacted by succeeding generations of folk. "Immigrant," invariably referring to recent arrivals in a new country, can also stress the continuities those people maintain with their homeland. It follows that "traditional immigrant music" can mean the oldtime music of newcomers who, despite displacement, remain practitioners of "foreign" ways. Self-described "folk festivals" generally, and "national" ones particularly, promote this interpretation—an interpretation that would exclude songs like "Newspaper Dress."

On the other hand, "tradition" can describe not static traits but a dynamic process, governed by essentially conservative yet adaptable rules, through which a people confront impinging historical and cultural forces—discarding, retaining, or extending certain parts of their own past while simultaneously resisting, acquiring, reinterpreting, or synthesizing aspects of the new. "Immigrant" can likewise connote not thoroughgoing attempts to sustain old world existence, but efforts to formulate an evolving identity that might combine—in the United States, for example—ethnic, American, regional, class, and occupational elements. Accordingly, "traditional immigrant music" can mean the contemporary music of immigrants and their offspring who at once draw upon their past and embrace their present. Art Moilanen's experience exemplifies this latter interpretation—an interpretation that will be illustrated in the paragraphs to come by a thorough reading of the musical tradition that produced "Newspaper Dress."

From the 1880s through the first two decades of the twentieth century, more than 300,000 Finns emigrated to the United States where jobs could be found chiefly in mills, mines, factories, and fisheries. Roughly half were drawn to the western Great Lakes region, more particularly to the mines of Michigan's "Copper Country" and of Minnesota's Mesabi Iron Range.[1] Here men worked underground, on ore docks jutting into Lake Superior, or on ore boats bound for smelting plants; women—few at first, but approaching parity with the number of men by the early twentieth century—found employment as domestic servants or in factories. Numerous religious, temperance, self-help, and socialist organizations were formed by newcomers to provide assistance and a sense of cultural cohesion.

Art Moilanen's parents were among the newcomers. Unskilled laborers hailing from the northern agrarian province of Oulu, they arrived independently, met, and married in Michigan's "Copper Country." In July 1913 the Western Federation of Miners called a strike against Upper Michigan's mining companies for a shorter workday, higher wages, and improved working conditions. The strike, in which Finns participated energetically, was bitter, violent, and unsuccessful. In the spring of 1914 many union families sought industrial employment elsewhere, or took up homesteading on land cut over by large scale logging companies. The Moilanens joined a cluster of Finns in the brush near Mass City, Michigan, a tiny hamlet in the Upper Peninsula's Ontonagon County, midway between Houghton-Hancock and Bruce Crossing. The family eked out a marginal existence as "stump farmers," but the senior Moilanen supplemented his income by felling second growth timber and running a small sawmill.

Art was born in 1916. Besides assisting with farm chores, he recalls, "I grew up with sawdust in my ears." Unlike some of his second generation neighbors who sought work in distant mines or in Detroit's auto plants, Art did not leave home after high school.[2] Like his father, he worked in the woods, except for a four and a half year stretch in the military during World War II, and eventually formed his own logging crew to cut pulpwood for the region's papermill at White Pine. In 1965, Art figured

> I was getting too old to do much logging anymore, so I started up the tavern in Rousseau [east of Mass]. It turned out to be such a fantastic place that—I had dancing three, four nights a week, sometimes all day and night long—it was just packed all the time. Then I retired at the age of fifty-five. I was five years retired.[3]

In 1977, at the age of sixty, Moilanen purchased "Art's Bar" in Mass City, along with an adjacent motel catering to highway maintenance crews, hunters, and snowmobilers. He and his wife Millie managed the two establishments until early 1983 when Art sold out to retire a second time.

Despite retirement, Art continues, as he has for more than half a century, to play dance music: "Music has always been great in my life." And just as the broad outlines of Art's life intersect with the experiences of those second generation Finnish-Americans who have remained in upper Michigan, so also does his music exemplify the workings of particular historical and cultural forces.

In late nineteenth- and early twentieth-century Finland, rural or folk or traditional music began to evolve in a rapid fashion that paralleled the sweeping developments encapsulated above. Non-stanzaic epic songs and ballads were gradually supplanted by "romantic waltz songs" and "humorous couplets" more attuned, in both form and content, to changing times.[4] Traditional reliance on the zither-like "kantele" and on the violin waned as the diatonic button accordion—introduced to Finland in the 1870s with the aid of itinerant Italian musicians—became "the most popular folk instrument." The Italian mandolin and, eventually, the Afro-American tenor banjo were likewise widely accepted. Old village ring dances, long integral to wedding rituals, likewise gave way in the late nineteenth century to the pan-European popularity of couple dances and their accompanying melodies: waltzes, schottisches, and polkas. Increased literacy led to the composition of new songs and to their preservation through handwritten songbooks.

With the dislocation of traditional rural society, both the context of music and the role of its performers altered. Secular halls abounded in rural communities and among the urban proletariat by the turn of the century, effectively replacing the home and yard as the locale for dancing to music. Professional musicians and singers emerged. Their performances—most frequently couplets derived from folk materials, and accordion-based dance tunes—were emulated widely by youthful amateurs, especially as printed songbooks and 78 rpm recordings became available. As innovators, many professional musicians developed eclectic repertoires influenced by "foreign" styles like "hot" Afro-American jazz.

The musical ferment in Finland was, perhaps, exceeded by the state of affairs in Finnish America. With very few exceptions, the "traditional immigrant music" brought by settlers to the western Great Lakes region was the "new folk music" of the old country.[5] The oldest tunes known by the second generation—learned from parents, an uncle, "an old lumberjack," a "man whistling in the hayfield"—are uniformly waltzes, polkas, schottisches, and humorous ditties. The opening verse of the waltz "Mustalainen" [The Gypsy] paints a doleful, sentimental picture of a migrant laborer equally homeless in old world or new.

> *Mustalaiseks' olen syntynyt, kotitonna kuljeskelen nyt,*
> *Luonnon lapsi, mitas huolinkaan, kuin vaan vapahanna olla saan.*

> [I was born a Gypsy, homeless, wandering now,
> A child of nature, I don't worry as long as I can be free.][6]

"Variksen Laulu" [The Crow Song] is a series of merry, hyperbolic, rural-flavored couplets combined with a nonsense chorus.[7] A man shoots an enormous crow in the woods and parts of its body are put to use: the wings make a boat's sail, the windpipe a funnel; the feathers stuff many pillows, the talons form powder horns.

> *Hoyhenista tuli hyvat vuodat patjat,*
> *Raikuma riuka rallal lei,*
> *Untuuista tyyny ja usiampi saataan,*
> *Ranttama rimu ramu rallala lei.*
>
> [From the toes they made a good harrow,
> *Raikuma riuka rallal lei,*
> Or they could have made a field rake.
> *Ranttamu rimu ramu rallala lei.*];

While such comic songs might be rendered a cappella, they were often backed by a button accordion—the primary instrument for early twentieth-century Finnish-American dance music.[8]

Like their old country counterparts caught up in the transformation of rural society, new world Finns gathered for song and dance in numerous socialist, temperance, or town halls.[9] Often literate and increasingly bilingual, they copied the words of favorite songs into lined notebooks.[10] Some wrote songs in changing Finland's dance tune/couplet tradition. J. Alfred Tanner's "Kulkurin Valssi" [Vagabond or Wanderer's Waltz], a melancholy celebration of footloose freedom, is dubbed the "Finnish-American National Anthem" in the western Great Lakes region where it has been performed for more than half a century.[11] Tanner, Wobbly lyricist Arthur Kylander, and "Copper Country" native Hiski Salomaa likewise penned humorous songs based on immigrant experiences.[12] Their efforts, not surprisingly, were marketed through published songbooks and commercial recordings. In the latter case, international recording companies like Victor and Columbia began to release Finnish-American performances, especially from the early 1920s until the onset of the Depression.[13]

The existence of halls, songbooks, and records likewise made it possible for some Finnish-American musicians to make a living as touring professionals. The greatest of these was Viola Turpeinen (Fig. 1), a native of Iron River, Michigan, whose career flourished from the 1920s through the 1950s.[14] Playing on a regular circuit that extended from Cape Ann, Massachusetts, to the Copper Country, to northern Wisconsin, to Minneapolis and Minnesota's Iron Range,

Courtesy of Anselm and Hilda Polso

Figure 1. Viola Turpeinen with her Excelsior accordion, 1930

Turpeinen exerted a wide and sustained influence on Finnish-American dance music. She abandoned the button accordion for the more expensive, louder, and more versatile piano accordion. Beginning with backing from the violin, mandolin, and banjo of John Rosendahl, Turpeinen expanded the instrumentation of her orchestra to include a second piano accordion and an occasional drummer. Her music was decidedly Finnish, but she was less a backwards-looking curator of tradition than a musician immersed in her times. She and her second accordionist wore racy flapper garb—above the keyboards of their instruments were "Viola" and "Sylvia" (Sylvia Polso) in flashy pearl inlay—and their playing was accomplished, crisp, full-bodied, and modern in the manner of Finnish "accordion orchestras" of the twenties and thirties (Fig. 2).Indeed, Turpeinen's band toured Finland while Finnish dance bands made annual American tours on the Cape Ann to Iron Range circuit.

The sustained influence of evolving Finnish dance music on its Finnish-American counterpart was paralleled in the western Great Lakes region by inter-ethnic contact both with fellow "foreigners" and with largely extra-regional Anglo-American culture. Slavs and Italians were drawn to mining and mill jobs in the late nineteenth

Courtesy of Anselm and Hilda Polso

Figure 2. L-R: Viola Turpeinen, Andy Kosola, William Syrjälä, Sylvia Polso, 1930.

and early twentieth centuries. They too were familiar with the accordion and with couple dances; and predictably, they traded tunes with Finnish-Americans to form a hybrid repertoire.[15] A similar process was occurring in other northern and midwestern communities settled by European ethnics during the same era. By the late 1930s second generation professional entertainers—utilizing tours, records, and songbooks—began to popularize a pan-ethnic polka music. Cleveland's Frankie Yankovic—a Slovenian-American accordion player whose bands typically included a second accordion, piano, banjo, and string bass—has played regularly, since the late 1940s, in the western Great Lakes region where he continues to be polka music's dominant proponent.[16]

Emergent country music likewise had a powerful affect on Finnish-American dance music.[17] Second-generation children learned the English language and an array of songs in schools, from records, or over the radio. In the 1930s "hillbilly" music—with its rural themes, string instrumentation, and energy—captivated many young Finnish-Americans who tuned in to "barn dances" broadcast on clear channel stations like Chicago's WLS. "Western swing," prevalent from the late thirties through the early fifties, was regarded as especially kindred. Spawned in Oklahoma and Texas, it drew not only upon hillbilly and Afro-American strains, but also upon the waltz and polka dance repertoire of southwestern Czechs, Germans, and Mexicans.[18] Such later forms as "honky tonk" or "hard country," with its emphasis on the ruralite adrift in the city, were especially appealing to displaced Finnish-Americans of Michigan who found themselves, like the figure in Danny Dill and Mell Tillis's "Detroit City," making cars by day and bars by night while lamenting "I wanna go home."

Art Moilanen's experiences and influences as a dance musician are inextricably bound to the preceding cultural and historical forces. His initial and most intimate musical training came from his immediate community. "Little country halls. . .the Simar Hall, the Rousseau Town Hall, and the East Branch Hall" surrounded Mass to serve, along with homes, as places to celebrate "weddings, anniversaries, birthday parties" and seasonal events with song and dance. Among the "older farmers and lumberjacks," first generation Finnish-Americans, there were button accordionists and "one or two that stuck out as very good singers." From such men as Konstu Sulkanen, Art learned a few songs "little by little as a kid," including "Villi Ruusu," "Rattikkoon," and "Kiikuri Kaakuri," couple dances widely known in old and new worlds. He also began "fooling around" with an older brother's "three row 'cordeen" while not yet in his teens: "I've never had a lesson in my life. It's all been home study, self-study." In other words, Art learned to play, in a typical folk fashion, by oral and imitative means. Yet his folk community was that of twice-uprooted Finnish-Americans and their offspring, and its traditional repertoire was the "new folk music" of button boxes, romantic waltz songs, humorous couplets, and couple dances enjoyed in a semi-institutional setting.

Not surprisingly, Art also "picked up lotta these Finn songs from a record that we had on an old phonograph at home." Indeed commercially recorded dance tunes constitute the bulk of Art's Finnish-American repertoire: "Itin Tiltu," "Kauhavan Polkka," "Kuuliaiset Kottilassa," "Maailman Matti," "Nujulan Talkoo Polkka," "Orpopojan Valssi," "Rannanjarvi," "Sak Jarven Polkka," and a handful of others.[19] Moilanen's encounter with recorded ethnic popular culture was augmented by the live appearances of Viola Turpeinen who

> . . .played the Mass Town Hall every year, [and] all the local halls: Mass, Bruce Crossing, Copper Country way, and up in the L'Anse area. When she was really in her prime, it was in my younger days. Of course, she's been dead for many years, but she was a really fine accordionist. She packed the halls with her music. . .I play just about all of the tunes that she used to do, biggest part of them anyway.

Inspired by what he heard and saw, Art, like others of his generation, longed to emulate Turpeinen's mastery of the piano accordion. He acquired his first piano keyboard when an older brother, who worked in a Virginia coal mine, purchased the instrument of a partner who was killed in an accident and sent it home to Art.

The young man practiced diligently and, in the middle of the Depression, began to realize that he could make a little money with his music. By the time Art was sixteen, in 1933, he was performing for local dances, especially weddings and anniversaries. He began working alone, but for a stretch in the thirties he fronted a band that included fiddle, mandolin, and drums. For several reasons, however, Art soon settled on

> . . .a two piece band. It's fairly simple and it furnishes pretty good music for what was required in areas around here. Of course, moneywise, it was always attractive to the people that hired you.

As a budding semiprofessional, Art was not only eager to play for as broad a regional audience as possible, but was also sparked by a young musician's desire to learn new tunes and techniques. His repertoire expanded accordingly.

Beyond Finnish-American numbers, he began to play the favorites of neighboring Swedes: Olle i Skratthult's Scandinavian vaudeville classic "Nikolina," "Johan Pa Snippen," a schottische, and the popular waltz "Livet i Finnskogarna" [Life in the Finnish Woods].[20] He learned the Croatian waltz "Kukavica," and that the "Polish polka is not too much different from [Finnish and] Croatian polkas." Accessible, like his Finnish-American repertoire, through face-to-face contact and 78 rpm recordings, Art also encountered other ethnic tunes through print. Like many an eclectic young blues or hillbilly performer of the mid- to late-thirties, Art taught himself to read notes in a rudimentary way while consulting sheet music and song books like *Eric Olzen's Scandinavian Dance Album*.[21] He also listened to extra-regional, pan-ethnic "polka" bands like those of "Whoopee John" Wilfahrt of New Ulm, Minnesota, and Cleveland's Frankie Yankovic. In Art's phrase, "Yankovic music" has been especially influential and a typical Moilanen performance incorporates such numbers as "Tick Tock Polka," "Sharpshooter's Polka," and "Helena Polka."

Incipient country music likewise made an impression on Moilanen. While the accordion has always been his main instrument, Art told me "I still get up and play the guitar every once in a while." His interest began in the early thirties when "hillbilly music" filled the airwaves and Art "used to tape the harmonica onto a chair back and play the guitar and harmonica too." The country songs in his working repertoire, however, date mostly from the late forties, following Art's tenure in the military, to the early sixties: "Born to Lose," "Detroit City," "From a Jack to a King," "Mocking Bird Hill," "Out Behind the Barn," "Your Cheatin Heart," and many others.

Country music, together with an occasional pop standard, also contributed to more than a dozen comic songs in Art's repertoire. "Born to Booze" was a parody or, in Art's phrase, an "ad lib" of "Born to Lose." "A Roomful of Roses," in like fashion, was rendered:

> If I gave a horse to you
> Every time you made me blue,
> I'd have a roomful of horses.

Sometimes limited to a mere chorus, other parodies extended to several verses. "Art's Barroom" paralleled "Detroit City" as a logger passes out in a tavern to dream about pulpwood piles, his chainsaw, and over-due payments. Still others, like "The Lumberjack Song," combined lyrics of Art's own invention—in this case, regarding a woodsman's tavern spree following a Spring payday—with a country tune reminiscent of Johnny Horton's "Sink the Bismarck."

At the same time, Art's comic songs harkened back to the Finnish and Finnish-American tradition of humorous couplets. Several acquaintances composed playful verses in Finnish which Art set to well-known American melodies. "Noan Arkki" [Noah's Ark] metrically and musically matched "The Battle Hymn of the Republic." The first two verses chronicle the cacophany of beasts and the amount they eat, while the third recounts the drunkenness of Noah.

> *Sade viimen takaisi ja jallen kuivi maa,*
> *Sitte han se aija raukka helpotusta saa,*
> *Juhli han ja juopotteli onnes yllahti,*
> *Pohnas paissaan Ryssan kirkoon viimein pyllahti.*
>
> [The rain finally stopped and land dried up,
> Then the poor fellow got respite.
> Drank too much wine in his joy,
> Tumbled over and fell asleep.][22]

At once ethnic and American, Art's comic songs were also overtly regional and personal. "Art's Barroom" and "The Lumberjack Song," both concerning loggers and tavern celebrations, not only described common Upper Peninsula activities, but also referred to Moilanen's own life as a pulpcutter and barkeeper. Through such songs, Art was able simultaneously to transform extra-regional songs and tunes into forms relevant to the lives of his audience, and to create a persona for himself. Art's motives in this regard derived partially from good business sense: "I always try to get Art's Bar into the song, part of my advertising campaign." (In like manner, Moilanen dispensed "Art's Bar" matchbooks, and sold T-shirts emblazoned with an accordion and the words "Where The Hell Is Art's Bar? / Mass City, Michigan.") But Art also used personalized songs to comment publicly, in a light-hearted and self-distancing yet realistic way, about his love of conviviality and his periodic bouts with alcohol.

The Story of My Life
It was way back last September, as far as I remember,
Walkin' the streets of Mass with lots of pride.

But I fell in the gutter and my heart is still a-flutter.
When a pig came by, it lay there by my side.
As I lay there in the gutter, and my heart is still a-flutter,
A lady walkin' by had a chance to say,
"You can tell a man that boozes by the company he chooses,"
And the pig got up and slowly walked away.[23]

Such songs predictably were oft-requested favorites of Art's clientele for they not only spoke certain truths about their singer, but they also reminded the assembled that—in a sparsely populated, climatically harsh, economically depressed region—people who fought cabin fever through intoxicated revelry risked an occasional spell "in the gutter."

Combining influences from a range of musical styles which span numerous cultures and several decades, Art's repertoire is not, however, all-inclusive. Indeed it rejects contemporary forms regularly heard and played in the U.P. Art "didn't go into the rock style of music at all"; he plays little or no country music from that period following the late 1950s; nor does he play any polka music from much later than the mid-1950s. Despite its obvious evolution and eclecticism, Art Moilanen's music is, in the 1980s, conservative, a definite throwback, exemplary of cultural lag.

Such an orientation toward the past and, more precisely, toward an era extending from the late 1920s to the late 1950s is partially explicable as the behavior of a musician who learned what he liked as a young man and who has maintained those preferences through middle-age and beyond. In this way, Art's playing of an old familiar tune not only satisfies an ingrained aesthetic, but it also conjures memories of other days—of a "golden age," perhaps, when times were better, or, at least, when Art Moilanen was a "rough and ready guy" more exuberantly alive. But the conservative nature of the man's repertoire is equally attributable to its immediate sociocultural context: to the usual events for which Art has played, to notions of appropriate performance on those occasions, and, most importantly, to the composition and orientation of his audience.

For most of the past half century Art has played within a limited area for a limited number of seasonal and life cycle events. Based chiefly in and around Mass City, he has ranged as far as forty miles in all directions: to Toivola and the outskirts of the "Copper Country" in the north, L'Anse in the east, Bruce Crossing in the south, and Ontonagon in the west. He has played for weekend dances, for annual bashes like late November "Hunter's Dances," New Year's Eve, galas marking the spring "break up" of winter logging, and, especially, for weddings and anniversaries. Although sometimes occurring in homes, these events are more often held in public halls and in taverns. Their physical settings, typified by Art's Bar in Mass City, were not modern night clubs but little more than large open rooms, often brightly lit, with a wooden floor, a few chairs and tables, plenty of space for dancers, and a corner for the musicians.

Amidst such events and surroundings, Art practiced the same conventions of performance he had learned half a century before. Like his first generation Finnish-American neighbors—farmers and loggers who happened to sing or play—Art was a local working man who could also entertain (Fig. 3). As someone "just like everybody else," he did not accentuate a unique status during dances by occupying an elevated stage, wearing special clothes, or affecting a formal act; rather, he stood on the same floor level as his audience, and wore everyday clothes. His dances were not organized into tight sets with standard openings and closings and a roughly fixed duration. Art would start to play whenever he and those gathered were

Figure 3. Art Moilanen

"in the mood," and he would continue or stop for irregular intervals depending on whether or not people wanted to dance or talk. As for following a particular sequence of tunes, Art reckoned

> I don't even carry a list of any kind. . .everything's in my head and I ask the audience what they want. Here at all my dances it's open for public requests. It happens that I know most of the requests that they call for, so we do it as it is. I never carry a program with me.

Eschewing a set program in deference to public taste, Art likewise did not treat his tunes as discrete artistic entities to be rendered just so; rather, he lengthened and shortened them, offered a commentary or sang a verse, so as to please dancers and listeners. Art also encouraged people in the audience to spell him or join in: "I always make the audience take part in the show if there is someone that is capable of doing anything." Rooted in the bygone neighborhood gatherings of his youth, Art's performance style was egalitarian, at odds with notions of the musician as elevated star, intended to stress that he and his fellows were equally important contributors to a common event.

Not surprisingly, the same kind of public has always comprised Art's audience. They are nowadays, like Art, "an older class of people," second generation Americans—roughly fifty percent Finn, but also of Croatian, Italian, Polish, and Swedish heritage—who have made their livings as miners, loggers, farmers, millworkers, tradesmen, and homemakers in the Upper Peninsula. Like Art, these people have eclectic musical tastes which embrace the range of styles often heard during that period from the late twenties through the fifties, when they were young. And so Art, as much to please his audience as to please himself, has fashioned a repertoire which is

> . . .a mixture of everything. I don't feature all polkas. I play some and I swing into some waltzes, country-western, and a schottische, and a *rattikko*. And, as you follow that through the night, you get something for everyone.

From the foregoing discussion of historical and cultural forces affecting Art Moilanen's existence, of his eclectic repertoire, and of his characteristic performances for a stable audience in recurrent contexts, it is clear that Art Moilanen's dance music is as much American as it is Finnish, as much pan-ethnic-American as it is Finnish-American, as much related to region and to class as it is to nationality, and it owes as much to the many external channels of popular culture—to touring artists, to records, to print, to hits of the forties and fifties—as it does to local face-to-face folk transmission. The tradition Art bears is actually that of ethnic-American-regional-working-class dance music shaped by a second generation sensibility and audience. Forsaking hyphens, Art plays vernacular music or, in Charles Keil's phrase, "people's music": music grounded in and embracing the *totality* of a particular era and area, including *all* of its varied peoples, and reflecting a continuum of events and experiences while reiterating age old themes and preserving the community values they articulate.[24]

Art Moilanen's sustained commitment to his dance music has, in recent years especially, won him wider fame. When Art's Bar was in operation it was often a stopping place for other musicians from beyond the radius of Moilanen's usual territory. Jimmy Andrietti or Elsie Nevala, Italian- and Finnish-American piano accordionists from Calumet and Ironwood, respectively, might pause for an impromptu jam session while passing through; as might northern Wisconsinites Tom Marincel of Ashland (a Croatian), Oulu's Lahti Brothers, and Walter and Aili Johnson of Bayfield County. In other words, beyond his geographically limited status as a people's musician, Art has become more broadly renowned—that is within a 100-mile radius—as a "musician's musician."

The circle of Art's constituency and his resultant status has been further widened and altered within the past decade by the rise of the new ethnicity. Explicable in simple terms as a self-conscious effort by post-immigrant generation ethnics to recapture, preserve, and promote their cultural heritage, often in idealized form, via formal institutions and public events (like folk festivals), this movement has affected Art Moilanen in a number of ways.[25] Within his own immediate region Art has performed for uncharacteristic audiences, including third graders from L'Anse to whom he taught the schottische and the rattikko during the school's "Finnish Day." Figuring that his "kind of music will pass away because the young people don't go much for it," Art also began in 1976 to teach Finnish-American tunes to three third-generation Finnish women: "They come along with me every once in a while to old age homes. . . and they go alone themselves" (fig. 4).

About the same time, Art began an involvement with institutionalized ethnic events sponsored by former Upper Peninsula inhabitants who had moved to lower Michigan. In the mid-1970s Art played for an annual "Ontonagon County Dance" at the Finnish Center in Detroit. His appearance there, for a benefit at the Wayne

Matthew Gallman

Figure 4. Art Moilanen jamming at Aura Jamboree with unknown Fiddler, 1979.

County Civic Center, and eventually for students in ethnic studies at Michigan State University, conferred upon Art the status of a relic, an endangered species, a preserver of near-extinct Finnish-American culture. In other words, Moilanen, people's musician and musician's musician, became a symbol of ethnicity: an entire culture's musician. As such he has subsequently gained national attention through appearances on National Public Radio, and in Michael Loukinen's film, *Tradition Bearers*, about the Finnish-American experience.[26] Indeed, national fame has become international through Moilanen's 1983 invitation to play in Finland.

Such accolades and attentions have understandably amplified Art's consciousness of his anachronistic style and of his historical and cultural role. He is fond, and rightly so, of stressing the folk and Finnish aspects of his music; these roots are his deepest. Yet within the man's fundamental tradition as a people's dance musician, "Newspaper Dress" and the tunes he heard the old lumberjack Konstu Sulkanen sing have the same validity. Certainly Art must think so too, for he invariably plays the former in any context—even when he might not be sure of "what they want me to." Indeed, the "Newspaper Dress" is the very tune through which the nature of Art's dance music can best be understood.

As a thinly disguised version of the "Tennessee Waltz," the "Newspaper Dress" is most obviously a country song. Yet its co-author, Pee Wee King was, as Bill C. Malone points out, "a decidedly untypical 'hillbilly.' "[27] King was a Pole from south Milwaukee who played accordion in polka bands before migrating to the National Barn Dance on WLS radio in Chicago and, eventually, to Nashville's Grand Ole Opry in 1937. He was also an exponent of western music with its debt to Czech and German dance tunes; moreover, King's rendition of "Tennessee Waltz" featured a piano accordion and took the form of a waltz. Art's substitute lyrics of "Newspaper Dress" quote King's original before interjecting the Moilanen fondness for parody and regional reference.

> I was dancing with my darling to the Tennessee waltz,
> At the annual fireman's ball.
> People, they were starin' and my girl she was wearin'
> A newspaper dress, that is all.

Mildly risque, locally apt in its mention of poverty and of the efforts of volunteer fire departments, the song also recalls, however faintly, the Finnish tradition of comic songs—a tradition Art acknowledged:

> If I see a comical verse in the paper, or I hear it somewhere, I put it to a tune. It always goes over pretty nice. And some of these real old Finnish tunes that I sing are comical. Course there're very few anymore that understand Finn and appreciate it anymore.

In short, "Tennessee Waltz / Newspaper Dress" is a country song of the forties, learned from a record, yet played on Art Moilanen's chosen instrument in a dance form which is popular with his Upper Peninsula audience; it also expresses, in English words inspired by a Finnish-American and regional perspective, its performer's playful, convivial, eclectic essence. Compressing all of Art's varied influences into a single song, illustrative of a dynamic process synthesizing old and new historical and cultural elements, "Newspaper Dress" epitomizes the simultaneously conservative and open-ended "traditional immigrant music" of those who settled and remained in the western Great Lakes region.

1. Matti E. Kaups, "The Finns in the Copper and Iron Ore Mines of the Western Great Lakes Region, 1864-1905: Some Preliminary Observations," in *The Finnish Experience in the Western Great Lakes Region: New Perspectives*, ed. Michael G. Karni, Matti E. Kaups, and Douglas J. Ollila, Jr. (Turku, Finland: Institute for Migration, 1975), 55-89.

2. Michael M. Loukinen, "Second-Generation Finnish-American Migration from the Northwoods to Detroit," in *Finnish Diaspora*, ed. Michael G. Karni (Toronto: The Multicultural Historical Society of Ontario, 1980), 107-26.

3. This quotation and all subsequent words from Art Moilanen were tape recorded by the author and Matthew Gallmann at Art's Bar, 23 March 1981. Original tapes are kept in the Vere P. and Rosa M. McDowell Ethnic Heritage Sound Archive and Resource Center, Northland College, Ashland, Wisconsin.

4. This sketch of musical change is drawn from Pekka Gronow, "Popular Music in Finland: A Preliminary Survey," *Ethnomusicology* 17 (1973): 52-71.

5. Observations are based on interviews conducted by Matthew Gallmann, Marina Herman, and the author with roughly three dozen Finnish-American musicians, from 1979 to 1981, under grants from the Folk Arts Division of the National Endowment for the Arts to Northland College.

6. Translation by Jingo Viitala Vachon of Toivola, Michigan, from the singing of Miriam Koskela of Ironwood, Michigan, 18 July 1983. Juho Koskela recorded "Mustalainen," Columbia E-3223, around 1917. References to this and subsequent recordings appear in Pekka Gronow, *Studies in Scandinavian-American Discography* (Helsinki: Finnish Institute of Recorded Sound, 1977), 2:56, 91, 111, 152. Miriam Koskela's version appears on a two record set—*Accordions in the Cutover: Field Recordings of Ethnic Music from Lake Superior's South Shore*—and accompanying booklet (Dodgeville: Wisconsin Folklife Center, 1986).

7. Vachon translation from the singing of Henry Luokkanen, Eagle Harbor, Michigan, 28 August 1979. Such facetious accounts of giant beasts are common in international folksong and folktale; Stith Thompson and Antti Aarne cite type 1960J, "The Great Bird," as a humorous "lying tale" in *The Types of the Folktale*, Folklore Fellows Communication, no. 184 (Helsinki: Academia Scientiarum Fennica, 1981), 520. Luokkanen's version appears on the record, *Accordions in the Cutover*.

8. Matthew Gallmann, "Matti Pelto: Finnish-American Button Accordion Player," *Midwestern Journal of Language and Folklore* 8, no. 1 (1982): 43-47.

9. Ellen Louma, "Courtship in Finland and America: Yojuoksu Versus the Dance Hall," *Finnish Americana* 2 (1979): 66-76.

10. I examined notebooks in the possession of Jingo Viitala Vachon, Anselm Polso of Kimball, Wisconsin, and Helmer Olavie Wintturi of Herbster, Wisconsin.

11. Discographic references appear in Pekka Gronow, *Studies in Scandinavian-American Discography* (Helsinki: Finnish Institute of Recorded Sound, 1977), 1:41, 44; and 2:72, 91, 146, 151.

12. Pekka Gronow, "Ethnic Recordings: An Introduction," in *Ethnic Recordings in America: A Neglected Heritage* (Washington, D.C.: American Folklife Center, 1982), 12, 24.

13. Pekka Gronow, "Finnish-American Records," *John Edwards Memorial Foundation Quarterly* 7, no. 24 (1971): 176-85.

14. Several of Turpeinen's performances from the 1920s have been reissued on *Siirtolaisen Muistoja: The Immigrant's Memories*, RCA PL 40115; LP recordings on the Standard-Colonial label include: *Holiday in Finland*, LP 650; *Songs and Dances of Finland*, LP 679; *Favorite Finnish Songs and Dances*, LP 682; and *Viola Turpeinen Sings and Plays Finnish Tunes*, LP 763. For more complete biography of Turpeinen, see James Leary, "The Legacy of Viola Turpeinen," *Finnish Americana* (in press).

15. The upper Midwest's hybrid European-American dance music is described in James Leary, "Old Time Music in Northern Wisconsin," *American Music* 2, no. 1 (1984): 71-88.

16. Robert Dolgan, *The Polka King, The Life of Frankie Yankovic* (Cleveland: Dillon/Liederbach, 1977).

17. See James Leary, "Ethnic Country Music Along Superior's South Shore," *John Edwards Memorial Foundation Quarterly* 19, no. 72 (1984), 219-30.

18. See Charles Townsend, *San Antonio Rose: The Life and Music of Bob Wills* (Urbana: University of Illinois Press, 1976); Clinton Machaan, "Country-Western Music and the 'New' Sound in Texas-Czech Polka Music," *John Edwards Memorial Foundation Quarterly* 19, no. 69 (1983): 3–7; and Chris Strachwitz's liner notes for *Texas Czech-Bohemian Bands, Early Readings 1928–1953*, Folk Lyric 9031.

19. Gronow's *Studies in Scandinavian-American Discography*, 1 and 2 provide recording data. Jousinen and Stein, "Itin Tildun," Columbia E 2417, 1915; and Hiski Salomaa, "Iitin Tiltu," Columbia 3158-F, 1930. John Rosendahl and Viola Turpeinen, "Kauhavan Polkka," Victor 3-80587, 1928; and Paul Norback, Viking 12, 1956. Leo Kauppi, "Kuulaiset Kottilassa," Columbia 3040-F, 1927; Leo Kauppi, "Maailman Matti," Columbia 3032-F, 1926; J. Alfred Tanner, "Nujulan Talkoopolkka," Victor 77610, 1924; and Tanner, Victor 80324, 1928. Juho Koskelo, "Orpopojan Valssi," Columbia E 9032, c. 1923; Koskelo, Victor 73870, 1923; and J. Alfred Tanner, Victor 1927. Otto Pyykkonen, "Isotalo ja Rannanjarvi," Columbia 3000-F, 1924; and Muhoksen Janne, "Isoo-Antti ja Rannanjarvi," Victor 78056, 1925. Willy Larson, "Sak Jarven Polkka," Columbia 3092-F, 1928; Suomi Jazz Orkesteri, Victor V4119, 1930; and Pohjolan Pojat, "Sakki Jarven," Standard F-5083, c. 1950.

20. Gronow offers complete discographic references in *Studies* 1 and 2; good introduction to Scandinavian-American dance music may be found in the booklet accompanying *From Sweden to America: Emigrant and Immigrant Songs*, Caprice 2011, 1981.

21. *Eric Olzen's Scandinavian Dance Album* (Chicago: Chart Music Publishing House, vol. 1, 1935; vol. 2, 1937; vol. 3, 1945; and vol. 4, 1951);

22. Translation by Jingo Viitala Vachon. Art's performance appears on *Accordions in the Cutover*.

23. Folklorist Tom Adler recalls hearing a slightly different version, played by a folk revival guitarist, on Chicago radio in the late 1950s; I have been unsuccessful in locating other versions.

24. Charles Keil, "Who Needs the Folk?" *Journal of the Folklore Institute* 15 (1978): 263–65.

25. Stephen Stern, "Ethnic Folklore and the Folklore of Ethnicity," *Western Folklore* 36, no. 1 (1977): 7–32.

26. *Tradition Bearers* (Marquette: Finnish-American Lives Project, Northern Michigan University, 1983), concerns the lives of four Finnish-Americans from northern Michigan and Minnesota.

27. Bill C. Malone, "A Shower of Stars," in *Stars of Country Music*, ed. Bill C. Malone and Judith McCulloh (Urbana: University of Illinois Press, 1975), 401–2; King recorded "Tennessee Waltz" in upper Midwest ethnic dance style on *Country Music Polkas*, Cuca K-2024.

House Parties and Shanty Boys: Michigan's Musical Traditions

Stephen R. Williams

rcheological evidence points to the use of such musical instruments as rattles, drums, and pan pipes by the Hopewell Indian culture as early as 100 B.C. Seventeenth century French explorers found the Woodlands Indians using these types of instruments to accompany dance, ceremony, and religious rite.[1] A drum and drum stick from the Woodlands Culture were probably integral elements in these occasions, whose music remains structurally the same today.[2]

French missionaries, fur traders, and explorers brought only small portable instruments such as Jew's harps with them,[3] but with the settling of Detroit in the early 18th century, French (and later British) military men provided regimental and social music with brass and percussion instruments, and an occasional flute or violin. Church music was initially provided by unaccompanied choruses; stringed and keyboard instruments were later introduced in some congregations.

The traditional music of fiddlers, fifers, and drummers undoubtedly lightened the hearts of settlers facing a rugged new life. As communities grew, the musical tastes and skills represented therein became broader in scope. Traveling "singing school" instructors stirred interest in music by staying in a community just long enough to produce a public concert. To meet the musicians' increasing demands for instruments, repairs, and published sheet music, entrepreneurs established shops where local and imported items were sold.[4] Among the first in Michigan was Couse's Music Saloon, which opened in Detroit in 1844 with over 1,500 pieces of sheet music, and "an assortment of 4 and 8 keyed Cocoa Flutes, 1 and 4 keyed box wood Flutes, Clarionets, Picolas, Fifes, Trumpets, keyed Bugles, Trombones, Cornopians, Concert Horns, Ophaclides, Guitars, French Accordions, Flageolets, Violins, Violoncellas, together with a general assortment of Musical Merchandise."[5] For nearly 40 years Adam Couse operated his store, taught dancing and composing, and in 1851 became the first music publisher in Michigan. He had amassed a fortune from his ventures in the music business by the time he died in 1885.[6]

Musical instruments appeared in many Michigan traditional settings. A day of toil often ended in song and dance at lumber and mining camps, barnraisings, aboard ships, and at husking bees. The house party became an important social event throughout rural Michigan, where neighbors gathered at one home, rolled up the carpet, pushed back the furniture, and danced to the music of neighborhood musicians and callers. House parties began late in the evening when chores were done and ended at sunrise when it was time to milk the cows.[7]

Two instruments most familiar to shanty boys in the lumber camps and participants of house parties were the hammered dulcimer and the fiddle. The DeLano Brothers of Oxford, who manufactured hammered dulcimers in the 1870s and 1880s, George Maurice, a fiddle maker from Detroit, D. S. Brown, a Port Huron mandolin maker, and Theophilus Osgood of Bedford Township, who took the skins of two calves to build a snare drum and a bass drum used in recruiting Civil War soldiers, are representative of the mid-19th and early 20th century musical fervor in Michigan. The fiddle figures predominantly in descriptions of house parties and life in the lumbercamps found in contemporary accounts taken from archival sources and reminiscences, as the following illustrates:

> The cook had an old instrument which Jessie had used for the present occasion. Of course it was not to be expected that the company assembled in that cook camp would be able to fully appreciate classical music, but they certainly did enjoy rendered cotillions, jigs, reels, strathspeys and hornpipes rendered by Jessie, with such exquisite skill that the camp went perfectly wild with enthusiasm. The shanty boys mixed freely with the visitors and danced with partners they never before had met or spoken to. Clog dancing, Scotch reels, French fours, Irish jigs and contra dances were all there indulged in to the fullest extent attached to their original music.[8]

Percussive bones may have been introduced by British settlers or blacks fleeing slavery.[9] In the mid-twentieth century Fenton J. Watkins of Birmingham fashioned a set of traditional musical bones out of the ribs of an animal, and added whistles in the ends of two of them.

Ethnic groups brought new music and instruments which became part of Michigan's musical heritage. Before 1900 the majority of immigrants came from the British Isles, Germany, other northwestern European countries, and Canada.[10] The German Harmonie Society was organized in 1849 to preserve the music of the fatherland in choral and instrumental performances at German beer halls, picnics, suppers, and dances. By 1865 the Harmonie Society staged operas for audiences beyond the German community, and remained one of Detroit's foremost music societies until 1976.[11]

Attracted by the possibility of jobs in automotive and other factories, immigrants from Poland, Italy, Russia, Hungary, Yugoslavia, Rumania, Greece, Finland, and the Near East came to Michigan cities in the 20th century.[12] When Gus Zoppi arrived in Michigan in the late 1920s, he brought with him not only the tools and skills acquired in an accordion factory, but also the traditional music of his native Castelfidardo, Italy. Today he builds custom-made accordions for Slavic and Spanish music and dance.[13] Eric Tapler's grandfather was a cymbalom tuner and repairer in Hungary, and continued to build them after he arrived in Detroit in 1915. The love of Hungarian music led Tapler to build several of his own cymbaloms.[14]

Some unique instruments—such as the large "Piano Harp" which was strung on both sides and difficult to play—were produced by anonymous Michigan builders. Quincy Ellis Ford from Benton Harbor fashioned "Shugalette" mandolins (fig. 1), and a bell-shaped "Belldola" guitar for his sister, Belle Ford Walton, who performed in vaudeville shows near the turn of the century.[15]

Old Traditions Revived Anew

"After a sleep of twenty-five years, old-fashioned dancing is being revived by Mr. and Mrs. Henry Ford," proclaimed the first edition of *Good Morning* (1926), a handbook of music, calls, and directions for old-time dancing.[16] In an effort to preserve the traditional music and dance forms of his youth, and as a response to what he perceived to be the lax morals of the "Roaring Twenties,"

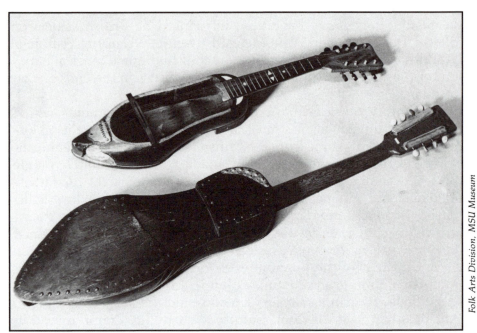

Folk Arts Division, MSU Museum

Figure 1. Shoegalletes made by Charles Ford, Benton Harbor area, c. 1900. MSU Museum collection

Henry Ford created the Early American Dance Orchestra in 1924, and engaged the services of Benjamin B. Lovett, a New England caller. Together they embarked on a program that included regular dance parties (for which Lovett Hall was built in 1937, with a ball-room complete with a springboard floor), radio programs and recordings, classes at the Edison Institute in Dearborn, and instruction in the public schools. "What we really teach is rhythm, grace, and appreciation of good music. Through these we teach our pupils to be courteous in a natural way," explained Lovett.[17] Ford also sponsored fiddlers' contests throughout the United States. The dance program came to an end with Lovett's departure in 1943, and with the death of Henry Ford in 1947 the fiddlers' contests were discontinued and the orchestra disbanded.[18]

Organizations such as the Original Dulcimer Players Club, the Original Michigan Fiddlers' Association, jazz preservation societies and square dance clubs have kept alive interest in traditional forms of music and dance. Contemporary craftsmen such as Ralph Flowers of Port Huron (fiddle), Percy Danforth of Ann Arbor (bones), and John Loxton of Port Huron (mountain dulcimer), revive the traditions of earlier generations of musical instrument makers from Michigan and other regions.

Elderly Instruments of Lansing is dedicated to the preservation of traditional music and dance forms and promotion of their revival among contemporary artists. More than just a music store, Elderly's is a nationally recognized center for rare and local recordings, sheet music, instruments, and instruction. The store features musical instruments built by contemporary Michigan craftspeople, and the staff includes repairers who keep pace with growing public demand for acoustic instruments.

They're Playing Our Song: The Proliferation Of Popular Music

The opening of the Erie Canal in 1825 made the transportation of keyboard instruments to Michigan much easier. Competition among eastern United States manufacturers grew fierce as technology improved in the mid-nineteenth century. The immense popularity of pianos and organs attracted manufacturers to Detroit as early as 1845.[19] Melodeons, reed organs and pianos became fixtures in many Michigan households as widespread mail-order catalogs developed and local keyboard manufacturers grew.[20] The Clough and Warren Organ Company, Detroit, had its beginnings in the 1850's, and by 1880 its melodeons and reed organs had achieved worldwide renown.[21] Keyboard manufacturers appeared in communities throughout Michigan, such as Pruden and Cordley (Adrian). Black legislator the Hon. Joseph Dickenson and his father-in-law Girard Gould formed the Dickenson and Gould Organ Company in Lexington.[22]

Companies such as Story and Clark (Grand Haven, 1884–1961), and Bush and Lane (Holland, 1901-1930) earned national reputations for their pianos.[23] Bush and Lane was well-known for producing player pianos. Grinnell Brothers, established in 1882 in Detroit as a musical merchandiser, began making their own pianos and player pianos in 1902 at a factory in Holly. Until 1960, Grinnell was the leading Michigan manufacturer of pianos.[24]

Local publishers capitalized on the mid-19th century craze for keyboard instruments and music. A virtual advertising war existed between two Detroit firms—J. Henry Whittemore (1858–1975) and C. J. Whitney (1857–1896)—as they vied for the public's patronage with songs such as "What Will They Say in Michigan" (J. H. Whittemore, 1862) and "Borders of Lake Michigan Waltz" (C. J. Whitney, 1866).

Polkas, schottisches, and waltzes, as well as parlor songs and instruction books were available locally and by mail-order.[25]

McKanlass and Marone Co. was formed in Port Huron to publish rags and tunes—such as "Evening Glow Waltzes" (1912)—written by William R. McKanlass (1879–1937). A much-beloved orchestra and band leader, music teacher, and musician, McKanlass had toured with minstrel and vaudeville shows in the late 19th century where he developed the great improvisational abilities necessary for a career in ragtime music. He played a number of instruments in the Port Huron City Band, where he probably met his business partner, violinist Rocco Marone.[26]

In 1911 two Albion College freshmen, Byron D. Stokes (1887–1974) and F. Vernor Dudleigh (1892–1974) hastily scribbled down the words and music for a song to commemorate their fraternity's 25th anniversary. "The Sweetheart of Sigma Chi" soon captured the nation, and to accommodate public demand, Dudleigh's brother Richard established a music publishing business in Albion that lasted from 1912 until 1923.[27]

The ragtime craze that swept the nation at the turn of the century was led in part by the Jerome H. Remick Publishing Company. Before its Detroit offices closed in the early 1920s, Remick produced over 350 tunes, many of them syncopated, spirited piano rags performed in saloons, dance halls, and on the New York stage.[28]

Religious music has passed among traditional, popular, and formal cultures. In 1912 traveling Evangelist George Bennard (1873–1958) set down the words and music to "The Old Rugged Cross," which has since become a favorite old-time hymn. Its popularity was immediate; radio stations all across the country were flooded with requests after it was first sung on the air. "I have trouble convincing people that it is not an old, old song and that I'm not 200 years old," remarked Reverend Bennard.[29] "The Old Rugged Cross" continues to enjoy wide appeal, and two Michigan communities, Albion and Reed City, now claim to be its birthplace.

Michigan musical instrument manufacturers also made stringed and wind instruments easily obtainable for home, community, and military use. Organizations such as city and school bands, orchestras, and choral groups flourished with the increased availability of a variety of instruments, published sheet music, and instruction.

In 1919 the American Violin Manufacturing Company moved to Manistee to produce violins "perfect in scale, of beautiful quality and tone, and which did not play out," desired by community and school orchestras.[30] Peter Christian Paulsen (1850–1920) had served an apprenticeship under a master violin maker in his native Denmark, and continued his research in the vibrational construction of the violin after arriving in the United States in 1882. He perfected his methods while employed in the violin department of Lyon and Healy (Chicago) and the Mills Novelty Company (maker of the automated violin and piano), and established his own company in Illinois before moving to Michigan. Production centered on six violin makers (probably including two of his sons), and nine additional laborers. They produced over 400 violins, priced between $45 and $100. The company folded a year after P. C. Paulsen's death in 1920.[31]

Another successful business venture was started in Grand Rapids by James Warren York (1839–1927), a brass band instrument maker and traveling musician. J. W. York and Sons began in 1882 as a music store—"The House of York"—and in 1885 began manufacturing cornets of York's own design, utilizing his experience gained as an apprentice to a New England brass instrument maker. The York cornet and trombone were initially hand-produced by European craftsmen brought to Michigan, until new technology allowed speedier manufacturing of brass instruments. By 1908 J. W. York and Sons employed 130 people in its own factory.[32] The company became the York Band Instrument Co. in 1926, and grew to be one of only six companies in the United States to manufacture an extensive line of instruments: cornets, trombones, trumpets, sousaphones, mellophones, French horns, and upright recording basses.[33] J. W. York and Sons entered the publishing business with tunes such as "The Grand Rapids Letter Carriers' Band March" (1900), and "The Furniture City Band: March and Two-Step for Band" (1903). Carl Fisher Musical Instrument Co. of New York purchased the business in 1940, and continued to produce musical instruments in Grand Rapids until 1971.[34]

The musical activity in Michigan provided a good business climate for the patent instrument industry. One-time violinist Henry C. Marx and his son, Charles, established the Marxochime Colony factory at New Troy about 1927, and produced various stringed instruments of their own design. The Violin-Uke, Marxolin, Pianolin, and Violin Guitar are all instruments which are simultaneously plucked and bowed to create melody and harmony. Marx dreamed of providing the non-musical student with an easy-to-play instrument, and devised a numbered notation system to replace standard musical notation. Marx instruments were sold door-to-door (and for one year through the Sears and Roebuck catalog), and enjoyed enough success to keep the factory open through the Great Depression. Production ceased in 1972 after Charles died; today his widow still sells a few instruments from the inventory left when the factory closed.[35] The Gibson Mandolin Guitar Manufacturing Company was formed in 1902 to produce and nationally distribute the fretted instruments of Kalamazoo inventor Orville H. Gibson (1856–1918), a craftsman who had gained a considerable reputation as a builder of fine handmade instruments. Gibson applied violin construction and acoustical concepts to make fretted plucked instruments fine enough for the concert stage.[36] His mandolin and harp guitar are prime examples of the attention he gave to shape, color, and visual detail as well. The Gibson Company developed and marketed families of instruments for banjo and mandolin orchestras that appeared on many stages in the early twentieth century. Gibson Mastertone banjos, developed in the 1920s, enjoyed a great wave of popularity that lasted nearly two decades. The tenor banjo could be heard in Dixieland bands, dance bands, college bands, in solo performances on the stage, and in the parlor.[37] Originally intended for formal use, Gibson guitars, banjos, and mandolins were integral elements in the popularization of country, bluegrass, and "pop" music, and in current revivals of old-time and traditional music. Gibson pioneered the electrification of musical instruments with its first electric guitar in 1924, and developed the solid body electric guitar in the 1950s.[38] Gibson continues to be a major manufacturer of quality electric guitars, as well as custom-made acoustic instruments. In 1984 the Kalamazoo factory was closed; all operations are now located in Nashville, Tennessee.

Traveling minstrel and vaudeville shows brought popular, ragtime, and formal music to urban audiences, while Chautauquas and the mass media spread many different styles of music to a wider rural audience whose music had been mainly traditional. Advances in transportation, especially the automobile, gave many people new opportunities to experience a wide variety of musical forms.

In 1934 Harold Rosier (1912–1980), musical saw player, actor, chalk talk artist, and magician, joined the Henderson Stock Company, a theatrical troupe. He purchased the company the following year, and created the Rosier Players, now the only traveling tent show of its kind in the United States.[39] The format has not been changed since the shows became popular sometime before the Civil War. The company remains in town for one week, staging a different play each evening with vaudeville skits between acts, and music before, during, and after the show. In the early twentieth century, Michigan boasted over forty professional shows of this type, which brought drama and music to communities throughout the state, and provided ample training opportunities for aspiring actors and musicians.[40] Today the Rosier Players continue to tour Michigan under the auspices of Jackson Community College, still featuring an occasional performance by Waunetta Rosier Oleferchik, Harold Rosier's widow.

One of the most popular ragtime songs ever composed was probably born in Deidrich's Saloon, Jackson, where a drifter named Hughie P. Cannon (1872–1912) played honky-tonk piano in exchange for nickels and dimes tossed his way—and a constantly-filled glass of liquor. Inspired by the marital troubles of his friend Willard G. Bailey, a local music teacher and dance hall musician, Cannon set down the words and music to "Bill Bailey, Won't You Please Come Home" in Jackson in 1902. The song soon became a popular hit, spawned many sequels such as "Since Bill Bailey Came Back Home," and led more than one person to claim to be the genuine Bill Bailey. Cannon, however, did not enjoy its success. He peddled it to a New York publisher for $350—the most he ever earned for one of his songs —and he spent his last days in a poorhouse in Wayne County. He died at age 39 in a hospital in Toledo, Ohio.[41]

Long, hard, working days in the mines and even longer winter nights were brightened with the opening of the Calumet Opera House in 1900. The Majestic Theatre held 1,200 people, and featured elaborate furnishings, Italian Renaissance ornamentation, and a large copper chandelier. Besides major attractions such as operas, operettas, and drama, the opera house booked touring stock companies and minstrel shows, which featured a grand parade to the theatre at noon, followed by a show in the evening. Calumet audiences enjoyed performances by Sarah Bernhardt, Lillian Russell, John Philip Sousa, and Irish tenor Chauncey Olcott, and many others. However, violence associated with the 1913 cooper strike forced the theatre to curtail its productions. By 1914, the Calumet Opera House had become a vaudeville house, and like so many other theatres throughout the state, succumbed to the lure of the motion picture. It remained a movie house— with occasional vaudeville shows—until the late 1960s, when local citizens embarked upon an ambitious restoration project. Now Michigan Technological University schedules musical and dramatic events there, and national touring companies once again grace the opera house's stage.[42]

Radio broadcasting was first made available on a large scale to the American public by a Detroit news station in 1920. Beginning with a broadcast of Michigan primary election results on August 31, the station 8MK (later WWJ) offered uninterrupted service to an ever-increasing audience. In the first week of broadcasting, the station aired baseball news, campaign proceedings, and recorded music which enlivened a party in a Detroit home, marking the beginning of this social aspect of radio broadcasting in the nation. By September 22, listeners enjoyed the first live vocal concert on the air in a performance by Miss Mabel Norton Ayers. As WWJ's signal began to reach audiences as far away as Georgia, programs expanded to include more musicians and theatrical talent from Detroit playhouses. WWJ scored other firsts in music broadcasting: the first complete symphony concert on February 10, 1922, with Ossip Gabrilowitch conducting the Detroit Symphony Orchestra, and live broadcasts from Belle Isle of Herman Schmenan and his thirty-piece concert band in June of 1923. Regular broadcasts of Julius Klein's orchestra from the Hotel Statler began in 1925. Through the years, WWJ continued to pioneer in broadcasting and to set standards for quality programming that were emulated by many other local stations which began to appear in the late 1920's.[43]

The rise of labor unions in Michigan was not untouched by music. Protest songs and music provided by groups such as the Fisher Strike Orchestra brought laborers together, blending traditional and popular cultures in a political context. The spirits of many strikers were lifted by familiar songs coupled with contemporary words, such as the following segment of "The Fisher Strike" (1937):

> Gather round me and I'll tell you all a story
> Of the Fisher Body Factory Number One,
> When the dies they started moving,
> The Union men they had a meeting
> To decide right then and there what must be done.
>
> (Chorus)
>
> These four thousand union boys,
> They made a lot of noise,
> They decided then and there to shut down tight.
> In the office they got snooty,
> So we started picket duty,
> Now the Fisher Body Shop is
> Out on strike. [44]

The rise of Motown Records in the turbulent 1960s and 1970s parallels the rise of urban, black, northern popular song. In 1959 songwriter, record producer, and auto worker Berry Gordy, Jr. founded a small rhythm-and-blues company in Detroit, which grew to be one of the largest black-owned corporations in the United States. The "Motown Sound," rooted in gospel and rhythm-and-blues, featured Detroit area talent such as Smokey Robinson and the Miracles, the Supremes, and Stevie Wonder, and became as popular with white audiences as black. During the mid- and late 1960s Motown sold over 12 million discs each year, providing an alternative sound to the very popular rock n' roll music. By 1972 the company had moved at least half of its operations to California, expanding into film and other areas of entertainment. Today Motown retains offices at "Hitsville, USA" in Detroit.[45]

A love for the music heard during his youth in Kentucky led pharmacist John Morris to start a collection of over 20,000 recordings of traditional, old-time, and bluegrass music. In an effort to preserve these musical forms and the radio programs which first spread them to a wider audience, he created "Old Homestead Records" in the basement of his Brighton home. "That's my main interest. I have some equipment which cleans up the hiss, and we've come out with nice collections of old-time performers which otherwise might not be available."[46] His company has grown in direct proportion to the current national interest in traditional and bluegrass music, and since 1971 has produced over 450 albums. Old Homestead Records has built such a fine reputation among contemporary bluegrass performers that Morris does not need to solicit many musicians to record for him. Active in bluegrass festivals in Charlotte and Whitmore Lake, Morris has also hosted a radio program, taught university classes, and co-authored a book on 1930s performer Molly O'Day. "I'm really in the business of promoting my kind of music, and I want Old Homestead to help out the performers rather than be just a big business."[47]

Precious Memories and Persistent Music:
A Profile of Music-making in the Thumb Area

The folk culture of Michigan's Thumb Area is rich and varied. The Thumb is outlined by the shore of Lake Huron, which has generated a wealth of marine lore in stories, songs, crafts, foods and thoughts. Inland, the fertile farmland has produced not only sugar beets and beans, but cultural traditions as well. Migrants from Canada and Europe, the southern United States, Mexico and most recently from Asia, have all come to the Thumb looking for employment on the Lakes, in the fields and in the towns. Generation by generation, they have added to the ethnic and religious complexity of the Thumb. From duck decoys to piñatas, from smoked fish to butter tarts, from Chippewa legends to Irish tales, and from the lone fiddler to a boisterous polka band, we find that there is much to enjoy in the folk culture of the Thumb.

One happy tradition worthy of examination is the house party—an informal gathering of folks at a neighbor's home. The house party provided an outlet for the creative energies of the musically talented. It served as a recreational opportunity and a vehicle for social interaction for people who labored.

Not all house parties were alike. They varied according to their respective neighborhoods, but there were common denominators, such as informal invitations, relatively small groups of close-knit families and friends, a potluck lunch at midnight, square dancing to local callers and musicians, talking and card-playing, spirits in varying amounts (depending on the local attitudes), and early-morning conclusions, so that the folks could go home to milk the cows.

Glen Westphal referred to himself as a thoroughbred German, and his family has a long tradition of music and dance. Glen colorfully describes the house parties of his youth in this way:

> My one uncle called. My Grandfather Albrecht called. My Grandfather Westphal played the accordion, and my Grandmother Westphal also played the organ. My uncle played fiddle, and then there was other fiddle players around the neighborhood. They weren't real good, but they'd set in and play, and you could make out what they were playing. But none of them were professionals. Once in a while somebody'd bring a guitar, but there wasn't too many guitars in our neighborhood. Accordion, organ and fiddle was about it. My Grandfather Albrecht called square dances. Pretty near everybody could call. Again, some was better than others, but pretty near everybody would call.
>
> They were all Germans and I guess 90% of them came from pretty much the same part of the country over in Germany. They talked the same German language. So they had their house parties, and from what I understand, that's the way it was in Germany. They would get together over there and have a party. Just a small community where there's a dozen homes or two dozen homes, whatever it would be, get together and have a party.

Wintertime more so than summertime, because summertime you was harvesting and planting. But occasionally right in the summertime—didn't make a difference—they'd have a party at least once a month even in the summertime. But in the wintertime it was every week. You were going to a party every week. And if there wasn't a wedding or wedding anniversary or a birthday party, they didn't need an excuse. They just had a party.

One time we were at a house party, and my dad wasn't there. My grandfather was playing, and I was 13 years old. And there was no caller available, and they wanted to square dance. They just filled up these two rooms, and I stood up on a chair and called. That was my first time. I remember that. Scared to death. But I liked it well enough that I wanted to try it. And I didn't call every Saturday night after that, but that more or less broke the ice to where it made me feel like I can do it, if I have to. . . . And then after the war, they started having hall parties up here in the township hall. And used to get me to call. Then I did put on dances up here at one time.

The war broke out and money got a little more plentiful, more cars in the community. The kids started driving to the shows in Sandusky and Port Huron. After the war, then dances started in halls and community buildings. Most of them was still the old-time dance. There used to be a hall in Lakeport. That was a modern dance. All round dances, all fox trots, and the younger crowd used to go there. And in Croswell, down at the railroad track, they had the hall they called the Croswell Arcadia. It was a big long hall, and every Saturday night they had old-time dances there. But after the war, house parties just faded away.[48]

In recent years the Port Huron Museum of Arts and History has developed a Traditional Music Program to recapture the house party experience in the Thumb area. The Traditional Music Program was spawned from the now obvious need for local people to enjoy their traditional songs and dances, and their desire to perpetuate this means of artistic expression by sharing it with others, especially younger members of the community. Recognizing its mission to preserve and promote the heritage and art of the local area, the museum has served as a catalyst for some exciting activity which has fallen under the umbrella of "traditional music."

In the beginning there was the Jamboree—the genesis of the museum's folklife programming. The first traditional music activity at the Museum of Arts and History was in June, 1981. In cooperation with the Original Michigan Fiddlers' Association, the museum hosted a fiddlers' jamboree. The OMFA has been holding jamborees around Michigan since 1976. That organization developed a successful method for ferreting out long-dormant musicians and callers, and the museum's Traditional Music Program has adopted the same procedure—simply get the word out that there's going to be a jamboree. Fiddlers' jamborees have, after ten years' time, a fairly rigid and predictable format. They almost always begin at about one o'clock on Saturday, at some local school gymnasium or hall. Musicians register at the door while spectators give a donation or pay a small admission price of $2 or so. Fiddlers are called to the microphone in the order they have signed in. All other musicians play back-up, and when time permits they may also have an opportunity to take the lead on a tune or two. At the end of the afternoon all the fiddlers play some tunes together on stage for a glorious finale. After a dinner break, the musicians return for the square dance, and this time the callers take turns at the microphone. It is not unusual for thirty or more fiddlers, fifty back-up musicians, and a dozen callers to attend a jamboree with three- to five-hundred or more in the audience.

The OMFA still sponsors jamborees all over the state but in no way could that organization begin to handle all the requests by local communities. So the Museum of Arts and History works with local groups to conduct about six jamborees a year in the Thumb area.

A modification of the jamboree has evolved into another highly successful activity at the museum itself—the monthly "Rap and Jam" session. During one Saturday evening each month, musicians and singers gather throughout our museum galleries to jam. A slightly more formal area is set aside with chairs and sound equipment for those musicians who opt to perform for a seated audience. Simultaneously other small jam sessions form throughout the museum galleries (fig. 2). At the same time, the museum's classroom area is turned into a dance hall accommodating six sets of square dancers. All this is done with an open invitation and without a firm commitment that anyone will attend these events. But a typical Rap and Jam session will have 30 or more musicians and an audience of 200 or more.

Why are so many people interested in this simple music and humble means of entertainment? The success of the current museum programs can be traced to their similarity to the traditional house party which was almost universally enjoyed by the folks of the rural Thumb, and many urban dwellers as well, until the disruption of life's routines by the Second World War. The house party was an often impromptu affair on a Saturday night where neighbors would

Folk Arts Division, MSU Museum

Figure 2. House Party Performers, Ann Arbor, 1984.

make their own music and fun. The museum's Traditional Music Program provides similar opportunities for entertainment and cultural expression in a changed world of the 1980s.

1. George Irving Quimby, *Indian Life in the Upper Great Lakes* (Chicago: University of Chicago Press, 1960), 75, 129.
2. Charles Hamm, *Music in the New World* (New York: W. W. Norton and Co., 1983), 10.
3. Jew's harps were found among other trade-related artifacts unearthed from a 1690 Indian burial at St. Ignace. See Eugene T. Petersen, *France at Mackinac* (Mackinac Island: Mackinac Island State Park Commission, 1968), 15.
4. Mary Evelyn Durden Teal, *Musical Activities in Detroit from 1701 through 1870* (Ann Arbor: School of Music, University of Michigan, 1964), 5, 8.
5. *Catalogue of Music and Musical Instruments for Sale at Couse's Music Saloon* (Detroit: Edward D. Ellis, 1844).
6. Teal, 11–13, 67–71.
7. Stephen R. Williams, ed., *House Party: Reminiscences by Traditional Musicians and Square Dance Callers in Michigan's Thumb Area* (Port Huron: Museum of Arts and History, 1982), 9.
8. John W. Fitzmaurice, *The Shanty Boy, or Life in a Lumber Camp*, Michigan Heritage Library Edition (Berrien Springs: Hardscrabble Books, 1979), 223.
9. Paul Gifford, personal letter, 1984.
10. Willis F. Dunbar, *Michigan: A History of the Wolverine State*, ed. George S. May (Grand Rapids: William B. Ferdmans Publishing Co., 1980), 590.
11. Teal, 204–12.
12. Dunbar, 590–92.
13. Vicki Zoppi Robasin, telephone conversation, 10 July 1984.
14. Eric Tapler, personal letter.
15. The Michigan State University Museum, provenance notes.
16. Benjamin B. Lovett, *Good Morning* (Dearborn, Mich: The Dearborn Publishing Co., 1926) quoted in Eva O'Neal Twork, *Henry Ford and Benjamin Lovett: The Dancing Billionaire and the Dancing Master* (Detroit: Harlo Press, 1982), 89.
17. *Orange and Black*, (Dearborn High School Newspaper), 17 January 1929, quoted in Twork.
18. Twork, 116–17.

19. Teal, 3, 105.
20. Jean Lincoln, "Music in Michigan Before 1860," (Master's thesis, Department of Music, Michigan State College, 1939), 48–64.
21. Teal, 102.
22. Arthur R. LaBrew, Historian, National Association of Negro Musicians, Inc., personal letter.
23. Robert Pierce, *Pierce's Piano Atlas* (Long Beach, Calif.: Bob Pierce, 1977), 51, 268.
24. Ibid., 110.
25. Teal, 131–58.
26. *Port Huron Times Herald*, 4 April 1937.
27. Leslie Stuart Carter, "The Sweetheart of Sigma Chi," *New England Senior Citizen*, reprinted in *Io Triumphe* (February-March 1984): 13–15.
28. Teal, 162.
29. Bill Markey, "Old Rugged Cross Composed at Albion," *Jackson Citizen Patriot*, 18 May 1948.
30. *Manistee News Advocate*, 1919.
31. *Manistee News Advocate*, 1920.
32. Edward Altenbrandt, ed., *The Men Behind the Guns in the Making of Greater Grand Rapids* (Grand Rapids: Dean-Hicks Publishing Co., 1909), 70–72.
33. Martin Krivin, *A Century of Wind Instrument Manufacturing in the United States: 1860-1960* (Iowa City: School of Music, State University of Iowa, 1961), 84–85.
34. Ralph Truax, "The Sound of Music is Stilled at York Instrument," *Grand Rapids Press*, 5 December 1971.
35. Scott Aiken, "Only the Melody Lingers on at Marxochine Plant," *Herald-Palladium*, 21 September 1981 (Benton Harbor-St. Joseph, Mich.).
36. William Ivey, "Every One a Gibsonite," Introduction to *The 1921 Gibson Catalog* (reprint, Nashville, Tenn.: The Country Music Foundation, 1973), iii, iv.
37. Julius Bellson, *The Gibson Story*, (Kalamazoo, Mich.: Julius Belloon, 1973), chapter 16.
38. Ibid., chapter 26.
39. Harold Rosier, Introduction to *The Rosier Players* program, (Jackson, Mich.: Jackson Community College, 1979), 2.
40. Ibid.
41. James A. Treloar, "Bill Bailey, Who Didn't Come Home," *Detroit News*, 17 June 1973.
42. Richard M. Goldstein and Charles W. Nelson, "The Calumet Theater: Music Hall or Opera House?" *Chronicle: The Magazine of the Historical Society of Michigan* (Winter 1983–84): 2–9.
43. Cynthia Boyes Young, "WWJ—Pioneer in Broadcasting," *Michigan History* (December 1960): 411–33.
44. Alan Lomax, comp., *Hard Hitting Songs for Hard-Hit People* (New York: Oak Publications, 1967), 240–41.
45. Charles Hamm, *Yesterdays: Popular Song in America* (New York: W. W. Norton and Co., 1979), 459–62.
46. Eric Zorn, "A 'Homestead' for Unsung Talent," *Bluegrass Unlimited* (December 1979): 24–26.
47. Ibid.
48. Glen Westphal interview with Stephen R. Williams, Port Huron, Michigan, 1984. See *House Party: Reminiscences by Traditional Musicians and Square Dance Callers in Michigan's Thumb Area* (Port Huron, Mich.: Museum of Arts and History, 1984), 2–4.

Occupational Folklore and Play

The Pottery &
the People

The Joy of Labor

Folklore of
Unemployed Workers

Waterfowling

Occupational folklore and play

are forms of cultural expression that reveal a great deal about the lives of Michiganders. Occupational experiences of lumberjacks, miners, and sailors in Michigan have been widely touted and popularized in recent years. However, scholarly attention has moved from often romanticized views of these early occupations to urban workers in cities who make their living in factories and on assembly lines. Every form of work or play has a set of associated traditions. Each participant in the occupations examined in this section has learned what Robert McCarl has termed "the canon of a technique" which refers to this "body of informal knowledge used to get the job done; at the same time, it establishes a hierarchy of skilled workers based on their individual abilities to exhibit that knowledge. The canon of work technique is not a law or a written set of rules but a standard that workers themselves create and control." Occupational folklore in Michigan work settings communicates an insider's view of the skills, stories, artistic creations, and customs that humanize the industrial workplace. While often playful in character, occupational folklore flows from the interaction of people at the workplace and challenges the outsiders' stereotypes about life in factories and on assembly lines.

The four articles offer some distinct opportunities to observe the culture of workers in Michigan. In the initial article, C. Kurt

Dewhurst focuses attention on the artistic output of workers in the workplace. These Grand Ledge worker-artists have applied the skills for which they were employed to produce sculpted creations for their own use, usually on their own time. The workers manipulate the materials of work, personalize the work environment, and engage their fellow workers in these creative activities as both aesthetic expression and as part of a community aesthetic. Yvonne R. Lockwood explores the creation of "homers," objects made with company materials and on company time. Unlike the Grand Ledge experience, these homers are frequently made without company approval. But like Grand Ledge pottery, these creations fulfill human creative needs and a sense of control over the work situation. Worker satisfaction comes in part from the control the worker asserts over the act of work, thereby creating an efficient utilization approach toward his or her work. Mark E. Workman demonstrates that the type of work one does shapes not only those days at work but even the way workers cope with unemployment. Narratives based on the experience of both a past work life and the search for a sense of self as unemployed can be rooted in a vital occupational folklore. Finally, the close interaction between work and play is presented in an article by C. Kurt Dewhurst and Marsha MacDowell that contrasts two waterfowling folk traditions that combine the occupation of guide and boat builder of Nate Quillen and Otto Misch, who also are engaged in what many would perceive to be an act of sport or play—duck hunting. Like many folk traditions, waterfowling practices are learned through small group or community folk processes in which the "canons of technique" are passed on only to the initiated. The traditions are sustained because they bond people together and give meaning to both work and play.

While there are many forms of occupational folklore and play in Michigan, the underlying premise is the same: members of any work group generate a body of traditional knowledge known as occupational folklore that helps us better understand our fellow Michiganders.

The Pottery and the People: A Community Experience

C. Kurt Dewhurst and Marsha MacDowell

ottery as material culture provides the point of focus and, at the same time, point of departure for this project. The purpose has been to redis-cover and further document the history of pottery production in Grand Ledge, Michigan, and the interrelationship of this activity and the people of the community. Conventional historical accounts rely primarily on census material, business directories, deeds, tax assessment records, newspapers, and diaries to reconstruct events. Although these tools played a considerable role in this project, the often-overlooked living resources—*the people*—have taken the central role in presenting the folklife of a community that has a distinctive past in pottery making.

James Deetz, an historical archeologist, recognized the need to look beyond the common objects of material culture to understand human experience. In a book that is titled for this approach, Deetz noted that early property tax records often concluded with a final entry by the appraiser that placed a monetary value on objects of seemingly less importance in this fashion: "In small things forgotten, eight shillings six pence."[1] The appraiser thus acknowledged "things that may have been overlooked but nonetheless had value."[2] In the course of this project, the pottery made in Grand Ledge might have

Reprinted from *Cast in Clay: The Folk Pottery of Grand Ledge, Michigan,* Michigan State University Museum Folk Culture Series 1, no. 4 (1980), 1–7.

found its way into the category "in small things forgotten" if an effort had not been taken to "read" the pottery as an artifact with "value." With the aid of many people in the community, the pottery activity of the past and the present came to life again, and a deeper understanding of the relationship between the pottery and the people emerged.

The initial pottery operations in Grand Ledge can now be acknowledged as among the earliest known sites of potteries in Michigan. Based near the rich deposits of clay along the Grand River, the Loveless (c. 1860) and Harrington (c. 1862) potteries provided a legacy for the industrial potteries that were to follow. The early pottery operations in Grand Ledge conformed to the traditional patterns of small-scale folk pottery making of New England. Pottery making was perceived to be part of a craft that was "governed by tradition and its practice required a long period of preparation."[3] Most of these family potteries were replaced by industrial pottery operations throughout the late nineteenth century, and the experience of Grand Ledge was typical of the practice. But the rich resources of clay in Grand Ledge made expanded pottery production a profitable enterprise for investors. In time, more local community residents began to find employment at these growing pottery concerns. The family potteries evolved into more expansive operations that became a source of common experience for the community.

The shared experiences of those who either worked at the potteries or knew those who worked there led to patterns of behavior communication, and customs that today are recognized by folklorists as "occupational folklore." Folklore is simply a term that describes "the traditional expressions and behavior which we have learned informally. Folklore usually expresses community values and it varies slightly, but constantly, as it is transmitted from generation to generation or from friend to friend."[4] The folklore that revolved around the life of work at the Grand Ledge potteries tells us much about life in that community. The human essence of the work experience cannot be measured simply in terms of years of employment or jobs performed. Thankfully, many community residents were able to help breathe life into the historical past and thereby enrich our understanding of life in a town with both a pottery past and a pottery present.

What is "Folk" about Grand Ledge Pottery?

To accurately label any object or group of objects as "folk," a number of conditions must be met. Folklorists frequently disagree on the purity of the folk object but almost universally agree that the culture that produces the folk object is conservative in its social values. Unlike the levels of culture that are considered popular (normative) or elite (progressive), folk culture retains a strong link with the past and carries forth past values into the future. Elite or popular cultural artifacts are subject to constant innovation or the capricious whims of those members of the cultural sets who are the agents for social change. Meanwhile, folk cultural artifacts experience "major variation over space and minor variation over time"[5] as these artifacts reflect locally defined community values.

In the communities where folklife proves most vital, traditional avenues for social intercourse exist between residents whether at home, at play, or at work. In Grand Ledge many residents contributed to the folklore of the workplace by passing along stories, behaviors, or, in the case of pottery, techniques for casting objects in clay. These folk patterns of life are usually transmitted orally, although at times they are recorded for informal aids in teaching. As workers with shared experiences in pottery making, the employees at the potteries in Grand Ledge formed what the folklorist would call a folk group. By examining the pottery and the process of learning to make pottery, one can detect the following conditions in the folk group: (1) clear identification with the folk group; (2) a distinct pattern of transmission of expressions and behaviors (primarily informal and oral); (3) a clearly identifiable traditional community aesthetic that governs the process of folk expression.

On the basis of these conditions of folk pottery making, certain types of Grand Ledge pottery that have been made, and are still being made, cannot be labeled folk pottery. The sewer pipe, drain tile, and conduit tile all conform to modes of pottery in popular culture, for these types of pottery are virtually identical to pieces made in the industrial potteries of Ohio. Although the workers who make these pieces identify themselves with the product, they are well aware that the industrial pottery they produce is identical to that produced elsewhere. Also, the techniques or procedures for making these utilitarian tiles are under constant scrutiny for potential improvement by those trained scientists and engineers who govern the introduction of new and improved technology. The worker thus has little room for creating a pottery that reflects a local community-based aesthetic. Although these production-line tiles cannot accurately be called folk pottery, their origin may have had strong roots in the folk tradition of pottery making. Also, this conclusion does not preclude the development of folklore that may still center around industrial pottery production or any occupation at all.

What, then, is "folk" about the pottery made in Grand Ledge, Michigan, in the last 120 years? As family enterprises, the early Loveless and Harrington potteries readily exhibit the established forms of a folk cultural organization: workers' identification with the community, distinct manner of transmitting the process, and an identifiable community aesthetic. As a consequence, one can call the early examples from these firms true folk pottery.

The more problematic forms of pottery are the many lions and other creations that were made along with the industrial tile-ware in the potteries of the twentieth century. When the same test is applied to these pieces, one reaches the conclusion that they too should be called folk pottery. The process of making these pieces was directly governed by the folk group that immediately surrounded the maker. Made according to the oral traditions passed on from fellow workers, lions in particular were created by successive generations of employees (fig. 1). The use of these pieces in the local community as doorstops, bookends, and for other purposes influenced the later pieces made by workers at the potteries. Umbrella stands, urns, and ashtrays were made as gifts for friends and relatives. Such pottery pieces, while varied, reflected the values of the workers and the community. Innovation occurred in limited steps, but new forms were encouraged. Some folklorists have qualms about the introduction of new ideas that are implanted in a conservative, tradition-bound community, and claim that tradition (and folk expression) stops where innovation begins. This notion is clearly misguided. Michael Owen Jones has noted that the belief that there is no virtue in originality is

> . . .an assumption that is based on a conception of folklore as necessarily static rather than *dynamic*. New discovery does not render the behavior or output of production non-folk. . .because what researchers have called folklore actually refers to a *process* of learning and utilizing modes of behavior in particular circumstances rather than to static texts or objects.[6]

The workers who made the variety of lions, animals, and assorted functional objects did so in the context of the folk process. They learned to make them from fellow workers and within the circumstances surrounding pottery making in Grand Ledge, Michigan.

Collection of the Grand Ledge Library

Figure 1. Grand Ledge Clay Products Workers, Grand Ledge, 1923.

The folklorist John Michael Vlach has written,

> Some have sought to distinguish between art that was culture and culture that was art, but what seems to be most significant is the broad and encompassing relationship between the two. Creativity reinforces identity: a sense of community is manifested between the maker and his artifact and other, like-minded individuals. This dynamic interaction of perceptions allows us to liken patterns in people to patterns in art.[7]

Folk Pottery in America

The art of the potter has a rich cultural history that can be traced back to the transitional phase between the Paleolithic and the Neolithic age or from approximately 8000 to 4000 B.C.[8] The fascination with pottery as a creative and utilitarian form was not only to flourish through the Middle Ages but also to find a fertile ground in the New World. A recent survey of early business records and diaries

in this country concluded that "the number of potters who were ply-
ing their trade in New England at an early date is astonishing. . .a list
of about seven hundred early potters has been compiled and at least
three hundred were at work before 1800."[9] Early American potteries
primarily produced pots for baking, serving, and storage. A typical
early American pottery was dependent on a local source of clay and
was operated by an individual potter who conducted work in his own
outbuilding or barn. An examination of some of the early accounts of
itinerant potters reveals that, because of the ready ease of transporting a potter's wheel, the potter moved according to the supply of clay
and local-level competition. Quite naturally, additional procedures
in potting lent themselves toward a more stable work environment,
since the kiln, grinding mill, glaze mill, drying shelves, and ever-
popular tubs for storing clay were not as easiy transported.

The process of throwing a pot always began with the digging of
clay, which was then washed to cleanse it of impurities before milling. Storage racks were filled with small quantities of clay that were
set aside for seasoning before use by the potter. Most pot shops were
one-man or family businesses, but apprentices or assistants were
often taken on to learn the trade. The common notion that a potter
produced one type of pottery at a time is accurate, but similar
objects were made in series such as jugs, crocks, or churns of identical size. Upon its completion, the pot was set out for drying in a
location that varied according to the season. Decoration of the pot
concluded with glazing and firing in what was virtually always a
roughly fashioned brick or stone kiln.

The folk tradition surrounding pottery making was well established and has led one scholar of American pottery to conclude:

> An important consideration in this craft is the fact that it was governed
> by tradition and that its practice required a long period of preparation.
> Apprentices were bound out to be master potters for a term of seven
> years; during that time they were taught every branch of the potter's
> art, from the preparation of clay to turning, glazing, and burning the
> ware. This long apprenticeship assured that the young craftsman
> would be able to turn a series of like forms rapidly without reference to
> measurements and that he also would have absolute control of the
> thickness of each form. A study of thousands of fragments shows that
> the latter skill was practically invariable.[10]

Two traditions of pottery making dominated early pottery
activity in early America: earthenware and stoneware. The heyday
of earthenware pottery has been roughly identified to be during the

period from 1640 to 1787. By the early 1700s, stoneware pottery had appeared on the American scene, eventually overtaking earthenware in popularity after the American Revolution and through the nineteenth century.[11] Some speculation has indicated that the "demand for sturdier vessels and the popular opposition to the use of toxic lead glazes" were responsible for the decline in the popularity of earthenware.

The centers for earthenware production in the eighteenth century were Charlestown and Boston. These two cities were responsible for spawning the potters that moved to other growing towns to set up potteries. Redware or earthenware pottery has been characterized as "soft and porous, oozing moisture from liquids placed in it and dangerous to health on account of its lead glaze," as compared to the "harder ceramic" or stoneware which is burned at a much "higher temperature and given a coating or glaze by means of salt thrown into the kiln at the greatest heat of burning."[12] The production of earthenware pottery required only a single firing, after which the pots were placed on the drying rack in preparation for the later steps of firing and glazing. Lead glazes, while clear in color, accentuated the yellow, brown, or red coloration of the original clay. The somewhat confusing names of redware, yellowware, brownware, and whiteware were all used to designate earthenware according to the primary color of the pottery produced.

Earthenware pottery is produced from simple clay fired at temperatures between 800° and 900°C. The amount of lime and other minerals in the firing temperature affect the final color of the pottery; it may be greyish or whitish, yellowish or reddish. High iron content in the clay, for example, accounts for the degree of redness in the earthenware after firing. Glazes were normally applied with a ladle or sprayed onto the pots. Incising of a decoration was popular and frequently resulted in revealing the color of the clay beneath the glaze. A particularly common method of decorating earthenware was the sgraffito technique in which two different colored slips were carefully poured on the pot to create an image or a word. Some potters even used a decorative process, comparable to applique work, in which small bits of molding clay were shaped by hand or molded and then applied to the pot before the glazing. Because glazes were considered relatively expensive to make, they were used sparingly and often with great care.

The stoneware tradition of pottery making followed the popularity of earthenware. The character of the clay required for stoneware is dramatically different from that used for earthenware. Whereas earthenware could be made from "common" clay, stoneware could be made only from a rarer high-quality clay. The temperatures up to and exceeding 1400°C that were used to fire stoneware produced a "vitrified" effect that gave almost a glass-like finish. The final application of a salt glaze over this effect resulted in a thin layer of natrium glass over the piece. New Jersey and Delaware were the early centers for stoneware since they were the locations of the supply of high-temperature firing clays. Because stoneware had a finer and less porous finish, it began to replace earthenware shortly after it was first produced.

Many earthenware potters experimented with local clays and imported better grades of clay in order to enter the stoneware market. Unfortunately, the supplies were limited and transportation was often complicated. Even where high-temperature firing clay was available, many folk potters found that raising the kiln temperatures to the necessary levels for stoneware was an insurmountable problem. New factory methods were tried to increase temperatures and improve techniques for loading kilns. The salt glazing technique was a traditional German technique that was readily adopted by the American potter. Throwing salt into the kiln after the pottery was completely fired caused "the salt to volatilize into a vapor which combined with the free silica in the clay body, covering the ware with a thin, mottled glaze."[13] The earliest forms of decoration on stoneware were rudimentary designs of letters, numbers, animals, birds, flowers, or stylized elements. After the introduction of cobalt, cobalt blue slips were popular, and they became more brush-like in quality. Responding to local demands, the stoneware potters produced a great volume of primarily durable and functional pots, such as jugs, bottles, urns, crocks, and churns. Technological innovations eventually led to standardization and the use of machinery to mold pottery. Before the end of the nineteenth century, these processes had replaced the local folk traditions that governed regional patterns of pottery making of earlier days. Some stoneware potteries in isolated communities retained their old distinctive ways; perhaps these potteries survived because they were part of a rich legacy of American folklife.

Cast in Clay: The Folk Pottery of Grand Ledge, Michigan

At the outset, it would be valuable to examine the history of Grand Ledge, Michigan, to set the stage for the development of folk pottery in that city. In June of 1836 a group of land speculators headed by a Mr. Zina Lloyd arrived in the Grand River Valley and purchased the section of land that is now Grand Ledge.[14] It is noted in the records of the *Grand Ledge Independent* that

> later surveys revealed a superior grade of sandstone, coal and clay, while the topography, which is the topography of the whole lower peninsula of the state, shows but eight points with a higher elevation than Grand Ledge, which is the summit of Eaton County, being 830 feet above sea level and 250 feet above Lake Michigan.[15]

Near where Grand Ledge was to develop, the Grand River Valley had carved a river bed that was approximately sixty feet below the surrounding terrain. The resulting sandstone ledges left exposed on the two sides of the Grand River were later to inspire the name of the town.

The Grand Ledge area had been called "Big Rocks" by the Ojibwa tribe who lived in wigwams throughout the area. Okemos was the chief of the Ojibwa tribe that hunted, trapped, made sugar, and fished in and along the Grand River. In 1848 the first white settlers appeared. Edmund L. Lamson, a native of Vermont, who had lived earlier in Pontiac and Farmington, Michigan, arrived with his family to settle on the land he had bought. Upon their arrival, the Lamsons discovered someone already living on their land. Little is known about the trespasser, Henry Trench, but records indicate that he was "an eccentric" who, although a college graduate, preferred the job of "tinkerer." Trench remained on the land for about eight years but finally gave up his eight acres along the Grand River and returned to Connecticut.

The Grand Ledge area was soon filled with settlers and in 1849 the Michigan state legislature authorized Abram Smith and John W. Russell to build a dam across the river. The dam was completed within a year, and a sawmill was soon in operation. In 1850 a meeting of the settlers was held to decide upon a name for their community and to petition the legislature for a post office. Several potential names were suggested, two of which were Trenchville and Lamsonville, but they were rejected because so many towns were "villes." Mrs. Lamson, a "cultured woman with a vision said, 'Why must we attach a "ville" to one of our names? Here we have this beautiful Grand River running through here and this grand ledge of rocks. Why not call it Grand Ledge?' "[16] Her suggestion met with approval and "Big Rocks" became Grand Ledge. In that same year the newly named community was granted its own post office.

The next fifty years were marked by rapid expansion and economic development in Grand Ledge. In 1853 the first wooden bridge was built to join the two sides of the town that were separated by the river. The *Grand Ledge Independent* was founded in 1870 and in the following year Grand Ledge was incorporated as a village by an act of the legislature. Yet, it is important to note that there was nothing but a dense forest between Lansing and Grand Ledge. Most of the time the road, an old Indian trail along the river, was almost impassable except on horseback.

In 1870 John Burtch undertook the development of the seven islands in the Grand River as a resort area. A few years later a Mr. Hewings bought the islands and expanded the facilities by enlarging the existing hotel, by buying a steamboat (which he christened "Gertie" in honor of his daughter), and by purchasing a large number of rowboats that were made available for a small rental fee. Along came another developer, J. S. Mudge, who bought the islands and made even more extensive improvements. A beautiful casino, added on one of the islands, made the seven islands "one of the most popular picnic places in Michigan." The seven islands were known to attract "as high as twelve train loads of people from various sections of Michigan and Chicago all in one day."[17] A colorful Indian legend contends that the seven islands were created when an Indian mother, fearing that an impending battle might harm her seven sons, decided to "give them to the Great Father." She supposedly threw her sons into the Grand River and shortly thereafter seven distinct islands appeared at the very locations where each of the Indian children had drowned.[18] Even though the resort business was to die down after the turn of the century with the invention of the automobile, Grand Ledge remained a thriving town.

What makes Grand Ledge so unusual is the fact that there were so few pottery towns in Michigan. Unlike other Eastern states that had numerous towns with potteries, only nine Michigan cities besides Grand Ledge had potteries: Burlington Township (Charles Gleason Pottery, c. 1868, known for redware when in Genesee County, New York); Corunna (John Neuffer Pottery, c. 1863–1864, known for its redware); Detroit (Martin Autretsch, c. 1863–1869, known for redware); Detroit (Theodore Blasley, c. 1865, known for redware); Grand Rapids (David Striven and Samuel Davis, c. 1859–1867); Hadley (Mortimer Price, c. 1863–1864); Hanover (Elijah Nichols, c. 1863–1865); Ionia (Sage and Dethrick, c. 1893–1903, known for earthenware, flower pots, and saucers); Marshall (Aaron Norris, c. 1862–1894), known for redware);[19] and Saginaw Clay Manufacturing Company (c. 1900).

By the end of the nineteenth century the city of Grand Ledge had experienced a dramatic change since the days when the area was populated by the Potawatomi Indians. For years the Potawatomi had moved in a north-south migration arriving in the Grand Ledge area in the spring to make maple syrup and sugar. Records show that following the Treaty of Saginaw, the Potawatomi Indians were among the tribes moved west to points beyond the Mississippi.[20] At that time, the Grand Ledge area became United States property, although a small number of the Ojibwa Indians continued to live in the region until about 1840.

In the early 1860s a pottery was built by a "Mr. Lew Harrington" on West Jefferson Street near the present site of the Grand Ledge Clay Products Company. A local legend contends that Indians in the area had used this site for pottery making, and it was soon discovered by homesteaders that the clay along the Grand River was suitable for the production of earthenware. Information about Mr. Harrington is scant, but it is known that he was the father of Edward, a painter,[21] and that he produced jars, churns, and crocks.[22] Another early potter, George Loveless, also built a pottery near or on this site. The 1860 census for the Township of Oneida (which includes Grand Ledge) listed George Loveless as a potter and his son George B. Loveless as a peddler. A colorful figure, George Loveless was too old to enlist at the outbreak of the Civil War. Undaunted by his age, he dyed his hair black and was able to join up. When the war ended, he returned home where he commenced a more personal kind of battle. The *Grand Ledge Independent* cites the incident in the following story:

> When the railroad was being built from here to Grand Rapids, the graders struck Mr. Loveless's land just at the end of the bridge by the chair factory; they had been allowed to complete the grade across his land without settling the right of way, and when they got the rails laid to the west end of the bridge, just before them on a pile of railroad ties which he had put up sat Mr. Loveless with a double barrelled shot gun. He had established a dead line at the end of the bridge and told them that the first man who crossed it would be shot. They settled. Loveless was eighty years old at the time.[23]

By 1869, work on the railroad was completed and trains began running through Grand Ledge on a regular basis.

The first organized clay product company was the Grand Ledge Sewer Pipe Company formed in the 1880s. In 1906, another business sprang up across the highway. A number of local businessmen, including R. E. Olds, founder of Oldsmobile, and John W. Fitzgerald, father of a Michigan governor and grandfather of the Michigan Supreme Court Justice John Fitzgerald, organized the new business, the Grand Ledge Clay Products Company, which has flourished until today. This firm was originally intended to produce only conduit pipe for underground wiring, but a disastrous fire in 1937 destroyed the dies for the pipes, and the company began to manufacture sewer pipes. This turn of events initiated a rivalry between the two companies which continued until the shut down of the first factory, leaving the Grand Ledge Clay Products Company the only remaining tile-producing firm in Michigan. During the years of competition, the original firm had changed hands, eventually becoming the American Vitrified Company, owned by the Ohio-based firm of the same name. Many sewer tile workers in Grand Ledge worked at various times in either firm. Because of its Ohio association, American Vitrified brought from Ohio many specialized workers, particularly molders and branchers. In the early teens, Grand Ledge Clay Products was employer of a large group of Syrian immigrants but, for the most part, the industries have found their labor force locally. Many of the workers' families still live close by.

Over the years, both companies worked out ingenious methods of removing the clay from the ledges and transporting the clay to their plants. For American Vitrified Products Company, this meant hand-loading the clay into a V-shaped narrow-gauge rail car, which was pulled by donkeys underneath the Pere-Marquette railroad, across the highway (Jefferson) to the factory. Grand Ledge Clay Products used a horse-drawn V-shaped rail car that ran on a narrow-gauge track to the main building, at one point crossing a trestle bridge built of conduit tiles. Since, for a long time, most of the clay was loaded by hand, the jobs at the sewer tile factories were arduous and demanding. One worker's widow, Mrs. Ray Poole, recalls, "It took a strong back and a weak mind to work there."[24] Yet it was at the end of their long days in this harsh setting that a small number of employees created their own artistic diversions and modes of self-expression in clay.

The Grand Ledge Lion

The folk pottery pieces in general, and the Grand Ledge clay lions in particular, were made to imitate what had been viewed by the makers or what had been learned through oral tradition. Some speculation has been offered by local antiquarians that the Grand Ledge lion was influenced by the earlier well-documented lions produced in Bennington, Vermont, or perhaps by examples imported from England. These more elaborate creations were complete with flint enamel or rockingham-glaze. The Bennington lions were often made without bases, with rough cast or smooth curly manes. Like the dogs, deer, and various animals made at Bennington or in other "industrial" potteries elsewhere, Bennington lions were beautifully rendered by highly skilled and trained potters. The figurative detail was carefully incised and shaped. It is no wonder that these figures would be remembered and perhaps copied in years to come.

There are many possible explanations for the appearance of folk pottery in Grand Ledge. The area was largely populated by New Englanders and especially by settlers from upstate New York. Settlers from Vermont who came to neighboring Vermontville, Michigan, may have carried with them the seeds of the idea or perhaps an actual example. But the most likely sources for the lion form produced in Grand Ledge are the many similar industrial potteries in Ohio that made sewer tile and drain pipe. The Zanesville, Ohio, area was especially noted for this type of pottery activity, and lions that resemble those made in Grand Ledge were also created by workers in these Ohio potteries. Quite naturally, there may have been some sharing from state to state because of the migration of workers to other potteries, as previously noted in the case of American Vitrified Products of Grand Ledge. Census listings and recollections of workers at both Grand Ledge Clay Products and American Vitrified recall molders and branchers coming up to Grand Ledge for work. The earlier explanation of the Bennington-type lion may still help explain the lion form whether it appeared first in Ohio or in Michigan.

Folk traditions are actually communication processes. Oral transmission and imitation are primary agents for communicating ideas of patterns of behavior in folk expression. Folklore or folklife is "true to its own nature when it takes place within the group (limited community) itself. In sum, folklore is artistic communication in small groups."[25] The form of the lion was the result of just this process of conception. Workers learned to make the vast number of lions by imitation and by following the oral lessons of their fellow workers. The earliest known lion made in Grand Ledge was made by Emery Marvin in 1901. From that early example, a steady stream of lions emerged from the kilns of both industrial potteries in Grand Ledge into the 1940s. Unlike the Bennington-type lion or rockingham-glazed lion on a base, the Michigan lion was transformed by the Grand Ledge workers from a naturalistic form to a more rigid sphinx-like figure resting on a flat clay base (fig. 2). The end result varied somewhat depending on the artist's ability to combine the necessary technical skill and the aesthetic elements. Among the many lions made, the most sophisticated pieces were achieved in direct contrast to the material used in their creation. One worker, Harry Poole, described the process of making a lion in this fashion:

> Just before noon some fellows would take some clay and pack the molds tightly. A lot of the molds were not filled properly and the lions never came out right. We would then set the mold aside until the next day when we would take the lion out of the mold and smooth it all out by licking your thumb. Some guys put tongues in their lions by using a knife to make the mouth open and then rolling some molding clay. The paws, tail, and mane were fixed by using a knife or pencil. Then the lion was placed on a sand-covered board and put in the kiln with the tile.[26]

Collection of the Grand Ledge Library

Figure 2. Grand Ledge Clay Lion, artist unknown, c. 1920.

The baking time for the production of tile and drain pipe was about three days in the large kilns, and the lions generally remained in the kilns for almost the entire period. According to Poole, some workers were less honest than others, for it was a fairly common event for lions to be stolen out of the kilns.

> I always put my lions up high because I was tall, just inside the door. When the kilns were just starting to cool some guys would wet their hands and put a handkerchief over their mouth . . . and when no one was lookin' slip into the kiln and steal a lion. . . . One time I saw someone get a shiner who had a lion in his dinner pail with someone else's initials on it. . . .[27]

The molds were made from plaster of Paris. During the time in the kiln the molded lions were usually subjected to the same salt glaze that the production pottery received. After they were dried and cooled they were taken home for the families and friends of the makers. One worker recalls that he could sell lions to people in town, and he remembers that he "made two lions one night and sold 'em for 25¢ and 50¢ each."[28] The bases of the lions were decorated with varied styles. Some bases were given a fluted or fringe-like effect by use of a knife, stick, or a rubber mold. Others were simply signed with the initials of the maker or in some cases the date and complete name of the maker. A few even displayed a more accomplished finish: they were stamped with the words "Grand Ledge, Michigan" along the base.

Banks were also made from the same lion molds by hollowing out the lion, cutting a slot on the top of the lion's head (just in front of the mane), and eliminating the conventional base. One such bank was given a two-tone finish by applying different color glazes to the body and the mane of the lion. Unlike the many lion door stops, lion banks were rarely produced and were especially susceptible to breakage because of their hollowness, not to mention the obvious breakage to retrieve money.

The lions made by the workers at both potteries were depicted in accurate proportions with a sculpted mane and strong facial character. The legs and paws seem to be relaxed and yet quite lifelike. The tail sweeps around and under the back of the left leg. Common practice dictated that the underside of the base be hollowed out somewhat to ensure even drying. The final results varied according to the subtle innovations of each worker. Often the strength of each lion's anthropomorphic character shone through in its smile and eyes.

Undoubtedly, the Grand Ledge lion became an outlet for artistic expression by the workers who were accustomed to rigorous nine-hour work days. Although the industrial revolution signaled the decline of many folk traditions in America, folk expression found new avenues. Industrial conditions such as those existing in Grand Ledge brought together a community of workers who established their own traditional patterns. Because of their local significance and their great number, the Grand Ledge lions were clearly the most identifiable form of material culture that resulted. In the words of one former worker, "Rarely a week went by without somethin' bein' made."[29]

"If You Have An Educated Thumb . . ."

Harry Poole claims that "if you have an educated thumb . . . you could make most anything. . . . You could throw some molding clay on the board an' then you could stand back and look at it . . . and then make something out of it."[30] It was just such unbridled enthusiasm for creating that was responsible for the variety of objects made by the pottery employees in their few spare moments. Even though lions were by far the most popular folk pottery subject, many other subjects were attempted. The work of one individual can help convey the personal exploration of varied subject matter.

Roy Poole, the brother of Harry, was born in Grand Ledge in 1898 and worked there his entire life. He was employed at both American Vitrified and the Grand Ledge Clay Products Companies. During his years at the potteries, he fashioned and fired numerous animals from "sewer tile for clay" for his own pleasure and to decorate his house and garden. He made turtles, alligators, frogs, coiled snakes, lamp bases, ashtrays, and assorted containers. Many of his pieces, such as his turtles, were large (twelve inches in diameter) and surprisingly heavy. His hand-fashioned turtles had shells incised with deeply scored shell-like patterns; extended appendages were also finished with decoratively incised claws. The head of each turtle was extended upward to convey a primitive expression of life. Its eyes seemed to be directed up at the human viewer. Perhaps Roy Poole was particularly attracted to the subjects of turtles and frogs because they were no doubt common along the Grand River, which ran through town. But his numerous other creations were seemingly the products of his imagination.

Other workers may have followed Roy Poole's example because numerous variations of frogs, for example, can still be found today. Harry Poole recalls, "I often took a handful of clay home to make snakes . . . they were never stolen [because of their lack of popularity]. . . . Some kids used to like to take them [clay snakes] to school."[31]

Animals were understandably popular subjects for the potter, but another popular subject was the sculpted tree trunk, which served as the form for urns, planters, umbrella stands, and other practical containers. These tree trunk shapes exhibit tremendous variation, but they share in common the attempt to simulate an exterior of bark and often stylized stumps of branches. For the creation of such a container one worker gave this explanation: "[I] took a section of pipe, then took molding clay to look like bark . . . you just go up like that [thumb motion] to make bark . . . then [use] molding clay to look like branches."[32] Practical and ingenious potters created variations of this form that were as endless as the imaginations of the potters themselves. Even cemetery planter urns and markers were made in Grand Ledge, much in the same spirit of the sewer tile cemetery markers that have been found in southern Ohio and in Kentucky. In later years, workers brought in molds made from other sculptured animal pieces such as a metal cast frog, human forms such as copperplated Abraham Lincoln mementos, or even religious articles such as the small figure of Jesus that was to serve as a mold for a number of clay replicas.[33] One can conclude, as Harry Poole has suggested, that "you can make anything out of clay."[34]

---

1. James Deetz, *In Small Things Forgotten* (New York: Doubleday, 1977), 4.
2. Ibid.
3. Lura Woodside Watkins, *Early New England Pottery* (Sturbridge, Mass.: Old Sturbridge Village, 1966), 2.
4. Suzi Jones, *Oregon Folklore* (Eugene: University of Oregon and the Oregon Arts Commission, 1977), 12.
5. See Henry Glassie, "Folk Art," in *Folklore and Folklife*, ed. Richard M. Dorson (Chicago: University of Chicago Press, 1972), 253–80.
6. Michael Owen Jones, *The Hand-made Object and Its Maker* (Berkeley: University of California, 1975), 68.
7. John Michael Vlach, *The Afro-American Tradition in Decorative Arts* (Cleveland, Ohio: Cleveland Museum of Art, 1978), 148.
8. Gerhard Kaufmann, *North German Folk Pottery of the 17th to the 20th Centuries* (Richmond, Va.: International Exhibitions Foundation, 1979), 13.
9. Watkins, 1.
10. Ibid.
11. Harold F. Guilland, *Early American Folk Pottery* (Philadelphia: Chilton Book Company, 1971), 3.

12. Watkins, 15.
13. Guilland, 57.
14. Grace Porter Pierce, "The History of Grand Ledge," *Grand Ledge Centennial Booklet*, 1936, 9.
15. "Speculators Came First," *Grand Ledge Independent* (special supplement), 13 May 1970, B-4.
16. "Potawatomi Indians Came Here First," *Grand Ledge Independent* (special supplement), 13 May 1970, B-4.
17. Grace Porter Pierce, *The History of Grand Ledge* (Grand Ledge: Grand Ledge Centennial Booklet, 1936), 11.
18. Ibid.
19. See William Ketchum Jr., *The Pottery and Porcelain Collector's Handbook* (New York: Funk and Wagnalls, 1971), 171; and *Geological Survey of Michigan*, vol. 8 (1900–1909).
20. "Potawatomi Indians Came Here First," B-4.
21. Michigan, Eaton County Census (Oneida Township), 1860.
22. Valorus M. Kent, "Recollections," Grand Ledge Library Files, 1922 (unpublished manuscript).
23. Mrs. Edward Kent, "Loveless Guarded Right of Way," *Grand Ledge Independent*, 1922.
24. Interview with Mrs. Roy Poole, 15 June 1976.
25. Dan Ben-Amos, "Toward a Definition of Folklore in Context," *Toward New Perspectives in Folklore* (Austin: University of Texas Press, 1972), 13.
26. Interview with Harry Poole, 17 February 1980.
27. Ibid.
28. Ibid.
29. Interview with Dale Brown, 2 January 1980.
30. Harry Poole.
31. Ibid.
32. Ibid.
33. Interview with Wayne Childs, 2 January 1980.
34. Harry Poole.

The Joy of Labor

Yvonne R. Lockwood

ohn Doe[1] was a production welder in an automobile plant when he submitted a piece of his metal sculpture in a contest sponsored by the United Auto Workers. The boredom of his welding job, he said, made him seek diversions. During the ten-second interval between cars on the assembly line, he welded together spare nuts, bolts, and scrap metal, transforming these useless materials into sculptures of small animals with crinkled hides and rumpled hair. Doe actually began to look forward to work and although it was exhausting to do "both jobs," he no longer was bored. At his welding job, Doe discovered the art of welding. Public recognition of his creative activities brought Doe to the attention of an enraged management. Before they could fire him, he quit and is now attending art school.

For Doe, the job was drudgery. Nonetheless, he perfected a job skill that allowed a form of expression that he and his co-workers regarded as art. Unlike Doe, however, other assembly line workers approach their jobs artistically.[2] Some see an aesthetic dimension to the skills required to fulfill their jobs.[3] And for others, play and work fuse into a game.[4] In Doe's case, however, artistry lay in creating sculpture, which, because of its illicit nature, intensified the experience. He found pleasure in both the homer process and the product.

Was management enraged by Doe's acts or by the acclaim resulting from his acts? His case raises familiar questions about the causes of worker alienation and how it is handled; about the distinction between work and leisure; and about "theft"—in other words, about the ownership of human time, proprietorship of machines and materials, and what constitutes capital. In an attempt to address these questions, this essay focuses on the meaning and implication of what are called "government jobs" or "homers," aesthetic creations "secretly" produced by workers on the job for their own pleasure with the tools and materials of their jobs.[5] This study of homers aims at increasing our understanding of occupational culture by broadening our knowledge about workplace behavior and ideology and our awareness of a type of occupational folk art.

According to Marx, the division of labor and the exploitation of employees results in the alienation of workers from their work and from the products of their work. Indeed, industrialization has made the work process more efficient; individual jobs became simplified and repetitive, no longer requiring workers' involvement in an entire project but, rather, focusing attention on one small part of the process. Thus, the assumption has been that the more repetitive the work, the greater the alienation, because dehumanizing work routines separate the worker physically and psychologically from the product. Blauner's classic study of industrial workers isolates four factors contributing to alienation: (1) powerlessness, the lack of autonomy and control over one's work; (2) meaninglessness, not knowing how one's job fits into the whole because of the production process; (3) isolation, a lack of satisfaction with the work group and a feeling of social separation; and (4) self-estrangement, a feeling that one's job is merely a way to make money and is neither of central interest nor a means of self-expression.[6]

Most workers in repetitive jobs on production lines acknowledge one or more of these factors in their work. They mention boredom and the lack of control over their jobs, a lack of intellectual challenge, and a lack of a sense of accomplishment. Their repetitive, unskilled jobs often do not permit them to demonstrate any skill, initiative, or resourcefulness. One auto worker vividly describes the singlemindedness of his job: "In the repair shop you clip on the color hose, bleed out the old color, and squirt. Clip, bleed, squirt, THINK; clip, bleed, squirt, YAWN; clip, bleed, squirt, SCRATCH YOUR NOSE."[7]

Some sociological studies of work still maintain that only individuals with low intelligence tend to be satisfied with repetitious jobs.[8] But studies based on participant observation and in-depth interviewing show that "satisfaction" means the successful integration of work and leisure. By repeating a job process, a worker becomes the master of the job, working easily and quickly, developing efficient techniques, gaining more free time while keeping up with or ahead of production goals. A female employee at an auto plastics plant, for example, has had the same job for some eight years, punching holes and assembling tiny metal parts for automobile dashboards. She knows her job so well that the movement of her body is perfectly synchronized with the machine at which she works.[9] Hers is an aesthetic of performance. Furthermore, she often works with her eyes closed, which is forbidden for safety reasons. But here lies the challenge. Workers, such as this woman, who are not on a conveyor belt can control their output by building up "banks"—visible, tangible, and controllable evidence of accomplishment.[10] This worker does not want another job; she "makes her daily production" of so many pieces and "earns relief," primarily time to make jewelry from the minute metal parts with which she works, to socialize and play cards in the cafeteria, or to exercise in the restroom. It is her choice; she has some control over her job, albeit the degree is miniscule. Significantly, this worker's satisfaction with her repetitious job has nothing to do with her IQ—or maybe it has everything to do with it. She has mastered her job, and thus controls her time; her leisure activities offer her social integration and identity.

Such examples are numerous, and they indicate that not all individuals passively accept the conditions of their jobs. Even in the case of auto assemblers like Doe, workers exercise job control, seek challenge, and gain a sense of accomplishment in various ways. They double up, work ahead, improve their tools, stall production, stop work, play pranks, and create objects of art. This behavior is a cultural response to a job situation. Culture is adaptive and serves to intercede between a person and the environment. Workers form groups for common cause; they also respond creatively by producing forms of expression that reflect an understanding and feeling of the worker-community.[11] A welder, for example, writes riddle poetry based on his own industrial experience and explains that "it's the way I have to express myself in my everyday routine work." An auto assembler says about her paintings of the assembly line, "You're told so many times by the boss to do something, they just treat you like you're not anything. You just come to work, do your job, and that's it. . . . I think with art you have a sense that you're somebody or something." A sheetmetal journeyman turned to metal sculpture when he became "frustrated working with metal in an uncreative way."[12]

These material art forms are prime examples of homers.[13] They are produced by workers who use their work experiences and skills with the machines, tools, and materials of their jobs in alternative, aesthetic ways. Thus, workers apply job skills to extraoccupational activity and consciously create art forms. With this kind of activity, the worker transforms the job and gains control over and freedom from the machine and automation. The worker scans the material at hand—these are usually scraps and leftovers no longer needed—weighs the capabilities of the machine or tools, and decides what to attempt. He or she does not otherwise have such control and possibility for decision-making on-the-job. This type of activity is the antithesis of mechanical, repetitive "real" work.[14] The fact that homers are made from scraps ensures that the satisfaction and beauty come from the labor itself. Some of this creative energy is said to be spent during coffee and lunch breaks or after work, but much of it also takes place on the job. As the Doe case demonstrates, management does not condone this on-the-job activity; therefore, his sculpting was done surreptitiously, between cars on the assembly line, when things were slow and when the foreman was not looking. Such activities are often negotiated with foremen, who turn their backs as long as work is done properly. In Doe's case, attention to his activity went beyond the plant foreman and forced management to take notice.

We find many examples of homers in auto plants. Welders and metal workers, for example, make chess sets, miniature tools, miniature automobiles and furniture, knives, sculptures, hash pipes, belt buckles, jewelry, and so on. A Kentucky migrant who works as a carpenter in an auto plant near Detroit illustrates the point. Wood carving is an old family tradition that he carried into the plant. Twice a day he checks the scrap woodpile at work; he whittles on breaks and when the "real" work is slow. Among his creations are wooden chains of various sizes and different toys, including automobiles and whistles.[15]

A very special type of sculpture made from black plastic is another example of homers at auto plants. The ejection molding machine oozes a soft plastic which, while still warm, the worker molds into abstract shiny black shapes. One example, named "Black Cobra" by the workers at the plant, is about ten inches high and looks like a snake ready to strike (fig. 1). Variants of these plastic sculptures are reportedly made in auto plants elsewhere in Michigan and Ohio; the sculptures apparently adorn work stations and are taken home as gifts. Paint departments of auto plants have also supplied workers with materials for their aesthetic impulses. After automobiles have been sprayed, the workers knock loose the paint that has accumulated on racks and sand the paint chips for use in jewelry. By feathering the pieces, the worker exposes the many layers of paint, creating a multicolored pendant or inset for belt buckles.[16]

Another case of creative homers occurs at a laundry that services industrial plants in the Detroit area. In the mid-1970s, several women employees began to salvage scraps of material used to clean machinery. The idea to make quilts came almost spontaneously: "We just got out our shears and started cutting." The entire quilting process from the washing of scraps to the sewing is done at the laundry with laundry equipment, sometimes even on company time when business is slow. Often the ideas for quilt patterns come from friends. One of the quilters explained why their quilts are special:

> The material is free. It's just nothing. It's being thrown away. So it makes it interesting to gather the stuff and wash it and sometimes there are beautiful patterns in it. . . . And when you . . . put it into a quilt, then you see what beauty comes out. . . . It's an art. And we like it. . . . It's relaxing.[17]

The plant atmosphere is not always as tolerant as it is at this laundry. When pleasure, beauty, and humor occur in places designated for work, officials tend to see workers' art as a threat to efficiency and as generally disruptive. In one automobile plant, workers made small figurines from dum-dum putty. According to a worker, every niche and possible work station was decorated with them. One weekend, management entered the plant and destroyed all figurines. Why? The worker's bitter answer was that the plant "had to look like a plant."[18]

Steelworkers also fall victim to management's housecleaning. According to one worker, everyone in the mill eventually decorates his or her hard hat. Sometimes decals are merely stuck on, or individuals' names and slogans are painted on. The more interesting examples are elaborate painted scenes covering the entire hat, scenes whose message often is meaningful only to other mill workers or is a social comment about the workplace. Management tolerates this

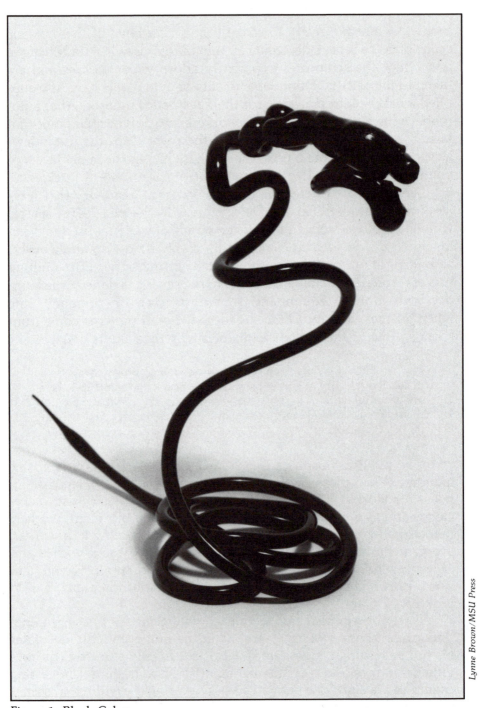

Figure 1. Black Cobra.

embellishment for a while, but eventually rounds up all hats for a "safety check" and at the same time cleans them up, like the janitor who cleans graffiti from bathroom walls.

While steelworkers and autoworkers strive to personalize their work environments, management enforces uniformity, a situation that recalls the early twentieth century and Henry Ford, who saw himself "more as a manufacturer of men than automobiles."[19] Ford's goal was uniformity, homogeneity, impersonality; his method was the assembly line. He maintained a Sociological Department whose duty it was to facilitate the melting pot. The staff went to the homes of immigrant workers, unannounced, to make sure that they were not eating spaghetti, because that was not American. Jonathan Schwartz reports, "It seems on reflection that the ideal of the Ford Sociological Department was a purely impersonal world, a world of interchangeable men who would operate like interchangeable parts of a machine. The 'melting pot' at Ford's was an assembly line."[20]

The embellishment of hard hats, beautification of the workplace, and the subsequent destruction of these artifacts are all part of an on-going struggle for control, where one side attempts to personalize and individualize the environment while the other strives to transform humans into replaceable parts of a large, humming machine.[21]

The attitude of company management is more understanding and accepting of employees' more conventional paintings and sculptures. Some companies display their workers' award-winning paintings, and some commission workers to paint murals in plants.[22] Other enlightened employers have established workshops in plants where employees use older machinery to make objects for personal use. Some employees have even set up easels near their work area and painted scenes of work. There are many more cases, however, of companies that have blocked that kind of activity. Unlike paintings, homers are usually discredited as junk; management neither encourages the making nor does it stop such activity so long as workers make homers on their own time.

The question here is one of ownership and "theft." When any worker uses the same materials, machines, or tools day-after-day, a sense of proprietorship develops over these items. In a plant setting, there is no clear division between company property and property of "uncertain ownership."[23] What is scrap and nonscrap or usable and nonusable is often ambiguous. Thus, the work group establishes its own boundaries. Usually property of uncertain ownership is designated "fair game." It includes company-owned materials that are small, inexpensive, and copious, often the by-products destined to be thrown out. A steel millworker explained about workers' use of company materials:

> When you say "theft," I think of that as stealing something to sell on the outside. There was only a few people doing this. I think most people felt they was a part of the steel mill, if they wanted a piece of steel. I never even thought about it as stealing. I used to get into the open-hearths, get in the stainless steel. We would take this and would lay it on a railroad track. We would mat it together. I don't know but what my wife may still have some of it. We'd make bracelets, we'd make knives. We'd bring the jewelry home. In fact, I think I have a knife now that I made in the steel mill. This is no secret. You don't hide it. I mean the superintendents and everyone saw us in our spare time making this stuff. I think when you speak of little articles being taken out, I don't think the company ever really cared. I used to enjoy making knives. We gave knives to some of the soldiers that they took with them to the service during WWII.[24]

Other examples contradict this worker's story and testify that employees must submit to body checks when they leave their plants. These workers must make their homers secretly because the materials are still valued as company property.

Most workers get part of their wages (or salary) in-kind. The meaning of this type of "benefit," however, varies widely. Scholars isolate different categories of in-kind payment; employers and white-collar employees get "perks," while blue-collar employees "pilfer."[25] The distinction is subtle but real. Someone caught pilfering is stopped but not necessarily prosecuted. In actuality, the employee is at the whim of the employer because pilferage is not a recognized offense; one's activity is defined as either theft or perk, and it makes little difference how workers view it. Employer designation varies for different industries, on different days, between different individuals.

A blatant example of this distinction between perk and pilferage is demonstrated in the case of a male supervisor who used company materials on company time to make large models of penises which, along with automobiles, were spray-painted and then presented to female autoworkers.[26]

There is nothing ambiguous about objects made for sale or profit; everyone agrees that this constitutes theft and, therefore, few admit to making homers for profit. The ambiguity of human capital control, however, makes it difficult to get straight information about whether homers are made on company time. It is my conclusion from many hours of interviewing workers that homers said to have been made on break time are often made on company time. The real issue is not control and use of material; rather, it is the ownership of human capital and control of leisure (or play). Does the company own the worker the entire eight-hour day? Should a secretary look busy when there isn't any work, rather than read a book? Should Doe have stood around being bored because those ten seconds were not his to dispense with in any other way?

When Calvinism sanctified work and industrialism enobled it, emphasis on economically productive functions and the separation of work and leisure became significant aspects of life.[27] Americans still hold the value that work is good and leisure is "free time." Thus, when work seems meaningless, the individual feels betrayed and begins to look away from work to find moral identification and loyalties. Work then becomes "just a job" while leisure takes on importance.

Although leisure is usually defined as a type of action easily distinguished from the act of working, the work of professionals— academics, artists, writers, and so on—is often indistinguishable from their leisure; their social activities, for example, abound with work. On the other hand, given the nature of industrial work, the stereotype persists that blue-color workers cannot possibly take pleasure in their jobs, and thus, their leisure activity must be confined to activities away from work.[28] Quite the contrary, work is more like leisure than scholars usually realize. Work and leisure are integrated in the lives of many industrial workers; they would be even more so if workers were left to their own devices, without management rules.

Homers help bring about integration in workers' lives. Whereas alienation stems mainly from the sense of separation, loss, and discontinuity that seems to characterize modern technical and bureaucratic process, both the homer process and the product give worker-artists a sense of mastery over the disconnected parts of their lives. The homer becomes an icon of that mastery and a symbol of continuity.

Homers assume still another role in the workplace, that is, as mediators in worker relations. The production of homers is not confined to isolated individual behavior; rather, there is cooperative effort, as for example, when workers comb the plant for materials for worker-artists. In laundries and steel and auto plants, workers share in homers both as creators and as audience. Like pranks and games, the making and sharing of homers undermines the status system reinforced by management. In plants where daily production levels must be filled, for instance, individuals might be offered special incentives to do more: they are promised overtime; they are promised easier jobs over hard ones. This causes dissension and competition among workers. In contrast, homers can function to stimulate cooperation between workers, reinforcing their relationship as a group vis-a-vis management and ameliorating their social alienation.

At the present time in the United States, our identities and sense of meaning and purpose are mainly based on work. "What do you do?" we ask of individuals we have just met. But within the group, identities are based increasingly on leisure pursuits. In the context of meaningless work, leisure becomes meaningful. Just as a good story-teller, joke-teller, and game player gains status, so worker-artists acquire a greater sense of accomplishment and appreciation. "It's nice," said one worker-artist. "People come up to me all the time to see what I'm doing. It gives me more recognition at work." Thus, aesthetic creativity fuses with his work to provide him dignity and a more positive self-perception.

Although homers have not been well-researched, there is mention of them throughout Europe. Even in the Socialist Republic of Hungary, factory workers are reported to have a "passion" for making homers, so much so that their decisions about job changes are based on whether the possibility exists to make them.[29] All such activity, however, is prohibited; consequently, workers make homers in great secrecy. Thus, it seems that homers are not the result of state ideology or policy—capitalism versus socialism—but, rather, the result of production methods and the organization of work. Ownership of the means of production seems not to matter in the homer process.

I have treated homers primarily as a response to worker alienation. It would be erroneous, however, to assume that workers' aesthetic impulses are expressed only under such conditions. At the same time, we must not underestimate the role of homers in counteracting the alienating aspects of work situations. As Kusterer argues, working knowledge about machines and materials and participation in the work community are two important strategies for overcoming alienation.[30] The act of making homers, in fact, requires both job know-how and group participation. Workers constantly struggle to breathe life into their work, to integrate work into their lives. Homers help accomplish this goal.

Note: This paper benefited greatly from the comments and suggestions of William G. Lockwood, Louis Berndt, John Beck, and Hyman Kornbluh.

1. This study was conducted in and around Michigan in 1981–82. The reader should be aware that much of the information about workers' art in this article is sensitive. Consequently, I have included information about informants sparingly and with caution. When individuals are named, I have used pseudonyms. Plant names and locations are not mentioned.

2. See Michael J. Bell, "Making Art Work," *Western Folklore* 43 (1984): 211–21. Elsewhere, Bell demonstrates that other work can also be creative; see his "Tending Bar at Brown's: Occupational Role as Performance," *Western Folklore* 30 (1976): 93–103. Similarly, Michael Owen Jones argues that some people "work at playing and others play at working, and still more create work as some work to create." See Jones' "A Feeling for Form, as Illustrated by People at Work," in *Folklore on Two Continents: Essays in Honor of Linda Degh*, ed. Nikolai Burlakoff and Carl Lindahl (Bloomington: Indiana University Press, 1980), 265.

3. Robert McCarl, "The Production Welder: Product, Process and the Industrial Craftsman," *New York Folklore Quarterly* 30 (1974): 243–53.

4. Donald Roy, "'Banana Time': Job Satisfaction and Informal Interaction," *Human Organization* 18 (1959–60): 158–68.

5. In this paper, these terms do not mean the same thing. "Homer" refers to art. Although in Michigan "government job" or "government work" refers to most "illegal" worker-controlled activity, from repairing a camera on-the-job to the creation of aesthetic objects, for the sake of discussion and clarity I have chosen to use the more common European term, "homer," to mean art, and "government work" to imply those activities which do not produce art and esoterically are considered theft, e.g., taking supplies of materials from work for personal use.

6. Robert Blauner, *Alienation and Freedom: The Factory Worker and His Industry* (Chicago: University of Chicago Press, 1964), 89–123.

7. Barbara Garson, *All the Live Long Day: The Meaning and Demeaning of Routine Work* (New York: Penguin Books, 1977), 88.

8. See discussion in Michael Argyle, *The Social Psychology of Work* (Harmondsworth, England or New York: Taplinger, 1972).

9. Wilhelm Baldamus refers to this type of pleasant feeling of being pulled along by an activity, i.e., "grooving," as "traction." See his *Efficiency and Effort* (London: Tavistock Publications, 1961), 59. Michael J. Bell calls this phenomenon "making art work."

10. Charles R. Walker and Robert Guest, *Man on the Assembly Line* (Cambridge: Harvard University Press, 1952), quoted by Blauner, 85.

11. Roger Abrahams, "Towards a Sociological Theory of Folklore: Performing Services," in *Working Americans: Contemporary Approaches to Occupational Folklore*, ed. Robert H. Byington (Los Angeles, 1978), 25.

12. These worker-artists were interviewed in conjunction with an exhibit of workers' art at the First Conference on Workers' Culture, 1980, University of Michigan, Ann Arbor.

13. A classic description of a homer appears in *The Korl Woman* by Rebecca Harding Davis, first published in the *Atlantic Monthly* in 1861. In his hours off from the furnace, Hugh Wolfe, a poor Irish immigrant and slave of the iron mills, sculpts life-sized figures from the light, porous refuse which remains after pig metal is run. Davis expresses her perception of the extreme alienation of this working class, and although her work is a fictionalized account, she too regarded the sculpture—a homer—a response to alienation.

14. See Miklos Haraszti, *A Worker in a Workers' State* (New York: Universe Books, 1978), 138–46.

15. At the time of the interviews (1980 and 1982), this informant (born ca. 1925) was beginning to attend local arts and crafts fairs. He has taught a number of his coworkers to carve chains, but only a small number have kept up the art. Simon Bronner has done extensive research on chain carvers. See his *Chain Carvers: Old Men Crafting Meaning* (Lexington: University of Kentucky Press, 1984).

16. Male Canadian auto worker and union official; interview conducted December 1981.

17. This interview was conducted in 1980 with one of the Afro-American quilters in preparation for an exhibit of workers' art. She was sixty years of age. Although she had watched her mother quilt, she never thought she would do it. Since the interview, the quilting activity of these women is no longer confined to the workplace.

18. The name of this informant and the plant are omitted to avoid any possible punitive action. Interview conducted January 1982.

19. "Henry Ford's Melting Pot," in *Ethnic Communities of Greater Detroit,* ed. Otto Feinstein (Detroit, 1970), 274.

20. Ibid., 279.

21. Another example of this struggle between management (for control) and workers (for personalization) is the worker-made versus company-made belt buckle described by C. Kurt Dewhurst in "The Arts of Working: Manipulating the Urban Work Environment," *Western Folklore,* 43 (1984): 192–202.

22. Ibid.

23. Donald Horning, "Blue-Collar Theft: Conceptions of Property, Attitudes toward Pilfering and Work Group Norms in a Modern Industrial Plant," in *Crimes Against Bureaucracy,* ed. Erwin Smigel and H. Lawrence Ross (New York: Van Nostrand Reinhold Co., 1970), 46–64.

24. Richard M. Dorson, *Land of the Millrats* (Cambridge: Harvard University Press, 1981), 67–68, 79–80.

25. Jason Ditton, "Perks, Pilferage and the Fiddle: The Historical Structure of Invisible Wages," *Theory and Society* 4 (1977): 39–71. See, also, Ditton's study of bakery workers, *Part-Time Crime: An Ethnography of Fiddling and Pilferage* (London: Macmillan, 1977); and Horning.

26. Personal communication from Michael Bell and information he learned in the course of his fieldwork on making art work.

27. Erwin O. Smigel, "Introduction," Bennett M. Berger, "The Sociology of Leisure," and William A. Faunce,, "Automation and Leisure," all in *Work and Leisure,* ed. Erwin O. Smigel (New Haven, Conn.: College and University Press, 1963).

28. Faunce, 91; Argyle, 261.

29. See Haraszti, *A Worker in a Workers' State* on this phenomenon.

30. Ken C. Kusterer, *Know-How on the Job: The Important Working Knowledge of "Unskilled" Workers* (Boulder, Colorado: 1978), 180–81.

A Bean on My Table and a Roof over My Head: The Folklore of Unemployed Workers

Mark E. Workman

ike Mark Twain's death, reports of Michigan's imminent demise are greatly exaggerated. Automobiles are rolling off assembly lines in increasing numbers, many huge corporations are based in the state, population is dense despite the southwestern migration and, in general, the ethnic and occupational representation is as diverse and rich as anywhere in America. Nevertheless, one cannot live in Michigan and be unaware of the depressed condition of the economy. The quintessential "rust belt" state, Michigan's problems run deep. Anachronistic tax structures, worker's compensation laws, powerful unions, and strong wages and benefits all have contributed to a climate unfavorable to existing businesses and unappealing to others that might consider locating there. Thus, despite the recent resurgence of the automobile industry, the long-term prognosis for full local recovery is guarded at best. It is not surprising, therefore, that while workers in many parts of the country are being called back to their jobs, the rate of unemployment in Michigan continues to remain among the highest in the nation—far above the national average.

To folklorists interested in occupational culture, this situation presents a peculiar opportunity. On the one hand, they can direct their attention toward the kinds of groups that have provided traditional focus of study. In a state as economically developed as Michigan these groups—rural, urban, and maritime—are present in abundance, and warrant continued investigation. On the other hand, folklorists can attempt to come to terms with the fact confronting them everywhere, that a significant percentage of Michigan's labor force is out of work. It seems to me that there is a moral imperative for pursuing this latter course, insofar as we claim responsibility for sharing with others our knowledge of how people display their values, beliefs, fears, and aspirations in folk expression. Further, there is the undeniable interest which results from venturing into areas as yet unexplored by folklorists.

Such a venture is problematic for folklorists, however, because in some ways their discipline does not prepare them to undertake it. One of the fundamental tenets of the field is that folk expression is communally grounded. Folklore is said to come about as disparate individuals begin to relocate the source of their previously distinct identities in some kind of shared experience—occupational, familial, ethnic, religious, or whatever. These shared experiences are transformed through ritual and narrative into a reservoir of memories which become a point of reference for the guidance of behavior in the present and future. From a folkloristic point of view, who one currently is and who one might someday become are very much a function of who one was. In this regard, to analogize to the study of literature, it is fair to say that folk studies have tended toward the comic rather than the tragic: that is, the discipline as a whole has been drawn to the celebration and study of integrative rather than disintegrative situations and processes.[1] But culture, however stable and functional it may appear to be in narrowly circumscribed situations, is in fact constituted of a dialectic between continuity and change. Just as memory is vital to the construction of identity, so is forgetting equally important in assuring that our identities remain open-ended rather than totally arrested by the past. Such forgetting may be subtle or violent, desired or imposed. However it may be regarded, it is just as much a part of folklore as the centripetal force of memorialization. On a local level it helps account for the fact that even the most tradition-bound performance is not a mere replication of an inviolable text but a re-creation of a dynamic construct; and on a broader basis it helps explain the ongoing transformations of society.[2]

Awareness of these contradictory tendencies is essential to an understanding of the particular plight of the unemployed worker. Curiously, jobless persons are defined on the basis of what they no longer are. Who they have become is not a continuation but an inversion of who they were, mere shadows of their former selves.

Forgetting has been thrust upon them, and thus they no longer speak from the center of an integrated community but at best from the margins of one from which they have become unbound. I am describing this predicament in dramatic terms, but of course unemployment is neither intrinsically good nor bad. A wide variety of factors can mitigate or exacerbate the loss of employment, such as the availability of alternative means of financial support, alternative groups for social support, and alternative means for occupying time. Nevertheless, whether it is painful or not, unemployed workers are now on the outside of a group to which they previously belonged.

What is of special interest to the folklorist is the range of expressive strategies that arise in response to the disintegrating experience of employment. To the extent that being jobless constitutes a kind of occupation—the business of one's life—these responses correspond in an ironic way to what Robert McCarl defines as "technique," the "shaping principle" of work. "Technique," according to McCarl, "is the pattern of manipulations, actions, and rhythms which are the result of the interaction between an individual and his or her work environment and which are prescribed by the group and used as criteria for the determination of membership and status within it."[3] It is a combination of "expertise and esoteric knowledge" which one needs to possess in order to perform a job in a manner acceptable to one's fellow employees.[4] In essence, technique is the "art of living" transferred to the workplace.

Without such a workplace, clearly, technique must take a different form. An indication of what that might be is contained in a statement made by Jerry White, who prior to his layoff eighteen months before our interview, was a production line worker and machinist for Pontiac Motors. "I don't *mind* not working," said Mr. White. "I'd like to be working and making more money. I'm living right now, but that's all I can do. But it's not that bad. You know, I guess I'm a lazy person in general, and I can handle it. As long as I've got a roof over my head and a bean on my table, I'm satisfied."[5] It seems to me that if there is in fact a technique of being unemployed, it is summed up in Mr. White's expression, "handling it." This might otherwise be phrased "getting by" or "passing the time." Obviously, it can assume myriad forms. Some people find odd jobs, some retire to the television, pursue hobbies, attend school, or generally "hang out" in one place and way or another. More importantly, they create and share the kind of knowledge they need to survive—physically and spiritually—their common ordeal.

The range of expression of the unemployed is broad. Some is benign and practical, such as the recipe for "Snow Cream" submitted to the *Solidarity Cookbook* by unemployed school bus builder Susan Counceller. The primary ingredient of this seasonal dessert is "one dutch oven full of freshly fallen snow," to which Mrs. Counceller adds the caution, "Beware of the yellow snow, 'cause that's where the huskies go." "Believe me, when we do eat," writes Mrs. Counceller, "it sure as hell isn't veal scallopini."[6] At the other extreme are crystallizations of sentiments which, despite their apparent humor, are much more foreboding in their implications. One sees many bumper stickers in Detroit that sound a note of doom: *Will The Last One Out Of Detroit Please Turn Off The Lights?"* and, more aggressively, *Real Americans Buy American.* Some, such as the sticker prominently displayed on the attendant's stand at the parking lot of Solidarity House, the UAW international headquarters in downtown Detroit, are overtly militant: *If You Bought It In Japan Park It In Japan.* Unfortunately, the xenophobia thus promoted is not confined to bumpers or parking lots: recently an American of Asian extraction was beaten to death by two disgruntled American auto workers because of their hatred for the Japanese. Thus, as Alan Dundes has so often demonstrated, even the smallest expression of folk attitudes can provide an accurate guide to world view.[7]

Many of the stories one hears from jobless workers concern the inevitable vagaries and ignominies of the unemployment line. If there is any benefit to be derived from standing in the line other than the money received, it is in the material provided for what is commonly referred to as "bitching." Further, the following transcription of a dialogue I had with Jerry White and several other laid-off Pontiac Motors' employees reveals not only an awareness of the need to participate in activities which may later be translated into narrative, but also something of the attitude that these particular people have toward their unemployed status:

> MARK: What happens? You all go down to collect benefits every two weeks?
>
> MARY: Yeah.
>
> MARK: And is that an ordeal?
>
> JERRY: It gives you something to do to stand there and bitch about it for two hours but it's not that bad when you consider: $400 for two hours worth of work. And the worst part is—it's not hard, it's just standing there—the worst part is you don't

have nothing to *lean* on. That's the biggest bitch of all. If they had chairs so everybody moved like musical chairs it'd be fine. There'd be people doing it for a living for the rest of their lives if they could! I went in and applied for unemployment back in about '74 or '75, and I took a lawn chair in with me, sat there in a lawn chair. Things were getting bad but not nearly as bad as they are now. I used to take a regular folding lawn chair with me, and people would want to rent it from me, you know. If you stand in line for four hours you get awful tired of standing.[8]

MARY: I get tired of standing for two hours. My back starts hurting. I can't wait to get to that wall! You know, to lean up against that wall.

JERRY: Yeah, you zigzag back and forth across the building, and every twenty minutes you get to lean up against the wall for about three minutes, and then you zip around.

AL: It seems that every time you get to the wall the line goes zooming around. You stand there and go, "Oh wow, I'm almost there!" And all of a sudden the line moves *fifty feet*! You stand there and look over your shoulder and say, "There goes my *wall!*"

GREG: You know, everybody bitches and moans about standing in line, but I mean, you walk up to anybody and say, "Tell you what, you work eighty hours in two weeks time—how'd you like to stand in the same place for three hours and make the same money once every two weeks." They'd all say "Yeah!" I mean, if you told them they had to stand in the same place *once a day* for three hours as opposed to working eight hours, they would do it. But it's not bad. It gives you something to bitch about.

JERRY: You're standing there waiting patiently, like a dog begging for your money, and then you get up there, and if they haven't lost your records then you're all set. You get your check and you're off for two weeks.

Contained in these words is a wealth of information about the real nature of the unemployment line. Related stories tell of the misplacement of records, interminable red tape, and general incompetence of the various welfare agencies. Much of the dialogue or bitching is stylized—Al artfully renders his fleeting encounters with the wall, and Jerry no doubt has gotten a lot of recurring pleasure from recounting his lawn chair experience—as is the behavior which it describes. Standing in line has thus become an instance, in narration and in fact, of what Kenneth Burke refers to as "the dancing of an attitude":[9] while one may wait as patiently as "a begging dog" for one's money, the maintenance of wit and perspective enables one to emerge from this strategic encounter with one's essential dignity intact. In fact, it is probably only through reframing this experience in the form of humorous anecdotes that the unemployed can distance themselves and laugh at what is in actuality both immediate and painful.

Another kind of knowledge which the jobless worker needs to possess in order to survive his encounters with the bureaucracy of unemployment concerns the compilation of a record of attempts to locate alternative means of support. As a prerequisite to receiving a check, the potential recipient of welfare is required to turn in a list every two weeks containing the names of personnel managers whom he has petitioned for work. Because the wages from any such job almost always would be considerably less than the amount of welfare, and because a search for such work more than likely would be fruitless anyway, no one with whom I spoke ever has taken this requirement very seriously. Al's following account describes one of the evidently few Michigan Employment Security Commission workers who is both aware of and sympathetic to the applicants' attitude toward this requirement, and Al's poignant reaction on one of the rare occasions when he actually did seek employment:

> The guy with the beard is really cool. You hand him your work sheet, one day he was signing my work sheet and he said, "What the hell do they make people do these things for, anyway." He goes, "Jesus Christ, half of 'em are out of the phone book anyway," and that's all he said. He knew. He'd been on unemployment himself. He knew that everybody writes down places out of a phone book, that nobody actually goes out looking. And when you do look, usually you can't find anything anyway. I filled out an application, the first one I filled out after looking lots of places. I thought, "Wow, the first place to take an application." It was for a forklift driver at a lumber place, and I says, "You think they're going to be taking somebody?" And the girl goes, and she kind of looks around and she goes, "Actually, we probably got anywhere between five hundred and a thousand applications, and the boss figures that it'll make people feel better if they can come in and at least fill one out." Because nobody else was taking any applications. "We're not really looking for anybody. We've got twenty people laid off right now." They just thought it might brighten up your day actually filling out an application—and *it did!*

Sadly, there is another kind of narrative heard around the Detroit area that tells of people even less fortunate than those on welfare. These are the people who have only their dignity to hang on to, since all aid has expired or been denied to them. Most often told about someone not present (because maintaining dignity requires maintaining face), such accounts provide the basis for the ubiquitous and maudlin "human interest" stories so cherished by news services; in the hands of the UAW they assume a form similar to certain kinds of legends and ballads and are used as potent political propaganda, as is the case with the following account from a union pamphlet boldly entitled *Ammo.* Under the caption, "Finally the Refrigerator Was Empty" the report read:

> In mid-January Ralph Brannan's refrigerator was empty. After a long hard struggle since he had been laid off from Ford's Flat Rock casting operations in March 1981, Brannan literally was cleaned out. He was being denied food stamps or general assistance. There just was no money coming in. Brannan's unemployment compensation had run out in late 1981. He was one of 33,000 Michiganders who lost an extra 13 weeks of extended benefits when President Reagan decided to revise the way the insured unemployment rate was figured. A Viet Nam war veteran, Brannan was forced to sell his possessions to survive because you can't collect food stamps or general assistance until you're certifiably poor.
>
> He sold his car, a flat boat, a snowmobile, a washer and dryer. His truck was repossessed. Delaying needed dental work, he opted to have teeth pulled rather than filled. And his dental problems continue. He had already seen his condominium go through foreclosure during an earlier layoff when a long-delayed check for several thousand dollars of backed-up Trade Readjustment Assistance arrived a week too late to satisfy his mortgage company. Finally Brannan was poor enough to get food stamps and general assistance. But when he decided to share a house with his brother to shave expenses, Social Services Department cut him off public help. Why? It was a new rule. In January his brother lost his job, too. With his food running out, Brannan was eligible once again for public help.
>
> During his long spell of unemployment Brannan has looked for jobs. But jobs are scarce in Michigan with Depression levels of unemployment. "I've gotten to places to apply for jobs and they'd already stopped taking applications," says Brannan, who has a typical problem of the unemployed—he can't afford a car, and during the spell from September to January when he was cut off all aid, he didn't have bus fare. And he didn't have a phone. . . . "Nothing's ever falling into place," Brannan says. "It's frustrating."[10]

It is not too difficult to articulate the kind of "technique" promoted by a narrative such as this. While there is little of practical value here to help the jobless worker attain what Jerry White referred to as the roof over his head, and the bean on his table, the story of Ralph Brannan was chosen for publication by the *Ammo* staff because of the abundant spiritual incentive it provides to readers of this pamphlet. The message is that if life is tough inside the workplace, it is even tougher outside; that President Reagan more than likely doesn't give a damn; and finally, and less overtly, that the unemployed person must be grateful for what he has that Ralph Brannan does not, but like Mr. Brannan, when pushed to the brink even then he must not fall over. Bend, perhaps be frustrated, but persist and never break.

There are other kinds of unemployment folklore, equally impractical, perhaps ultimately as sad, but much more immediately entertaining. This is achieved by embedding the tendentious material of the various kinds of narratives in humorous frameworks. In a cartoon in another union publication, for instance, two men are depicted walking along: one says to the other, "Can't deny it; President Reagan promised to get us back on our feet. . .." On the next level of the cartoon this sentence is concluded with the words, "and here we are," just as the two men arrive at the end of a long line of people waiting under a sign which says, predictably, "Unemployment Office."[11] A similar sentiment is expressed in an item of xeroxlore[12] presented to me by an unemployed auto worker. This is a parody of the Twenty-third Psalm, satirically called, "Psalm for Reagan":

> Reagan is my shepherd, I shall now want.
> He leadeth me beside the still factories.
> He restoreth my doubts in the Republican Party.
> I do not fear evil for thou art against me.
> Thou annointest my wages with freezes so that my expenses run over my income.
> Surely poverty and hard living shall follow the Republican party, and I shall live in a rented house forever.

Five thousand years ago Moses said, "Park your camel, pick up your shovel, mount your ass, and I shall lead you to the promised land.

Five thousand years later, F. D. Roosevelt said, "Lay down your shovel, sit on your ass, light up a Camel, this is the promised land."

Today Reagan will take your shovel, sell your camel, kick your ass, and tell you *this* is the promised land:

I am glad I am an American
I am glad that I am free
But I wish I was a little doggie
And Reagan was a tree.

Another medium in which the plight of the jobless has been commemorated is music. Songwriters have long displayed a sensitivity to social inequities, and it is not surprising, given the permeable boundary between folklore and mass culture, to find several rock 'n' roll musicians giving popular voice to the attitudes of the unemployed. Recent songs by Billy Joel and Detroit native Bob Seger have centered on the difficulty of finding work in this time of economic crisis. More substantively, Bruce Springsteen has gone on in his music to explore some of the social ramifications of unemployment. One of his songs, "Johnny 99," is about an auto worker turned criminal:

Well they closed down the auto plant in Mahway late that month,
Ralph went out looking for a job but he couldn't find none,
He came home drunk from mixin' Tanqueray and wine,
He got a gun, shot a night-clerk; now they call him Johnny 99.

According to *Solidarity* reporter Joe Lawrence,

The many studies correlating the increase in unemployment with increased illness, death, and crime are fleshed out in "Johnny 99," so named for his prison sentence. Most cope without breaking down; but with the devastating stress unemployment brings, there are many who snap. "Now I ain't saying that makes me an honest man," Johnny tells the judge. "But it was more 'n all this that put that gun in my hand."[13]

The life chronicled by Springsteen is one leading ultimately to fragmentation, isolation, and despair and, as Lawrence indicates, the accuracy of this vision, while distorted here for the sake of the song, is generally borne out by the increasing incidence of child and spousal abuse, alcoholism, depression, suicide, homicide, and other forms of socially induced problems of the unemployed.[14] Here we must confront a point I made earlier which has perhaps been obscured by the emphasis on communally-shared techniques for handling unemployment. Unemployment entails exclusion, and while some people are fortunate enough to be absorbed into groups unrelated to work, others find the absence of a job to be a void that not only cannot be filled, but into which the rest of their lives collapse as well.

Filling the void would seem to be a social obligation of high priority. According to all my informants, the UAW has been terribly negligent in this regard. ("The union had a picnic, but *I* never got invited," said Jerry White. "They're just as glad to see us gone; that's one less person they've got to worry about.") At a meeting of union officials and representatives which I attended at Solidarity House in February 1983, everyone acknowledged the urgency of this need, but little of a practical nature was suggested to remedy it.[15] One might suppose that even without the facilitation of the union, the jobless workers themselves would seek out one another for companionship, solace, support, and entertainment. Such a function is fulfilled by the ad hoc group depicted by George Orwell in his ethnographic novel, *Down and Out in Paris and London.* The unnamed narrator tramps about the outskirts of London, finding shelter either in publically supported "spikes" or in the cheapest of lodginghouses. The narrator particularly likes the kitchen of one such house:

> It was a low-ceilinged cellar deep underground, very hot and drowsy with coke fumes, and lighted only by the fires, which cast black velvet shadows in the corners. Ragged washing hung on strings from the ceiling. Red-lit men, stevedores mostly, moved about the fires with cooking-pots; some of them were quite naked, for they had been laundering and were waiting for their clothes to dry. At night there were games of nap and draughts, and songs—"I'm a chap what's done wrong by my parents," was a favorite, and so was another popular song about a shipwreck. Sometimes late at night men would come in with a pail of winkles they had bought cheap, and share them out. There was a general sharing of food, and it was taken for granted to feed men who were out of work. A little pale, wizened creature, obviously dying, referred to as "pore Brown, bin under the doctor and cut open three times," was regularly fed by the others.[16]

This kind of communitarian ideal in which food and folklore are selflessly shared does not commonly exist in Detroit, at least not in the experience of my informants. Perhaps the tramps with whom Orwell traveled as a young man inhabited a more blatantly hierarchical society and thus were more dependent on one another. Perhaps, too, the nature of contemporary American society is such that people are culturally less inclined and less able to reveal their vulnerabilities to one another and prefer, instead, to suffer in isolation. Yet another reason suggests itself from my fieldwork, and I suspect that it is not peculiar to the automobile industry. It is simply that people who work together often just do not wish to socialize together. This attitude is stated explicitly by Russ Salfi and Rick Sanches, two tool and die machinists who had been out of work approximately six months at the time I interviewed them:

> *RUSS:* For me there was work and then there was the time I was out of work. For the most part, the majority of people that I worked with I really didn't socialize with that much. I socialized with Rick and three or four other people from out of about forty people. So I really couldn't say that I actually socialized outside of work with the people I worked with.

> *RICK:* You can't really say you're in two different worlds, but it almost is because uh, these are the same people you see every day for eight hours, which is, you know, a third of your lifetime and I guess you get to know people pretty well and what they're like and, uh, while you're there you're friends with 'em and everything, but outside in the real world you really don't socialize with them that much.

> *RUSS:* Yeah, you're in a situation where you know you have to maintain a congenial atmosphere with the people you work with, you know you have to be able to work with 'em but as far as, like, choosing these people as associates outside of the work area, for the most part the majority of people you run into, at least I've found, while you're working, are not the kind of people that you would want to socialize with. I'm not saying that they're low-lifes or, you know, unacceptable people in society; I'm just saying when you choose your friends, you choose your friends.

If it is the case that many unemployed workers do not socialize with one another except on a casual and haphazard basis (Russ occasionally associates with several jobless auto workers because they all frequent the same bar in downtown Pontiac), then it is unreasonable to look for anything other than a casual and haphazard folklore of unemployment. This is accurate to a point, but requires qualification. As my survey indicates, there is a substantial body of material which grows directly out of the loss of work; it appears to be common and necessary folk knowledge among the jobless and therefore constitutes a technique of unemployment. While this occupational culture may not be as tightly organized or as extensive as the folklore of more cohesive and intimate societies, it does serve to distinguish as an identifiable group people who have experienced exclusion from work. There are still others, however, who experience not only exclusion from jobs, but exclusion from the jobless as well. Except perhaps on the unemployment line, these individuals do not share the time and space or inclination necessary for the production of routinized displays of esoteric knowledge.

It is interesting that during our several evenings together Mr. Salfi and Mr. Sanchez quite naturally produced a great many stories and anecdotes concerning fellow machinists and techniques of their trade. Indeed, part of their repertoire consists of tales which they themselves identify as "Beltz stories": Russ describes this character as a "living legend, about 6'2", 270 pounds; he looks very eerie and he's got blond hair, extremely light complected, blond mustache and, uh, he's a madman, he's just a total madman." Both speak with authority about technical matters such as the intricacies of installing heads on engines—the prescribed way and the assembly line work-ers' way—and the conflicts with upper management which result from too much innovation. Yet as we have seen, both Russ and Rick indicate that they do not engage in such nostalgic performances on any regular basis. Capable of reviving the past, it seems that they prefer instead to forget it, or perhaps more precisely, to allow it to remain dormant until they are reunited with it more fully and permanently.

There is evidence here of an ambivalence toward their occupa-tional identities, and it is displayed by all the other jobless auto work-ers I have interviewed as well. This perhaps is the ultimate factor determining the degree to which one participates in the occupational culture of the unemployed: not everyone feels equally secure or happy or comfortable with his identity as an automobile worker in the first place. According to unemployed worker Greg Blue, many assembly line workers, especially those who work in the foundry, regard their work merely as something to get behind them: "You know," said Greg, "when you have ten years in you say, 'Goddamn, only got twenty more years to go and I'm out of this place.' Not that you hate it. But you can leave your job when it's three o'clock or five o'clock, you know you're going home and you're done, and you don't have to think about that point until tomorrow morning. All you have to do is get up and put your eight hours in. And no matter what kind of job it is it's only eight hours, and everybody gets paid."

This loose commitment to work felt by some workers can only be undermined further by the abundant scorn directed at the auto-mobile workers—laid off or employed—by the general public. Russ Salfi, who is justifiably proud of his considerable training and skill, describes an encounter he recently had in a local bar in which the mere mention of his occupation was sufficient to elicit just such a condescending opinion:

> I was at Kennedy's one night and there was a lady there and I was talking to her and I said that I worked for the automotive industry and, out of the blue, I mean this was like a comet that came out of the blue and I've heard this *several* times, this lady goes, "I have absolutely no compassion for the American auto worker." Out of the blue. And I said, "Well, under what circumstances do you mean that? I mean, do you just not have any compassion for all auto workers?" And she goes, "Well, I've heard so much, so many complaints from the American auto worker how the unemployment afflicts them and their job is, you know, mentally fatiguing. . . ." She cited the reasons why she had no compassion for the American auto worker but, I don't know, I just thought it was extremely uncalled for, because I have absolutely no negative feelings towards any occupation in general, but it seems to me that for some reason the auto worker gets a lot of antipathy from other fields.

In an ideal world everyone would have a job, everyone would like the job he had, and everyone would appreciate the jobs performed by his fellows. The world of the unemployed auto worker is ideal on none of these counts. He is jobless, he is ambivalent toward his work, and his is regarded with considerable aversion by others. The factors which produce unemployment—and more generally a stratified society in which people who inhabit the most worn regions of the country face the greatest likelihood of ejection from jobs which they are not fully committed to in the first place—are many and complex. As the lyrics of "Johnny 99" ominously proclaim, more than just a mixture of gin and wine lead Johnny to shoot a clerk. The folk expressions of the unemployed, dialogues with all the forces conspiring against them, reflect an awareness of the depth and profundity of the crisis.

I have been trying to suggest here some of the enormous and complicated forces which bear upon the jobless auto worker and consequently determine at least part of his repertoire of expression. I have also suggested that these same forces just as conceivably might tear people apart as bind them together. From the latter we should expect to witness a folklore of unemployment, the techniques—multiformly expressed—whereby people contend with the physical and mental dilemma of being out of work. From the former, our discipline—focused as it is upon community—leads us to expect to hear nothing at all, or at best only isolated expressions of despair. For people alone are people without language, and people without language are people dehumanized. Because they do not count themselves as members of a group, however, does not give us license to turn from them. On the contrary, as humanists and as students of culture, folklorists must be sensitive not only to those safely ensconced within, but to those on the outside as well; they too have a story to tell, if we will but take the time to listen.

An abridged version of this paper was presented at the December 1983 meeting of the Modern Language Association in New York City. I could not have written this paper without the gracious assistance of Ms. Ruth Eberle, who at that time was president of UAW Local 1925; she greatly facilitated my fieldwork, and generally clarified my conception of the problems resulting from unemployment. While conditions in the automobile industry have improved substantially since this paper was first written, there is a distressing likelihood that, with the next recession, all the experiences recounted in this paper will unfortunately be relived.

1. I elaborate on the fundamental orientation of the discipline in "Mapping the Center: Toward a Sociopoetics of Folklore," presented to the Conference on Narrative Poetics, Columbus, Ohio, April 1986.
2. On the role of dynamism in folklore, see Barre Toelken, *The Dynamics of Folklore* (Boston: Houghton, Mifflin, and Co., 1979), chapter 2.
3. Robert S. McCarl, Jr., "Occupational Folklife: A Theoretical Hypothesis," in *Working Americans: Contemporary Approaches to Occupational Folklife*, ed. Robert H. Byington, Smithsonian Folklife Studies 3 (1978): 7.
4. Compare the general definition of culture proposed by Ward Goodenough, *Description and Comparison in Cultural Anthropology* (Chicago: Aldine Publishing Company, 1970), 98–103.
5. All transcriptions in this article are from interviews conducted by the author in the Detroit area during 1982 and 1983. Some informants are identified by pseudonyms. I extend my appreciation to all my informants for their gracious assistance.
6. Susan Counceller, "Solidarity Cookbook," *Solidarity* (February 1983): 23.
7. Alan Dundes, "Folk Ideas as Units of World View," in *Toward New Perspectives in Folklore*, ed. Americo Parades and Richard Bauman (Austin: University of Texas Press, 1972), 93–103.
8. Yvonne Lockwood has pointed out that this comment is as applicable to line work as it is to the unemployment line.
9. Kenneth Burke, *The Philosophy of Literary Form*, 3d ed. (Berkeley: University of California Press, 1973), 9.
10. "Finally the Refrigerator was Empty," *Ammo* 22, no. 19 (1983): 6–7.
11. *Solidarity* (April 1982): 20.
12. On the subject of folklore produced by copymachine, see Alan Dundes and Carl R. Pagter, *Work Hard and You Shall Be Rewarded: Urban Folklore from the Paperwork Empire* (Bloomington: Indiana University Press, 1978).
13. Joe Lawrence, "Recession Rock," *Solidarity* (February 1983): 16–17.
14. According to a report prepared by UAW Community Services Department Director Tom Snover, a Johns Hopkins University researcher contends that "for each one percent increase in joblessness in the national economy, the following events result: 38,886 deaths; 20,240 cardiovascular failures; 494 cases of death from cirrhosis of the liver attendant upon alcoholism; 920 more suicides; and 648 additional homicides." "Call to Action on Unemployment," 28 February 1983. See also the week-long report (31 August–6 September 1986) by Stephen Franklin and Marcia Stepanek, "Blue Collar Casualties," *Detroit Free Press*.
15. In all fairness to the UAW, it must be acknowledged that the union is very active in lobbying for social reforms at all levels of government. It is less well equipped for assisting the individual worker in dealing with the everyday problems of unemployment, the ultimate solution for which is, of course, the return to work. For a record of the social consciousness of the UAW see John Barnard, *Walter Reuther and the Rise of the Auto Workers* (Boston: Little, Brown, and Company, 1983).
16. George Orwell, *Down and Out in Paris and London* (New York: Harcourt, Brace, Jovanovich, 1961), 133–34.

Downriver and Thumb Area Michigan Waterfowling: The Folk Arts of Nate Quillen and Otto Misch

C. Kurt Dewhurst and
Marsha MacDowell

ichigan's location between many of the important nesting places and wintering resorts of wild ducks and geese brings about an abundance and variety of waterfowl which is exceeded in few states. Opportunities to hunt or study waterfowl in this state are many, and these birds deserve increased appreciation by the public as well as greater attention to the new program for wildlife management. Nearly two dozen kinds of duck, three species of geese and one swan migrate through the Great Lakes region. Michigan's own crop of "local" ducks, although as yet not well inventoried, is certainly far greater than is commonly realized.[1]

This observation was written by Dr. Miles David Pirnie in 1935 in his now classic book, *Michigan Waterfowl Management.* Since that time, a concerted effort has been made to inventory the waterfowl population of Michigan during the migratory seasons, and the general public has continued to develop a fuller understanding of the prominence of waterfowl in this Great Lakes state.

For the sportsman, waterfowling has had a rich but often overlooked cultural heritage in Michigan. Today, the fall season in Michigan is welcomed by the waterfowler as an opportunity to carry on traditions that were learned from past generations. Fathers taught sons the nuances of the successful day of hunting in their own favorite hunting sites. Beyond the most obvious aspect of the

Reprinted by permission of the Michigan State University Museum, *Downriver and Thumb Area Waterfowling* 2, no. 1 (1983): 1–9.

hunt—the shoot—the day of hunting was long prepared for, and the traditional patterns of behavior that were prescribed by previous generations were carefully observed. Quite naturally, over time, some of these traditional activities began to fade because of lack of practice. But vestiges do survive in locally defined hunting communities around Michigan.

We will examine two differing geographical hunting traditions in Michigan that can be represented by the artistry of two Michigan waterfowlers: Nate Quillen of Rockwood, Michigan, and Otto Misch of Weale, Michigan. Quillen represents the "downriver" tradition that reached its most fruitful years in the latter part of the nineteenth and early part of the twentieth century, when the waterfowl population was at its peak and shooting clubs were being established in the downriver area. Otto Misch, in contrast, represents the traditional hunting life of those who hunted in the Saginaw Bay area. Weale is in the "thumb" of Michigan, near Sebewaing, an area that has proven to be an active hunting location up to the current day. Even though the waterfowl population has declined, primarily because of lack of feeding beds, the Saginaw Bay area has remained a popular hunting place for the average Michigan waterfowler.

Folklorists are often drawn to pursuits such as waterfowling because of the strong sense of continuity that exists from one generation to the next in carrying out such activities. Waterfowling as it has historically been practiced in Michigan is a folk cultural activity. The young learn the necessary skills and behaviors orally or by demonstration from their parents and those members of their local community who participate as hunters. Rarely does an initiate learn how to function as a waterfowler from a book; this activity has traditionally been a person-to-person learning and sharing experience. Such is the very nature of folk culture. Whereas popular and elite culture are introduced through formal organized patterns of transmission such as magazines or schools, folk patterns are learned informally—but in an organized way. Folk patterns are powerful and resilient over years. These lasting lessons are preserved in the forms of what to do, what not to do, and how to do. Stories or tales often embellish the learning process, and the process itself serves an important role in sustaining the quality of local community life because these folk activities provide for meaningful time with friends and family.

In addition to identifying the nature of the folk process of learning traditional behaviors, folklorists usually identify distinctive characteristics of each folk group that is studied. For example, hunting traditions differ considerably between the downriver and the thumb areas. Beyond the obvious geographical differences, people learn different traditions in different places. It has been noted by folklorist Henry Glassie that folk culture experiences "major variation over space and minor variation over time."[2] The locally established traditions of areas of Michigan have remained relatively the same over a number of decades, whereas they differ dramatically from those traditions established by another local community not far removed in terms of space. It is this principle that is clearly at work in the folk traditions of Nate Quillen and Otto Misch.

The material culture—the objects—and the makers of decoys and boats that were used widely within their own local communities, can tell us much about a people and their values. Neither Quillen nor Misch intended to create objects that would appeal to a wider audience than those people whom they knew as fellow hunters. Their creations were influenced by the traditions of the past but were also the results of their own sense of innovation within the traditionally prescribed behaviors of waterfowling that they knew as they grew up. Most significantly, their work was a synthesis of the past and present concern for functionally effective decoys and boats—and their creations in turn have provided a legacy for those generations that have followed.

Nate Quillen: A Downriver Waterfowler (1839–1908)

The downriver waterfowling tradition has been shaped by the natural character of the shoal delta known as Pointe Mouillee. This site was once a thriving marsh area with channels and islands that continued to the point where both the Detroit and Huron rivers debouch into Lake Erie. According to W. T. Barbour's account, entitled *A Story of Pointe Mouillee*:

> 'Pointe Mouillee,' meaning 'Wet Point,' was named by the early French settlers. . .a local name after the English or Americans settled in this section was 'Dead Man's Point.' This name was given because some, if not many, who were drowned in the waters above, floated down the River and fetched up on this shoal.[3]

In the years that followed, a number of well-known shooting clubs were established in this area, the most notable being the Pointe Mouillee Shooting Club.

Nate Quillen has been remembered as a locksmith and cabinet maker,[4] but in the eyes of sportsmen he is best remembered for his service at the Pointe Mouillee Shooting Club, where he carried on the functions of the hired guide working in the employ of a series of different club members. The making of decoys and hunting boats was only part of his work as a guide, but these objects are the lasting examples of material culture that are perhaps the best reminders of the nature of the man.

Little evidence exists of the daily life of the punter and guide for the major shooting clubs. Beyond the obvious contrasts between the wealthy club members and the locally born and raised guides, life at these clubs invites the curiosity of waterfowlers from all levels of society. Hy Dahlka has attempted to record much of the oral accounts of the club life, and his efforts provide some fascinating insights. Dahlka reports that at the turn of the century, the punter at the Pointe Mouillee Shooting Club received $1.65 a day during hunting season, including room and board. On occasion, a club member on a three-day hunt, such as John Newell, would also give his guide a $3.00 tip—and "he was considered a big tipper."[5] Hy Dahlka also has noted that the work of the guide was not restrictive to the preparation and the hunt itself, but was a full day's work:

> The punters not only had to load shells; after supper they also had to pick and often dress their birds before going to bed. If the kill had been excessive the particular day, any of the punters who did not have guests shooting the next day had to turn to and pick and dress the remainder of the previous kill.[6]

Edward Lezotte is another valuable personal resource with much to share on the life of the punter. Lezotte worked as a punter in the early part of this century at the Pointe Mouillee Shooting Club. "Each person had their job. . .you worked for a member and if he had a guest. . .and if your member was not down [at the Club]. . .you got an extra day's pay."[7] But the responsibilities of the guide and punter were not restricted to the duck hunting seasons, as Ed Lezotte recalled:

> Before duck season, we had to make the blinds, paint the boats and paint the decoys. . .[we used] live decoys until about the 30s. . .the live decoys were kept at the club, and guides took live decoys out in their boats and used iron anchors made by W. T. Barbour at the Detroit Stove Works. . .a piece of leather was made for around one leg and was strapped on. . .[we] used usually three or four live decoys with other wood ducks when [hunting] with members.[8]

The actual hunt was demanding work for a guide. Lezotte described the day of the hunt this way:

Guides were up at 6:00 a.m. and went into each member's cottage and built a fire. Guides lived in hospital-like barracks with four beds to a side and then a hallway to a cook's room in the back. Members got up at 8:00 a.m. While they were eating breakfast, [the guide] got guns, shells, and put the boats in the water—also got live decoys from the little fenced off area and put them in the box. . . .. Guides used to shake peas for position; 'first position,' etc. was marked on the black board outside. . .the last guide could go anywhere. . . . Every night when they came in, [we] washed out the boats, paired up the ducks and hanged them in the member's cooler. Each member had a cooler that looked like a corn crib. . .[we] hanged them by the neck until pretty near a week.[9]

Clearly, the life of the guide was a colorful one that is best captured in this story, also told by Edward Lezotte:

Jim Barrow [was] one of the best shots and duck hunters I ever knew— he taught me a lot—he was a guide himself. He would go on top of one of the boat houses and he would sit up there every night and study the ducks. We used to go to him when we was young—we'd go up to him and ask him where we should go and he'd say, 'Go down to the north end—you'll get a good shoot down there,' But he'd take his man and go to the south end.[10]

Nate Quillen: Decoy Maker

Nate Quillen, the punter and guide at the Pointe Mouillee Shooting Club, has a lasting reputation for his skill in fashioning his own particular style of decoys and for his distinctive duck hunting boats, which he fashioned in his workshop on Huron River Drive in Rockwood. His decoy making was described by W. T. Barbour in *A Story of Pointe Mouillee:*

During the winter time, after selecting his wood, he [Quillen] built boats and decoys. Many of his decoys are still at the Marsh. They were all handmade. We used to pay a dollar apiece for them. Nate Quillen was an artist as well as an artisan. He took great pride in all the work he did. As models for his decoys he used birds that were shot on the marsh. He was very neat, and everything had to be in perfect order. Not only would he make the decoys but he also painted them, every bit of color was applied with great exactness and care. His appearance and temperament were those of an artist.[11]

The decoys made by Quillen conform in many respects to the traditional folk forms of other late nineteenth-century decoys of the downriver area. As Hy Dahlka has observed,

The earliest handmade decoys found in southeastern Michigan are smaller, narrower, and higher than those customarily thought of as being typical of this area [today]. They are, in concept, much like our Mason Factory Decoy except that the hollow hand-made decoy is scooped out from the bottom and the opening fitted with a thin board. The Mason decoy is split across the middle, hollowed out, and then fitted back together. The decoys of Nate Quillen are typical of this early phase in Michigan decoy carving and seem to be the only ones found in any quantity. A great variety of species is represented in his work, both solid and hollow, including many marsh ducks.[12]

The significant number of Quillen decoys still extant may be attributed to Quillen's care in craftsmanship and to the high regard in which the hunters held them.

Quillen's decoys are truly creations of a dedicated and meticulous artist. In a pioneering biography of Quillen's decoy making, Bernard W. Crandell quotes from an interview he recorded with James N. Foote, Jr. on Quillen's technique:

Quillen first dried the Michigan white cedar logs for a year in his barn. . . . Then he rough-cut the logs into sizes suitable for decoys and put them back into the barn to dry another year. After finishing the carving of the decoy, Quillen dried it another year before painting.[13]

Crandell also learned that, although Quillen preferred to make hollow decoys, which he later generally sold to Pointe Mouillee Shooting Club members for one dollar, on occasion when he found decoys that could not be hollowed out because of knots in the wood, he left them solid and sold them for twenty-five cents. His production has been estimated at approximately one decoy a day and perhaps as many as two hundred decoys a year during the last two decades of the nineteenth century.[14]

In his workshop, Quillen used three basic colors to paint his decoys. Ed Lezotte recalled that as a young boy he used to go to Quillen's workshop after Quillen's death where Quillen's friend Jim Wiseman continued to make decoys from the old Quillen patterns. Lezotte learned then that Quillen relied on willow green, roseate, and tobacco brown in combination to replicate the colors of each species of duck for his decoys. Lezotte also stressed the practical advantages of Quillen's setting the entire piece that comprised the head and neck into the body. This practice resulted in a more durable construction, for most hunters "grabbed and pitched" their decoys by the head. Many of the "high neck" Quillen heads were likely designed to be inset for strength because of the narrow shape of neck that Quillen favored in his carving style.

Little has been gathered about Quillen's character beyond his reputation as a waterfowler and craftsman, but perhaps it was in these realms that his true character emerged. Two descriptions of the man have been offered. This one was recorded by Bernard Crandell in an interview with Quillen's nephew, Edward Burgess:

> Uncle Nate was a thin, raw-boned fellow, about 5 feet 8 inches tall, and very pleasant. I went and played in the shavins in his shop many a time when I was a kid. He always seemed to have a boat a-building on his saw horses, and one of them was for my dad.[15]

Obviously, Nate Quillen's workshop was a fairly well-known community attraction. Ed Richardson recalls his father telling him that as a boy, he was told to "stop at Nate Quillen's and pick up five or six punting paddles on [your] return from Rockwood" (by horse and wagon after getting the groceries and mail). He said,

> Nate had his home and workshop on the north side of Huron River Drive just before Silver Creek crosses the road on the way to Rockwood. There was a flowing spring just about 100 feet west of Quillen's shop where Nate used to cool his pop, as he was a great pop drinker. Kreger's horse-drawn pop wagon from Wyandotte used to stop at Quillen's every week—with Nate's orange pop.[16]

Nate Quillen: Boat Builder

Nate Quillen's decoys are fairly widely appreciated, but his duck boat construction is often either overlooked or taken for granted. Quillen made boats as he made decoys, with careful attention to detail and with little regard for those who might want to rush the time needed for construction. W. T. Barbour has given much credit to Nate Quillen as an innovator in boat making in the downriver area:

> Pointe Mouillee without boats wouldn't mean much. A new type of boat was developed for use at the marsh by one Nate Quillen. During the winter time he used to go about the country picking up tamarack stumps, from which he carved out the braces for the boats. He likewise selected his lumber with great care, most of which was clear white pine free from knots and grained to his taste. Many of his boats we are using now [1940] were made by him fifty years and more ago.[17]

The two types of duck boats that Quillen is best remembered for were the punt boat (a guide's boat) and the monitor boat (a member's boat) (figs. 1 and 2). These boats were originally used primarily during hunting season by those who were employed at or those who were members of the Pointe Mouillee Shooting Club. The differences between these two boats are significant, and they can be traced to the corresponding functions of the guide and the member while on a shoot. Punt boats were open, flat-bottomed boats designed for travel at great speed. They could hold two men and were known to be extremely "tippy." The monitor boat was custom-made for the size and weight of each club member. It was a much more stable boat with front and back rails for stabilizing the hunter. The front and back deck area provided a location for decoys to be secured since the weight of the hunter brought the water level up above the deck level. Both the punt boat and the monitor had a series of holes around the coaming of the passenger area for wooden posts to hold a duck blind in position if a blind of this type was used. (Another technique was to create a blind in a marsh area for the boat to move into and then anchor.)

The boats contained a shell box or a small bench to sit on and false bottom flooring, and the monitor often had a rolled-up piece of

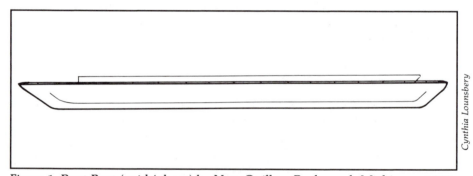

Figure 1. Punt Boat (guide's boat) by Nate Quillen, Rockwood, Michigan c.1890.

Cynthia Lounsbery

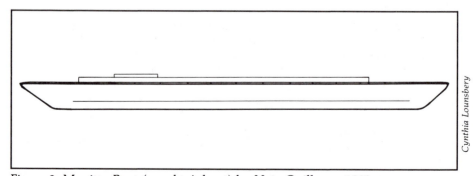

Figure 2. Monitor Boat (member's boat) by Nate Quillen c. 1890.

Cynthia Lounsbery

carpeting, sickles, paddles, guns, and decoys. The standard practice was for the punt boat to carry the decoys, including the live decoys, as it was the guide's job to arrange the rig in the water. If a floating blind was to be mounted upon arrival at the hunting site, it would be carried by the punt boat and put in place by the guide. But this was often accomplished before setting out. The punter spent his time preparing for the actual shoot and assembling the catch, often with the assistance of the member's dog. Thus the boats played a critical role in the success of the shoot.

Physically, the punt boat and the monitor differ dramatically upon close inspection. The punt boat is a much narrower boat with a shallow draft. It is propelled by using a punt pole or push pole, which the punter manipulates while in a standing position in the stern of the boat. Although most punt boats can hold two men, they are essentially designed to hold one man and the necessary equipment for the hunt. Leo Pospishal has indicated that the punt boat was a much more difficult boat to build, and the Quillen punt boats were made with 24" wide white pine, obviously a rare commodity today.[18] Ed Lezotte, when asked to describe the difference between the Quillen boat and other examples, remarked: "Give it a push and it would go straight—the weight made it easier to move—it did not swivel."[19] Pospishal concurred: "The most outstanding feature probably was the weight—after they picked up water they were very heavy but the weight helps maintain momentum."[20] It is generally accepted that the fact that these boats were painted twice a year helped preserve a number of examples of Quillen boats.

The traditional boat forms that Quillen originally modified and further developed were retained for years after Quillen's death. But according to local hunters, no one could completely copy a Quillen boat. In the words of one hunter, "From a distance, it looked okay but not when you got up and looked them over."[21] Ed Lezotte suggested two tests for the true Quillen boat: "(1) If it has a batten seam down the center—it's *not* a Quillen, and (2) if the coaming around the passenger area is squared, not rounded off, it is not a Quillen."[22]

Otto Misch: A "Thumb" Area Waterfowler (1910–1965)

The waterfowler in the "thumb" area hunted primarily in the Saginaw Bay, Sebewaing Bay, and in an area known as Wildfowl Bay. During the early part of the twentieth century, this region was an especially popular hunting location. In an interview, Herb Miller recalled that a shoot was accomplished with relative ease and without sophisticated decoys, boats, or techniques:

Fred Luft had the first sneak boat and it was not used on the Saginaw Bay or Sebewaing Bay until about 1928—you did not need to use a sneak boat as food was very abundant—[there were] lots of birds. You could shoot all the birds you wanted without all that elaborate equipment.

The most obvious difference between the downriver and the thumb area waterfowling traditions centered on the contrasting characteristics of river hunting and bay hunting. Decoys made for use in the thumb area bays were not refined and narrow in form. The decoys from the thumb area shared the following features in common: (1) they were flat bottomed; (2) they were wider, verging on oblong or even round shapes when viewed from above; (3) they were much heavier; (4) the heads were mounted much further back toward the middle of the body and the heads were primarily in a very upright position; and (5) the decoys were generally fitted with a drop keel, a keel that was suspended down from the decoy by wire approximately four to six inches into the water. These keels were a response to the need for a stable decoy in the active waters in the bay areas. Needless to say, there were variations within the traditional pattern of decoy making in this region, but the locally established principles were transmitted from generation to generation through the conventional folk process—word of mouth.

Otto Misch: Decoy Maker

Otto Misch moved to Weale, Michigan, from the Port Huron area. He worked for years as a shipwright for Gar Wood Racing Hulls and, like many of his fellow workers, he maintained a passion for life on the water. His decoy making began when he started to make decoys for his personal friends and hunting partners. A small cabin in Weale served as his workshop and, although his reputation was established, he never advertised his decoys. Like many other decoy makers, he relied on a series of patterns that were fashioned for each species of duck that he chose to create in wood.

It is apparent that Misch, known locally as Ott, was influenced by his years in the St. Clair flats area because his decoys vary somewhat from the traditional thumb area decoys. Misch decoys were certainly wider than their nineteenth-century downriver predecessors but they were not quite as wide as the other decoys made by his contemporaries in the Sebewaing area. Also, the heads on his decoys were not set back nearly as far as those on other decoys from the shops of his fellow carvers.

A close personal friend of Misch, Maynard Smith, also made decoys, and the two often shared ideas. Both Smith and Misch lived originally in the Port Huron area. Many accounts indicate that this relationship was a particularly close one that encouraged Otto Misch to produce both decoys and duck boats.

Otto Misch: Boat Builder

Otto Misch's experience as a shipwright was especially evident in his boats. Like Nate Quillen, Misch has been remembered as a cabinet maker in his approach to boat building. Unlike his decoy making, Misch did make boats for sale to his hunting friends and acquaintances in the community. Even today, Misch's duck boats are recognized as among the best duck boats made in the thumb area.

Unlike Quillen, Misch relied on some of the construction traditions of the locale in which he worked. The majority of the duck boats made by Misch were round bottomed, not flat bottomed. Most significantly, Misch made his boats with strips of wood that would be nailed and laminated together around a solid mold or form. Misch cut two strips at a time and put the same bevel on them before securing them around the form. This was a complete departure from Quillen's downriver practice of building the boats with long, wide planks that ran the length of the boat and were shaped to create the hull and sides without a form. Both Quillen and Misch, however, did share a penchant for fine craftsmanship.

The types of boats for which Misch is remembered are primarily punt boats and, later in his life, sneak boats (fig. 3). Herb Miller has described Misch's punt boats as being

> . . .made in generally the same pattern of the St. Clair Flats sneak boat but smaller in scale—they were a little higher in dimension from the bottom of the boat to the deck. While the St. Clair Flats sneak boats were 18 to 20 feet in length, Misch made his punt boats 12 to 14 feet in length. The nose of the boat was stubbier and the bow and stern were generally semiround.[23]

The Misch sneak boats were made primarily in the late 1940s. One of these boats is in the collection of the Folk Arts Division, The Museum, Michigan State University. This boat, made in 1948–49 and donated by John Arnsman, displays the canoe-type hull construction that Misch used. Made with cedar strips and bent ash ribs, this 16-foot bottomed sneak boat was the first boat on which Misch used Fiberglas on the hull. The ingenious construction provided special motor mounts for use on this boat.

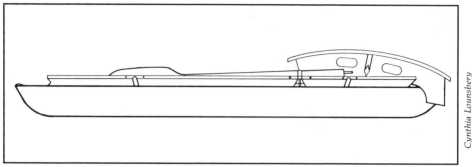

Cynthia Lounsbery

Figure 3. Sneak Boat by Otto Misch, Weale, Michigan 1948-49.

The sneak boat was named for a particular hunting technique that incorporated the following steps: (1) the decoys were set out and the boat was then anchored at a distance directly upwind; (2) the canvas shield was put in place and secured in the bow of the boat to conceal the hunters; (3) when the ducks landed among the decoys, the anchor was released and the hunters paddled downwind into the decoys; (4) the live birds usually would retreat in front of the boat to the downwind edge of the decoys; (5) when the ducks flushed they had to take off into the wind back past the hunters; and (6) after the shooting, the hunters retrieved the birds and returned to their original location. . .to wait again (fig. 4).

Misch made his first boats at his home in the Port Huron area, but later, after he began to spend more time at his "camp" at Weale, his boat building blossomed. By 1940, he had settled in Weale and continued to make boats through the 1950s. His boats retained the conventions of other boats made in the thumb area: false flooring, coaming around the decking, and the popular "dead grass brown" paint throughout the boat. Many of Misch's durable boats remain in service in the bay areas in the thumb region.

Conclusion

Many of the traditional practices of waterfowling remain intact in both the downriver and thumb area hunting communities of Michigan. The greatest threat to the traditional folk culture surrounding waterfowling must be recognized as not the imposition of nonfolk traditions, but rather the decline in sufficient feeding areas to maintain the waterfowl populations. The days of skies "darkened with flocks" have virtually passed. Herb Miller has reminisced on that time with deep regret:

Figure 4. Downriver Sneak-Shooting by Jim Foote.

Phyllis Ellison Collection, MSU Museum

> When I was in high school (in the twenties), vegetation was very dense. Clouds of migrant birds, mostly divers—thousands of divers—filled the sky. By 1940, there were fewer birds and by 1945 without feed, the waterfowl population began to disappear."[24]

Attempts have been undertaken to restore the feeding grounds in the downriver, thumb, and other hunting sites around Michigan, but the task is a painfully slow process.

Still, many of the elements of the human processes involved in waterfowling—especially the material culture traditions—have been transmitted to successive generations. The ingrained decoy making traditions are alive and well as demonstrated by the informal hunting practices in the downriver and thumb areas. Each area retains the distinctive characteristics of those waterfowlers from previous generations. The folk arts of decoy-making and boat building as practiced by Nate Quillen and Otto Misch offer instructive lessons on the nature of folk culture. Each successive generation prospers from the oral and behavioral traditions of the previous generations and not only practices what has been learned but also enriches the traditions with personal innovations. Folklife, while primarily conservative and trusting of proven traditional patterns of behavior, depends upon the process of strengthening people's interaction with each other. Material folk culture demonstrates the collaborative efforts of successive generations, and the study of folk art traditions reveals a great deal about community life both in Michigan and throughout the world. Bernard Herman and David Orr have perhaps summed up this opportunity for cultural investigation best:

> The objectives of the past cannot redeem us, but they can be made to yield the heart and thought of bygone hands and days slipping into the night of forgetfulness—and that is what the study of the decoy and all culture is about."[25]

1. Miles David Pirnie, *Michigan Waterfowl Management* (Lansing: Michigan Department of Conservation, 1935), 3.
2. Henry Glassie, "Folk Art," in *Folklore and Folklife,* ed. Richard M. Dorson (Chicago: University of Chicago Press, 1972), 253–80.
3. W. T. Barbour, "A Story of Pointe Mouillee," unpublished manuscript, 1.
4. Bernard W. Crandell, "Nate Quillen Decoys/1839–1903," in *North American Decoys* (Spring 1972), 2–11.
5. Hy Dahlka, unpublished manuscript, 7.
6. Ibid.
7. Interview with Edward Lezotte, 15 November 1979.
8. Ibid.
9. Ibid.
10. Ibid.
11. Barbour, 19.
12. Dahlka, 33.
13. James Foote, in Crandell, 4-7.
14. Crandell, 7.
15. Edward Burgess, in Crandell, 8.
16. Ed Richardson, in Hy Dahlka.
17. Barbour, 18–19.
18. Interview with Leo Pospishal, 19 January 1981.
19. Interview with Edward Lezotte, 16 January 1981.
20. Leo Pospishal.
21. Edward Lezotte, 16 January 1981.
22. Ibid.
23. Interview with Herb Miller, 15 July 1980.
24. Interview with Herb Miller, 20 January 1981.
25. Bernard Herman and David Orr, "Decoys and Their Use: A Cultural Interpretation," in *Frontiers,* Annual of the Academy of Natural Sciences of Philadelphia 1 (1979): 30.

Symbols and Identity

The Sauna

The French-Canadian Community

Ice Cutting

The Cornish Pasty

any symbols and signs

are forms of communication. Scholars of semiotics have established that there are differences between signs, symbols, and the scope of the term "communication." However, it is clear that in various settings, symbols and signs serve to communicate group and individual identity. The articles selected for this section convey the power of particular folk forms which are imbued with special meaning by folk groups and are truly symbols of identity for some Michiganders.

In the opening article, Yvonne R. Lockwood builds the tie between ethnicity, ritual process, and the concepts of space and time. Sauna is both a physical building and a folk process. Still widely practiced in the Upper Peninsula, sauna is more than a cultural survival of the past; rather, it is a dynamic functioning tradition and a vital symbol of Finnish-Americans' identity today.

Dennis M. Au and Joanna N. Brode trace the history of the French in the community of Monroe. This complex cultural portrait stresses those folk traditions that have been lost, as well as those that have been elevated as symbols of French-American identity in this historic community.

The role of festivals in perpetuating and celebrating community identity provides the focus for John F. Moe's study of the Remus Ice-Cutting Festival. Moe establishes the link with the past, stressing the nature of community festivals as a service of community pride and meaning in Michigan. Centering the study on the repetition of annual events and the acute awareness of past festivals in the community, the article underscores the critical role festivals play in providing symbols of identity in the late twentieth century.

The section concludes with an analysis of a Michigan regional food tradition, the pasty, by William G. Lockwood and Yvonne R. Lockwood. The transformation of the pasty from its mono-ethnic Cornish origin to a multi-ethnic specialty and finally to a symbol of Upper Peninsula regional identity illustrates the dynamic nature of cultural expression and the fact that the pasty can be redefined as a symbol of ethnic or regional identity, depending on context.

The assimilation of ethnic groups in America has often been wrongly described by the metaphor of the "melting pot." In reality, the process can be better described as a "tossed salad," a term offered by John Michael Vlach. While symbols of identity are often rooted in folk culture, some forms of expressive culture become more prominent or visible both to those within the culture and to those looking in from the outside. As the following essays demonstrate, identity is complex.

The Sauna: An Expression of Finnish-American Identity

Yvonne R. Lockwood

he sauna is the Finnish hot air bath, often called "steam bath" in colloquial English. The term refers both to the place where one bathes and the act of bathing itself; for example, one goes to the sauna and one takes a sauna. There has been a proliferation of saunas all over the western world since the 1950s; its high marketing potential has attracted a variety of entrepreneurs. Saunas are now special features of many hotels, motels, and health clubs; public saunas exist in numerous cities, some displaying names expressing the multi-ethnic distribution of the term—Bangkok Sauna, Maggies Midnight Sauna, Japanese Sauna, Pancho's Siesta Sauna. In addition, more and more affluent Americans of different ethnic backgrounds are installing saunas in their own homes.

This study of the sauna is part of a more extensive project which attempts to identify, analyze, and interpret the roles of traditional expressive culture in Finnish-American ethnic identity.[1] That is, what elements of Finnish-American culture do individuals, especially second and third generations, recognize, maintain, and enact as expressions of being Finnish? What is the function, role, and symbolic significance of these expressions? And how do they compare and relate to parallel traits in "mainstream" American culture? In

Reprinted with permission of the California Folklore Society from *Western Folklore*, 36 (1977), 71–84.

other words, what does it mean to be Finnish-American today and in what ways is this identity expressed? To answer these questions, we shall approach the sauna from the Finnish-American perspective and concern ourselves with the emic concept of this cultural complex.

The sauna is one of the most viable expressions of Finnish-American identity. As a physical object it is a characteristic feature of Finnish-American material culture. For example, the greatest density and largest number of Finnish-Americans are located in the Lake Superior regions of Michigan, Wisconsin, and Minnesota, and cultural geographers working in these regions have utilized it as an index to Finnish-American settlement zones.[2] In 1962, 77% of the Minnesota Finnish residents and 88% of the Michigan Finnish residents had saunas, as compared with 6% and 9%, respectively, for non-Finnish residents.[3] Even today there is a high probability that when one sees a sauna in the Upper Peninsula of Michigan it is a part of a Finnish cultural complex, especially if it is the traditional, detached structure set apart from the house.

The earliest Finnish-American saunas were one room and made from squared logs, hewn and mortised at the ends and then placed horizontally on top of each other, log-cabin style. This early type of sauna is idealized in Finnish-American culture although very few exist today. It is called a *savu*-sauna (smoke-sauna), so named because the firebox has no chimney; smoke from the wood fire encircles the walls, ceiling, and tiered benches and escapes through a small vent near the ceiling or through the door. The interior is black from years of use. The sauna is ready for use when the room is good and hot, i.e., 170–230° Fahrenheit; then the fire is allowed to go out and the smoke to escape. Finnish-Americans describe the fragrance as "fresh and healing" and the smoke as "pure and cleansing,"[4] "keeping everything sanitary."[5] One informant remembers calling this type of sauna "devil's sauna" as a child, probably because of the dark, hot interior. This expression, however, seems to be a family tradition unknown to others, but, nevertheless, the term does depict something of the atmosphere of the smoke-sauna.

The modern sauna more often is a plank-wall construction and has an attached dressing room. Within living memory of second-generation Finnish-Americans, before dressing rooms were added, people undressed in the house and streaked naked to the sauna which stood some distance away. Adding a dressing room to the one-room sauna was in partial response to outside pressure, just as

308

at one time chimneys were constructed on the smoke-saunas to conform with local safety regulations[6] (fig. 1). The dressing room is usually rectangular; the walls are lined with benches, with pegs on the walls for clothing and homewoven rag rugs on the floor. A door opens into the bath chamber, a room about fifteen by eight feet, with a stove in the corner heaped with Lake Superior rocks and a two or three tiered wooden platform, like bleachers, extending from wall to wall at one end. There is a small window in each room; ideally the sauna should be dimly lighted. Water is either carried to the sauna and stored in large drums or piped in. Utensils include dippers, basins and/or buckets, and whisks, which are often made of young leafy birch branches in spring and early summer but of cedar boughs the rest of the year.[7]

The conceptual significance of the sauna event varies according to whether the person is Finnish-American or one of the many other Americans now participating in the sauna. For the latter, a sauna is a quaint, perhaps healthful, way of bathing, but for Finnish-

Folk Arts Division, MSU Museum

Figure 1. Log Sauna built by Lauri Lipponen, Keweenaw Peninsula.

Americans, a sauna is a ritualized enactment of cultural expression. The process of bathing itself is enacted by highly redundant sets of behaviors and accompanied by specific rules and tradition. The sauna event is both spatially and temporally removed from ordinary daily activity. There also is a psychological sense of separation from the social order. Participants are outside or on the periphery of everyday life in a transition from one state, usually characterized as disorder, to another, that of order. Arnold van Gennep and Victor Turner have termed this state liminality, which usually refers to the transitional condition of ritual participants who are between defined states or statuses in the social structure.[8] Van Gennep outlines the three primary stages of transitional rituals, or rites of passage, as separation from the social order, the transitional stage itself, and finally reintegration into society. These stages clearly structure the sauna performance. Turner goes on to examine the bonding of these liminal entities which he calls communitas. He maintains that persons sharing this liminal state during ritual develop bonds of comradeship and egalitarianism. Sauna participants sharing a liminal state also maintain strong social bonds. However, unlike Turner's concept of spontaneous, antistructural communitas, which occurs in a homogeneous social order without status and roles,[9] the social bonds between sauna participants exist prior to the actual performance. Nonetheless, these pre-existing bonds are strengthened and reinforced in the sauna event.

In Finnish-American culture the ritual use of the sauna has changed over the years.[10] The early Finnish immigrants, as in Finland, associated the sauna with the life cycle and with its rites of passage. Traditionally, one was both born in the sauna and prepared for burial in the sauna. Prior to weddings the bride and groom ritually cleansed themselves in the sauna. It is no surprise that it was often the first building erected, for it provided a sense of order and stability to the communities. Often the Finnish immigrant family lived in the sauna while they built the house. Today, however, these life crisis events do not take place in the sauna, except in cases of ethnic revitalization. In recent years, for example, a few third-generation women have given birth in the sauna as their grandmothers did, and have expressed their Finnish identity in this revival of an ancient sauna ritual.[11] Aside from this exception there is little association between the sauna and the life cycle and rite of passage in modern Finnish-American culture. In contemporary North America the primary social function of the sauna has become manifestation

310

and reassertion of Finnish-American ethnic identity. In order to understand this phenomenon, it is necessary to describe the sauna process.

The sauna is physically removed from everyday activities—usually as a separate structure away from the house or at least in the basement. It is dimly lit, quiet, and hot. The fragrance is unusual and peculiar to the sauna. After removing one's clothing in the dressing room, one enters the sauna naked, closing the door behind. These acts symbolically detach the sauna participant from everyday life, as if one were stepping into another world. This spatial and temporal removal, called separation by Van Gennep, is further emphasized in sauna behavior.

Once inside, people may sit wherever they wish. There is no formal rule about where to sit, but there are patterns; for example, the "bravest" go directly to the top where it is hottest. Children under ten or twelve, however, are usually not yet active participants. Most sit as low to the floor as possible and try to get out as fast as they can, which is not as soon as they would like. When perspiring freely, one leaves the sauna to cool off. Today one sits in the dressing room, but before the two-room sauna, one stood or sat naked outside. This practice shocked and annoyed passing non-Finns; to stand naked outdoors in any season was anti-normative American behavior, but it was especially abnormal behavior in the winter. It was, however, appropriate Finnish sauna behavior.

The bather again enters the sauna and begins the process all over. Now and then water is thrown on the hot rocks; the water sizzles on impact and hot steam encircles the bathers, their skin tingling. An unstated rule of the sauna is that anyone who desires more heat may throw on water. If it gets too hot for the others, they either move down or out. A proverb in Finnish validates this behavior: "the taker rules the sauna." In actual practice, however, one asks the others if they would mind, knowing that they must and will agree, because, as it will become clear, it is difficult to admit that one cannot take more heat. Along with the steam comes the whisk, which should be green and from a living tree. It is soaked in warm water and then lightly toasted on the hot stones "to kill germs."[12] The bather energetically beats herself/himself, causing an additional sense of tingling. An outsider might interpret this act as masochistic, the tingling as discomfort; a Finn regards it as feeling good, that every inch of the body feels alive. This pleasure is learned. One third-generation Finn stated that he never attempts to push himself to the limit of his tolerance in the sauna, but, he added, "I just don't feel right until there is a certain measure of pain."[13]

The bather then steps out to cool off again. This pattern is usually repeated three or four times, but it may occur only once, for example when one is in a hurry or during menstruation, or one can remain several hours sweating, flagellating, and rinsing. Finally one scrubs down well with a very stiff brush, either in the sauna or in an adjoining shower, so that "every groove and pore in the skin is scraped."[14] Then, after rinsing in cool water, the bather may, if desired, warm up in the sauna heat just enough to dry off. Ideally one would dip in a cold lake or river to cool off, but usually one must be content with lying down in the dressing room to relax and rest. Earlier, winter bathers rolled in the snow or jumped into an icy nearby lake or river to cool off. Michael Karni writes that there are "documented instances" of suspicious non-Finnish neighbors complaining to religious and civil authorities that the Finns were worshipping pagan gods in their strange log house and performing naked dances outside.[15] Similarly, another Finn, recalling his childhood, stated that non-Finns looked upon them "as foreigners, sinners."[16] Whether substantiated or not, these reports are esoteric expressions of Finnish-American uniqueness.

This, then, is the ideal sauna performance. Coming out of the sauna, clothed, is to re-emerge, to join once again normal activities, which is analogous to the third phase of Van Gennep's transition ritual, reintegration. One re-enters society feeling like a "new person," fresh, clean, and "invigorated." The sauna event concludes with sharing refreshments in the house, affirming, in a symbolic sense, the restoration of order.

A common cross-cultural feature of ritual is the transitional condition of the participants between states or statuses in the social structure. This aspect was particularly evident when a pregnant woman went into the sauna to give birth, in which case her transitional pregnant state was changed to one of normalcy and her status elevated or changed to that of mother. A similar transition occurred when one went into the sauna to die or when bodies were prepared there for burial. Although the sauna no longer plays a viable role in rites of passage, the event is ritualized on other levels when participants are in a transitional state.[17] In contemporary tradition the sauna performance transforms a situation of disorder into order. Examples of such transformation are illness to health, drunkenness to sobriety, impurity to purity, dirtiness to cleanliness, anger to calm, weakness to strength. In the case of the latter, giving birth in the sauna with its warmth and pure, healing fragrance was thought to give the new mother strength so that she was up on her feet and at work in a matter of hours. In the minds of many Finnish-Americans there is a link between the sauna and the strength of Finnish soldiers, the stamina and skill of Olympic champions, and the beauty of Finnish women. A Finnish-American writes:

> The [Finnish national] soldiers, their vitality forged by sauna heat, were victorious against both the Russians and the cold. . . . The sauna may not have been the decisive factor in the Finns winning the winter war, but it probably contributed much to the strength and energy of the soldiers.[18]

The Finnish national epic, the *Kalevala*, contains many references to the sauna and its attributes, one of which is the magical curing property of the steam. It also describes sauna rituals which cured the afflicted of diseases. Today it is still common knowledge that "the sauna is a cure for anything."[19] When one has a bad cold or the flu, one takes a sauna, sips whisky, and sweats out the fever. A Finnish-American proverb runs, "if a drink of liquor and a sauna won't cure an ailment, it is a fatal one." Finns are known as hard drinkers. One informant reported that when her husband had been on a long hard drunk, "he would go to sauna, to sweat it out of his system, and I mean he really cooked himself."[20] According to folk belief, the sauna cures psychological as well as physical ills. When Finns in the Upper Peninsula learned of another Finn's low spirits and general depression, they advised him to take a hot sauna. In a similar vein, a Finnish national writes, "The sauna banishes psychological troubles and ill humor. . . . In its heat the mind is relieved of all pressures and recovers its true balance. . . . In the sauna anger cools and hatred burns away."[21] To what degree the transformation of disorder to order is merely psychological and temporary is not known, but the belief in the power of the sauna to transform is very strong.[22] Many a person enters the sauna feeling tired, depressed, and ill, and emerges pink, shiny, and revitalized. To partake in the sauna is the Finnish way to restore order.

There are rules and traditions which govern, justify, and strengthen the role of the sauna. At one time the church and the sauna were regarded as equally sacred places.[23] Although today this sacred association is seldom explicitly stated, the codes governing sauna behavior still emphasize a sense of sacredness. A study published in 1951 reports that many older people in the Upper Peninsula stated that "the sauna brings you a little nearer to God."[24] Only recently a young, third-generation Finnish-American described the sauna experience as "spiritual" and "almost sacred."[25] A definite concept of correct behavior regulates sauna activities. Children are scolded when they misbehave and reminded that they are in the sauna and to act accordingly: no boisterous activity, such as playing, singing, whistling; even talk is soft and kept to a minimum. Cursing and violent behavior are not condoned. Contrary to popular non-Finnish presumptions, sex in the sauna is not possible from the Finnish perspective. One informant was horrified when asked if this was part of Finnish mixed-sex sauna behavior. "Not in a Finnish sauna," she said. "Only crazy Americans would try something like that."[26]

Sharing a sauna is significant socially. The sauna event is most often associated with the closest kin, one's own nuclear family. After the family, one shares sauna with close friends and more distant relatives of the same sex. Very seldom, if ever, do Finnish-Americans today mix sexes in the sauna beyond the nuclear family. One does not share the sauna experience with just anyone outside the closely knit kin-based group. The act of sauna-sharing is an intimate experience which strengthens social bonds. This relationship is reinforced even further by mutual assistance in the sauna. Bathers wash each others' backs, pour rinse water over each other if there is no shower, and beat each other with whisks.

In the past the Saturday night bath, either in preparation for the Sabbath or merely because it was the end of the work week, was clearly ritualized cleansing. Today, sauna may be taken on any day, but traditional sauna day is still Saturday. This custom has been reinforced in part by the fact that the sauna event may also serve as recreation and a way of socializing at the end of the week. Friends may be specifically invited for sauna at which time refreshments and visiting are part of the entire event, like inviting friends over to play cards in other American subcultures. Sharing food after the sauna is an important part of the event, and usually includes coffee and/or beer and pastries, or even a complete meal. Finnish-Americans who do not have their own sauna often have customary use of a relative's or a friend's. Saturday, for example, may be both sauna day and the traditional day to spend with grandparents. Not uncommonly, friends and relatives may have a standing invitation to drop in on "sauna night." Informants describe the "sauna party" as a social event: the house is full of people with the coffee pot going constantly as guests drink coffee and visit while waiting their turn for the sauna. Social connotations of the sauna are strong enough that coffee and pastry are even offered at neighborhood saunas in the Upper Peninsula where one pays a small fee to bathe.[27]

Offering sauna to out-of-town guests is the expected norm in extending hospitality and the practice is closely observed (fig. 2). During my own visits in the Upper Peninsula, the sauna has been heated every day and even those who do not have their own have offered me a relative's. There are signs of this tradition weakening, and sometimes the offer of sauna on a day when it would not normally be heated is half-hearted. Generally, however, violation of this code of hospitality is severely criticized by others.

A most important aspect of the sauna is its role in enculturation. A child is taken to the sauna while only a toddler and continues to accompany one or both parents until about ten to twelve years old. Adults are the agents of social order and in the sauna under their guidance the child learns about personal hygiene, the facts of life, and the human body, but most importantly, the child learns about Finnishness. Many children go through a stage of rebelling against being in the sauna, hating the heat, the flagellation, and so on. Informants remember that as children they sat low to the floor and as far from the stove as possible while adults encouraged them to sit on the top tier and to stay a long time so that they would

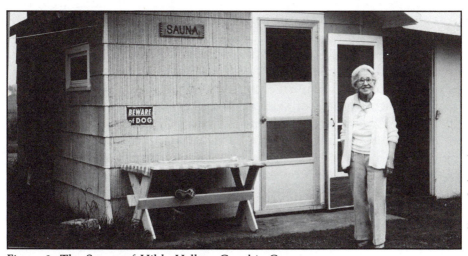

Figure 2. The Sauna of Hilda Hellen, Gogebic County.

be strong. At about the age of ten, children began to go to the sauna with their own peers, with cousins and friends. They have learned proper sauna behavior and are expected to act accordingly. Young males tend to compete with each other to see who can outlast the others. He who does so gains a reputation for being strong. To grow up Finn is to partake properly in the weekly sauna. But to be Finn also means to persevere, to stick it out in the heat, not to give up. This culturally learned characteristic is called *sisu*; to be Finn is to have *sisu*. The term has no exact translation in English and has been defined as "sheer, unadulterated tenacious bull-headedness," as "fortitude," as "unyielding persistence and determination," as "having guts to the *n*th degree." One Finn explicitly relates *sisu* and sauna:

> The Finns have been known throughout history as being a tough, hardy race. Perhaps the sauna has something to do with it. . . . To the Finns development of the human body and mind is synonymous. A healthy body and a healthy mind produces athletes with brains and intellectuals with healthy bodies. . . . Sometimes I think the incomparable Finnish "sisu" . . . was born in the infernal heat of a primitive sauna where [the Finns] were tested for endurance.[28]

The implication in this quote of God testing a people is significant.

Finnish-Americans themselves identify Finnishness with sauna participation; the sauna is a emic category of Finnish ethnic identity. For example, a couple doing research in an Upper Peninsula community was invariably asked the same set of questions by newly encountered inhabitants: (1) How do you like it up here? (i.e., the weather, the pace of life, the isolation, the food, the people), and (2) do you like to sauna?[29] In other words, when people were concerned with how well this couple was adapting to the community, they phrased their concern in terms of the sauna. Their questions are an expression of basic Finnish-American values.

Another example of such expression focuses on cleanliness, an important Finnish value. Despite various available modern methods of bathing, more than one Finn has stated that only a sauna makes her/him feel clean inside and out. One informant contrasted her children with those of a non-Finnish neighbor, saying, "I don't think those kids ever were as clean as a sauna would get my children. They were always so dirty. Their mother was a Finn, but their father was not. They didn't go for any of our customs."[30] The evaluation is clearly an esoteric statement of Finnish ethnic identity phrased in terms of the sauna.

In another case, a second-generation Finn discussed the self-consciousness he experienced as a child:

> As I got older I wanted to bathe like our American friends, in the kitchen in an old tin tub. Our neighbors were all Americans and our sauna habit didn't impress them so we kept it to ourselves. . . . I didn't realize it then, but I was too eager to get Americanized and too eager to cast aside old country habits.[31]

In yet another case, a Finnish-American, who has lived in Detroit some thirty years, said that he has given up the sauna, and because he has, he is now healthier than his siblings in the Upper Peninsula.[32] His rejection of the sauna is implied proof of his acculturation into "mainstream" American life. And the fact that he is healthier because he did so is affirmation that he did the right thing.

An interesting example of the sauna as a symbol of Finnishness is evidenced in ethnic revitalization. Informants for whom the sauna had become an almost inactive cultural expression, often because of weak ties to a Finnish community, are again active sauna participants by conscious choice. In another instance, a Finnish-American family that has maintained the sauna tradition and has its own sauna is now building a smoke sauna, the idealized, even romanticized bathhouse of yesterday. This revitalization phenomenon is somewhat analogous to nineteenth-century nationalist movements in Europe, in which the intellectual and "progressive" individuals revitalized traditional cultural expression by looking to the peasantry, the guardians of tradition and ethnicity, for lost roots, for soul. These intellectuals donned peasant costume, collected folksongs and tales from the peasantry, and wrote poetry using oral tradition as their model. This activity gave new respect to folk traditions and other compatriots followed their suit.

A parallel may be cited in contemporary Finnish-American culture. In the Upper Peninsula sauna tradition has not waned; it is still a viable Finnish-American cultural expression. Outside the traditional area of Finnish-American settlement, however, sauna and other aspects of Finnish-American culture are usually not as strong. Generally, the Finnish-Americans of these regions are more assimilated into mainstream American culture than are their Upper Peninsula kinfolk. Moreover, the sauna's role and function differ among Finns in predominantly Finnish communities and Finns in predominantly non-Finnish communities. In the Finnish communities sauna provides a regular means of bathing whether or not there is access to a modern bathroom. The Finn in this community regularly uses the sauna to get clean. The Finn outside the Finnish community usually does not go to the sauna regularly. Even if there is a sauna in the home, it may not be utilized on a weekly basis. However, the desire to do so is often expressed. This Finn looks forward to saunas and is entertained by them whenever he/she visits Finnish communities. For this Finn, the sauna is no longer a regular method of cleansing. Rather, it has become a self-conscious act of Finnishness as opposed to mainstream American behavior. In these colonies sauna revitalization occurs as part of the awakening of ethnic identity. In the process of discovering their Finnish-American background, these displaced people of the second and third generations consciously turn to the sauna as an expression of their new ethnicity. In large part the intellectuals have led this revitalizing movement by publishing studies on the sauna. The large number of publications on the phenomenon by Finnish-Americans in recent years is an indication of the extent of sauna revitalization.

The following exuberant quote appeared in a bulletin of Suomi College, the Finnish Lutheran college in Hancock, Michigan. The author's purpose was to announce a new sauna in the college dormitory:

> Finns and saunas belong together. . . . Furnishing other peoples, tribes, nations and kindred the benefits of the Finnish bathhouse is culture extension of the highest degree. . . . There is a school of thought that believes the quiet relaxing one attains while lying languidly on the sauna platform, soaking in the heat, perspiring freely, then occasionally flicking oneself with the . . . twigs, sloshing water around, washing, rinsing . . . is the best thing in the world to make the mind keen, so that thoughts race rapidly and the inventive faculties are sharp, and that school of thought will be happy with the Suomi College sauna—more "A" students. . . . Behind Sibelius . . . [was] the sauna![33]

These are but a few of the cases which single out the sauna as an important Finnish-American emic cultural sign.

Adult Finnish sauna behavior and attitudes are models for children. When one takes a sauna according to the model, it is an act of Finnishness. The sauna is ritualized performance, not just a method of bathing. Nor is the sauna comparable to a bathtub or shower, which every modern Finnish-American home has. Only to a non-Finn are the bathroom and the sauna generically the same. These are Finnish attitudes with which children are enculturated and which non-Finns, unlike Finnish children, seldom adopt.

The opposition of non-Finnish to Finnish behavior is equivalent to the unsocialized child and the socialized adult in the sauna. A series of binary oppositions illustrate these two poles and emphasize the emic views about ideal Finnish-American sauna behavior and Finnishness itself. Just as the sauna is to the bathroom, the Finn to the non-Finn and adult to child, the quality of dimness contrasts with light, fragrance with lack of fragrance, quiet with noise, hot with cool; the act of flagellation contrasts with no flagellation, high seating with low, long duration with short; the emphasized result of braveness contrasts with cowardliness, strength with weakness, and pleasure with discomfort. The Finnish national characteristics of *sisu* and cleanliness are played out in proper sauna behavior.

Finnish-Americans generally do not recognize many of the commercial and private establishments called "sauna" as the real thing: people talk too much and too loudly, it is not hot enough, and the management often does not allow water on the rocks or the use of whisks. Others are indignant and offended by the association of saunas with massage parlors. In other words, the Finnish code of sauna behavior is violated. This code is the essence of the Finnish sauna.

From the perspective of a Finn, the term sauna means particular behavior in a particular context. Despite the variables in individual performance, there is a shared general concept of an "ideal" sauna event just as there is for the sauna structure itself. Not only is the sauna Finnish, but Finns define themselves as such in terms of sauna participation. The affirmation of their identity is communicated in the sauna performance.

A shorter version of this paper was read before the Michigan Folklore Society at the 1976 meetings of the Michigan Academy of Science in Lansing, Michigan. I would like to thank Michael Loukinen and William G. Lockwood for their comments and suggestions.

1. Research was conducted in 1976 among second- and third-generation Finnish-Americans in or from the Upper Peninsula of Michigan. Many of the informants reside in densely populated Finnish areas in the western part of the Peninsula. Others (as well as the author) no longer reside in their natal ethnic enclaves but do maintain ties with these communities. Methodology consisted of directed interviews with a tape recorder, informal questioning during normal discourse, and observation of and participation in the sauna process. Literature published by Finnish-Americans about the sauna provide another source of information, which, for the most part, is descriptive and esoteric.
2. A popular name for the Copper Country of the Upper Peninsula of Michigan, for example, is "Finn-Land."
3. Cotton Mather and Matti Kaups, "The Finnish Sauna: A Cultural Index to Settlement," *Annals of the Association of American Geographers* 53 (1963): 500.
4. Aili K. Johnson, "Lore of the Finnish-American Sauna," *Midwest Folklore* 1 (1951): 34.

5. Second-generation female informant, 59 years of age, a resident of California for approximately twenty-five years.

6. Johnson, 33.

7. In other parts of the country whisks are also made of leafy maple, oak, and even eucalyptus branches.

8. Arnold van Gennep, *The Rites of Passage*, trans. Monika B. Vizedom and Gabrielle L. Caffee (Chicago: University of Chicago Press, 1960); and Victor W. Turner, *The Ritual Process: Structure and Anti-Structure* (Chicago: University of Chicago Press, 1969).

9. Turner, 177.

10. Although the first Finnish immigrants came to the region of the Delaware River in 1638, Finnish immigration was limited until the 1860s; the greatest number arrived during the first decade of this century. For information on Finnish migration and settlement the following studies are recommended: A. William Hoglund, *Finnish Immigrants in America, 1880–1920* (Madison: University of Wisconsin Press, 1960); Michael Karni, Matti E. Kaups, Douglas J. Ollila, eds., *The Finnish Experience in the Western Great Lakes Region: New Perspectives* (Turku, Finland: Institute for Migration, 1975); and John Wargelin, *The Americanization of the Finns* (Hancock, Mich.: The Finnish Lutheran Book Concern, 1924).

11. Third-generation male, a new resident of the Upper Peninsula, formerly from the region of Detroit, Michigan.

12. Second-generation male, approximately 70 years of age, resident of the Upper Peninsula.

13. See note 11.

14. Jingo Viitala Vachon, *Tall Timber Tales* (L'Anse, Mich.: L'Anse Sentinel, 1973), 77.

15. Michael G. Karni, "Honey Heat and Healing Vapors," *Northwest Architecture* (1973): 79.

16. John O. Virtanen, *The Finnish Sauna* (Portland, 1974), 95–97.

17. There is some evidence, as yet not adequately investigated, that ritual cleansing takes place after the consummation of marriage. This occasion would be the couple's first shared sauna.

18. Virtanen, 129.

19. See note 5.

20. Ibid.

21. H. J. Viherjuuri, *Sauna: The Finnish Bath* (Helsinki, 1960), 95.

22. There are many studies concerning the effects of the sauna on the body and health. One of these deals with the physiological benefits and the use of the sauna in therapy: Victor R. Ott, *Die Sauna* (Basel, 1948). In both the United States and Finland the sauna has been the object of recent medical research. One such study is by Marjorie A. Clement, "Variations in Blood Gases, Serum Potassium, and Blood Lactate Levels during Hyperthermia (The Finnish Sauna) and Their Relationships to Observed Cardiac Abnormalities" (M.S. thesis, Michigan Technological University, 1976).

23. Johnson, 37; Karni, 69.

24. Johnson, 39.

25. Third-generation female, thirty-six years of age, a resident of Arizona.

26. See note 5.

27. The public Finnish sauna is an old institution, which may be merely a family's sauna open to the neighborhood during certain hours or a larger commercial establishment equipped to handle many customers at once. It can be found in urban regions and small towns with sizable Finnish populations; the clientele are predominantly Finns who do not have regular access to private saunas. These bathhouses are traditional saunas in terms of both behavior and function.

28. Vachon, 80.

29. See note 11.

30. See note 5.

31. Virtanen, 96–97.

32. Second-generation male, sixty years of age.

33. Arnold Stadius, "The New Student Center Has a Sauna," *The Finnish-American Blue-White Book*, ed. Reino J. Minkkinen and J. William Pellinen (Brooklyn, 1966), 80–81.

The Lingering Shadow of New France: The French-Canadian Community of Monroe County, Michigan

Dennis M. Au and
Joanna Brode

 oven throughout the geographic fabric of the United States are communities rich in folk tradition that has imparted a cultural distinctiveness to the landscape and its inhabitants. The Hudson River Dutch, the Louisiana Cajuns, the Pennsylvania Germans and the Hispanic cultures of the American southwest are such communities. Michigan likewise harbors a centuries-old folk culture: the French-Canadian. Having taken root in the waning years of the seventeenth century, remnants of this early culture linger in pockets of the state, giving these communities a distinctive "personality of place" that geographers and folklorists term an "ethnic culture region."

One of the most visible French-Canadian communities in Michigan is found in the southeastern corner of the state in present-day Monroe County. We shall attempt to identify its distinctive character by examining specific living cultural traits that date from the period of initial occupation. These traits consist of material culture and oral traditions specific to Monroe and reflect the French-Canadian folk origins of the community. In viewing these examples one can trace the evolution of the ethnic group, and in so doing provide a model to identify other cultural groups in similar environments.

With minor exceptions, the French-Canadians of Monroe County trace their roots to northern France. As early as the seventeenth century their ancestors left France for Canada, bringing with them their language and traditions. Their initial settlements were centered around the Quebec City region, but as time passed their descendants moved westward towards Montreal. The founding of Detroit in 1701 by Antoine de la Mothe Cadillac, and the subsequent settlement of the Detroit-Windsor border region by these French-Canadians, was merely a continuation of their westward expansion.

The Detroit settlement grew steadily under the French and, after 1760, the British. However, by the 1780s its French character began to fade as it was gradually supplanted by elements of the more dominant English culture. Toward the final decades of the eighteenth century, many French-Detroiters had begun to seek out new homesteads where their language and customs could better be preserved. They sent offshoots into the river regions north and south of Detroit. The River Raisin settlement due south of Detroit (roughly present-day Monroe County) was one of the first of such enclaves founded within the Michigan Territory.

From 1784, when Colonel François Navarre constructed the first home on the River Raisin, until the outset of the War of 1812, the French community of Monroe grew rapidly. The 1811 census listed 1,340 inhabitants, the vast majority French-Canadians from Detroit (only a small minority hailed directly from Quebec). During the first three decades of settlement the inhabitants of the Raisin settlement enjoyed relative freedom to nurture their native culture. They built homes and laid out farms according to the traditions of their ancestors.

But, alas, the continuity of this French community was short-lived, for within its midst was enacted one of the bloodiest actions of the War of 1812: the Battle and Massacre of the River Raisin. In three short years the settlement was destroyed, its inhabitants left destitute, and the majority scattered as far afield as Ohio and Canada. Nevertheless, at the war's conclusion in 1814, these undaunted souls returned to begin their lives anew. Again they sowed and nurtured the seeds of their native culture, but this time they reaped a different harvest. The American war victory had altered the cultural complexion of the River Raisin for all time.

By the year 1817, the community had acquired an American name—Monroe. And by the 1830s the French were again outnumbered by an influx of Eastern "Yankees" who had arrived via the newly-opened Erie Canal. French political, cultural and economic hegemony in Monroe was broken. French craftsmen and carpenters were either supplanted by or assimilated into the new American fashions. With the exception of homemade commodities such as straw hats, the material culture produced by and for the French no longer retained its distinctive identity. In a short time, the region began to appear more like Boston and New York and less like Quebec and Montreal.[1]

However, the cultural legacy of the first settlers is never totally extinguished. Elements of the original culture often go underground or survive in curious customs and artifacts that offer intriguing clues for the cultural historian. The intent of this article is to expose these cultural remnants in Monroe County as an archaeologist might excavate a prehistoric site—to trace them to their roots from the past to the present and by so doing to pay respect to a vibrant community that was one of the few European outposts in the Northwest Territory.

Cultural traditions may be grouped into material and verbal aspects of culture. Material aspects comprise such elements as settlement patterns, architecture, foodways, and home furnishings; verbal aspects of the culture include folksongs, folktales, language, and place-names. The primary focus will be upon the most visible exponents in each category; namely, those elements which still impart to the region a "personality of place." However, mention also will be made of specific items that denote the French legacy but are best defined as "relics." These relics usually exist singularly or in such small quantity that they impart only a small degree of distinctive regional flavor, yet serve as mileposts in understanding a community's genesis.

In the two hundred years that the French have lived in Monroe County they have left an indelible mark. Today the most prominent reminder of their presence lies in land patterns. The geographic settlement of a people is an aspect of folk culture studies that is frequently neglected. Yet often it is the one cultural legacy that remains most visible and unchanged over time. It encompasses the use of the land, the setting of property boundaries and the location of buildings, roads and fields. In the initial period of occupation this may be governed by custom and law. So it was, that when Frenchmen came to Monroe County in the eighteenth century, they followed a settlement tradition dating to twelfth century France, one which had already been adapted successfully to the new world in the Canadian wilderness.

This culturally distinctive settlement pattern used in Monroe and in most other French settlements in North America has been named the *"roture"* or "French long lot" system.[2] The claims were long narrow strips of land which fronted on the major rivers and creeks. Although many claims in Monroe did not conform, the custom was for an individual *roture* to measure four *arpents* wide by forty *arpents* long (roughly 710 feet by 7,096 feet) with the longer axis always perpendicular to the river.

Following established custom, the buildings, roads and fields were arranged on the *rotures* in prescribed fashion. On both sides of the river, a road, called the *chemin*, ran parallel to and followed the river's course. These roads provided the major land routes into the community. With few exceptions, the houses were located on the first rise above the floodplain fronting the road, with the road sandwiched between the house and the river. Summer kitchens, major barns, stables and other outbuildings were situated just beyond the house. Behind the outbuildings lay the orchard, then the fields and pasture, and in the farthest perimeter, the wood lot.

This French landscape pattern contrasts sharply to the early New England metes and bounds or the later Township and Range division that prevails in the rest of Michigan. Nevertheless, the long lot worked well for these early settlers on the Raisin, as all of the dwellings were within shouting distance of the adjacent farms, an important defense factor in frontier days. Likewise, the system helped foster a close-knit community which was and still is important to the French. Finally, this land division made ecological sense. The long narrow parcels cut across the geological zones in the river valleys to give each person a wood lot in the back, prime farm land from the trees to the floodplain and frontage along the river, the major transportation artery.

Some aspects of this French landscape pattern have survived in Monroe County and have been well adapted to contemporary land use. The boundaries of the individual *rotures* are still the basic property divisions in many parts of the county. Five major highways follow the routes originally carved out by the *chemins*. Likewise, many of the houses along these roads are still on the rise above the floodplain and just behind the road as they were in the eighteenth century. In many instances the farms of today follow the ancient French pattern: river, road, buildings, orchards, fields, and timber. As one drives east from Dundee to Monroe on Route 50, the landscape is strongly reminiscent of the river valleys which border Montreal. The Raisin at this juncture looks more like the Richeleau of French Canada and less like its American cousin, the Huron River, which merely shares a closer geographic relationship.

Leaving the land division for a moment, the cultural landscape affords twenty buildings with identifiable French traits still extant in Monroe County which exemplify three surviving architectural types. These three examples represent the final stages of evolution in the vernacular idiom before all variants of French folk architecture disappeared from Michigan.

At the end of the eighteenth century, when the French settled the River Raisin, their architectural traditions had already undergone one hundred and fifty years of evolution in North America. Identifiable regional traits were easily distinguishable, from the galleries of the French Indies to the one-and-a-half story cottages of Quebec.[3] The Navarre-Anderson Trading Post (fig. 1) is an excellent example of late eighteenth century French-Canadian architecture. This structure, erected along the River Raisin in 1789 for François

Dennis Au

Figure 1. The Navarre-Anderson Trading Post under restoration. This structure was built in 1789.

Marie Navarre *dit* Heutrau, has recently been restored by the Monroe County Historical Commission and will take its place as a significant testimony to one of the earliest chapters in Michigan's heritage.[4]

This one-and-a-half story structure reveals a front façade with nearly symmetrical door and windows. Typically, both façade and roof axes parallel the river and the road. The gable ends comprise the shortest sides of the nearly square edifice supporting the roof with its distinctive pitch. Architectural historians in Canada have chronicled the evolution of pitch from the earliest settlements in the seventeenth century when they measured fifty degrees to the early decades of the nineteenth century when they were about thirty degrees. As such, roof pitch is usually a reliable determinant of age. The roof of the Navarre-Anderson Trading Post measures forty-five degrees which, according to the Canadian chronology, is typical of the late eighteenth century. As this was the time period within which the Trading Post was completed, we can reasonably assume a direct cultural link from Monroe to Montreal of the late eighteenth century.

While form and style are important indicators, construction technique is often the critical determinant in establishing a cultural association. In the years preceding the 1830s (before balloon framing swept over North America), most ethnic groups maintained their own distinct construction methodology. As with building form and style, French-Canadian construction techniques had undergone a century and a half of evolution by the time the Navarre-Anderson Trading Post was built in 1789. Of the various building techniques known and used by the French, the one selected by Navarre's carpenters was the most fashionable in the Montreal region of that day.[5]

Pièce sur pièce, as the method is called, is precisely what the translation states: log on log. The exterior walls of a house constructed in this manner consist of hewn timbers laid horizontally, one on top of the other. These logs are then secured into place by vertical posts called *coulisse*, which divide the façades into sections. The *coulisse* has grooves or mortice joints cut into the entire length on both sides. Tongues or tennons on the ends of the horizontal logs are fitted into these mortice joints and secured into place by wooden pegs. Two important variations exist for corner treatments. In one, the corners of the logs are morticed and tennoned into another *coulisse* at the corner. In the other, logs are either dove-tailed or lap-notched at the corner. The Navarre-Anderson building is lap-notched.

The Labadie house, located on LaPlaisance Creek just south of the River Raisin, represents a later stage of architectural evolution from the Navarre-Anderson Trading Post. Erected about 1818 by Medard Labadie on the site of another home that had been destroyed during the War of 1812, this structure reveals many distinguishing French architectural traits. Perhaps the most striking difference between the Labadie house and the Navarre-Anderson Trading Post is in construction methods. Labadie's house was built using a method known as *maison colombage*. This technique consists of vertical timbers set into a sill log. The material used to fill the spaces between the vertical timbers consists of a mixture of stone, brick and mortar called, in French, *pierrote*. The selection of this construction technique again falls into a chronology that reflects the prevailing fashion of the cultural hearth: Montreal. Furthermore the use of *pierrote* distinguishes the Monroe structure from *maison colombage* of the Mississippi Valley, where a fill-in of mud and straw, referred to as *bousiller*, was favored.

In the years following the erection of the Labadie house, the number of buildings constructed following French traditions declined rapidly. By 1825 when Edward Loranger, a local brick mason of French origin, built his home on Stony Creek, north of Monroe, the building tradition was nearly at an end. At first glance, the house would not be classified as French stylistically, because its cornice, cornice returns, and roof pitch mark it as an example of the early classic revival style.

The classic details listed, however, are largely decorative. The basics of the building are French: the one-and-a-half story construction; symmetrical placement of door and windows; and the landscape scheme in which the house is located on the first rise above the creek with its roof axis and façade parallel to the creek and the road, with the road bisecting the two. Structurally, the French theme continues. The first floor interior walls consist of vertical timbers with brick laid between them, much like the traditional *maison colombage*. This is a construction technique the French called *brique entre poteau*.

The floor plan, an important indicator in classifying folk architecture, follows the same basic pattern in the Loranger house as it does in Navarre's and Labadie's, all typical of the French folk structures of the Montreal hearth. An almost square plan is bisected by a main interior wall running from the right of the front entry to a doorway diametrically opposite at the rear of the structure. Commonly, this two room plan features a stairway located on the far corner from the entry leading to a commodious loft. Variations in the plan have evolved over time and frequently the two-room plan is divided into three or possibly four rooms. Later, a hallway might be created from front to rear entry, essentially dividing the house into two equal portions, enclosing and formalizing the rooms.

In essence, the Loranger house constitutes a symbolic representation of the cultural history of Monroe County, Michigan, in its infancy. We see a structure quite American in appearance which, at its core, is French. This curious blend reflects what was occurring in the culture of the day. The English-speaking culture had asserted its dominance in society, politics, and commerce. And like Loranger's house, if a Frenchman were to succeed, at least his public (exterior) façade must appear Anglo-American.

While the surviving architecture provides the most recognizable examples of French material culture in Monroe County today, there are, nevertheless, a number of artifacts which reveal important associations. These are the cultural relics spoken of earlier. While they may no longer impart a "personality of place" that distinguishes the community in the present day, as relics they help document the "personality of place" at specific points in the past. One such item is the chair pictured in figure 2. Constructed circa 1795 for Colonel François Navarre, nephew of the first occupant of the Trading Post, it is one of a set of three in the collection of the Monroe County Historical Museum.

In furniture, as in architecture, form and construction are important elements in ascribing cultural origin. In style, the Navarre chair recalls the *chaise a la Capucine* (Capucine monk's chair), popular in France during the reign of Louis XIV. It is a simple, but sturdy, ladder back chair with a rush seat. The important identifying construction details to note are that the wood used for the stiles and front legs is rived not sawn, and the stretchers are not turned, but rounded with a drawshave. As was traditional in French Canada, the stretchers penetrate the stiles and legs and the slats on the chairback pierce the stiles. The legs extend above the seat, another French trait to note. In an attempt to diminish the chair's severity, the legs and stiles are chamfered. Rush seats, while not as common in French Canada as rawhide, were the standard in Normandy, the Canadian ancestral homeland.[6]

Figure 2. Ladder back side chair made for Col. Francois Navarre about 1795.

The crude simplicity of the chair is contrasted with the silver spoons that also belonged to Colonel François Navarre. The spoons convey a certain cultural aspiration not exhibited by the chairs. The housing of more formal objects with homely ones under a common roof was a noted feature of frontier New France. The spoons, crafted by Israel Ruland and his son Joseph between 1790 and 1820, might seem unrelated to the French-Canadian material culture made by silversmiths with obvious English surnames. However, research firmly identifies Ruland as an apprentice to the noted Detroit silver-smith, Gerrit Greverat.[7]

When Ruland, and later his son, moved to the River Raisin set-tlement in the 1790s, they continued their trade following the meth-ods of their French-Canadian teacher. The obvious crudeness of the spoons can probably be attributed to the fact that the Rulands, as frontier silversmiths, were primarily engaged in producing trinkets for the Indian trade and lacked experience in producing decorative household silver.

The final item of French material culture to be discussed, is the long handled frying pan, *poêle à queue* (fig. 3). Made about 1835 for Samuel Navarre, the youngest son of Colonel François Navarre, it is now in the collection of the Monroe County Historical Museum. The handle, one continuous piece of wrought iron, was formed on a blacksmith's anvil. Its long beveled sides terminate in a tapered, looping tail by which it could be hung. So that it could be riveted securely, the opposing end of the handle is bent downward and flattened to conform to the upright side of the pan. Used for cooking in a fireplace, this implement had a special holiday associa-tion in the French kitchens of America: it was the cooking utensil used for flipping the traditional *Mardi Gras* pancakes.[8]

Utensils, chairs, buildings, and settlement patterns have survived for nearly two hundred years and help identify the corner of southeast Michigan as a French culture region. Each testifies to the French-Canadian influence in the county. By careful examination and com-parison we can conclude that in the eighteenth century the community at the River Raisin was an extension of the Quebec-Montreal cultural hearth. Second, the paucity of identifiable objects of French culture originating after the 1830s confirms a historical reality. As the nine-teenth century progressed, the influence of Quebec diminished while Yankee America made significant inroads into the cultural, technical and economic aspects of the local French community.

By the opening years of the twentieth century, the distinctive craft culture of the French-Canadians had all but disappeared, while in homes the language, songs, legends, tales and foodways remained strong. Though many of these traditions exist today, most are no longer part of daily life. Rather, they are remembered from child-hood when these traditions played a role in family life. An examina-tion of these cultural survivals, however, affords additional insights into the French-Canadian community of Monroe County. There has been no systematic attempt to record these aspects of culture, and

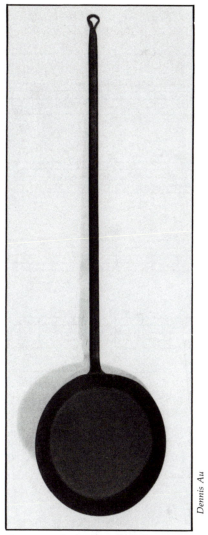

Dennis Au

Figure 3. Long handled fry pan
from the family of Samuel Navarre.

the following discussion is based on a sampling of what has been
collected by the authors.

Perhaps the most engaging of the oral traditions among French-
Canadians in Monroe County are folksongs. As late as the 1930s,
an amazingly large repertoire of traditional French songs was an
active part of family tradition. The three songs which follow are
representative samples of the music that has been collected. Today
these songs are part of memory culture and seldom if ever are sung
in public.

Prendre un petit coup
[Take a Little Swig]

1. Oh, Mr. Moses smoked his pipe so much,
   Smoked his pipe so much.
   Smoking so much gives you consumption.
   For I tell you he smoked his pipe so much.
   Smoked his pipe so much.
2. Let's go to the woods my friend Annette.
   Let's go to the woods us two.
   There I will pick you the prettiest of flowers.
   Let's go to the woods my friend Annette.
   Let's go to the woods us two.
3. A little swig, that's fine.
   A little swig, that's sweet.
   A big swig, dizzies the mind.
   A little swig, that's fine.
   A little swig, that's sweet. Salute!

1. *Prendre un petit coup*
   Oh Monsieur Moïse fumez donc pas tant la pipe,
   Fumez donc pas tant la pipe
   À tant fumez, c'est donner la chichite.
   Car je vous dis fumez donc pas tant la pipe
   Fumez donc pas tant la pipe.

332

2. *Allons au bois m'amie Annette,*
   Allons au bois tous deux.
   J'estime mieux la chere de marguerites.
   Allons au bois m'amie Annette,
   Allons au bois tous deux.
3. *Un p'ti coup, c'est agréable,*
   Un p'ti coup, c'est doux.
   Un gros coup, ça rend l'esprit malade.
   Un p'ti coup, c'est agréable.
   Un p'ti coup, c'est doux. Salut!

The refrain of this song is by far the most commonly remembered bit of music in the community. Considered a drinking song, it was usually sung at large, festive gatherings. It is known in France and is especially popular in Quebec where it has been sung for centuries. Drinking songs constitute the largest genre of music collected by the authors. The above version was recorded from Father Lambert LaVoy in 1976, who learned it from his father, Gilbert LaVoy. Long a central figure in the French-Canadian community, Father LaVoy was born in Erie, Michigan, in the southern portion of the county and served as a parish priest there for several years.

Quand le diable est venu sur le terre
[When the Devil Came to Earth]

When the Devil came to Earth,
You can see if he didn't have an effect.
He went to a baker's.
And the baker played a trick.
He stuffed the Devil into his oven.
But the Big One to play a trick back,
He broke out the back of his oven.

Quand le diable est venu sur la terre,
Vous pouvez voir s'il ne fasse un effet.
Il a été chez le boulanger,
Et le boulanger a joué un tour.
Il a fourré le diable dans son four.
Mail le gros pour jourer a lui un tour,
Il a cassé le dierriere de son four.

333

This version was recorded in 1975 from Clarence "Putsie" Reaume of Monroe Township, who learned it from his grandmother, Mary Navarre-Reaume. It appears that the song was sung by both adults and children. When Mr. Reaume sang this song for the author, his wife of many years said she had never before heard her husband sing in French.

The song, *"Quand le diable est venu sur le terre"* ("When the Devil Came Back to Earth") has an unusual slant and is part of a song known as "Le diable dans le sac" ("The Devil in a Sack"). It tells of the devil coming to earth where he becomes the victim of a mortal's trick. In retaliation, the devil finds an opportunity to play a trick upon the mortal. This theme of the devil as a trickster, rather than the tempter, was current throughout medieval Europe.

"Le petit coq gris"
[The Little Gray Cock]

1. The little gray cock there.
   He laid in the church there.
   He laid a little egg . . .
   For *(child's name)* to go beddie-by.
   Da dish a da doe.
2. The little black cock there.
   He laid in the cupboard there.
   He laid a little egg . . .
   For *(child's name)* to go beddie-by.
   Da dish a da doe.

1. *Le p'ti coq la gris la.*
   Il pond dans l'église la.
   Il pond un p'ti coco pour (child's name) *a faire a dodo*
   Da dish a da doe.
2. *Le p'ti coq la noir la.*
   Il pond dans l'armoire la.
   Il pond un p'ti coco
   Pour (child's name) *a faire a dodo*
   Da dish a da doe.

"The Little Gray Chicken" is a delightful version of the classic lullaby of French America entitled, *"La poulette blanche"* ("The Little White Hen"). The Monroe version presents the rather incongruous substitution of the *coq* (cock) laying the egg instead of the *poulette* (hen). The informant who sang this version in 1977, Mr. Edward Labadie of Monroe Township, said that he learned it from his parents. They would sing as many verses as were necessary to put their children to sleep, changing the color of the chicken and the place where the egg was laid in each verse.

These three songs contain important evidence that links the French community in Monroe County to French Canada and to Old France. While all of the songs can be traced to the traditional Quebec repertoire, there is a curious anomaly. The folksongs which popular culture has made into classics in Quebec, like *Alouette* and *En roulant ma Boule*, are almost totally unknown among the French in Monroe. This seems to confirm research indicating that the Monroe French had severed their cultural links with Quebec early in the nineteenth century, the time when these folksongs were popularized there. Thus, the songs of the Monroe repertoire may be more representative of the eighteenth century than those now found in Quebec.[9]

In rare instances, traditional French folktales are still part of family life. Most, however, are relegated to memory culture. In many cases, the themes and characters in the tales can be traced to medieval France. Although the *lutin* (goblin) and *feu follet* (will-o-the-wisp) are occasionally remembered, the *loup garou* (were-wolf or were-animal) and the devil are the most popular subjects of the tales collected to date.

Loup garou tales date back to at least the Middle Ages and share a similar theme in which a man, or his soul, becomes embodied in a fierce animal that repeatedly confronts a specific person. Frightened, that person consults an elder who explains that the vicious animal is the *loup garou*. The way to end the confrontations is to draw blood from the animal, thus delivering the soul which is embodied within it. Care must be taken, however, for if the animal draws blood first, the attacker will also become a *loup garou*. The tale concludes with a scheme devised to wound the animal. Once wounded, the animal is miraculously changed back into a human.[10] The following narrative was told in 1976 by Edward Labadie, who heard it from his parents as a true story:

The people were troubled. They would hear a knock on the door, answer the door and every time they would answer the door it would be nothing more than a police dog standing there. And this would happen every once in a while throughout the weeks and months and they got to where they discussed it with their neighbors. And one man said, he said, "Listen." He said, "Do you have a set of keys to the outbuildings and to the house." He said, "The next time you hear the knock on this door and you open it and the police dog is standing there, take the keys and hit the dog in the face. Make sure you draw blood." And he said, "You will be surprised what you see. It'll be somebody you know or one of your neighbors sure!" And they said they did this, and there was a person that appeared whom they had known.

A tale recorded in 1986 from Lora Gray concerns the other popular subject, the devil. As preadolescents in the 1960s, Lora and her sisters spent many weekends with their grandfather, Eli Cooley, a master raconteur. As a warmly anticipated bedtime ritual, he delighted them with stories of his youthful experiences growing up around the Lake Erie swamps. He told and retold "spooky" yarns woven from the fabric of old French legends that he had inherited from his father. The best remembered of his repertoire is the following tale, which has its roots in ancient France and is among the most popular folktales of French North America:[11]

I remember it as the story of the girl who danced with the Devil. And it starts out with a young girl in her, I would say in her middle teens . . . and she would read things or hear things from people who would come through Monroe from other big cities. And she became disenchanted with the rural atmosphere around here. And she would long for some excitement and some boy friends who were more sophisticated than the farmers that she was meeting at school and at church here.

And so one night in her room she just kind of said a prayer, like that, said, "I'd give anything to get out of Monroe!" And instead of the Lord hearing the prayer, the Enemy, the Devil, heard that. And it was soon after she said that that a very distinguished looking gentleman ended up in Monroe with a beautiful black carriage, with a buggy that was just spiffy. And a beautiful black horse pulling it. And this man caught her eye right away.

And there was a dance coming up in the community and she wanted to go to it. And this gentleman befriended her. . .and he asked her to this dance. Now her parents didn't know why they didn't like him but they didn't, and they forbid her to go to the dance with him, because there was just something about him they didn't like.

But, she wanted to go anyways, so the night of the dance, without her parents knowing it, she snuck out of the house and went with him. And her parents later came to the dance and found out she was there but they didn't say anything. So she was at the dance with this man. And my grandfather told us that back then, they didn't use babysitters and things. When you came to a dance or community function everybody came. And in the corner they had a baby sleeping which was one of their neighbor's babies. And every time this couple—this young girl and this stranger to Monroe—would dance by this crib the baby would cry. And the parents began to notice that something was wrong. But they didn't know what, and they noticed that every time they danced by this baby it would cry.

Well, towards the end of the dance, the gentleman whispered something into her ear that made her scream and cause a little commotion. And my grandfather would say in a voice, "It's time for you to leave Monroe," and he would say it in a spooky voice about how the Devil had finally said, "You said you'd give anything to leave Monroe. Well, now you're coming!" And she began to cry out to her father for help. This man was exceptionally strong and no one could do anything. He had her in a corner and he was going to leave with her. Well, the father just instinctively knew that there was something evil about this man. And so you know, because of the baby and all the different things. . . .

So they called for the priest. And he came and he brought holy water and he began to take authority over him with the power that the Church has over the Devil. And he would say . . . scripture or something, to tell him to leave through the authority the Lord has over the Enemy. And he would throw holy water on him. Now . . . something happened to him when the water hit him . . . and he would back up and back up, until they were in a corner. And finally . . . he ran through the wall to get away from the priest. . . . And the wall was destroyed and could never be rebuilt.

And so there was an ultimate victory of good over evil and the daughter then ran back to her father saying, "I'll obey you now; I'll do what you say!" And I guess the moral of the story was, obey your parents, they really do watch out for you and when they tell you not to hang around with certain people they have intuition about them; but that's the jist of it. But, that was the night she danced with the Devil.

Historical legends about tragic events constitute an important surviving genre. These stories usually have some basis in truth, but over the years they have become embellished and their story lines altered to conform to a few accepted themes. The Battles and Massacre of the River Raisin, which took place in January 1813 during the War of 1812, is one such historical event remembered in legend. A version recently collected from George M. Smith of Monroe concerns his ancestors, Captain Ambroise Charland and his wife Marie Angelique, both of whom witnessed the terrible events. Some of the details of the narrative, such as the time of the battle, the placement of Ambroise Charland in the fighting, and the statement about soldiers being killed along the trail, can be verified.[12] However, Mrs. Charland did not rescue General Winchester, although she might have saved another officer and mistaken him for Winchester.

The plot of this legend is similar to that of numerous stories about the War of 1812 printed locally in the nineteenth century. A man is sheltered from hostile Indians by a French woman; Indians come to the woman, making demands for food or liquor; she gives the Indians just enough to satisfy them and then sends them on their way; saved from the Indians, the man escapes to safety. This theme continues in the French community as evidenced by Mr. Smith's version of the legend:

> My great grandmother told this story to my mother when I was small. . . . Just before dawn [Marie Angelique Charland] was feeding her daughter, Monique, when she heard the cannon firing. . .and it seemed like hours before it stopped. Her husband Ambroise was away somewhere with his men and she didn't know if he was in the fighting again or not. Later in the afternoon, she said General Winchester came to the door and told her that the soldiers were being killed and scalped and they were dead all over the trail. Just then, she saw three Indians coming down the creek. She knew that they wouldn't hurt the French women or children so she hid the General under a barrel used for pickling pork, in a corner of the cabin. The Indians walked in demanding whiskey, but she didn't give them any. She had none. She gave them a fresh loaf of bread she had been baking and they walked out and headed down the creek. And the General waited until dark and then left heading toward the Maumee settlement.

In a broader perspective, these oral traditions are important in that they help impart a distinctive cultural identity to the French community. The *loup garou* and devil narratives link the French in Monroe to Quebec and Old France. The legend about the War of 1812 links them to the pioneer days of the territory of Michigan. As these tales cease to be remembered, their function as markers of local French culture will be diminished.

Another area that identifies Monroe County as a French cultural region is language, of which place-names are the most visible legacy. The 1810 Land Claims Map lists French names for rivers, creeks, and shore features. Of these, *Pointe Mouiler*, *Pointe aux Peaux*, and *La Plaisance* still retain their French nomenclature. The others, with one exception, have been literally translated from French to English. *Rivière aux Raisins*, the exception, has been anglicized, not to the literal translation, Grape River, but to River Raisin. Monroe people insist that the name is River Raisin and not Raisin River, thus retaining the French word order. In fact, Monroe people can spot non-natives simply by their usage of "Raisin River," rather than River Raisin.

As late as the 1930s many members of the old French community spoke only French. Today, however, French is the remembered language of their childhood and is rarely, if ever, used in conversation. As it is spoken and remembered today, the Monroe dialect is distinctive.[13] When the speakers of the local dialect encounter French nationals they usually revert to English, because they cannot be understood.

Discussion of the French dialect of Monroe will focus upon two areas: pronunciation and vocabulary. As the language has evolved in Monroe, there are some definite differences in pronunciation from modern European French. A good example is the phrase *bon soir* (good evening). In modern French it is pronounced "boneh swah." The Monroe French consistently pronounce it "boe swaer," with a heavy nasal accent on *soir*. This accent and pronunciation is somewhat consistent with that found in rural Quebec today. Indeed, as this example illustrates, the French spoken in Monroe is a derivation of Quebec French, which in turn is descended from seventeenth century Norman French.

Vocabulary, the other aspect of the spoken language is also important as a cultural determinant. The French in Monroe met a curious predicament early in this century when many new inventions such as cars, threshing machines, and washing machines came into common use. Isolated from other French speakers, they were completely on their own in selecting names for new objects. Their solution was simple. The new mechanical devices would all receive a generic name: *le machine* for the machine. The word *voiture*, for example, Parisian French for car, is completely unknown to the Monroe people. This and similar vocabulary selections all point to an independent evolution of the language in Monroe. Taken together, vocabulary, pronunciation, and place-names support the idea that this French community has developed from its Quebec roots to something separate and distinct.

Foodways also illustrate the distinctiveness of French culture in Monroe. The French-Canadians of Monroe, like many ethnic groups, are closely identified with their foods. Some of these foods remain confined to the cultural group, while others have spread to the larger community.

Tourière, or meat pie, is a favorite among the Monroe French. Originating in France, *tourtière* was brought to Quebec in the seventeenth century. While evidence indicates it has been a staple for nearly two centuries in Monroe, its popularity has not spread beyond the ethnic community. Today it is considered a holiday treat reserved for Christmas and New Year's Day and the recipe is passed on from mother to daughter. The following recipe was collected from Mrs. Elnora Krueger (nee Bomia) of LaSalle, Michigan in 1975. Typical of the local *tourtière* recipes, the following has been modernized: ground pork sausage and hamburger have replaced the diced pork which was once the main ingredient:

TOURTIÈRE
1 pound of bulk pork sausage
1/2 pound of hamburger
l cup of diced onion
2 cups of chopped raw potato

Allow the ingredients to steam in a skillet until soft. Then place mixture into a pie shell. Cover with a top crust with a half inch hole in the center. Bake at 350 degrees until brown. Can also be served cold topped with maple syrup.

More than any other food, muskrat identifies French folk culture in Monroe. Indeed, this symbol is so potent that the local French were often derisively referred to as "Mushrat French" by their Anglo-American brethren. Nevertheless, the culinary appeal of a good muskrat supper, while having clearly originated with Frenchmen in the fur trapping era of the eighteenth century, has spread beyond the indigenous French community. By the opening of the twentieth century, muskrat carnivals and dinners were in local vogue. These events are continued to this day by Monroe County's many sportsmen's and recreation clubs, churches, and veterans' organizations sponsoring annual muskrat dinners as fundraisers.

In the spring of 1987, muskrat served in restaurants of the downriver area south of Detroit was brought to the attention of the Michigan Health Department. Consequently, the sale of muskrat has been banned in restaurants and meat markets. Residents are protesting this infringement on a very old cultural tradition, but to date the ban has not been dropped.

There is rich folklore about the local French love affair with this rodent. The most fascinating narrative dates back to the War of 1812. As the story goes, food was very scarce during the war, especially in the winter months when muskrat was in season. In this exclusively Catholic region, the lack of food was complicated in the late winter and spring by the numerous fast days in the Catholic calendar when the people were forbidden to eat meat. Because the muskrat lives in the water, the French petitioned the bishop to formally declare the muskrat a fish to supplement their food supply. Tradition states that this petition was granted. To this day, local French descendants who observe meat abstinence on fast days consider the muskrat a fish and often make it a point to partake of it at these times.

Father Lambert Lavoy, a local priest who grew up with this tradition, was informed by his bishop that in truth no such dispensation had ever been granted. But, the bishop continued, while the people may not be observing the fast to the letter of the law, they were observing it in spirit. Hence the eating of muskrat on fast days would be tolerated. While muskrat can be prepared in several ways, the following recipe, collected from Mrs. Henry Duby of Monroe in 1956, is generally the most popular:[14]

MUSKRAT

After removing all musk glands and fat from the carcass, soak the muskrat for about two hours in salt water to which two tablespoons of vinegar has been added. Drain.

Put onion, celery, salt, pepper and muskrat in a pan of cold water. Bring to a boil. When a scum has formed, drain and rinse with cold water. Repeat the process until scum no longer forms.

Keep the muskrat in the boiling water and allow it to cook until tender.

Drain the water and then fry the meat, or place it in a roaster, cover it with cream-style corn and top it with crumbs.

Bake for a minimum of 1/2 hour. The result is a tender dish that tastes like a combination of sweet beef and duck.

Two varieties of fruit are often identified with the French-Canadians of Monroe County. Historically, the orchards were considered among the most important components of the French farmsteads in southeastern Michigan. Grown in these orchards were fruit varieties unique to the French culinary heritage. Today, two strains, the snow apple and the French pear, are still cultivated and in local demand.

The snow apple, called the *famuse* in French, is a rather small, red, striped dessert apple. Sweet and especially good for eating out of hand, this apple is best known for its snow-white flesh. Like the ancestors of Monroe's French community, the snow apple first took root in Quebec in the seventeenth century. As these Canadians moved west and into southeastern Michigan, they took this apple variety with them.[15] In the nineteenth century, the *famuse* became popular throughout the United States. With the decline of the small farm orchards in the twentieth century, the snow apple has all but disappeared except in areas such as Monroe where they are fondly remembered and valued.

The French pear, much like the snow apple, is a small dessert fruit. It is an egg-shaped pear with sugar-sweet flesh. The tree itself is unusual among fruit varieties, growing over sixty feet tall and on occasion living for well over a century. Its origins harken back to the first years of the French settlement at Detroit. Although it was a locally favored variety, this pear never spread beyond the boundaries of the French settlements in southeastern Michigan. Like the French people themselves, this native Michigan fruit has tenaciously hung on and while its numbers are dwindling, those who know the fruit well are nurturing the old trees and propagating a new generation.[16]

The culinary traditions of the folk culture of Monroe compare with the other items of oral traditions. Foods like the *tourtière* and the snow apple document the local community's ties to Quebec and Old France as do certain folksongs and folktales. Other comestibles such as the muskrat and the French pear, akin to the tale from the War of 1812, developed within this region more or less spontaneously. These food items, language, narrative, music and song set off the community from the larger culture and lend to the region a distinctive "personality of place" which is peculiarly Michigan French.

We have divided the French folk-cultural contributions into two major categories: the material and oral traditions. While the modes of survival for the material and non-material items are vastly different, the stories they tell are remarkably parallel. Most of the items discussed in each category are relics which reflect primarily the state of a past culture, yet some items like settlement patterns and muskrat feasts have come into the twentieth century as recognizable parts of today's life.

Individual items discussed were selected to give as broad a representation of the French-Canadian community as possible. By definition a folklife study should encompass many aspects of a culture. As demonstrated, folklife can be a tool to give people and places an identity and to highlight and explain a community's roots. Folklife study also demonstrates that culture is not a captive of historical periods, but that traditions are part of a continuum evolving through time.

It is clear that material and verbal traditions help compile a composite picture of the French-Canadian culture enclave in Monroe, Michigan. We know that the first permanent European settlers in Michigan were French from the Montreal region of Quebec, who came to Detroit, and from there settled Monroe County in the waning years of the eighteenth century. Their folk culture has left an imprint upon the region and if we read the geography and the culture carefully, we will see and hear evidence of their presence even today. Although many aspects of this folk culture are changing, its legacy enriches our understanding of Michigan's history and her people.

1. Russell E. Bidlack, *The Yankee Meets the Frenchman: River Raisin 1817–1830* (Ann Arbor: Historical Society of Michigan, 1965), passim.
2. Richard Colebrook Harris, *The Seigneurial System in Early Canada: A Geographic Study* (Québec: Les presses de l'université Laval, 1968), 117–68, and David C. McCauley, "The River Raisin Settlement, 1796–1812: A French Culture Area" (Masters Thesis, Department of Geography, Eastern Michigan University, 1968), passim.
3. Georges Gauthier-Larouche, *Évolution de la maison rurale traditionnelle dans la region de Québec* (Québec: Les presses de l'université Laval, 1974), 23–97, and Michel Lessard and Gilles Vilandre, *La maison traditionnelle au Québec* (Montréal: Les editions de l'homme, 1974), 29–78 and 101–292.
4. Matthew C. Switlik, *Research Summary: Navarre-Anderson Trading Post Structure, Monroe, Michigan*, Monroe County Historical Commission, 1971.
5. In the eighteenth century French-Canadian carpenters in North America utilized three basic construction techniques in building houses. Each technique had several variants. The construction techniques are: (a) *Poteaux en terre*: literally this means "posts in the ground." Walls are formed by placing vertical timbers in a trench with the top secured by a plate. The spaces between the vertical timbers—a space which could be less than an inch or over two feet—are daubed with mud, mortar, or brick and mortar; (b) *Maison colombage*: this construction is similar to *poteaux en terre*, except the vertical wall timbers are set into a sill which rests upon a foundation; and (c) *Pièce sur pièce*: buildings made of this technique have walls consisting of horizontally laid timbers which are joined together at vertical posts which are set into the sill and plate.
6. Jean Palardy, *The Early Furniture of French Canada*, 4th ed. (Toronto: Macmillan of Canada, 1978), 213–26.
7. Walter E. Simmons III, "The Silversmiths of Old Detroit" (M.A. thesis, Wayne State University, 1969), 46–50, 70.
8. Louise Décarie-Audet, Nicole Genêt, and Luce Vermette, *Les objects familiers de nos ancêtres* (Montréal: Les editions de l'homme, 1974), 194.
9. Charles Marius Barbeau, *Folk Songs of Old Quebec*, Anthropological Series, No. 16, Bulletin 75 (Ottawa: National Museum of Canada, 1943), passim, and Conrad Laforte, *Le catalog de la chanson folklorique française* (Québec: Les presses de l'université Laval, 1958), passim.
10. Marie Caroline Watson Hamlin, *Legends of Le Détroit*, 2d ed. (Detroit: Throndike Nourse, 1884), 113–21.

11. Edward C. Woodley, *Legends of French Canada*, 2d ed. (Toronto: Benjamin Blom, Inc., 1971; reprint, New York: Arno Press, 1978), 26–33.

12. Ambrose Charland left this interesting account of some of his activities in the War of 1812: Deposition of Ambrose Charland, Monroe County, Michigan, 15 July 1853, Gabriel Godfroy Papers, Burton Historical Collection, Detroit Public Library, Detroit, Michigan.

13. Edgar Brandon, "A French Colony in Michigan," *Modern Language Notes* 12 (April 1898): 121–24.

14. Dennis M. Au, "God Bless dee Mushrat: She's a Fish! *1987 Festival of American Folklife* (Washington, D.C.: Smithsonian Institution/National Park Service, 1987), 73–76.

15. Bela Hubbard, "The Early Colonization of Detroit," in *Michigan Pioneer and Historical Collections*, vol. 1 (Lansing: W. S. George & Co., Printers and Binders, 1877), 352.

16. Dennis M. Au, *Romance of the French Pear Tree* (Monroe: Monroe County Historical Society, 1979), passim.

Meaning in Community Events: An Ice-cutting Festival in Michigan

John F. Moe

During the winter of 1978–79 I was teaching at Central Michigan University. I had just come from southern Indiana and was not prepared for the intensity of the harsh Michigan winter and the snow that would for months conceal the picnic bench outside my window. I had trouble understanding how Michigan folks endured the cold and the snow with such ease and equanimity. During January and the first part of February I kept inside, venturing out only for essentials and to teach my classes. Finally, when the walls began to close in, I searched for ways to survive with dignity. A headline in the weekly advertiser newspaper caught my attention. "Remus Ice Cutting Set," it read. The title thawed my fieldworker's juices. As a folklorist and student of American culture, I had to investigate this event.

The announcement noted that preparations were under way for the annual Remus Ice Day festivities scheduled for February 17th. I was fascinated that not only would folks be celebrating the ice and cold, but that they made it an annual event. I had written previously on festivals, but they were primarily celebrations in southern Indiana held during the summer when people went outside to be with one another. An Ice Day was a unique opportunity.

I read further. About 20 tons of ice were to be cut and stored for the Remus Heritage Days and for various church functions and family reunions. Remus Heritage Days were celebrated in July, but the ice cutting festival was held for the entire community and for events coming up in the spring and summer. The ice was to be cut from Gene Flachs' pond, two miles east and a quarter mile north of Remus.

Ice Day activities were to begin at 1:00 p.m. with the Snowmobile Club and firemen providing refreshments and a bonfire. The Ice Committee had extended an invitation to anyone who would like to cut or handle the ice. Following the ice cutting activities in the afternoon, an "ice dance" was to follow with entertainment provided by the Rural Electric Band. In addition, a raffle at the end of the afternoon would offer a chain saw, a homemade quilt and a pair of snowshoes as prizes. Tickets for the raffle could be purchased from Ice Committee members and local merchants in the town of Remus. In short, the entire event was not dissimilar from a traditional folk festival including a central activity, food and drink for the participants, music and dance for entertainment, and games in the form of a raffle.

As a folklorist I knew much about how traditional festivals worked and functioned in the community; I knew a lot less about ice cutting as a form of activity in a traditional community. The newspaper indicated that ice cutting had some local, albeit fairly recent, history. Ice Day had begun in 1977 when more than thirty tons of ice had been cut for the Remus Centennial. The following year ten tons of ice supplied the Remus Heritage Days. But this year the output was to be doubled and made available to local organizations. Prices would be determined at a "later date." One piece of information encouraged me to feel that there was more to this event than I might have initially realized. The statement that the "pond has been plowed periodically this winter and storage arrangements have been made to preserve the ice"[1] indicated that there was a process involved in this event, and that the community would indeed know what "plowing" the ice meant in terms of the production of ice blocks for the harvest.

Ice cutting properly belongs in the fields of folklore and history as part of the broad range of material folk culture study. The study of material folk culture, whether folk building, harvesting, events on the landscape or foodways, seeks meaning in artifact that reveals our past and illuminates our present. The gentle tug, as folklorist Henry Glassie put it, between thought and gesture, idea and object, offers us an opportunity to see the uncommon meaning in common objects. The rules for behavior that govern the flow from thought and plan to gesture and object tell us much about the event in the community and the community itself. Inescapably embedded in objects like houses, town plans, quilts, and showshoes, the inscribed message of history can be deciphered through material culture study. The range of material folk culture objects and gestures that make up the process of ice harvesting tells us much about the history of those regions that at one time performed the ritual of ice cutting as a meaningful part of the cycle of life in rural America.

Ice harvesting, like many activities that once dominated the routines of ordinary citizens, has disappeared as a necessary form of individual, family or group enterprise within the folk culture. The winter months of January and February were once the time of the annual ice cutting and harvest in early America. As the cold deepened and the days shortened, people prepared for a harvest as significant as the gathering of the fall agricultural crops. Currier and Ives immortalized the ice harvest in their large 1864 folio print entitled, "Winter in the Country: Getting Ice." One of their most popular prints, it depicted the tools, equipment and setting of the traditional ice cutting harvest. The Currier and Ives print serves as a generic reminder of the image of ice cutting and harvesting that encouraged contemporary rural people of central Michigan to resume the traditional agricultural activity.[2] Current residents, in the process of remembering this activity through older informants, reenact the work and play rituals of their ancestors who used the blocks of ice as a means of food preservation during summer months.

In traditional America ice harvesting was imbued with a special meaning that went beyond the simple preservation of food. In *Walden*, Henry David Thoreau wrote about the clear winter morning that his solitude was disrupted by the sounds of men engaging in ice cutting.[3] Ice cutting in his woods was as expected as the other activities of man and nature, and was not nearly as disruptive and unnatural as the intrusive tracks of the railroad that invaded his peace.

The study of ice cutting and harvesting reflects the effects of change and modernizing influences on a traditional folk occupation in a regional community in central Michigan. The folk craft of ice cutting was both a family enterprise and a revenue-producing occupation during the end of the nineteenth century and the beginning of the twentieth century. As the process of modernization occurred in central Michigan and throughout the midwest, the traditional occupation of ice cutting was eventually supplanted by the advent of mechanized production of ice blocks and modern refrigeration. By the 1920s and 1930s it was cheaper and more efficient to rely on ice companies for the production of ice. Though ice cutting was no longer used as a folk occupational technique, its value as a traditional folk craft was not lost. In personal narratives, local history, material culture and folk festivals, ice cutting activity remained an important part of the community. Traditional narratives and examples of material culture, such as ice saws and ice houses, illustrate the value of the folk craft of ice cutting. As Michigan and other midwestern states moved from a traditional to a modernized society, the traditional crafts remained in the memories of the people of the community.

In a lecture I once gave in Cleveland, I talked about the Remus Ice Day. After the lecture, June Phypers, a woman in her late seventies who lived in northern Ohio, told me that "at one time in our township every farm had an ice house. You had to have an ice house," she explained, "if you wanted meat that wasn't salted. Besides," she added with a youthful chuckle, "you needed ice to make ice cream with in the summer." She remembered that until about 1914, the farmers in her neighborhood got together every winter and harvested enough ice to fill all their ice houses, which on most farms were near the barn. The event was a community-oriented activity. "That's the only way you could get those things done. It was like the hay harvest. Everyone had to work together in order to have enough hands to get a lot of work done. Everyone had to pitch in. That's all done now," she continued, somewhat wistfully. "After the war, we began to buy our ice."[4]

Historians have noted the importance of ice harvesting to the cycle of rural and urban life. From 1800 to 1920, nearly every community of any size in the northeastern United States had its local ice company since people wanted something better than dried and salted meats.[5] The importance of ice storage and maintenance from winter to summer for meat packers, dairies, farmers and beer breweries made the ice business prominent among the early industries in the United States. Dewey Hill, last owner of the Utica Ice Company and co-author of *Ice Harvesting in Early America*, commented on the size of the industry when he noted that, by 1850, New York City required 300,000 tons of ice per year.[6]

Clearly, the harvesting of ice was a dominant seasonal activity in those geographical areas where it was cold enough to freeze the ponds and lakes deep enough for blocks of preservable ice to be cut. Cutting ice was a social occasion and work activity that required work teams of varying sizes. For example, during the 1930s in

Otsego County, New York, a small scale harvest for a dairy industry enlisted only five to six men. By contrast, the local Cooperstown Ice Company at Otsego Lake employed thirty men to supply enough ice.[7]

The event of ice cutting was closely associated with the traditional notion of "harvesting" as in harvesting a field crop or wild fruit and vegetables. In fact, the ice blocks, or "kegs" as they were called, were referred to in New York as a "crop."[8] One tribute to the ice harvest in 1848 characterized ice blocks as a harvestable commodity much like corn or hay. "Cooperstown has a winter harvest time," the commentary read, "in January or February, when the ice is cut from the lake for the summer supply. This industry occupies a large force of men, with plows, saws, hooks, crowbars, horses and bobsleds, for several weeks."[9]

In general, the residents of New England during the nineteenth century were well acquainted with both the idea and the event of ice harvesting. The Currier and Ives print and Thoreau's comment on the arrival of the ice harvesters at Walden attest to this. Roger Abrahams commented on the importance of those events which dominate the community life. "Discussions of culture and society," he wrote, "commonly center on the systems by which we live with each other and with the environments in which we find ourselves."[10] Abrahams' work with hay harvesting, recounted in journals and recollections, certainly attests to the commonality and importance of group efforts in the traditional setting of community harvesting.[11] June Phypers was describing just such a system when she related how ice was "put up" in her community.

The annual rite of the ice harvest was one of the systems by which people in the northeastern and the north central United States lived. The ice harvest ritual allowed people to work together and to share the ice in the summer. It was a means for these people to live within their environment and to cope fruitfully with the harsh northern winters. The enactment of the winter harvest ritual served to enhance a sense of community to those familiar with the ice cutting. The ice cutting harvest was certainly not remotely a religious ritual; nonetheless, the experience of the harvest, employing the shared knowledge needed to cope with the difficulty of the task, served to reenact a performance that would strengthen a sense of community.[12] Oral and written narratives affirm this community strengthening aspect of the annual rite of the ice cutting and harvesting.

The ice house itself conjures up romantic images related to the ice harvest. Henry Beetle Hough, who was for fifty years a newspaper editor and resident of Martha's Vineyard, gave stirring testimony to this romantic vision. "The most conspicuous landmark in our view," he wrote, "was the Sheriff's Meadow Pond icehouse, a gray-weathered monster of a building that shouldered high, its roofline sharp against the blue of far sky and sea. At one end a lean-to had been built to shelter a horse and ice wagon and close by stood a boarded shack for the engine that powered a hoist to lift ice cakes up the incline of the ladderlike ramp, into the constant blackness and biting cold of the icehouse itself."[13] His observations coincided with those of Mrs. Phyper in Ohio and my own fieldwork in central Michigan. When I talked with people about the ice harvesting they invariably pointed out where one could find ice houses still standing.

The process of ice harvesting is a regional activity that offers a unique perspective to the study of material culture folklife and foodways. The enduring nature of traditional foodway systems provides deep insight into the areas of primary concern for the community. Food preservation, as well as food preparation and the oral folklore of recipes and foods, opens up areas of discussion leading to different approaches to traditional foodways.[14]

The Ice Day harvest in the small community of Remus, Michigan (population approximately 600) is primarily concerned with the reenactment of the annual ritual and work of producing ice for food and liquid preservation. Through the Ice Committee the residents of Remus created a festival of ice cutting that enhanced the actual work activity and developed a reenactment of a traditional winter ritual. It was my impression that the residents were easily able to identify with this ritualistic harvest because of the local interest in and knowledge of the ice harvest as it had occurred years earlier. To some degree, the people of central Michigan shared the experience of "winter things" and, more specifically, they shared the experience of the ice cutting harvest. What made this event special, in Victor Turner's terms, was the fact that this event was a shared experience in which the community together was able to work out meaning. The system of signification for the meaning of the ice cutting harvest was woven by the community itself. As social beings, the function of the ice cutting event provided for community residents an opportunity to tell what they had learned about the meaning of winter and the cycle of the year, from winter to summer. The ice cutting harvest provided a cultural mirroring of the "meaning-seeking process at the public generalizing level."[15]

Ice Day proved to be just that—the temperature dipped to 20 degrees below zero by the time that the ice cutting began. However, by the time the ice cutting was well underway, 150 Remus residents, mostly males, were there to participate. The day revolved around three primary activities. First, of course, the participants paid primary attention to the ice cutting. Next, many of the people huddled around the bonfire and drank wine, or in some cases, coffee. At 20 degrees below, beer and soft drinks froze and one had to consume the coffee quickly in order to keep it from freezing. Finally, other festival activities included the raffle and snowmobile races.

There were two community heroes on Ice Day. Arnold Lehnert, the Mecosta Schools custodian, was the patriarch of the occasion. In his seventies, he was a veteran ice cutter and remembered how his family had cut ice when he was young. Lehnert provided leadership in the way the old veteran blue grass singer might lead a crowd through the lessons of music. While Lehnert was not the strongest or most agile of the men, he showed others how the ice should be cut and, in fact, did a large share of the cutting himself. The other community heroes were the members of the highly successful Remus Snowmobile Team. For the most part, in typical festival fashion, they made up a second level of primary males and did not take as much a part in the ice cutting; instead, they exhibited their snowmobile skills by taking turns driving around the pond. It was appropriate that they held such a prominent role in the ice cutting festival because the town was singularly proud of this team that had distinguished itself in competition against better financed teams from larger towns. (Later in the summer, the Remus Snowmobile Team was one of the most popular floats in the Remus Heritage Days parade.) Although their position in the community was firmly established, during the ice cutting event they stood aside and Arnold Lehnert served as the primary male of the community.

Lehnert brought a standard ice saw and bar or packing chisel for cutting and moving the ice, and hoisting-tongs for hauling the blocks. When the cutting began, he demonstrated to the rest of the men—even though they had done it for three years—how to score the ice for cutting and how to begin. He established a routine in which each man had to begin cutting ice with the long ice saw. When tired, the men went on to cut the ice with a chain saw, but it was important that each one start with the manual saw. Mr. Lehnert

John Moe

continued to use the manual saw for the remainder of the day and teased the rest for using chain saws. "They ain't men enough to use an ice saw," he challenged in a gaming tone. "A chain saw will go through that ice easily. I remember years ago when ice like this was the only cooling system we had." Lehnert recalled, during the times when he rested by leaning on the long ice saw, how he and his father had cut ice for their own ice house. "Wasn't that long ago when this was the only way to keep things cold in the summer. Everyone had small ponds to cut their ice from and if they didn't have a pond then they could go in with a neighbor and help cut the ice so that they would have some in the summer." That day Lehnert relished teaching lessons about how to live in a community of the past. His instruction was not forgotten, for in the summer the people of Remus talked about the same forms of community behavior when they worked together in the Heritage Days celebration.

When the first load of ice kegs was finished, the men ceremoniously stacked it on Lawrence Orr's horse drawn sleigh. Larry Karchert, whose wife Nancy sold the raffle tickets, explained that it was "just too cold to use those horses. They aren't used to it and the hard work in the cold could hurt them. We only used them once just to have the old flavor." The rest of the ice was piled on pickups and driven to Albert Young's barn a couple of miles north where Joe Simon organized the storage of the ice. Simon was the barn boss, much like Lehnert was the cutting boss. By day's end they had stored 400 kegs of ice ranging in weight from 110 pounds at the beginning of the day to 300 pounds at the end. Simon and his crew of six used 70 pounds of sawdust for insulation around the kegs of ice. "You put the brown cured sawdust in between the kegs of ice and put the green sawdust on top of the ice. That way when the green sawdust cures it will heat some of the ice. The melted ice around the outside will re-freeze and form a shell around the ice and it will act like a refrigerator until we take it out in the summer. She'll never melt until next summer," he added. Simon then instructed his crew to put the "old grey stuff (the brown sawdust) six inches to a foot thick" on top of the green sawdust to create a shell around the ice keg pile.

Nancy Karchert continued to sell raffle tickets all day. It was appropriate that first prize in the drawing was a chain saw. Second prize, a handmade quilt, was probably worth more money but was less valued by northerners than the chain saw. (Mrs. Karchert also ran the raffle during the summer Heritage Days and first prize then was also a chain saw.) A community enthusiast, she reflected on the

Ice Day activities while she stood by the bonfire trying to keep warm. "Arnold's the one that really got this thing off the ground. We discovered that ice was much more expensive than it needed to be. It's a good time for everybody. It must be for them to stand out here in this weather."[16]

Karchert's observations indicate an understanding of the role that the ice cutting harvest played in the community's awareness of the importance of "getting together" to create the event. When I returned to attend the Remus summer Heritage Days, Nancy and her husband presented me with a Heritage Days t-shirt "for having come the greatest distance to Heritage Days." She was pleased and somewhat surprised that someone outside the community showed such interest in the town's activities. For her own participation, she did not seek acclaim, but rather the satisfaction of making something better for the town.

Ice harvesting in Michigan was a normal activity until well into the twentieth century. Much of the commercial activity existed around Barron Lake[17] near Niles, Michigan. But ice harvesting for non-commercial use was prevalent all over Michigan where there were small ponds and cold winters. The activities in Remus for Ice Day were but one example of the ice harvest being reenacted for contemporary people. At the same time as the Remus Ice Day, Blanchard, Michigan celebrated its "Millpond Madness." Further south, citizens of Spirit Lake, Iowa, celebrated their centennial with an ice harvest. Many communities had their own Arnold Lehnert to show the young ones how to use an ice saw and to scoff in jest when they had trouble sustaining their sawing efforts.

The Ice Day celebration grew quickly from an event designed to save the town money into an event that took the form of a traditional folk festival. In the summer, I witnessed a town celebrating the day they took the ice out of Gene Flach's Tenth Avenue pond, for the summer parade and festivities were geared toward the coming once again of the long harsh winter.

Note: My work concentrates primarily on fieldwork completed in the area of Remus, Michigan, with additional fieldwork in northern Ohio, Iowa and central New York State.

1. *Mount Pleasant Sun*, February 1979.

2. Harry T. Peters, *Currier and Ives: Printmakers to the American People* (New York: 1942).

3. Henry David Thoreau, *Walden: A Life in the Woods* (New York: Modern Library, 1981).

4. This interview took place in October 1979 at Case Western Reserve University in Cleveland, Ohio.

5. Dewey D. Hill and Elliott R. Hughes. *Ice Harvesting in Early America* (New Hartford, New York: New Hartford Historical Society, 1977), 4.

6. Ibid.
7. Carol Eve Kohan, "Ice Harvesting on Otsego Lake," in *Bicentennial Essays*, ed. Wendell Tripp (Cooperstown and Fly Creek, N.Y.: Cooperstown-Town of Otsego Bicentennial Essays, 1976), 44–45.
8. Ibid., 44.
9. Ibid., 46.
10. Roger D. Abrahams, "Rituals in Culture," *Folklore Reprint Series* 5, no. 1 (February 1977): 1.
11. The material referred to here under investigation by Roger Abrahams was loaned to me by Abrahams.
12. Ibid., 46–47. See also Victor Turner, *The Ritual Process* (New York), for seminal work in the area of describing and assessing the importance of the ritual process in community shared events. Turner's work is crucial in understanding the importance of such events.
13. Henry Beetle Hough, "Icehouse Lost," *Country Journal* 6, no. 3 (March 1979): 40.
14. See Anne Kaplan, et al., *Minnesota Ethnic Foodways* (Minneapolis: The Minnesota Historical Society Press, 1986), for a discussion of the importance of traditional foodways operating in ethnic folk culture.
15. Victor W. Turner, "Dewey, Dilthey, and Drama: An Essay in the Anthropology of Experience," in *The Anthropology of Experience*, ed. Victor W. Turner and Edward M. Bruner (Urbana and Chicago: University of Illinois Press, 1986), 36–37.
16. Pat Farnan, "Even readings of 20 below can't chill cutter's spirits," *Mount Pleasant Sun*, February 1979.
17. Lee Dodd and Barbara Wood, "Ice Was for Harvesting at Barron Lake," *Chronicle* 12, no. 4 (Winter 1976–77): 16–24.

The Cornish Pasty in Northern Michigan

William G. Lockwood and
Yvonne R. Lockwood

The once popular image of the "melting pot" is now all but dead in the United States.[1] The model was developed early in this century in reaction to those who demanded immigrant conformity to the culture of the Anglo-Saxon majority. The idea envisaged a merger of the various peoples who had made their way to the United States, and "a blending of their respective cultures into a new indigenous American type."[2] The melting pot notion was, in its turn, supplanted by a pluralistic model which emphasizes the preservation of the communal life and significant portions of the culture of later immigrant groups. The idea of the American melting pot is now in disrepute, and is considered by many ethnic leaders to be not only erroneous but demeaning. Perhaps this is an overreaction. We should remember that all these models are ideal types. Truth, as is so often the case, lies somewhere in between. The melting pot did work, in its way. In no other aspect of cultural activity is this so graphically demonstrated as in American foodways.

It is doubtful that a food diffused is ever adopted in quite the same form in which it existed in the Old Country. Nor does it maintain the same symbolic meaning. This should not surprise us. Culture is always in flux, and more so when population movement and

An earlier version of this article was printed in *Food in Motion,*, Oxford Symposium Documents (1983).

the cultural displacement and confrontation which result are involved. To demonstrate these points we will examine one food—the Cornish pasty—and its diffusion, adoption, and alteration in one region of the United States—the Upper Peninsula of Michigan. We will focus on two contemporaneous processes—one having to do with form and the other with function. Regarding form, we will show that the pasty, which existed in diverse forms in Cornwall, was first standardized in America, then later rediversified. With regard to function, we will demonstrate a transition of symbolic meaning from ethnic to multi-ethnic to regional.

The state of Michigan consists of two large peninsulas separated by the Straits of Mackinac and the Great Lakes Michigan and Huron. The southern, larger, portion includes all the major population centers, all the most important industries, and all the major cultural institutions of the state. It was not until 1957, when the Mackinac Bridge was finally completed, that there were direct connections between the Upper Peninsula (the "U.P." as it is usually called by Michiganders) and the Lower Peninsula. Previously, one could get from one peninsula to the other only by ferry or by traveling the length of Wisconsin through Chicago. As a consequence, the U.P. is a region much more closely related culturally, historically and demographically to northern Wisconsin and, to some extent, northeastern Minnesota, than to the Lower Peninsula of Michigan. Inhabitants of the U.P. (they call themselves "Yoopers") have a highly-developed regional consciousness. They feel looked down upon by the people of the Lower Peninsula, and neglected by the state government. They even talk—only partly in jest—of breaking away and establishing a 51st state to be called "Superior."

Soon after Michigan became a state in 1837 some residents traveled north to investigate the Upper Peninsula that the American Congress had included in the state's territory. The reports they brought back triggered the first major mining boom in the United States. From the very beginning of the industry, a major role was played by Cornish immigrants.[3] By 1844, two copper mining companies were already in operation with some twenty Cornish employees. These Cornishmen were valuable to the developing mining industry since they arrived already having had experience with deep mining techniques and machinery in the tin mines of Cornwall. As a consequence, the Cornish tended to set the pattern of mine work in the U.P. By the time of mass migration—the so-called "New Immigration"—to the United States, the Cornish were already well established in the mines as skilled workers, foremen, bosses, and mining captains. The recently arrived Finns, Italians, Poles, Croats, and Serbs provided the unskilled labor.

Just as the Cornish influence was felt in methods of mining, the Cornish also established the social and cultural life of the mining communities. The new immigrants looked upon the Cornish as established American citizens. They had status and their habits and ways were noted, if not imitated, models of American life. This relationship was typical of cultural relations between members of the New and Old Immigration. Elsewhere, it was particularly common that the Irish—as the most numerous of the "Old Immigrants"— were emulated by newly-arrived eastern and southern Europeans.

Cultural geographers Wilbur Zelinsky and Raymond Gastil[4] have argued that in the United States the first European or American white populations to establish the economic and social basis of an area usually had a decisive influence on later patterns which came to define it as a cultural region. A similar argument has been used by George Foster[5] in his analysis of the diffusion of Spanish culture to Mexico. Although immigrants from throughout Spain contributed to the colonial population of Mexico, the cultural patterns established there were nearly all Andalusian in origin. Foster attributes this to a process of cultural crystalization. Since Andalusians were the first to arrive in Mexico, because the conquest of Mexico directly followed the reconquest of Andalucia, they were the ones to establish the cultural patterns for later arrivals.

In a similar manner, the earlier immigrants of northern Europe sometimes established the cultural patterns of later-arriving immigrants from southern and eastern Europe. From the perspective of "greenhorns" from the other side of Europe, the practices of earlier arrivals, whose immigrant cultures had already been transformed to ethnic cultures, were accepted as "the American way." These were the Americans, after all, with whom new immigrants were most likely to have contact. It was likely to be their neighborhoods into which new immigrants settled, and they who were most likely to be the foremen and supervisors in the mills and mines where the immigrants went to work. Thus, it is not surprising that the ethnic culture which took shape was profoundly influenced by that of earlier immigrants. In no aspect of culture has this been more apparent than in foodways.

The pasty is a turnover of pie-like crust filled with a variety of food combinations. It is the national dish of Cornwall,[6] and it continued to play an important role in the diet of Cornish-Americans wherever they settled. It was no surprise that the pasty was quickly adopted by newer immigrants who worked by their sides and under their direction in the mines of the U.P. It was not just a recipe that was passed from one ethnic group to another, but an entire cultural complex: the use, the way of eating, and so on— all diffused as a package. At the same time, some significant alterations and innovations took place in the process of this diffusion and adopted by non-Cornish.

The particular use of the Cornish pasty was an important reason it was so readily adopted by members of other ethnic groups in the U.P. In both Cornwall and among Cornish-Americans, the pasty was traditionally associated with work:

> The Cornish pasty is one of the best examples in the world of what one might call *functional food*. For the Cornish pasty. . .is not merely delicious food, it was designed for a certain quite definite purpose; it was designed to be carried to work and eaten in the hand, to be taken down the mine, to sea, to the fields. You will see a Cornishman munching his tasty pasty squatting in the narrow tin-mine workings, sitting in the nets of his leaping fishing-boat, leaning against a grassy bank while his patient plough-horses wait.[7]

In the United States the pasty was particularly associated with mining.[8] It is very well suited to this use: it is easily carried in pails or specially-made sacks; it retains its heat for a long time; it is eaten with the hands; and it is a heavy meal-in-one. Little wonder that the Finns, Italians, and Slavs who saw their Cornish foremen eating pasties soon were demanding the same from their own wives.

Cornishmen now make up a relatively small ethnic component of the U.P., the predominant ethnic group being the Finns. The first Finnish immigrants to the U.P. began to arrive in 1864, well after the main Cornish immigration, but thirty years before the massive Finnish immigration which began around the turn of the century. By 1880 there were over one thousand foreign-born Finns in the U.P. The first arrivals were skilled workers who were employed as carpenters, blacksmiths, or skilled yardsmen at the mines. Thus, they were already established and partially acculturated by the time of the mass immigration. Later Finnish immigrants probably adopted the pasty from these earlier Finnish arrivals, rather than from the Cornish themselves.

The gradual development of a Finnish-American culture drew not only upon Finnish and mainstream "American" culture but also upon the cultural traditions of other ethnic groups with whom the Finns came in contact. The appropriation of the Cornish pasty by Finns in the U.P. is one of our best examples of this process.

The transformation of Finnish immigrants to Finnish-American ethnics was, of course, a very gradual process. It involved not only the adoption of cultural practices from both mainstream American culture and other American ethnic groups, but also an amalgamation of different regional traditions from Finland. No doubt many Finnish immigrants had their first experience of certain Finnish regional dishes in the American context. The closest approximations to the pasty in Finland are *piiraat* and *kukko*—dough-enveloped specialties filled with meat, fish, vegetables, rice and so on, varying in size from individual turnovers to large loaves.[9] The existence of these somewhat similar foods may have meant easier adoption of the pasty for those unfamiliar with it. How was a Finn, newly arrived in America, upon seeing a pasty in the lunchpail of a fellow countryman arrived some twenty years before, to know that this was not merely a regional variant of food he was already familiar with? Thus, many Finns came to believe the pasty was of Finnish origin. In the same way, some Italians in the U.P. regarded the pasty as Italian.

While regionalization meant general participation and sharing in a food tradition, the pasty has maintained a sense of ethnic propriety. By and large, Yoopers know the Cornish origin of the pasty because of education and mass media. Some even refer to it as a "Cousin Jack mouth organ" (Cousin Jack being a popular synonym for Cornishmen). However, the association of pasties with Finns cannot be ignored. Raymond Sokolov, a former Michigander and ethno-culinary journalist, writes of the "Finnish flavor" of pasties.[10] Among U.P. Finns themselves, some still regard the pasty as Finnish food. This belief is perpetuated by family tradition, Finnish church suppers, and annual Finnish traditional celebrations where the pasty is featured as a Finnish specialty. This association probably results from the importance of the Finns in the diffusion of the pasty, which is even further reinforced today by the predominance of Finns in the U.P. Many pasty shops, for example, are owned and operated by Finns. On the other hand, family tradition is an important factor in the issue of propriety: the pasty is first and foremost a family tradition. Yoopers make and eat pasties according to the recipes and tradition of their mothers and grandmothers. We know many Michigan Finns who were totally unaware that other ethnic groups also eat pasties. This is particularly true of non-Finnish in-laws who are not from the U.P. but assume the pasty is Finnish because the spouse's Finnish family serves it.

In the course of its transformation from mono-ethnic to multi-ethnic, the pasty in the U.P. has undergone a process from diversification to standardization, and finally, to rediversification. In Cornwall, as in the U.P. at the turn of the century, it has many possible ingredients: rice and leeks, egg and bacon, beef and potatoes, lamb and parsley, venison, fish, apple, and so on . The possible variants are so endless that it is said that "the devil never dared cross the Tamar River from Devonshire to Cornwall for fear of the Cornish women's habit of putting anything and everything into a pasty."[11]

Although the old country pasty is a multi-variant food, the U.P. pasty became a standardization of but one of these forms. The range of variation narrowed to a basic mixture of meat, potatoes, onions, rutabagas and/or carrots. Although some variation remained, it could not deviate far from this particular combination and still qualify as a pasty. Meat may consist of beef, a beef and pork combination, or even venison when available; some may add parsley, and a few omit both carrots and rutabagas. But today, the U.P. pasty has become this particular meat and root vegetable specialty.

One area ripe with variation—and controversy—is the crust. Crust recipes are usually guarded secrets. In Cornwall, pasties are made of either puff pastry or a crust similar to that used for American pie; it is only the latter that is used in the U.P. The dough, according to Yoopers, should be light and short and hold together, yet not be as flaky as pie crust. Its secret lies in the proportion of shortening and water to flour, and the type of shortening. Traditionalists claim that suet is the original—and best—shortening, Others use lard because it is more convenient and "just as good as" suet. With today's emphasis on lighter foods, some now use vegetable shortening, which purists claim produces an inferior, tough, and tasteless crust.

The pasty seal, another place for variation, is one of the few distinctive ethnic features. According to the older Cousin Jacks and Cousin Jennies, a "real" Cornish pasty is sealed by "making a rope," a particular method of tightly closing the dough, usually across the top of the pasty. In Great Britain this is sometimes called "the Cornish Crimp." Today few Yoopers—including Cornish—know this technique. Instead, most make a seal by pinching, folding, or crimping the edge as they would for a pie. Those Cornish who do use "the Cornish Crimp" take great ethnic pride is doing so.

Another distinctively Cornish feature is the designation of each pasty with an individual's initials made from dough and baked onto one end. This serves to identify pasties made to suit individual likes and dislikes, e.g., omission or greater amounts of certain ingredients, and to mark leftovers of uneaten pasties for later consumption. It is still practiced by a few Cornish families in the U.P. In some Cornish households the code has been translated into toothpicks: one, two, or three toothpicks stuck into the crust designate the child to whom it belongs.

Adaptation to the U.P. context has produced variations in pasty construction and consumption, and in attitudes and values about pasties. Most Yoopers would agree, in theory, that for the best flavor all ingredients—including the meat—should be chopped with a knife and layered: potatoes topped by rutabagas (and/or carrots), followed by onions, and finally meat, salt, pepper, and perhaps butter or suet. However most pasties are made today with ground meat—usually hamburger or ground chuck—although most butchers in the U.P. still sell coarsely ground beef (with or without pork) labeled "pasty meat." In practice, ingredients are almost always mixed rather than layered.

Accompaniments and condiments with the pasty have become highly variable with patterns strongly linked to family tradition. A great many Yoopers would not enjoy a pasty without catsup. Other accompaniments are equally essential for some individuals or families: chow-chow pickles, crisp vegetables, tea, buttermilk, beer, tomato juice. Each has its advocates. These ingredients are not casual choices. Quite the contrary, one of several of these accompaniments is absolutely necessary to complete a satisfactory pasty meal.

Originally, the pasty was hand food. Its traditional shape, size, and substantial crust attest to its function as a working person's meal, intended to be carried in a pocket or lunchpail. The "real way" to eat a pasty is to begin at the end, holding it parallel with the body so the juices keep the remainder moist. Increasingly, Yoopers eat pasties on plates with forks, a manner which expands its original function and opens the door to still more variations (fig. 1). Once a pasty rests on a plate, it lends itself to innovations that some regard as abuse: its crust is broken in the center, releasing its moisture and heat, and it is smothered with butter, gravy, or other substances.

365

William Lockwood

Figure 1. One of the many pasty shops that have opened to serve local and tourist needs.

Change also occurred in structure. Although the characteristic half-moon shape remained standard, some housewives began to save time by baking "pasty pies": pasty ingredients baked in a pie shell with a top crust and served in wedges on plates. This was done at least as early as the interwar period and has increased in frequency since. Others have speeded up the process by making over-size pasties in the traditional shape, which are then cut in half to be served. Both of these unorthodox forms are reserved for family, never being utilized either for commercial production or for company dinners.

Some innovations are associated with particular ethnic groups. Thus, according to some sources, dousing pasties with gravy was begun in the U.P. Mennonite community. The accompaniment of pasties with buttermilk is said to be Finnish. Similarly, the replacement of rutabagas (considered Cornish) by carrots is said to be Finnish. This is hardly the case—many Finns use rutabagas and many non-Finns use carrots—but the stereotype remains, even to the extent that "carrot pasty" is a derisive term for Finnish-made pasties. It is commonly said of the pasty that "the Cornish originated it, the Finns disseminated it, and the Italians improved it." This apparently arose because some of the most popular pasty shops in the U.P. are owned by Italians. No one we spoke to could attribute specific differences to Italian-made pasties. Only one Yooper designated his Italian mother-in-law's pasty as different from others—because she added hot peppers to the filling.

The first pasties available outside the home were sold at church pasty sales, most probably those held at the Methodist churches of the Cornish, but they have now long since been institutionalized by churches of all denominations in the region, including Catholic and Finnish Lutheran. In addition to raising funds, the church pasty preparation and sale is a social event. Despite long hours of work, participants speak of these activities as both enjoyable and as an effective way to initiate newcomers to church functions and U.P. traditions. In this context, knowledge about pasties is exchanged between individuals so that the church sale helps to maintain the pasty tradition. Even women who bake their own pasties will buy at church sales. The product is regarded as "homemade," and even as "the real thing," because older women usually dominate these affairs. Either they are deferred to because of their experience and age, or they themselves take a supervisory and authoritative role and actively monitor the work of younger women. Consequently, some young women are intimidated and hesitate to volunteer because of possible criticism about the way they make pasties. One of these guardians of tradition, a ninety-year-old Cousin Jenny, stated emphatically that she could not eat anyone's pasties but her own and those from her church because all others are only poor imitations.

Although there are many commercial pasty shops, opinions about them are mixed. Most Yoopers regard homemade pasties as best. Nonetheless, most women who make pasties will buy them on occasion: when they need a large number, as for a wedding supper; when they go fishing or hunting; or when they are feeling lazy or tired or rushed—like sending out for a pizza elsewhere in the United States.

The first commercial pasty shops appeared just after World War II. Yoopers recall that in Hurley, Wisconsin (located at the Michigan state line and then known as "Sin City"), an entrepreneur baked pies in his kitchen and peddled them from bar to bar in the early morning hours. In about 1938 he opened a pasty shop. After the war other shops appeared across the border in Ironwood. Today pasties are made and sold in at least one place in nearly every community: special pasty shops, bakeries, restaurants, bars, fast food counters, ice cream stands, and grocery stores. They can be purchased hot, cold, partially baked, frozen, and day-old.

The post-World War II period brought drastic economic change to the U.P., and this brought about consequent change in both function and form of the pasty. During earlier decades of industrial expansion in the United States, the U.P. experienced an economic boom. However, because growth was based on extractive industry—the primary production of iron, copper, and lumber—the area was directly and immediately affected when production fell off and the large corporations were pulled out by their absentee owners. The U.P. was exploited and then abandoned. The economy began a gradual but steady decline about 1920 and despite occasional spurts of activity, never recovered. The subsequent secondary status felt by Yoopers contributed negatively to their self-image and resulted in a group inferiority complex. Particularly after completion in 1957 of the bridge allowing access to the U.P. from the south, the local economy became reoriented toward tourism. One consequence was the proliferation of pasty shops.

Tourism is presently the major industry in the U.P., and the pasty figures large in the regional culture offered tourists by their Yooper hosts (fig. 2). Today, along a seven-mile stretch of highway going west from the bridge, at least thirteen pasty shops, some

Yvonne Lockwood

Figure 2. Using a fork is not considered the 'real' way to eat a pasty, but it makes it easier. (Notice a common accompaniment–tomato juice.)

advertising in three-foot high, glow-in-the-dark letters, exist to the virtual exclusion of other eateries. The personal names of the establishments—Granny's, Lehto's, DeRich's, Clyde's—assures strangers of a "homemade" treat. The latest step in the evolution of the pasty in the U.P., then, is to become a regional symbol.

In historical context, the regionalization of the pasty can be viewed as a rhetorical strategy to enhance the self-image of the U.P.[12] According to Kenneth Burke,[13] one of the leading exponents of rhetoric as the art of persuasion, rhetoric embodies a message which is capable of imbuing individuals with heightened consciousness and of persuasion when materials are manipulated and ideas are asserted by aesthetic techniques to produce pleasure. Expressive culture is an important persuasive tool whose strategy is to elicit a desired response through the use of aesthetic techniques.[14] All expressive culture can be a form of argument, but traditional expressive forms are especially effective in the art of persuasion, because the techniques which were developed in or have reference to the past, bear the test of time and elicit a sympathetic response. Serving pasties to outsiders is a conscious, predictable act intended to impress them, and to persuade them of the quality of U.P. life. The acceptance of pasties by outsiders is a symbolic validation of Yooper culture in general.

The pasty's regional affinity is communicated by various means. Narratives regionalize the pasty by emphasizing ties with occupation and environment. Legends tell of hardworking miners who warmed pasties on shovels held over the candles of their mining lamps. Others claim that miners carried hot pasties wrapped in cloth or newspaper in their shirts and were thus kept warm on cold U.P. mornings and in damp, chilly mines. In turn, miners warmed their pasties as they worked. Warm pasties undoubtedly are comforting next to the body in severe temperatures. Hunters and fishermen, probably influenced by the legend, sometimes carry pasties this way. However, the physical exertion of mine work would certainly transform any pasty really carried inside their clothing into a crumbled mess.

Much of current lore about the pasty has to do with crust. Take, for example, a narrative that explains the origin of the pasty:

> In Cornwall, the women searched for a good meal for the miners other than sandwiches; the men were tired of sandwiches. They experimented with potatoes, meat and onions wrapped in dough and were pleased with the results. It was a whole meal in one. At meal time, the women brought their pasties to the mine and dropped them down the shaft to the men below. They didn't even break.

When a folklorist collected a variant of this in 1946, it was told in jest.[15] When we heard it in 1981, it was presented as fact.

The pasty-as-missile is a recurring motif in popular expression. Upon hearing the above legend, one former resident of the U.P. expressed disbelief about its authenticity, but recalled that his own mother could toss her pasties into the air and catch them with no breakage. Local cartoonists play with this same image. The text accompanying a comic strip in Michigan by Cliff Wirth reads:

> Blue is the color of my dear gramma's skin.
> When standing by Superior old grampa pushed her in.
> She evened up the score, or so I was told,
> When she beaned him with a pasty that was nine days old.

A recent manifestation of all this was the First Annual Pasty Throwing Contest, held in April 1983.[16] It was sponsored by the owners of a local source of pasties, the Finlandia Cafe and Bakery, who cited the U.P. belief that "a good pasty can be dropped to the bottom of a mine shaft without splitting open." The winner—a Cornishman, appropriately—made a throw of 155 feet, bringing him a trophy topped by a gilded pasty.

At the same time pasties are offered as a symbolic representation of the region, manipulation of pasty lore is utilized to express group boundaries. Folk terms, like "gut buster" and "ulcer bun," are used in familiar fashion by Yoopers, thereby distinguishing themselves from outsiders. The shared knowledge of pasty characteristics which such terms imply is an expression of social solidarity. In-jokes, like referring to pasties at one shop as "Catholic" because they are skimpy on meat, serves the same purpose. On the other hand, curious tourists identify themselves as outsiders when they inquire about *"pasteys,"* thereby providing more grist for the folklore mill. Yoopers never cease to be amused by this pronunciation and the resultant confusion with the accouterment for striptease dancers. Nor do they tire of recounting such incidents and ridiculing the outsider, who otherwise contributes to the Yoopers' negative self-image. When a U.P. newspaper sponsored a contest for limericks about the U.P., the winning verse focused on this widely-shared regional joke:

> A Casper widow named Patsy,
> Earned her living by the selling of pasties,
> When a fudgy hasty demanded a pastey,
> Her response was rather nasty.[17]

"Fudgy," incidentally, is a derogatory term used by Yoopers for other Michiganders. It is derived from yet another regional food specialty, Mackinac Island fudge, which is purchased in great quantities by outsiders.

The idea that the pasty is unique to the U.P. is maintained in various ways. Residents' esoteric beliefs about the enigmatic pasty reinforce its symbolic regional meaning. For example, during and after World War II, many individuals and families left the U.P. for industrial centers in the Midwest and West. With them went the pasty. Numerous accounts are related of individuals who tried to start shops but were unsuccessful because, according to folk belief, people elsewhere were ignorant of the pasty. Similarly, one pasty shop owner in the U.P. delights in telling of all the problems he has when he orders matches printed with his shop's name and address. Invariably, printers who are not local change "pasty" to "pastry."

Detroit, however, is another story. Large numbers of Yoopers moved to Detroit to work in the automotive industry and as a community developed, their regional self-awareness heightened, possibly even before a sense of regionalism emerged in the U.P. itself. At such times, knowledge of regional esoteric folklife fosters self-conscious awareness of membership in a regional folk group and the pasty was an important part of this. Thus, Detroit became the home of a U.P. social club, a Finnish social club—dominated by a U.P. clique—and an Episcopalian church whose congregation is almost entirely Cornish Yoopers. Like their friends and relatives in the U.P., these groups continue U.P. customer of fund-raising pasty dinners and bakesales. Pasty shops owned by former Yoopers have been part of the Detroit scene for decades. According to one of these owners, about ninety percent of his customers are from the U.P. or have spent considerable time there:

> That's where the pasty came from. It didn't come to Detroit from Cornwall, but from the U.P. Pasty is the tie to the U.P. Invariably, a customer will tell me he's from the U.P., as if that's any surprise. I certainly didn't think he was from Alabama![18]

The same informants who recall business failures thirty years ago are now predicting that pasty shops will soon exist all over the United States. America's Bicentennial, with its emphasis on local and ethnic pride, was a significant catalyst in this process. The change of mind was also influenced in 1968 when Governor Romney designated 24 May as "Michigan Pasty Day." The media play no small role in the new consciousness. Newspapers all over Michigan feature articles about pasties in the U.P. At least one such story, "U.P. 'Adopts' Miners' Meal," sparked a long and heated debate in letters to the editor about what constituted a genuine pasty.[19] In 1979, WLUC Television in Marquette, Michigan, aired a short promotional spot, "Stay For It," with local folk historian, Frank Matthews.[20] Looking like a stereotypic miner, this elderly Yooper informs viewers about the pasty's Cornish origin and function. This program was an attempt to build regional pride by stressing the pasty's aesthetic qualities and its historical and occupational tie to the U.P. As Mr. Matthews bites down on a tempting pasty, he urges viewers that "pasties are part of the Upper Peninsula heritage and that's why you should stay for it and try one!" Finally, Yoopers are witnessing the pasty's increasing popularity among tourists: skiers, hunters, fishers, campers take twenty, thirty, fifty pasties home to freeze. Indeed, some residents now refer to the pasty as "U.P.'s contribution to American culture."[21]

The U.P. pasty that evolved in the early twentieth century remained relatively stable in form and content for many decades. During this period only a narrow range of variance was permitted. Popularization and commercialization, however, have led to significant changes in form. Earlier, one heard stories about people who put peas into pasties secretly, knowing that their neighbors would not approve. Now similar "violations" of tradition are openly admitted: pasty of kidney, pasty made with condensed onion or mushroom soup, pasty with gravy. These variants are still repugnant to many Yoopers and often are attributed to specific groups, i.e., "it's those other guys." Gravy, for example, is said to be Cornish by some Finns, Mennonite by other, but, by general Yooper consensus, is eaten only by non-Yoopers. In all cases, these views are exoteric beliefs about "them" and explain, in a fashion, a violation of tradition.

Commercial competition has been instrumental in this movement toward rediversification. Both health food stores and a few standard pasty shops have begun to offer a vegetarian version, often with whole wheat crust. Other less-than-traditional versions are found in commercial establishments that cater largely to tourists. For example, in some restaurants pasties can be ordered with cheese, bacon, or chili topping. Some pizza parlors offer 'pizza pasty'— pasty ingredients enfolded by pizza dough, much like the Italian calzone. Thus, from its varied origin in Cornwall, the pasty, which had become standardized within relatively narrow limits in the process of becoming Americanized, is now once again appearing in a wide variety of types.

The pasty always seems to have been a link between generations and between different groups. But since the mid-1960s it has emerged with new meaning as a public regional symbol that recalls the past, speaks of the present, and implies the future. Connotations of history, multi-ethnicity, occupation, and region, as well as aesthetics and association with ritualized events have bestowed the pasty with new status. Hence, when the pasty is spoken of, made, and consumed, the "performers" also achieve status. To participate now in pasty foodways not only reinforces tradition, but is also a manifestation of regional membership. Regional identity is still strongly held in the U.P. and pasty eating—either at home or away—has become a way of demonstrating one's allegiance.

Identity, however, is a complex issue. The pasty has become symbolic of the U.P., but at the same time remains deeply rooted in ethnic and family tradition. Although the pasty's ethnic association has become secondary to region, it continues to be available for Yoopers seeking to demonstrate their ethnic roots. Thus, there is a certain ambiguity regarding ethnic versus regional culture, but these associations need not be mutually exclusive. Identity is always contextual and these separate identities, existing as they do at different levels of organization, are seldom brought into conflict. At the same time that the pasty is an integral part of U.P. Finn, Cornish, or Italian culture, the regional status of the pasty is demonstrated each time it is served to visitors from outside. As Finns, Italians, and Slavs of the U.P. each made the pasty their own, it became both the ethnic specialty of each and—first implicitly, later explicitly—a specialty of the region.[22]

1. We wish to thank all those Yoopers and former Yoopers for their assistance and support in this study. Fieldwork was conducted during 1980 and 1981.

2. Milton M. Gordon, *Assimilation in American Life* (New York: Oxford University Press, 1964).

3. Jane Fisher, "Michigan's Cornish People," *Michigan History* 29 (1945). See also John Rowe, *The Hard-Rock Men: Cornish Immigrants and the North American Mining Frontier* (Liverpool: Liverpool University Press, 1974), especially 62-95 and A. L. Rowse, *The Cousing Jacks: The Cornish in America* (New York: Charles Scribner's Sons, 1969).

4. Wilbur Zelinsky, *The Cultural Geography of the United States* (Englewood Cliffs, N.J.: Prentice-Hall, Inc., 1973), 5-35; and Raymond D. Gastil, *Cultural Regions of the United States* Seattle: University of Washington Press, 1975), 26-27.

5. George Foster, *Culture and Conquest* (Chicago: Quadrangle Books, 1960).

6. Philip Harben, *Traditional Dishes of Britain* (London: The Bodley Head, 1953), 9–13; W. R. Roberts, *Cornish Recipes* (St. Ives: James Pike, Ltd., 1977), 3, 16; Marika Hanbury Tenison, *West Country Cooking* (London: Mayflower Granada Publishing, 1978), 77–105; Kathleen Thomas, *West Country Cookery* (London: B. T. Batsford, Ltd., 1979), 57–58; and Adrian Bailey, *The Cooking of the British Isles* (New York: Time-Life Books, 1971), 20–21.

7. Harben, 9–10.

8. Roberts, 3; Tenison, 78; Bailey, 20. Also see Richard Dorson, *Bloodstoppers and Bearwalkers* (Cambridge: Harvard University Press, 1952), 117–18, for the association of the pasty with mining as communicated in folk narrative.

9. Kirsti Tolvanen, *Finnish Food* (Helsinki: Kustannusosakeyhti;umo Otava, 1959), 81–85.

10. "Tasty Pasty in Michigan, A Cornish Delicacy is Given a Finnish Flavor," *Natural History,* January 1980, 101–3.

11. Tenison, 78; Bailey, 20.

12. See Roger Abrahams, "Introductory Remarks to a Rhetorical Theory of Folklore," *Journal of American Folklore* 81, no. 320 (1968): 143–58; and Suzi Jones, "Regionalization: A Rhetorical Strategy," *Journal of the Folklore Institute* 13, no. 1 (1976): 105–20.

13. *A Rhetoric of Motives* (New York: Prentice-Hall, Inc., 1950), 46.

14. Abrahams, 145–47.

15. See Dorson, 107, 109,. 117–18, for folklore collected about the pasty. He also mentions the folk explanation of the origin of pasties on p. 117.

16. "Add rutabagas to a meat pie and you may end up in Guinness," *Ann Arbor News,* 10 April 1983.

17. Published in *The Pick an Axe,* 1976 (now defunct). We collected the limerick from the author, who asked to remain anonymous. We have not located the original newspaper article.

18. Wayne State University Folklore Archives, no. 119, 1970.

19. *Upbeat,* the Sunday magazine section of the *U.P. Times,* Escanaba, Michigan, 16 April 1978. The debate continued sporadically until December 1979.

20. Mr. and Mrs. Matthews also served as informants for *American Cooking: The Eastern Heartland* (New York: Time-Life Books, 1971), 25–29.

21. Since this article was written, the pasty has been franchised in California.

22. It would be enlightening but beyond the scope of this paper to compare the U.P. pasty with various other local and regional foods derived from a single ethnic group of the area. One of the best studied of these is Cincinnati chili (see Timothy Charles Lloyd, "The Cincinnati Chili Culinary Complex," *Western Folklore,* 40, no. 1 [1981], 28–40). Basically an elaborated version of chili mac with Near Eastern spicing of the chili, it was originated by Macedonians and is now disseminated almost entirely by Greeks. Nevertheless, it is thought of as a local food, devoid of ethnic connotations. And Cincinnatians utilize it symbolically in much the same manner as Yoopers do pasty. The beerock (a cabbage, onion and beef mixture enveloped in dough and baked) is popular food in all Volga Deutsch-American communities. But in Fresno, California, it is now becoming a local rather than an ethnic specialty. Beerock shops, a recent phenomenon, are run by Armenians (another large group of the area) or by those without claim to a specific ethnic heritage. Spiedi (small skewers of grilled meat) are a popular food prepared in homes or served in bars of Binghamton, New York. Grocers there carry "spiedi meat" and hardware stores offer "spiedi skewers." Judging by the name, they are of Italian origin ("spiedini" denotes a similar dish in Italy), but no one the authors could find in Binghamton was aware of the fact of original. The Binghamton Italian community is eclipsed by the much more numerous Slavs.

A Brief Guide to Michigan Folklife Resources

ichigan has a number of archives and museums that house collections of Michigan folklife materials. Because fieldwork efforts of folklorists are usually community-based and the focus is often on local experience, these collections of diaries, local newspaper accounts, letters, taped oral histories, photographs, and artifacts held in local libraries and small local museums are highly valued and essential to research efforts. Many communities also sponsor annual festivals and community celebrations, or mark religious and secular holidays in distinctive ways, with the documentation of these events or the material culture connected with these events often found in local depositories. Virtually every small library with archival holdings or small historical museum in Michigan should be regarded as a potential folklife resource.

Beyond this segment of community resources, archives and museums in Michigan have assumed a major role in the documentation, preservation, and presentation of Michigan folklife. The Wayne State University Folklore Archives, for example, has had a long and distinguished history in the collection of photographs, manuscripts, reference materials, field notes, ethnic materials, tapes, recordings, films, and video-tapes. The Bentley Historical Library, Michigan Historical Collections has collected primarily Michigan historical archival material but also houses the Ivan Walton collection which includes field notes and papers of this pioneer Michigan folklorist, proceedings of the Michigan Folklore Society, bibliographies of Michigan traditions, and so on. Still other programs, such as the University of Detroit Computerized Folklore Archives, provide access to a wide assortment of collected folklore genres from Michigan and around the world. Clearly, the resources available to students, teachers, and scholars in Michigan are substantial and diverse. The colleges and universities of the state also offer an assortment of resources in the holdings of libraries and in private research collections of faculty members who teach folklore on Michigan campuses.

The state of Michigan, thanks to its many ethnic groups, has a wide array of ethnic archival resources and international centers. The International Institute of Metropolitan Detroit, the Ukrainian-American Archives and Museum in Hamtramck, and the Michigan Ethnic Heritage Center, are among the prime resources for ethnic studies in Michigan. The Michigan Ethnic Heritage Center has published two ethnic directories (a third is planned) that provide a listing of community clubs, organizations, and individuals and a brief history of each group in the Detroit area.

Many folk musical organizations have made a commitment to documentation and collection development. Some that deserve special mention are the Michigan Dance Association, the Original Dulcimer Players Club, and the Original Michigan Fiddler's Association. There are many organizations that sponsor concerts and folklore-related activities such as The Ark and Ann Arbor Council for Traditional Music and Dance in Ann Arbor, the Ten Pound Fiddle in East Lansing, and folk music societies around the state. In addition to these state resources, the Archive of Folk Culture at the Library of Congress, Washington, D.C., has field recordings of traditional songs and stories of Michigan ethnic and minority cultures preserved on cylinders and discs collected in the 1930s and 1940s.

Since 1974 the MSU Museum has been involved in collection and documentation activities related to Michigan folklife. State survey exhibitions, publications, and research have resulted in a Michigan Folk Arts Archives at the MSU Museum. The Michigan State University Museum developed *Michigan Folklife: A Resource Guide* which lists libraries, archives, museums, and individual and organizational resources in Michigan. Published jointly by the MSU Museum and the Michigan State University Cooperative Extension Service (Bulletin #4-H 1263), this directory is available through the

Cooperative Extension Service. In partnership with the Michigan Council for the Arts, the MSU Museum houses the Michigan Traditional Arts Program for the state.

The following is a selected summary of some of the primary folklife resources available in Michigan. For further information see *Michigan Folklife: A Resource Guide* or *The Peoples of Michigan* (ethnic resource directories of the Michigan Ethnic Heritage Center) or consult the Michigan Folklore Society (see below for information).

Michigan Folklife Resources

The following code indicates the type of folklore and folklife with which each organization or institution is concerned:

AR Folk architecture
AT Folk art
CO Folk cooking
CR Folk crafts
DA Folk dance
EC Ethnic
FL Folklife—hunting, trapping, farming, lumbering, sugaring, barn raising, ice fishing, dowsing, etc.
ME Folk medicine
MU Folk music
VA Verbal folk arts—narratives, beliefs, anecdotes, place names, customs, riddles, stories, etc.

Ann Arbor Council for Traditional Music and Dance
Attention: Don Theyken
875 S. First Street
Ann Arbor, MI 48103 (Washtenaw County)

EC, FL

Holdings and Collections: photographs, manuscripts, business accounts, ethnic materials, postcards, family albums, private papers, tapes, recordings, films, other materials relating to the lives and institutions of the people of Michigan. *Facilities:* library, archives. *Educational Programs:* newsletters, publications. *Services:* publications, newsletters, research.

Bentley Historical Library
Michigan Historical Collections
1150 Beal Avenue
Ann Arbor, MI 48109 (Washtenaw County)

EC, FL

Holdings and Collections: photographs, manuscripts, business accounts, ethnic materials, postcards, family albums, private papers, tapes/recordings, films, other materials relating to the livesa and institutions of the people of Michigan. *Facilities:* library, archives. *Educational Programs:* newsletters, publications. *Services:* publications, newsletters, research.

A guide to the Bentley Historical Library is available on request. Young adults are asked to supply a letter from their teacher stating the student's ability to use the library's unique materials. Of special interest is the Ivan Walton collection which includes field notes and papers of this pioneer Michigan folklorist.

The Edison Institute
Greenfield Village and Henry Ford Museum
Dearborn, MI 48121 (Wayne County)

AR, AT, CO, CR, CA, EC, FL, ME, MU, VA

Holdings and Collections: photographs, reference materials, field notes, ethnic materials, tapes/recordings, films, objects. *Facilities:* archives/library, museum, public meeting space. *Educational Programs:* courses, public programs, festivals/fairs, newsletters, demonstrations, workshops, lecture/concert series, traveling displays, publications. *Services:* teaching, information services, film/recording production, research, youth programs.

Elderly Instruments
1100 N. Washington
Lansing, MI 48906 (Ingham County)
517/372-7880

DA, MU

Holdings and Collections: tapes, recordings, objects. *Facilities:* meeting space. *Educational Programs:* courses, workshops. *Services:* teaching, youth programs.

A hub of folk music information, the Elderly School is part of Elderly Instruments, a complete folk music and bluegrass center.

In addition to selling music, records, and instruments and doing repairs, the school offers lessons in folk dance and music. Special classes on folk music are also offered to parents and teachers.

Grand Rapids Public Library
Michigan Room
60 Library Plaza N.E.
Grand Rapids, MI 49503 (Kent County)
616/456–3640

AT, CO, CR, CA, FL, ME, MU, VA, EC

Holdings and Collections: microfilms of records of Bureau of Indian Affairs, censuses, correspondence, taped/transcribed interviews with west Michigan Native Americans, photos, publications, and manuscripts pertaining to Native Americans, Dutch materials. *Facilities:* meeting space, archives/library. *Educational Programs:* exhibits, public programs. *Services:* information services, research.

Grand Rapids Public Museum
54 Jefferson S.E.
Grand Rapids, MI 49503 (Kent County)
616/456–3977

Holdings and Collections: manuscripts, photos, artifacts of Native Americans (local and national). *Facilities:* archives. *Educational Programs:* exhibits, public and educational programming. *Services:* information services, research, school programs, films, lectures.

The International Institute of Metropolitan Detroit, Inc.
111 East Kirby
Detroit, MI 48202 (Wayne County)
313/871–8600

AR, DA, EC

Holdings and Collections: ethnic artifacts, reference materials. *Facilities:* exhibit areas, classrooms, cafeteria, gift shop. *Educational Programs:* English as a second language classes, citizenship classes, ethnic exhibits, Old World market, folk arts and dance classes. *Services:* counseling, information services.

Michigan Ethnic Heritage Center
The Rackham Educational Memorial Center
60 Farnsworth
Detroit, MI 48202 (Wayne County)
EC

Holdings and Collections: reference materials, ethnic materials. *Facilities:* archives, library. *Educational Programs:* ethnic tours of Detroit. *Services:* publications/newsletters, information services, consulting.

The Michigan Ethnic Heritage Center is affiliated with the University of Michigan and Wayne State University. The center has published several ethnic tour guides of the Detroit area and three ethnic directories of Detroit

Michigan Council for the Arts (MCA)
1200 Sixth Avenue
Detroit, MI 48221 (Wayne County)
313/256-3731

AR, AT, CO, CR, DA, EC, FL, MU, VA

Holdings and Collections: reference materials, program development materials. *Facilities:* meeting space. *Educational Programs:* public programs, internships. *Services:* publications/ newsletters, information services, consulting, financial services.

Michigan Council for the Humanities (MCH)
Suite 30, Nisbet Building
1407 S. Harrison
East Lansing, MI 48823 (Ingham County)
517/355-0160

AR, AT, EC, FL, ME, VA

Holdings and Collections: reference materials, program development materials. *Facilities:* reference library. *Educational Programs:* public programs/forums. *Services:* newsletter, information services, consulting, financial services.

Michigan Department of State
Bureau of History

Affiliated Program:
Michigan (State of) Library
735 East Michigan
P.O. Box 30007
Lansing, MI 48909 (Ingham County)
517/373–1592

AR, AT, CO, CR, DA, EC, FL, ME, MU, VA

Holdings and Collections: reference materials, ethnic materials, family albums, film, publications, periodicals. *Facilities:* archives/library. *Educational Programs:* publications. *Services:* information services.

Affiliated Program:
Michigan Historical Museum
208 North Capitol
Lansing, MI 48933 (Ingham County)
517/373–3559

AR, AT, CO, CR, DA, EC, FL, ME, MU, VA

Holdings and Collections: photographs, reference materials, field notes, ethnic materials, postcards, family albums, private papers, objects. *Facilities:* museum, branch offices, meeting space. *Educational Programs:* public programs, festivals/fairs. *Services:* information services.

The Michigan Historical Museum is one of Michigan's oldest museums. It is an educational and cultural institution dedicated to the study, preservation, and presentation of the heritage of the people of Michigan. Through a variety of exhibits, programs, and special events, the museum tells the story of Michigan and its people.

Michigan Folklore Society
Yvonne Lockwood, Current President
Michigan State University Museum
Michigan State University
East Lansing, MI 48824 (Ingham County)
517/355–2370

AR, AT, CO, CR, DA, EC, FL, ME, MU, VA

Educational Programs: workshops. *Services:* teaching, information services, research.

Michigan State University Museum
Michigan State University
East Lansing, MI 48824 (Ingham County)
517/355-2370

AR, AT, CO, CR, DA, EC, FL, ME, MU, VA

Holdings and Collections: photographs, manuscripts, business accounts, reference materials, ethnic materials, postcards, family albums, private papers, tapes/recordings, films, folklife materials, Michigan Quilt Project files, objects. *Facilities:* archives, museum, folklore archives, meeting space. *Educational Programs:* public programs, exhibits, traveling exhibits, internships, outreach programs, publications, newsletters related to Michigan folklife. *Services:* publications/newsletters, information services, research, consulting, youth programs.

Affiliated Programs:
Michigan Traditional Arts Program

The staff of the Michigan Traditional Arts Program conducts research on Michigan traditions, provides technical assistance to organizations concerned with programming related to tourism, education, and community-oriented issues, and serves as a liaison to other state folklife programs. The MSU Museum maintains an archive on Michigan folk arts and artists, organizes exhibits on folk arts, sponsors educational programs, publishes information on Michigan folk arts, and coordinates the Michigan Quilt Project, the Michigan Traditional Arts Apprenticeship Program, and the Festival of Michigan Folklife.

The Michigan Quilt Project (MQP)

In 1984, the MSU Museum launched a major statewide quilt project to locate, document, and collect information and materials on Michigan quilts and quilters. Information on over 5,000 quilts, representing the work of over 3,500 quilters, has now been deposited in the Michigan Folk Arts Archive at the MSU Museum. The MQP also features quilt exhibits, publications, and a statewide quilting conference. Supported in part through the Harriet Clarke Endowment, the MQP continues to research and present information on Michigan quiltmaking traditions.

The FOLKPATTERNS Project

"FOLKPATTERNS: Michigan's Living Traditions" began in 1979 as a joint project of the MSU Museum and the 4-H Youth

Programs of the Michigan Cooperative Extension Service. Originally funded by a grant from the National Endowment for the Humanities, this project involves youth in the exploration and documentation of historical and living traditional patterns in their communities. The FOLKPATTERNS program gives youth valuable skills in learning from people and places around them and helps them become aware of Michigan's rich cultural heritage. FOLKPATTERNS publications are used in Michigan 4-H Youth Programs, in schools and by other youth organizations.

Finnish American Historical Archives
Suomi College
Hancock, MI 49930 (Houghton County)

AT, CO, CR, EC, MU

Holdings and Collections: manuscripts, reference materials and ethnic materials. *Facilities:* archives and library. *Educational Programs:* classes and workshops. *Services:* information services.

Ukrainian-American Archives and Museum
11756 Charest
Hamtramck, MI (Wayne County)
313/366–9764

AT, CO, CR, EC, FL, MU

Holdings and Collections: manuscripts, reference materials, ethnic materials, objects. *Facilities:* archives, library, museum. *Educational Programs:* festivals/fairs. *Services:* information services.

University of Detroit Computerized Folklore Archives
Jim Callow
4001 West McNichols Road
Detroit, MI 48221 (Wayne County)
313/927–1000

EC, FL, VA

Facilities: folklore archives. *Services:* information services, research.

Wayne State University Folklore Archives
448 Purdy Library
Wayne State University
Detroit, MI 48202 (Wayne County)
313/577-4053

AR, AT, CO, CR, DA, EC, FL, ME, MU, VA

Holdings and Collections: photographs, manuscripts, reference materials, field notes, ethnic materials, tapes, recordings, films, videotapes. *Facilities:* archives/library, folklore archives. *Educational Programs:* courses, public programs, festivals/fairs, internships, newsletters, demonstrations, workshops, inservice training, lecture/concert series, traveling displays, publications. *Services:* teaching, publications, newsletters, communication/mass media networks, film/recording production, research, consulting, financial expertise, recruiting volunteers, youth programs.

The archives are open from 9 a.m. to 5 p.m. during the regular school year.

Wheatland Music Organization
c/o Bruce Bowman
1120 6 Mile Road
Remus, MI 49340 (Mecosta County)
517/561-2308

DA, MU

Holdings and Collections: tapes, recordings. *Facilities:* archives, library. *Educational Programs:* courses, public programs, festivals, fairs, demonstrations, workshops, dances. *Services:* teaching, information services, recording production, research.

Introduction to the Bibliography

The items cited in this selected bibliography represent a range of Michigan folklife. Some are articles by non-folklorists; others are journalistic and more popularized in their presentation; and still others are academic folklore studies. In recent years efforts have been made to identify the shifting paradigms of American scholarly folklore research. In describing material culture studies, for example, Thomas J. Schlereth has proposed three periods in the United States: (1) The Age of Collecting (1876–1948); (2) The Age of Description (1948–1965); and (3) The Age of Analysis (1966-present). In each period there has been a particular intellectual emphasis such as historical association and artistic uniqueness in the Age of Collecting; classification systems and the search for American uniqueness in the Age of Description; and vernacularism and methodological fascination, in the Age of Analysis. Despite the material culture focus to Schlereth's categorization, one can also place many of the writings in this bibliography in one of these periods according to its intellectual emphasis. However, the most notable characteristic of the items included in this bibliography is that many of them rely on *fieldwork*.

There exists an extensive body of fiction, autobiographical accounts, and regional, local, and occupational history about Michigan people, containing varying degrees of information on the folklife of a past era, and at its best communicating an accurate sense of the lifestyles, beliefs, attitudes and values of the people.

Because these publications are not concerned with folklore or folklife, per se, they have not been included. Although a list here cannot do justice to what is available, the reader might make note of the works of Lewis Reiman, E. J. (Pete) Peterson, and Stuart Holbrook on life in the Upper Peninsula, northern Michigan, and the lumber era; Jingo Viitala Vachon's tongue-in-cheek accounts of Finnish-American life; the short stories about Upper Peninsula life by Cully Gage, and novels and autobiographical accounts by Robert Travers.

Note: The articles reprinted in this volume are not all included in the bibliography. The reader is advised to consult the references to each of the readings in this volume.

1. Edward B. Tylor, *Primitive Culture*, 2 vols. (London: John Murray, 1871), 1:16.
2. Ambrose Merton [W. J. Thoms]. *The Athenaeum* 982 (1846): 862–63.
3. Thomas J. Schlereth, *Material Culture Studies in America* (Nashville, Tenn.: American Association of State and Local History, 1982), 1–75.
4. Richard M. Dorson, *American Folklore and the Historian* (Chicago: University of Chicago, 1971), 85.
5. Ibid., 85.

Books and Articles

Au, Dennis M. "God Bless dee Mushrat: She's a Fish!" *Festival of American Folklife Program Book* (Washington, D.C.: Smithsonian Institution, 1987), 73–76. Reprinted in *Festival of Michigan Folklife Program Book* (East Lansing: Michigan State University Museum, 1987), 39–42.

—— Au, Dennis M., and Patricia Jodry Vincent, eds. *Old French Town Cookery.* 2d ed. Monroe, Mich.: Monroe County Historical Society, 1985.

Beck, E. C. *Lore of the Lumber Camps.* Ann Arbor: University of Michigan Press, 1948.

——. *Songs of the Michigan Lumberjacks.* Ann Arbor: University of Michigan Press, 1942.

——. *They Knew Paul Bunyan.* Ann Arbor: University of Michigan Press, 1956.

——. "'Ze Skunk." *Journal of American Folklore* 57 (1944): 211–12.

Bell, Michael. "Making Art Work." *Western Folklore,* 43 (1984): 211–21.

——. "Working on the Line." *Festival of American Folklife Book* (Washington, D.C.: Smithsonian Institution, 1987), 55–59. Reprinted in *Festival of Michigan Folklife Program Book* (East Lansing: Michigan State University Museum, 1987), 21–25.

Clifton, James, George Cornell, and James McClurken. *People of the Three Fires. The Ottawa, Potawatomi and Ojibwa of Michigan.* Grand Rapids, Mich.: Grand Rapids Inter-Tribal Council, 1986.

Cochrane, Timothy S. "The Folklife Expressions of Three Isle Royale Fishermen: A Sense of Place Examination." M.A. thesis, Western Kentucky University, 1982.

Crockett, Dolores N. "Children's Rhymes from Michigan." *Journal of American Folklore* 44 (1931): 116.

"Detroit's Most Amazing Stories." *Monthly Detroit* 3 (March 1986): 65–73.

Dandekar, Hemalata C. and Daniel F. Schoof. "Michigan Farms and Farm Buildings. 150 Years of Transformation." *Inland Architect* (January/February 1988): 61–67.

Dewhurst, C. Kurt. "The Arts of Working: Manipulating the Urban Work Environment." *Western Folklore* 43 (1984): 192–202.

—— , ed. "Downriver Decoy-Making Traditions: Recollections by Hy Dahlka." *Ward Foundation News,* Summer 1984.

——. *The Folk Pottery of Grand Ledge, Michigan: Traditions at Work.* Ann Arbor: UMI Research Press, 1986.

——. "Paths of Folk Art Study in Michigan." *Researching Art in Michigan: Michigan in Books.* Library of Michigan, 1984.

——. "River Guides, Long Boats, and Bait Shops: Michigan River Culture." *American Folklife Festival Program Book.* Smithsonian Institution, 1987. Reprinted in *Festival of Michigan Folklife Program Book* (East Lansing: Michigan State University Museum, 1987), 31–34.

——. "Sneak Shooting in the Downriver Tradition." *Wildfowl Art,* Summer 1985.

Dewhurst, C. Kurt and Marsha MacDowell. *Cast in Clay. The Folk Pottery of Grand Ledge, Michigan*. East Lansing: Michigan State University Museum, 1980.

———. *Downriver and Thumb Area Michigan Waterfowling. The Folk Arts of Nate Quillen and Otto Misch*. East Lansing: Michigan State University Museum, 1981.

———. "Expanding Frontiers: The Michigan Folk Art Project." In *Perspectives on American Folk Art*, edited by Ian M. G. Quimby and Scott T. Swank. New York: W. W. Norton and Company, 1980.

———, eds. *Folklife in the Greater Lansing Area*. East Lansing: Michigan State University, 1982.

———. "Michigan Folk Art, Treasures from Untrained Hands." *The Michigan Natural Resources Magazine* 46, no. 2 (1977): 17–32.

———, eds. *Michigan Hmong Arts. Textiles in Transition*. East Lansing: Michigan State University Museum, 1983.

———. "Oscar Peterson: The Carving Fisherman." *Michigan Natural Resources Magazine* 51, no. 6 (1982).

———. *Rainbows in the Sky: The Folk Art of Michigan in the Twentieth Century*. East Lansing: Michigan State University Museum, 1978.

Dewhurst, C. Kurt, Betty MacDowell, and Marsha MacDowell. "A Stitch or Sketch in Time: Michigan's Women Folk Artists." *Michigan History* 66 (1982): 8–10.

Dobson, Pamela J., ed. *The Tree That Never Dies. Oral History of the Michigan Indians*. Grand Rapids, Mich.: Grand Rapids Public Library, 1978.

Dorson, Richard M. *America in Legend: Folklore from the Colonial Period to the Present*. New York: Pantheon, 1983, 69, 151, 161–168, 180–182, 184, 202, 243.

———. *American Folklore and the Historian*. Chicago: University of Chicago Press, 1971), 85.

———. "Aunt Jane Goudreau, Loup-Garou Storyteller." *Western Folklore* 6 (1947): 13–27.

———. *Bloodstoppers and Bearwalkers. Folk Traditions of the Upper Peninsula*. Cambridge: Harvard University Press, 1956.

———. "Canadiens in the Upper Peninsula of Michigan." *Les Archive de Folklore* 4 (1949): 17–27.

———. "Dialect Stories of the Upper Peninsula. A New Form of American Folklore." *Journal of American Folklore* 61 (1948): 113–50.

———. "Folk Traditions of the Upper Peninsula." *Michigan History* 31 (1947): 48–65.

———. "Immigrant Folklore." In *American Folklore*, 135–65. Chicago: University of Chicago Press, 1959.

———. "Jewish-American Dialect Stories on Tape." In *Studies in Biblical and Jewish Folklore*, edited by Raphale Patai, Francis Less Utley and Dov Noy, 111–74. Indiana University Folklore Series no. 13. Bloomington: Indiana University Press, 1960.

———. *Negro Folktales in Michigan*. Cambridge: Harvard University Press, 1956.

———. "Negro Tales of Mary Richardson." *Midwest Folklore* 6 (1956): 5–26.

———. "Polish Wonder Tales of Joe Woods." *Western Folklore* 8 (1949): 25–52.

———. "Tales of a Greek-American Family on Tape." *Fabula* 1 (1957): 114–43; 2 (1958): 202–3.

Dorson, Richard, George List, and Neil Rosenberg. "Negro Folksongs in Michigan from the Repertoire of J. D. Suggs." *The Folklore and Folk Music Archivist* 9 (1966): 1–41.

Eberly, Carol, ed. *Our Michigan: Ethnic Tales and Recipes*. East Lansing: Eberly Press, 1979.

Festival of American Folklife (Program Book). Washington, D.C.: Smithsonian Institution and National Park Service, 1987, 45–86.

Festival of Michigan Folklife (Program Book). East Lansing: Michigan State University Museum, 1987.

Finley, Robert, and E. M. Scott. "A Great Lakes-to-Gulf Profile of Dispersed Dwelling Types." *The Geographical Review* 30 (1940): 412–19.

First, Joan M. "Folklore in Michigan." *Michigan Education Journal* 36 (1959): 291–95.

Gallacher, Stuart A. "Superstitions in the Michigan State University Archives." *Midwest Folklore* 5 (1955): 60–62.

Gardner, Emelyn. "Some Counting-Out Rhymes in Michigan." *Journal of American Folklore* 31 (1918): 521–36.

———. "Some Play-Party Games in Michigan." *Journal of American Folklore* 33 (1920): 91–133.

Gardner, Emelyn Elizabeth, and Geraldine Jencks Chickering, eds. *Ballads and Songs of Southern Michigan*. 1939. Hatboro, Penn.: Folklore Associates, 1967.

Gilmore, Janet C. "Fishing for a Living on the Great Lakes." *Festival of American Folklife Book* (Washington, D.C.: Smithsonian Institution, 1987), 60–64. Reprinted in *Festival of Michigan Folklife Program Book* (East Lansing: Michigan State University Museum, 1987), 26–30.

Gray, John. "Milltown Name Tags." *Michigan Natural Resources* 43 (1974): 14–15.

Groce, Nancy. "The Hammered Dulcimer or the Lumberjack's Piano." *Chronicle* 10 (1984): 9–12.

Harris, Pauline Beatrice. "Spanish and Mexican Folklore as Represented in Two Families in the Detroit Area." M.A. thesis, Wayne State University, 1949.

Hartikka, Helen Johnson. "Finnish Folksongs Collected in and about Detroit, Michigan." M.A. thesis, Wayne State University, 1944.

Hartman, Lee. "Michigan Barns, Our Vanishing Landmarks." *Michigan Natural Resources* 45 (1976): 17–32.

Helbig, Alethea. *Manabozho, Giver of Life*. Brighton, Mich.: Green Oak Press, 1985.

———. "Manabozho of the Great Lakes Indians: As He Was, As He Is." *Michigan Academician* 11 (1978): 49–58.

———. "Manabozho: Trickster, Guide, and Alter Ego." *Michigan Academician* 7 (1975): 357–71.

Hoogasian-Villa, Susie. *100 Armenian Tales*. Detroit: Wayne State University Press, 1966.

Humphrey, Norman D. "Some Dietary and Health Practices of Detroit Mexicans." *Journal of American Folklore* 58 (1945): 255–58.

Ivey, William. "'The 1913 Disaster': Michigan Local Legend." *Folklore Forum* 3 (1970): 100–14.

Jackson, Joyce M., and James T. Jones, IV. "Good News for the Motor City: Black Gospel Music in Detroit." *Festival of American Folklife Book* (Washington, D.C.: Smithsonian Institution, 1987), 83–86. Reprinted in *Festival of Michigan Folklife Program Book* (East Lansing: Michigan State University Museum, 1987), 49–52.

Johnson, Aili Kolehmainen. "Finnish Labor Songs from Northern Michigan." *Michigan History* 31 (1947): 331–43.

———. "Lore of the Finnish-American Sauna." *Midwest Folklore* 1 (1951): 33–40.

Kaups, Matti. "Finnish Place-Names in Michigan." *Michigan History* 4 (1967): 335–47.

Kidder, H. R. "Why the Poplar Stars—Superstitions of Miners in Michigan." *Journal of American Folklore* 13 (1900): 26.

Kurath, Gertrude Prokosch. *Michigan Indian Festivals.* Ann Arbor, Mich.: Ann Arbor Publishers, 1966.

Langlois, Janet L. "The Belle Isle Bridge Incident: Legend Dialectic and Semiotic System in the 1943 Detroit Race Riots." *Journal of American Folklore* 96 (1983): 183–99.

Larsen, Sarah, and Stephen Williams. *House Party to Concert Hall. An Exhibition of Michigan-Made Musical Instruments.* Port Huron, Mich.: Museum of Arts and History, 1984.

Leary, James. "Ethnic Country Music Along Superior's South Shore." *John Edwards Memorial Foundation Quarterly* 19 (1984).

———. "Folklore of the Upper Peninsula." *Festival of American Folklife Book* (Washington, D.C.: Smithsonian Institution, 1987), 51–54. Reprinted in *Festival of Michigan Folklife Program Book* (East Lansing: Michigan State University Museum, 1987), 17–20.

Lockwood, Yvonne R. "Immigrant to Ethnic: Folk Symbols of Identity Among Finnish-Americans." In *Folklife Annual 1986,* edited by Alan Jabbour and James Hardin. Washington, D.C.: Library of Congress, 1987.

———. "The Joy of Labor." *Western Folklore* 43 (1984): 202–11.

———. "Michigan Traditions: Ethnic or Folk?" *Festival of Michigan Folklife Program Book* (East Lansing: Michigan State University Museum, 1987), 61–65.

———. "The Sauna: An Expression of Finnish-American Identity." *Western Folklore* 36 (1977): 71–84.

Lockwood, William G. and Yvonne R. Lockwood. "The Cornish Pasty in Northern Michigan. In *Food in Motion. The Migration of Foodstuffs and Cookery Techniques.* Proceedings of Oxford Symposium, 1983, edited by Alan Davidson, 84–94. London: Prospect Books, 1983.

Lockwood, Yvonne R., C. Kurt Dewhurst, and Marsha MacDowell. *Michigan Whose Story: A Celebration of the State's Traditions.* East Lansing: Michigan State University Museum, 1985.

MacDowell, Marsha. "Country Fairs, Roadside Stands, and Community Harvest Festivals: Outward Signs of Michigan Agricultural Traditions." *Festival of Michigan Folklife Program Book* (East Lansing: Michigan State University Museum, 1987), 57–60.

———. "Here's the Work of an Unusual Folk Artist and Wood-Carver Named Oscar Peterson." *Michigan Natural Resources* 51 (1982): 58–63.

———. *Michigan Folk Art. Its Beginnings to 1941*. East Lansing: Michigan State University Museum, 1976.

———. *Michigan Folklife: A Resource Guide*. East Lansing: Michigan State University Museum and Cooperative Extension Service, 1983.

———. "Visual Descriptions of the Work Experience: Insider vs. Outsider Views of Art and Work." *Western Folklore*, 43 (1984): 178–92.

MacDowell, Marsha, and Rutho D. Fitzgerald, eds. *Michigan Quilts. 150 Years of a Textile Tradition*. East Lansing: Michigan State University Museum, 1987), 61–65.Mathias, Elizabeth, and Richard Raspa. *Italian Folktales in America*. Detroit: Wayne State University Press, 1985.

McClurken, James M. "Crafts of Survival: The Materials of Ottawa, Ojibway, and Potawatomi Culture." *Festival of American Folklife Book* (Washington, D.C.: Smithsonian Institution, 1987), 77–82. Reprinted in *Festival of Michigan Folklife Program Book* (East Lansing: Michigan State University Museum, 1987), 43–48.

McEwen, George M. "Ivan H. Walton, A Pioneer Michigan Folklorist." *Michigan Academician* 2 (1970): 73–77.

Nettl, Bruno, and Ivo Moravcik. "Czech and Slovak Songs Collected in Detroit." *Midwest Folklore* 5 (1955): 37–49.

Olmstead, Carrie. "Cedar Craft Lives." *Michigan Natural Resources* 51 (1982): 46–51.

Ottawa Quillwork on Birchbark. An Historical Exhibition of Ottawa Quillwork on Birchbark Executed Between 1830 and 1983. Harbor Springs Historical Commission, 1983.

Pawlowska, Harriet, ed. and coll. *Merrily We Sing. 105 Polish Folksongs*. 1961. Detroit: Wayne State University Press, 1983.

Paxson, Barbara. "Potawatomi Indian Black Ash Basketry," *American Indian Basketry* 17 (1984): 6–11.

Penti, Marsha. "Copper Country: Snow Country." *Festival of Michigan Folklife Program Book* (East Lansing: Michigan State University Museum, 1987), 53–56.

Rizzo, Lydia. "Folklore Collected from Italian Americans in Detroit." M.A. thesis, Wayne State University, 1945.

Rollman, Wil and Cheryl Baker. *An Inventory of the Ivan H. Walton Collection*. Michigan Historical Collections, Bentley Library, 1979.

Romig, Walter. *Michigan Place Names*. Grosse Pointe, Mich.: Walter Romig, 1972.

Rowe, John. "Cornish Emigration to America." *Folk-Life* 3 (1965): 26–38.

Schlereth, Thomas J. *Material Culture Studies in America*. Nashville, Tenn.: American Association for State and Local History, 1982.

Schoolcraft, Henry R. *Algic Researches*. 1839.

———. *The Myth of Hiawatha*. Philadelphia: 1856.

Sidwa, Anne. "The Devil and the Long, Long Thread." *Polish Folklore* 3 (1958): 28–29.

Singer, Eliot A. "Life in the Michigan Northwoods." *Festival of American Folklife Book* (Washington, D.C.: Smithsonian Institution, 1987), 69–72. Reprinted in *Festival of Michigan Folklife Program Book* (East Lansing: Michigan State University Museum, 1987), 35–38.

Smyka, Mary Solomon. "Spirits of Detroit." *Monthly Detroit* (October 1982): 48–51.

Sokolov, Raymond. "Tasty Pasty: Michigan's Finnish-Cornish Meat Pie." In *Fading Feast. A Compendium of Disappearing American Regional Foods*, 64–72. New York: Farrar, Straus, Giroux, 1981.

Sommers, Laurie Kay. "Migration to Michigan: An Introduction to the State's Folklife." *Festival of American Folklife Book* (Washington, D.C.: Smithsonian Institution, 1987), 45–50. Reprinted in *Festival of Michigan Folklife Program Book* (East Lansing: Michigan State University Museum, 1987), 11–16.

Stekert, Ellen J. "The Wayne State University Folklore Archive: In Process." *Folklore and Folk Music Archivist* 9 (1967): 61–78.

———. "Focus for Conflict: Southern Mountain Medical Beliefs in Detroit." In *The Urban Experience and Folk Tradition*, edited by Americo Parades and Ellen Stekert, 95–127. Austin: University of Texas Press, 1971.

"Superstition Relating to Crossed Feathers." *Journal of American Folklore* 10 (1897): 76.

Thigpen, Kenneth A. "Romanian-American Folklore in Detroit." In *Immigrant and Migrant: The Detroit Ethnic Experience*, edited by D. W. Hartmann, 189–201. Detroit: New University Thought Publishing Co., 1974.

Tylor, Edward B. *Primitive Culture*, 2 vols. London: John Murray, 1871.

Walton, Ivan. "Folk Singing on Beaver Island." *Midwest Folklore* 2 (1952): 243–50.

———. "Indian Place Names in Michigan." *Midwest Folklore* 5, no. 1 (1955).

———. "Marine Lore." In *Michigan. A Guide to the Wolverine State*, compiled by the Workers' Projects Administration, 113–34. New York: Oxford University Press, 1941.

Williams, Steve R., ed. *House Party: Reminiscences by Traditional Musicians and Square Dance Callers in Michigan's Thumb Area*. Port Huron, Mich.: Museum of Arts and History, 1982.

Wilson, Ben. "The Amazing Curative Powers of Black Home Remedies and Other Elements of Folk Wisdom in Rural Southwestern Michigan." *Negro History Bulletin* (1982).

FIELD RECORDINGS

Accordions in the Cutover: Field Recordings of Ethnic Music from Superior's South Shore. Collected by Jim Leary. Northland College and Wisconsin Folklife Center. Dodgeville, Wisc., 1986.

Songs and Dances of Great Lakes Indians. Recorded by Gertrude Kurath. Ethnic Folkways Records LP4003. New York, 1956.

Songs of the Great Lakes. Recorded by Edith Fowke, Folkways Records FM4018. New York, 1964.

Songs of the Michigan Lumberjacks. Recorded by Alan Lomax and Harry B. Welliver, edited by E. C. Beck. Archive of Folk Song (now Archive of Folk Culture), Library of Congress. AFSL56. Washington, D.C., 1960.

FILMS

Finnish-American Lives. 16mm, color, 47 min. Produced and directed by Michael Loukinen. Marquette: U.P. North Films, Northern Michigan University, 1982. (Revised with epilogue to 59 minutes, 1984.)

Good Man in the Woods. 16mm, color, 88 min., 30 sec. 1987. Produced and directed by Michael Loukinen. Marquette: U.P. North Films, Northern Michigan University.

Great Lakes Indian Beadwork. Super 8mm and 1/2" VHS, color, 20 min. 1977. Produced and distributed by the Grand Rapids Public Museum, 54 Jefferson, S.E., Grand Rapids, MI 49503.

Porcupine Quillboxes. 1/2" VHS, color, 45 min. 1985. Distributed by Grand Rapids Intertribal Council.

Tradition Bearers. 16mm, color, 47 min. 1983. Produced and directed by Michael Loukinen. Marquette: U.P. North Films, Northern Michigan University.

Wiigwaasijiimaan ("The Birchbark Canoe"). Produced by Saginaw Chippewa Tribe, Mt. Pleasant, Michigan and Bemidji State University, 1978.

Woodland Indian Basketmaking. Super 8mm and 1/2" VHS, color, 15 min. 1975. Produced and distributed by the Grand Rapids Public Museum, 54 Jefferson, S.E., Grand Rapids, MI 49503.